Library of
Davidson College

The Dynamics of Human Rights in U.S. Foreign Policy

The Dynamics of Human Rights in U.S. Foreign Policy

Edited by
Natalie Kaufman Hevener

Transaction Books
New Brunswick (U.S.A.) and London (U.K.)

Second printing, 1983.
Copyright © 1981 by Transaction, Inc.
New Brunswick, New Jersey 08903

All rights reserved under International and Pan-American Copyright Conventions. No part of this book may be reproduced or transmitted in any form or by any means, electronic or mechanical, including photocopy, recording, or any information storage and retrieval system, without prior permission in writing from the publisher. All inquiries should be addressed to Transaction Books, Rutgers — The State University, New Brunswick, New Jersey 08903.

Library of Congress Catalog Number: 79-66435
ISBN: 0-87855-347-9
Printed in the United States of America

Library of Congress Cataloging in Publication Data

Main entry under title:

Human rights in United States foreign policy.

    Includes index.
1. Civil rights — Addresses, essays, lectures.
2. United States — Foreign relations — 1977 — Addresses, essays, lectures.
3. Civil rights — United States — Addresses, essays, lectures.
I. Hevener, Natalie Kaufman.
K3240.6.U54   341.48'1   79—66435
ISBN O-87855-347-9

TO CARROLLEE
And All Our Children

Contents

Acknowledgments ix

Introduction i

Part I   **Introductory Perspectives** 9

    1. Moral Dilemmas in the Development of United
       States Human Rights Policies 11
       Paul M. Kattenburg

    2. Ideological Patterns in the United States Human
       Rights Debate: 1945-1978 29
       Richard A. Falk

    3. Domestic Consequences of United States Human
       Rights Policies 53
       Robert L. Borosage

    4. International Consequences of United States
       Human Rights Policies 63
       Louis B. Sohn

Part II   **United States Participation in the Identification and
Definition of International Human Rights** 75

    5. The United States and International Codification
       of Human Rights: A Case of Split Personality 77
       Bruno V. Bitker

    6. The United States and the Right of
       Self-Determination 101
       Walker F. Connor

    7. The United States and Recognition of New
       Human Rights: Economic and Social Needs 123
       Peter Weiss

    8. The United States, International War, and the
       Preservation of Human Rights: The Control of Arms . 135
       Marcus G. Raskin and Ann Wilcox

Part III **Human Rights Policies of the United States in International Organizations** 155

9. The United States and the International Protection of Minorities 157
   Robert G. Wirsing

10. The United States, the United Nations and the Struggle Against Racial Apartheid 203
    C. Clyde Ferguson

11. The United States, the Organization of American States, and Political Repression in the Western Hemisphere 215
    Martin Weinstein

Part IV **Formulation and Implementation of United States Human Rights Policies** 227

12. The Influence of Interest Groups on the Development of United States Human Rights Policies 229
    David Weissbrodt

13. The Role of Congress in Deciding United States Human Rights Policies 279
    Robert B. Boettcher

14. The Contribution of the United States to the Promotion and Protection of International Human Rights 291
    Richard B. Lillich

APPENDICES

    A. Universal Declaration of Human Rights 321
    B. International Covenant on Civil and Political Rights, 1966 327
    C. International Covenant on Economic, Social, and Cultural Rights, 1966 346
    D. Table of Signatures and Ratifications 356
    E. Sections 502B and 116 of the Foreign Assistance Act .. 358

Contributors 362

Index 369

Acknowledgments

This volume grew out of a colloquia series held in the Department of Government and International Studies of the University of South Carolina. The series was made possible through grants from the United States Department of State, Bureau of External Research, the University's Faculty and Productive Scholarship Fund, and the Office of the Dean of the University's College of Humanities and Social Sciences. I am grateful for this financial support which enabled me to bring a number of outstanding scholars and practitioners to the campus to discuss their work on human rights. I owe a special debt to authors Richard Falk, Louis Sohn, Robert Borosage, Peter Weiss, and Robert Boettcher for taking the time to come to South Carolina and for sharing their ideas and experience with us; I am also grateful to the faculty and graduate student participants from the department whose informed, provocative, and constructive comments were invaluable to the editor and to the visiting contributors. To Dean Chester Bain, and the department chairmen, James Holland and James Kuhlman, I wish to express my thanks for their help and support during the colloquia series.

My task of transforming the colloquia papers into a finished volume was greatly aided by the extensive review, suggested revisions, and persistent optimism of Robert G. Wirsing and Paul M. Kattenburg. Also my two graduate assistants, Steven Mosher and Carl Young, worked well beyond their normal hours diligently and cheerfully helping me with the entire process of manuscript preparation.

Finally, I wish to thank my family, especially Suzy and Sam, and my friends, William P. Kreml, Carolyn Matalene, William Matalene, and Mary Bryan for our many enlightening and enjoyable discussions and for their abiding confidence in me and my work.

Introduction

In recent years "human rights" has become one of the most used phrases in the American political lexicon. Its popularity—not only in the United States but also abroad—had been increasingly visible throughout the 1970s. But the turnover in Washington in 1976 from Republican to Democratic administrations gave it vastly more official sponsorship and undoubtedly quickened the tempo of its public acceptance.

In sharp contrast to its Republican predecessors, the Carter administration advanced human rights as an explicit and prominent part of its announced foreign policy agenda. Largely unanticipated, and by no means fully understood or approved, this unusually emphatic endorsement of human rights has been given a great many explanations. Among the most commonly cited are:

1. Earlier congressional human rights initiatives, including a series of hearings, resulted in structural and policy action which the Carter administration inherited. Congressional committees and a Department of State bureaucratic division on human rights were already established.
2. Public disillusionment with the Nixon-Watergate revelations and, to a lesser extent, Kissinger's ultrarealistic foreign policy set the stage for dramatic change. The new avowedly moral policy distinctly separated Carter from the previous administration in a particularly effective fashion: the policy was claimed to be moral in content and implementation.
3. United States world leadership had been damaged by the defeat in Vietnam. Through the human rights policy, the Carter administration was able to draw on a domestically acceptable source for reviving American stature in international affairs: the American tradition reflected in the Declaration of Independence and the Bill of Rights.
4. A further response to Vietnam, as well as to United States economic difficulties, was a domestic tendency toward isolationism. The human rights emphasis provided a rationale for the revival of an activist, if not interventionist, foreign policy.
5. Carter, himself, as an apparently deeply religious man appears to have personally charted his human rights policy in the hope of creating a new sense of "national integrity" to parallel the "personal integrity" so much a part of his public as well as personal image.
6. International organizations, both public and private, have significantly increased their discussion of and action on human rights, particularly in light of intensified concern over racist policies in Africa. The Carter administra-

tion may have felt the need to respond favorably to this rather strong international pressure.

The response to Carter's concentration on human rights, however, may appear to the interested observer to have created a hodgepodge of contradictory forces: accusations and defenses; revelations and concealments; sincere investigations and manipulative inquiries; legitimate concern and pious posturing; cynical resignation and naive optimism. One might conclude that the energy expended on this subject has produced more confusion than clarification, more harm than help. There are some who are already convinced that the human rights issue suffers from overexposure. They would be relieved, no doubt, to see the fading from public attention of this intensely complex, highly controversial, and personally disturbing subject. Their uneasiness is well-founded: a full, open national debate on human rights has the potential of revealing fundamental disparities between stated nationally shared values and their contemporary level of implementation.

Concern with human rights will continue to be a major characteristic of domestic and global politics and will, therefore, have a significant impact on the formulation, implementation, and evaluation of United States foreign policy. The contributors to this volume have felt from the beginning that the discussion of this subject although difficult and hazardous was worth pursuing. In addition, they agreed to the necessity of placing the debate in an international context aware that this added dimension would compound the problems already existent at the national level.

Fundamental to *international* concern with human rights is an acceptance of the idea that there is an essential commonality among human beings, reflected in the concept of human kind. It is this shared bond of common humanity that both provides the basis for and legitimizes a consideration of the rights and well-being of peoples other than those with whom one shares nationality. The international consideration of human rights since 1945 has been predicated on a belief in the ability to identify and define a set of basic rights to which all people are entitled. This commitment assumes a recognition of the concept that there are limits to state action, restrictions on the discretion of the state which arise from the fundamental rights of human beings. Clearly, unless individuals and groups are viewed as fully in possession of rights, there can be little justification for international concern over rights violations within domestic societies. In discussing human rights, therefore, the ultimate source or authority should be an understanding of human nature; the mode of definition is reason; and the purpose of inquiry can be nothing less than the maintenance and advancement of the dignity of mankind. The basic assumption, as C. Wilfred Jenks has suggested, is that the ultimate members of the society of states are, first and foremost, human beings.

Clearly, the historical, cultural, economic, and social variation which exists among and even within states will result in varying interpretations and applications of the full range of human rights. Within all legal systems there will probably always be some disparity between binding and effective law. Nevertheless, the rights in the Universal Declaration of Human Rights have been legitimized by international positive law of custom, convention, or general principles of law, and therefore form a *minimum* core of rights regarded as legitimate by the governments of states in today's world. There is, moreover, a clear distinction between general moral precepts and legal rights and obligations, although one hopes that the former are well represented among the latter.

Given the existence of a minimal international consensus, state action which violates these rights becomes of *special concern* for U.S. foreign policymakers when: (1) there is a clear pattern of consistent violation, a pattern which implies governmental complicity or tacit consent; (2) there are no local remedies available to those whose rights have been violated or such remedies have been exhausted; (3) the violations are "gross" in nature, such that any reasonable observers would concur on the severity of the commission or omission.

Many would agree that in spite of the difficulties and conceding the evolutionary nature of the task, U.S. decisionmakers can and should make a determined effort to formulate an informed, carefully designed, intelligent foreign policy which sincerely and sensitively takes into account the inevitable and troublesome complexities of internationally recognized human rights. The United States can play a role in the maintenance and expansion of the realization of this set of basic rights—some of which the United States has accepted as domestic law, some as international law, and some as emergent global commitment; it is understood that to do so will require a serious effort to clarify, understand, and intelligently create the means of increasingly incorporating respect for these rights into U.S. foreign policy—into its actual content and into the strategies used for its implementation.

Part I of this volume, Introductory Perspectives, provides the background information, formulates the basic concepts, and sets out the critical controversies which are necessary for an understanding of the nature of international human rights and their relation to U.S. foreign policy. The initial dramatic announcement of commitment to human rights has been followed by a period of painful awareness of the complexities of conceptualizing policy objectives and constructing policy strategies into which human rights considerations can be genuinely incorporated.

In the first essay, Paul Kattenburg perceptively and sympathetically probes the serious problem of reconciling personal ethics with actions in the service of an amoral state. His experience as chargé and political counselor in U.S. embassies abroad, as an early opponent to the Vietnam War, and as a continuing participant in the training of foreign service officers, enables him to infuse his analysis with first-hand knowledge of the political pressures and bureaucratic restraints of foreign policy decision makers. He seeks humane guidelines which would aid the policymaker, suggesting a combination of nationally accepted standards and globally recognized principles. And he reminds us that behind the search for national and international norms of human rights lies the basic moral tenet of individual responsibility for individual behavior.

From the realm of morality, we move to that of politics with Professor Richard Falk's exceptionally discerning review of the United States' human rights record since 1945. He explains why action on human rights by official governmental organs of the United States is limited by the political spectrum of relevant elites and the publics to whom they appeal. He organizes a system of categorization for placing human rights advocates along an ideological continuum and discusses the mixed and contradictory uses of human rights rhetoric which result in confused, often unrealistic expectations from human rights movements. He concludes with a checklist of United States human rights actions which he has devised to assist in clarification of public expectations and intelligent assessment of U.S. policies.

Professor Falk shows us that the domestic political environment delineates the boundaries of actual foreign policy alternatives; Robert Borosage is concerned with how that domestic environment is in turn affected by the human rights content of foreign policy. He examines the strategy of implementation as well as the policy goals, indicating the necessity of subjecting foreign policy means as well as ends to a human rights standard. With particular emphasis on the intelligence community and national security interests, he then explicates the linkages between human rights violations in foreign policy and the potential for erosion of rights here at home.

As Robert Borosage's essay indicates, the domestic consequences of the presence or absence of a human rights standard in foreign policy are not normally given adequate attention. The global ramifications are also often overlooked. Usually the primary concern is with bilateral relations, the direct impact of U.S. action on a given foreign government's internal or external affairs. Professor Louis Sohn studies the general implications of United States human rights policies for the world community. He stresses the limited effectiveness of the U.S. bilateral approach of rewards and sanctions and develops the case for the United States' use of multilateral channels, regional and global, as the means for expanding world consensus and advancing the fulfillment of international human rights.

Part II examines the United States' participation in the identification and definition of international human rights. The adoption in 1948 of the Universal Declaration of Human Rights by the United Nations General Assembly was in one sense a culmination of serious U.S. efforts to regain a position of principled international leadership vacated during the post-World War I period. This document has become a touchstone of human rights activity to which innumerable United Nations resolutions, national foreign policy statements, and bilateral and multilateral treaties make reference. Eighteen years after its adoption, two draft treaties were concluded: the International Covenant on Civil and Political Rights and the International Covenant on Economic, Social, and Cultural Rights. They had received enough ratifications to come into force in 1976. (See Appendix for text and table of ratifications.)

But although the covenants are the most comprehensive codification response to the Universal Declaration and the movement which produced it, numerous other international agreements pertaining to human rights have been negotiated and brought into force. Unfortunately these treaties have been almost entirely ignored by the U.S. Senate; they have not received serious attention based on the merits of the substantive contents, but have since the early 1950s been set aside as inconsistent with the treaty-making powers, on the grounds that human rights are essentially within our domestic jurisdiction.

Bruno Bitker, who has been directly involved in the ongoing effort to promote serious consideration of human rights instruments, traces the development of human rights consideration by the United States. He believes there is a deep American ambivalence toward international legal codification of human rights and he identifies the contradictory human rights positions which have been adopted by U.S. representatives in international and national arenas.

The Universal Declaration was not meant to be a definitive or complete statement of human rights. The most significant omission from the Universal Declaration was the right of self-determination which appears in both covenants as Article I. The idea of self-determination, however, has proved easier for most states to accept in principle than to apply, particularly when its application would adversely affect their own domestic affairs. Walker Connor, who has written extensively on this topic, reviews the historical and political development of the self-determination doctrine and places it in relation to other human rights. The United

States traditionally has cherished this idea, reflected in our own Declaration of Independence, but as Professor Connor indicates, we have not consistently applied it in our relations with other states. He suggests how the United States might contribute to the challenging task of developing a meaningful doctrine of self-determination which could actually be applied within the context of the nation-state system.

The Universal Declaration includes several articles dealing with social and economic rights; these were elaborated and codified in the Covenant on Economic, Social, and Cultural Rights. The Carter administration's acceptance of the importance of economic rights has been a major innovation in U.S. foreign policy. Peter Weiss focuses on these particular rights which the Third World and Eastern bloc nations view as fundamental and indeed necessary for any meaningful exercise of civil and political rights. He provides the historical and legal reasons for their emphasis on these rights and explains how public and private U.S. economic activity contributes to the deterioration rather than the enhancement of human rights conditions in developing nations. He concludes with the thesis that the two sets of rights are interdependent and recommends various means by which the United States' verbal acceptance of economic rights can be translated into actual policy.

Other basic human rights, not included in the Universal Declaration, are also now being discussed. Marcus Raskin and Ann Wilcox give a persuasive introduction to the still novel idea that the enjoyment of all human rights depends on the creation of an international climate of basic security; freedom from war is a prerequisite for freedom from fear. The authors discuss the past and present role of the United States in the process of world armament and offer studied realistic steps by which U.S. decision makers might move toward the achievement of global arms control.

Part III considers the human rights policies pursued by the United States in international organizations. As Professor Sohn has pointed out, international human rights are most appropriately implemented through multilateral institutions. It would be difficult to discern a clear pattern in U.S. action on human rights within international organizations. The authors of the in-depth studies included here reveal the changes in U.S. attitudes and practices and they make recommendations for this nation's future policy.

One basic set of rights discussed extensively after World War I and greatly neglected since is that pertaining to minorities. Professor Wirsing traces the role of the United States in the development of international protection of minorities under both the League of Nations and the United Nations. He lucidly discusses both sides of the controversy over international minority protection and assesses the options available to American policymakers in light of the renewed global interest in minority rights.

Minority protection is only beginning to receive serious international attention; the dominant human rights issue in recent years has been the struggle against racial apartheid. Clyde Ferguson, who has represented the United States in black African states and at the United Nations, explains the political and economic nature of the United States' involvement in South Africa and the detrimental effect this involvement has had on the United States' status in international organizations. From his study it is clear that the development of a viable policy toward South Africa will require an understanding of the role of the United Nations both in influencing and providing a channel for U.S. foreign policy.

While antiapartheid holds priority in the human rights agenda of the United Nations, political repression dominates human rights discussions at the Organization of American States and throughout the Western hemisphere. Professor Weinstein's essay offers new insights into the unique problems and opportunities surrounding the pursuit of U.S. human rights policies in Latin America. He reviews and evaluates the impact which past and present policies have had and are likely to have on repressive governments and on the treatment of political prisoners.

The final section treats the formulation and implementation of U.S. human rights policies. We are familiar with, have seen numerous references throughout the preceding chapters to, the central role of the Carter administration. Foreign policy is appropriately seen by most to be essentially within the domain of the executive branch. Others are, however, intimately involved in designing and carrying out official U.S. policy.

Robert Boettcher reviews the early congressional initiatives on human rights (in which he played an important part) and analyzes the pre- and post-Carter legislation aimed at altering the content, operation, and process of implementing human rights policy. He describes the pattern of executive-legislative relations in this area and observes new creative efforts by the legislature since the advent of an administration more interested in human rights action.

David Weissbrodt provides an appraisal of the strategies and techniques which various ethnic, racial, national, religious, economic, and political interest groups have employed in the pursuit of their specialized human rights objectives. He considers the means available to the groups in their effort to influence U.S. foreign policy and foreign governments through official and unofficial, public and private channels. He elucidates the advantages and difficulties, especially the possibility of cooptation, for interest group activity directed at a government which has gone on record in support of human rights.

The concluding essay by Richard Lillich carefully examines the full range of policy options available to the United States for the implementation of human rights policies. The author is particularly concerned with humanitarian intervention and intercession and his chapter provides a useful framework for analysis. He also offers suggestive criteria for determining which options are likely to be most appropriate, available, efficacious, and consonant with international legal norms.

Part I
Introductory Perspectives

Chapter 1
Moral Dilemmas in the Development of United States Human Rights Policies

Paul M. Kattenburg

Recent emphasis on human rights in U.S. foreign policy has sharply heightened awareness and prompted discussion of the role of morality in our foreign policy. This is hardly surprising. The overwhelming feeling among the public at large and among political leaders that recent American policy, during and after the Vietnam War and particularly during the Nixon-Kissinger period, had been at least amoral if not downright immoral inspired much of the emphasis on human rights in the successor Carter administration. President Jimmy Carter's repeated stress on human rights in turn focused commentary on still broader questions of the role of morality.

Even though more than three decades have elapsed since the Nuremberg judgments established the principle that state leaders are themselves accountable for state actions desecrating presumed norms of acceptable civilized human behavior, most of the American foreign policy elite has continued until quite recently to be basically comfortable with some of the fundamental assumptions of *realpolitik*. These include the belief that a state's morality in international affairs cannot be judged by the same standards applied to ordinary individuals in orderly society, and that special rules apply. Yet this outlook—most always assumed, rarely examined—has seemed faulty in a host of recent cases. In respect to Vietnam, ITT, Lockheed, and, above all, the abuses of the FBI and the CIA, the pretext of "national security" interest covering the actions of leaders has been mercilessly stripped off by popular scrutiny with ensuing public accounting on the part of individual leaders. Except in the case of Watergate, this has not yet led to public prosecutions, but the threat of these in future cases hangs unmistakably in the atmosphere. It is, after all, undeniable that the former attorney general of the United States is presently imprisoned for authorizing actions which, in his own mind, were designed at least as much to protect "the national security" as to advance the political interests of his cohorts.

It seems plausible that it was at least in part because the claim of immunity from morality by statesmen presumably acting in the interest of national security seemed wrong to many people that "a new morality" became the campaign slogan of the victorious candidate in the 1976 elections. Are the claims of leaders that they act under cover of the national interest, and accordingly need not account for their actions like ordinary mortals, ever again to be taken seriously by their peers in government or by the people? Would such claims be sustained were the veil of secrecy to be permanently lifted to expose the means employed in successful actions? Even the long buried and seemingly advantageous bribery by the CIA of the Italian Christian Democrats after World War II does not now seem immune from *post-facto* judgments of immorality, much less so the unsuccessful efforts to assassinate Fidel Castro or to keep Salvador Allende from taking power.

We do not have a great deal in the literature of international relations to help guide us on the path of answers to the vexing questions raised by the problem of morality in foreign policy. The general subject was explored with great wisdom by Arnold Wolfers nearly 30 years ago[1] while Hans Morgenthau both thundered on the inevitable evils of power[2] and masterfully arraigned the powerful on moral grounds in essays published at the height of the Vietnam War.[3] Richard Falk, Charles Frankel, Maurice Cranston, Ernest Lefever, Inis Claude, Paul Ramsey, and John Courtney Murray, S.J. are among those who have provided advice on morality to statesmen, which the latter have largely ignored. But we seem yet far from definitive answers to the fundamental problems the subject raises, some of which the present essay attempts to further explore.

The Pervasiveness of Reification

Reification is the treatment of abstract concepts as if they had concrete material existence. The use by leaders and peoples of such symbols as "national security," "national interest," even "state," "nation," "government," or "law," tends to blind us all to the real people and real situations which are implicit within these symbols. If we do not return to human beings, the problem of morality in foreign policy—which is a problem of values and principles held by human beings, and the conduct of such human beings in interactions with others who also hold values—remains obscure and meaningful answers cannot be found.

Concepts like "the state," "national security and interest," even "law" and "government" are after all only abstractions which when reified shield the real people who, whatever their titles or elite roles, actually guide human affairs. In the last analysis we are always dealing with leaders who speak for people so long as the latter consent, or in case of tyrannies or autocracies, so long as the leaders can maintain their control. Only leaders, in the name of "law," apply commonly agreed-to standards that remain valid only so long as the values underlying them are shared and accepted—for example, was the leaking of secret government communications the illegal activity or were the means used to prevent such leaking that which was illegal? Only leaders tell other people on their behalf or as their targets what the "national interest" is supposed to be. Leaders are, in the end, only human beings with all their capacities and flaws, as we are so painfully reminded when we contemplate a Nixon or a Carter—or a Charles de Gaulle, a Henry Kissinger, or an Idi Amin.

Is there such a thing, really, as "national survival"? Who, what survives? If one hundred million or more Americans were killed in a nuclear holocaust, would the United States have survived even if there were no further damage? It certainly would not be the United States we know now.[4]

If, as Charles Frankel has suggested[5] a dictatorial regime came to power in the United States which established a ruthless and ubiquitous secret police and incarcerated, say, "only" three million people as "enemies of the regime," would the United States have survived? It certainly would not be the United States we know now. On the other hand, if the United States kept its present democratic system of government unchanged but agreed like India to belong to the British Commonwealth as a republic, would the United States have survived?

Reification is what makes possible the phenomenon of "bureaucratic detachment," so elegantly described in the following quotation from James Thomson about Vietnam:

> In quiet, air-conditioned, thick-carpeted rooms, such terms as "systematic pressure," "armed reconnaissance," "targets of opportunity," and even "body count" seemed to breed a sort of games-theory detachment. Most memorable to me was a moment in late 1964 target planning when the question under discussion was how heavy our bombing should be, and how extensive our strafing, at some midpoint in the projected pattern of systematic pressure. An Assisant Secretary of State resolved the point in the following words: "It seems to me that our orchestration should be mainly violins, but with periodic touches of brass."[6]

"Games-theory detachment" enables decision makers to engage in what Irving Horowitz once dubbed "the Howard Johnson sanitized vision of conflict."[7] Abstract concepts and distant human relationships are linked into imaginary "problem situations" wholly distinct in the minds of many statesmen and decision makers of lesser breed from their own "real" world. Thus, the savage fighting in Vietnamese villages turns into "pacification"; the terrors of North Vietnamese civilians into "graduated pressure"; the bribing of Chilean publishers into "preservation of press freedom"; the smearing of Martin Luther King into "cointellpro"; the tapping of subordinates' phones into "leak plumbing." In each instance, the effects on individuals are submerged into the necessities of "programs" which run on momentum, impervious to review, dictated by the alleged requirements of the higher abstractions. Owing to the reified presumption of national security interest, the question of morality, of the personal suffering of some and the possible personal responsibility of others, simply need not arise. Real people, whether the victims of such actions or the consciences of those who perpetrate them, simply cease to count—all in the name of a "higher morality," that of the interests of the state.

This is what is changing. If we wish to come to grips with the problem of morality today, we must return to human beings and realize that in fact it was Nixon and Kissinger (with Geneen of ITT, Helms of CIA, and various lesser fry) who sabotaged Allende, and were and are accountable for the actions of "the United States in Chile"; that it was Castro who may have done in Kennedy because the latter may have tried to do in Castro, making them both accountable for the actions of "Cuba" and "the United States." Nuremberg may have been early though not necessarily premature in convicting men whose defense it was that they acted in the name of the state. But by the end of the twentieth century, it had become apparent that such defenses would no longer be accepted by publics, at least in the Western world. From this point on, men are to be judged with all the complexities such judgments imply, not the reified abstractions under which they have been acting in the past.

The Cloaking of Power in False Virtue

Why are the moral foundations of *realpolitik* crumbling in the test of time? There is certainly no denying the empirical finding in the world today of an overwhelming and almost universal tendency on the part of leaders to "seize what they can get," as Machiavelli advised, "and hold what they have acquired."[8] The "drive to power" seems to remain as firm a motivating force in international politics today as at any time in history, whether for state leaders or for opponents of existing regimes—whether these are national or social revolutionaries, or a mix of both, or transnational actors such as multinational corporations

(MNCs), individuals operating across boundaries, or international public or private organizations. The "haves" continue satisfied with, and trying to expand the reach of, their grasp on the sinews of world power; the "have nots" endeavor to see the goods redistributed, frequently saying they are overthrowing injustice, but fundamentally animated in most instances by the same self-interest. In an extreme view, the world seems to remain Hobbesian enough to justify both the sin and redemption schools of theology and the famed statement in reference to diplomacy that "the act of acting (by the state) is itself evil."[9]

Yet what is crumbling in the midst of all this activity is the acceptability of proffered justification by those speaking for the state. Selfish actions taken in the "national interest" continue to be cloaked in noble language, virtuous principles, and high moral sentiments. Thus, Kennedy was not extending the American empire to the Southeast Asian mainland, but making it possible for the less developed world to build independent nations and achieve development. In this rhetoric, he was reminiscent of Teddy Roosevelt and Lloyd George who did not avow to imperialism but to the "emancipation of peoples," or of Benito Mussolini who was not aggrandizing Italy but saving Ethiopia from tribal barbarism. De Gaulle was not avowedly creating spheres of influence, but preserving European civilization from the "twin hegemonies of the Giants," reminding one that Woodrow Wilson was supposedly occupying parts of the Caribbean, Mexico, and the new Soviet Union to strengthen democracy and hopes of self-determination. Nixon, in 1969 and after, was not preserving in Vietnam his best options for reelection, but giving the South Vietnamese a final chance to achieve "peace with honor"; just as Clemenceau, intent on the paralysis of Germany or Bismark, concerned with Prussia's hegemonic aspirations, claimed they were "assuring the peace of Europe." To this day, Brezhnev is not consolidating Soviet control in East Europe behind detente but "building world peace through coexistence." Fewer and fewer people in the world today accept and believe these multiple deceptions.

Since the early 19th century, leaders have become ever more sharply aware that this is an age in which the masses of their peoples perceive themselves increasingly more deeply affected by the interactions and interrelationships of a multiplicity of nation states—after all, they will suffer the consequences of international economic crises or shed the blood in international wars. Accordingly, the masses of people have to believe or be made to believe in causes, principles, norms, virtues, and justice—as seen in their own codes. Leaders themselves have to do so. They are therefore not necessarily or always consciously lying or deceiving themselves or others. They are in fact practicing *Staatsräson*, reasons of state, under the growing constraints of popular scrutiny and their increasing needs for popular support. The result is the massive dependence of leaders on noble and moralistic rhetoric, whether such rhetoric is founded on the alleged necessities of the preservation of the state, or on those preserving peace in the community of nations.

Cloaking conduct governed by statesmen's relatively temporary judgments of *Staatsräson*, or by their relatively narrowly conceived judgments of justice in the international community, in the unmitigated expression of its moral validity is an extreme temptation of leaders, which they follow to their peril. Conversely, as we shall note below, cynicism among their publics leading to disbelief that morality really does or even can play any role in the behavior of leaders of states is an equally dangerous tendency. Under these conditions, publics will gnaw at the state and its leaders until they destroy each other by ceasing to share common values altogether. The United States came perilously close to such circumstances in the years 1973-75.

The Perils of Rule and the Fickleness of Public Values

Why are moral principles and the presumed universal norms underlying them so often overplayed by many leaders, as already suggested, thus leading to cynicism when illusions are shattered? Why are overarching principles invoked, rather than more modest ones that stand at least a minimal chance of credibility when policies are judged? One may have to search for answers in the perilous nature of rule in the world today. Governing has become risky everywhere because of the enormous growth in the twentieth century of individual and group will assertions. This in turn derives from the latent effects of universal mass education—a phenomenon less than a century old.

Since the legitimacy of political leaders tends to be increasingly questioned in so many places by more and more of their subjects, whose growing level of education enables them to question their governors' competence and whose increasingly participatory role in society elevates their ambition, authority at all levels and in all societies tends to be constantly undermined and under fire. This is another long-term result of the historic change wrought by the French Revolution—in the Western world at least—from monarchic, hereditary, and aristocratic-elite rule to representative republics, universal suffrage, and popular democracies or dictatorships. We must now live with the fact that individuals and groups at all echelons of society will make increasing assertions of "rights" and will make these assertions felt.

At the same time, and paradoxically because of the same phenomena of multiplying group and individual will assertions, almost always intensively reported by the mass media, it is more than ever difficult for leaders or lesser decision makers to "stick by principle" and yet retain command. The increasingly complicated nature of politics in the late 20th century obliges leaders in practice to construct compromises straddling the widest possible range of ideolgoically or even morally principled positions simply to safeguard their rule. We may safely propose that this is true in socialist, autocratic, or other types of political systems, as well as in pluralistic ones.

Thus, Nixon led the rapprochement with China which in turn, permanently we may hope, ended the "good versus evil" cast of international politics which Nixon himself had done so much to propagate in the post-World War II cold war, and led to the present relative deideolization of international affairs. President Gerald Ford accepted substantial portions of detente diplomacy and turned from an apostle of conservatism into an apostle of pragmatic compromise. Jimmy Carter moves easily from liberalism to conservatism and from a certain type of neoisolationalist passivity to activist internationalism and back again. The justification for such compromises becomes extremely difficult to accomplish without misty, vague, and frequently overarching rhetoric. The latter is used freely whenever possible.

Grandiloquent explanations are then all too easily disbelieved, compounding the existing public cynicism. If leaders stand for well-defined values, and have attained positions of power preaching these values, why do they not always act in accordance with them? If, on the other hand, they are prone to compromise, offering a variety of pragmatic explanations rooted in the necessity of securing consensual support for their rule, then what real role do morality and values play? The public in that case turns to sensing politics as in fact only an ever-fluctuating and evanescent pursuit of power for its own sake. But publics generally refuse to legitimize leaders who seek only to exercise power over them; they yearn for and seek leaders who will presumably use power on behalf of ends in which the publics believe.

Yet public values are themselves changing at such rapid pace that, even with the best of goodwill, leaders would find it difficult to adapt to their flux. This is not likely to diminish in an increasingly modernistic, rational, protoscientific, and semieducated world. Education and new technologies, along with the new mobility, are constantly instilling deviant or varying behavior, changing mores and lifestyles and bringing forth new notions of "good" and "evil," propagating new morality and new values. The "great American virtues" of the recent past, for example, did not include "gay liberation" or "chairpersons" in state legislatures. In the Muslim world, many today who were themselves educated in Western schools laugh at the notion that Christianity stands for justice, charity, and the brotherhood of man. Even values in the so-called socialist world are changing radically when leaders of major Communist parties in advanced countries abjure the class struggle, and the thought of Mao attracts as many as that of Marx.

It is at least worth proposing that publics proceed on the basis of a far more skeptical perception of morality than do ruling elites in general. Publics generally do not expect killings, brutality, or wanton destruction to cease overnight; nor do they believe there is any millenium around the corner. Leaders, however, especially in the nuclear age, tend to be mesmerized by the rhetoric of universalistic moral standards. The media and press, with scholars and worldly observers in tow, if not prompting them, trumpet an age of universal human rights along with "an age of interdependence" and a general reign of goodwill. But what are these presumably universally valid ethical or moral standards which are to bind the peoples across frontiers?

Despite the existence of a Universal Declaration of Human Rights subscribed to by most of the world's governments, even the simplest and most fundamental of all human rights, "the right to be free," remains *de facto* an aspirational quest rather than an established right in positive law throughout most of the world. Stating this is not to deny the validity of a higher natural law upon which the aspiration for the widespread establishment of human rights must of necessity be promised.[10] It is simply to call attention to the reality that often men, who should be free and live in dignity, in fact are not and do not.

The problem is compounded by the pervasiveness and persistence of culture-bound and therefore relative standards of behavior. What is moral and acceptable in *X* can be regarded as highly immoral behavior in *Z*, and vice versa. Under almost endlessly varying sets of behavioral norms and in the prevalence of culture-bound moral standards, leaders would appear better served to exercise extreme caution in preaching and advancing solutions premised in universalistic standards of morality. Perhaps the ethic of the Sermon on the Mount is coming closer to universal acceptance in an age of rapidly homogenizing communications, mass media like TV, and of a shared educational foundation in at least the three Rs. But neither the standards of the Sermon, nor those of the Universal Declaration of Human Rights are as yet anywhere close to being universally practiced. Even slavery continues to exist in parts of the world, as Eldridge Cleaver recently reminded us,[11] and many societies continue to judge a human right to be unquestioning female obedience to males. How does one in fact distinguish among "human rights"? The torture of political prisoners in Brazil or the Philippines is indeed reprehensible in the extreme, and should be condemned in the most vigorous terms; but this cannot condone silence on the equally reprehensible treatement of peons or peasants who are routinely subject to dispossession or manhandling by landlords or rulers in these same or other countries.

Since there do not yet exist firmly accepted and established universal standards, temptations by governmental leaders to speak as if they were already established are not only unrealistic but potentially dangerous when applied to interactions among leaders of states; as Arnold Wolfers suggested 30 years ago, an absolutist or perfectionistic ethic on the part of leaders of one or more states in international relations tends to generate more conflict than it mitigates and may cause more pain than it relieves.[12] Once more, this is not to argue that civilized state leaders should in any sense acquiesce silently to some of the more hideous practices which indeed do exist throughout the world—such as the detention or torture of political opponents, or the practice of apartheid—but only to point out that human rights must be approached with great caution and prudence by governments, even those themselves least guilty of possible infractions.

The Search for Moral Foreign Policy

The absence of as yet universally applied moral standards does not relieve the obligation of leaders and statesmen to act morally within their own time- and culture-bound codes. This is prudent and expedient in statescraft if the character of state interaction is to be as predictable as possible and to remain as consonant as possible with humanity's aspirations for progress. And it is ethical because it is the best that can be achieved, up to this point. A rational foreign policy is therefore a moral one and conversely, among statesmen of the West, at least, such a policy must seek—though prudently and discerningly—to advance the gradual implementation of the Universal Declaration of Human Rights.

The question in international affairs can never be "Can a state's behavior be judged normatively, or expected to be normative?" for all rational behavior including that of the state is logically normative in that it seeks to advance or delay certain ends and proceeds on the expectation of some value realization. Moreover, the state is a reified abstraction hiding the reality of human beings acting for the state. The real question has to do with the kinds of ethical standards and norms which govern the behavior of a state's leaders. It might be asked as follows, both as a problem in practical statecraft and as a moral test of a state's policy: "Does the behavior of a given state's leaders conform with the values and norms that prevail both among that state's people as well as with those that prevail generally in the world at the time they are acting?" So tested,

20 THE DYNAMICS OF HUMAN RIGHTS IN U.S. FOREIGN POLICY

Hitler's policies would have failed on at least the second part of the test for both the self-determination of peoples and the elimination of racism—among others—had become widely accepted aspirational norms of the international community at the time he was acting.

We can thus begin to equate "moral foreign policy" with behavior by state's leaders which conforms to the prevailing ethical and value standards of their time. "Time" provides the key to the understanding of values which may help explain why the value of resisting aggression in Europe in the 1930s and early 1940s could not be automatically transferred to the civil wars of Southeast Asia in the 1960s. The shift of values with time also helps explain why it is so unlikely that statesmen—contrary to their general conviction—can in fact learn from the "lessons of history." History, regrettably, is a very poor teacher since values, as well as the identification of events as manifestations of particular values, are constantly in flux. It is almost impossible today to imagine that the Zulu War or the repression of East Indian rebellions could look righteous to men of rectitude in pre-World War I Britain, or that the eradication of native Americans could be applauded as heroism in frontier America. Bringing civilization to the heathen was the rationale in these cases, a rationale as little accepted in today's world as is "resistance to aggression," since many in today's world tend to see "justice" in certain national liberation wars regarded by others as "aggression," and since the search for "justice" has climbed to predominance in today's prevailing pattern of values.

The inseparability of morality and foreign policy is demonstrable in innumerable examples. Solzhenitsyn reminds us of it when he speaks from an ethically absolute platform after his departure from Russia and pillories the West for resisting the notion "Better Dead Than Red." Yet it is of course never "better" to be dead in the literal sense than to be anything else; but it may be "better" not to be "red" assuming "red" is that necessarily "bad" state incompatible with the "good" life men can enjoy. For the world as a whole, it is probably in fact "better" that 300 million or so people in East Europe and the Soviet Union be "red" and thus politically "dead" (assuming they all concur with Solzhenitsyn, which is by no means demonstrated) than for it to suffer the consequences of a nuclear holocaust. The absolutist language employed by Solzhenitsyn is therefore morally ineffectual and his argument flounders in futility.

Benes faced a basic moral problem when as Czech foreign minister he twice (1938 and 1948) failed to engage his country in armed warfare against vastly superior enemy forces. But in the absence of assured Franco-British and later Allied support, Benes made a possibly wise moral choice by avoiding the needless sacrifice of lives. This in no way justifies "appeasement" or "surrender" in every circumstance; it merely points to the need for judging in each situation which course of action is most likely to minimize suffering and pain. Faulty analysis, not immorality, led Chamberlain to "appease" in 1938; but by 1939, when Poland was invaded, the only moral course of action left was to declare war on an international outlaw. American leaders, judging by their own lights and perceptions, analyzed faultily though did not act immorally by involving themselves against what they perceived as aggression in Vietnam in the early 1960s. By 1969, however, once they had recognized faulty analysis and declared their intention to withdraw from the war, their decision to spread this withdrawal over a four-year period was immoral in the extreme. More American and Vietnamese lives were lost in 1969-72 in Vietnam than in the preceding period. Immorality was compounded by further reversion to faulty (or, one might say phony) analysis, in that there were no rational grounds whatever for believing during 1969-72 that the South Vietnamese could achieve on their own what they could not achieve together with the U.S. in 1965-69.

In the perceptions prevailing among world leaders today, armed forces and even nuclear stockpiles remain necessary to ensure the protection of their peoples. The possession of such instruments, in light of these perceptions, is not immoral *per se*. It would become so only if the analysis underlying the perceptions were demonstrably shown to be false. While it is possibly false to analyze "counterforce targeted" nuclear weapons as providing an effective deterrent to attack—they would in fact enhance prospects of a "first strike"—it has certainly not been demonstrated that "mutual assured destruction" rests on a faulty premise. Accordingly, to disarm unilaterally in the area of nuclear weapons might in fact prove far less moral than maintaining a so-called "balance of power" which has preserved peace between the superpowers for nearly 30 years.

Again, it is plainly immoral to support a policy of ignoring the perils of environmental desecration, and to oppose one minimizing such perils. This is because common-sense and prudential ethics command that clean rivers, clean oceans, clean air are "better" for human existence than polluted ones. The problem, of course, arises in execution and when the promotion of one set of values appears to demand sacrifice of another. Is it "moral" to support policies of environmental control when the latter might further damage the welfare of people in a less developed country or region?

In such dilemmas, the ends in choice must ultimately be compared situationally. The end of environmental control is no doubt good, but is it less good or better than the end of promoting development "in such and such a place at such and such a time"? If the question is asked without the last portion placed in quotation marks—that is, if we ask whether it is better that the world be reasonably clean or that we avoid a world of have nots growing constantly more conflictual with the haves—we are led right back to fundamentally unreal choices between abstract ends, returning us to reification and to absolute ethics. Real answers to such dilemmas involve situational ethics that are place-, culture-, and above all time-bound. They also involve choices of means. The particular question at issue might be rephrased: "Which means will contribute most to minimizing environmental problems in country or region X at this or in the reasonably proximate future, while at the same time doing most to promote its peoples' welfare through economic development?"

In such examples, we see that choices of ends and means in foreign policy are invariably normative and that moral choices—choices conditioned by prevailing culture- and time-bound norms—do not, in fact, should not, require consideration of absolute ethical standards. Thus we conclude that morality in foreign policy (as in other domains) is not synonymous with "perfection" but minimalist in nature; to achieve the best possible (i.e., the most conducive to the mitigation of tragedy in the human condition) under the circumstances.

The Vehicles of Moral Choice

There are three major vehicles of state and human behavior through which we can hope that leaders of states with vastly differing value structures and political systems will tend toward moral choices in foreign policies. First, however slowly and painfully, a gradual but undeniable accretion of universally acceptable norms is occuring largely through the role of public and private international organizations. The United Nations General Assembly continues in this respect to perform an indispensible role in providing the world community with advanced announcements of what is wanted and what is no longer tolerable. In the words of Inis Claude, it is "writing the graffiti on the wall of history."[13] The United Nations General Assembly and other like bodies demonstrate for us month by month and year by year what the prevailing code words and underlying norms are: "national liberation," "a measure of economic redistribution," "increasing welfare in developing countries," "abolition of racism," "interdependence if it does not serve only the rich," etc. In this general area, the "affective motivation" of statesmen and leaders, or their desire to put their fingers on the pulse of history and to move it forward toward the realization of the values they hold, is a most powerful motivating force. But this cannot progress very far in advance of a process of rational intercommunications between state leaders, in which these ends and values can be realized and advanced in practice.

Rational diplomacy, the second vehicle, may be viewed as a continuous process of communications between all actors in the international system for the purpose—as Roger Fisher so persuasively summed up[14]—of fractionating conflict, solving problems, and managing the world through increasingly clearly stated "tasks." The tasks are tackled by means which diplomacy can fashion through rationality. Here the "effective" motivation of statesmen—their professional desire to make things run smoothly and well—is the most powerful motivating force.

For example, the vexing problem of international terrorism can probably not really be solved until relevant universal norms, the absence of which causes expressions of terrorism in the first place, are more firmly established. But in the interim, diplomacy can gear itself up for the operational or managerial resolution of such problems. It can, for example, attain a minimally acceptable definition of the "terrorism" that is to be eliminated. Such a minimally acceptable definition, which remains as close as possible to the task of elimination and as far away as possible from evaluating the ultimate ends which terrorists pursue, could perhaps be drafted as follows: "Terrorism is the apprehension of the persons or the property of others by individuals not authorized to do so by and through means not valid under existing municipal and international laws." The problem of elimination then might become entirely one of means for this task. Nonetheless, terrorism would not be solved as an international problem until norms such as the unfettered right of national liberation for each group demonstrably capable and desirous of statehood were more firmly and universally established.

A third vehicle available for the promotion of moral if not necessarily perfectionist behavior on the part of states is continuing popular scrutiny of leadership actions in all states and culture areas by means directly available to private individuals and groups, whether in the media or press, the professions, or organized groups of the general public. Such popular scrutiny can only be based on the value patterns, norms, and codes prevailing in each polity or political region at the time perceived abuses occur. It is the task and the glory of writers like Solzhenitsyn—even if the world does not always espouse the extremist solutions they sometimes propose; of organizations such as Amnesty International which report and denounce the evils of rulers; or parties, like the Japanese, who strain to rid themselves of leaders caught in corruption or malfeasance; or of journalists like those of the American press who energized the Congress and other authoritative bodies to bring down a chief executive engaged in ruthless abuse of power.

Similarly, on a world-wide scale, "international public opinion"—for much that it has been decried as a sham and considered by hard-nosed observers as an object worthy only of flouting—has played an enormous role over many decades in setting the outer limits of the possible for statesmen. This is particularly so when international opinion finds spokesmen that can concretize it. It may be hard to admit but foolish to deny that Bertrand Russell or Olav Palme ultimately exercised great influence on U.S. Vietnam policy, or that Idi Amin united much of the world behind his enemies. Far from ignoring this often inchoate and diffuse expression, statesmen tend on the contrary, and because their antennae in protection of their rule stretch far, to perceive it sooner and more sharply than others.

The Tests of Morality

We come finally to the question of how the American people can judge whether or not their foreign policy can be accepted as genuinely moral. We assume it is to be constructed within the limitations of a nonperfectionist ethic and within the bounds of its own culture and time-prevailing norms, which today include acceptance of the principles of the Universal Declaration of Human Rights as positive law.

At least part of the answer must lie in the continuous application of a test of means to ends in our foreign policy. Are the means we use commensurate and in harmony with the ends we seek? Is this relationship of means to ends proportionate and humane, or disproportinate and thus inhumane? In our culture the ends do not and cannot justify the means. Were we to begin claims to the contrary—and abortive efforts have occasionally pointed in that direction—our own value structure would quite quickly begin to disintegrate. This must be one of the principal lessons of Vietnam, and also of Watergate, where means like wholesale wiretapping and "enemies lists" proved quite disproportionate to the relatively low-threshold threat that may have existed in the perceptions of our leaders.

In Vietnam, the use of means disproportionate to the ends sought led to the polarization and subsequent potential disintegration of our domestic value structure, particularly after the decision had in fact been made in 1968-69 to get out of the war with or without victory, and this decision had been sanctioned by elections. The means finally proved disproportionate to the ends sought in Vietnam, not because they were insufficient, but because they were too large, too costly, and ultimately perceived as too inhumane for the ends advanced to justify them. The war in Vietnam was lost at home and not because of inadequate means in

Vietnam. Twice the means used in Vietnam would have lost the war even faster at home, because of the aggravation of the existing perceptual disproportionality that would have ensued. A test of means to ends is thus quite useless without, and dependent on, a direct test of the ends of policy.

The test of ends lies in finding out whether the policy objectives to which their affective motivations drive our statesmen and leaders, and for which they seek to earn public acceptance, are in fact properly in harmony (1) with fundamental, though culture- and time-bound, norms in our domestic value structure; (2) with prevailing international standards of opinion and conduct. When the affective behavior of leaders is allowed to serve abstract ends of *Staatsräson* devised in the sometimes remote scenarios leaders conjure up in their role of self-confident elites, the chances are strong that the ends of policy will fail to justify the means used, that the latter will cease to be further forthcoming, and that policies will fail.

On the contrary, when leaders set course on and explain policy objectives, tangibly and palpably related to prevailing world standards and to sentiments and currents pulsating among our people, the chances are strong that the means forthcoming will be commensurate with the ends sought, and that policies will succeed.

The sentiments, currents, thoughts, and feelings pulsating through the American public—even though the public is not generally well-informed until the proper effort of honest education has been made—must be assumed by leaders, and virtually on faith, to be basically generous, decent, rational, and humane. When leaders start from the opposite outlook, that the people are not only crass and ignorant, but inherently badly disposed or unconstructive—as perhaps Nixon did—the temptation to veil policy objectives in secrecy is overwhelming; and though policies so premised may succeed for a while, they will eventually fail in democracies because they do not rest on an assumed bond of mutual confidence, trust, and respect.

Conversely, and unless demagogues have been at work, sentiments pulsating in the public inherently tend to reject base or pure profit-seeking motives, or bloodthirstiness. The American people rarely condone "doing in the other guy," unless they have the strongest reasons to suppose he is doing it to them. Thus, today, there is little left of the sentiment so strongly held during, and for a period after, the Korean War that the Soviets would "do us in" if given the chance. Inchoately perhaps, but perceptibly nonetheless, Americans have sensed since the Vietnam War and the development of the Sino-Soviet conflict, that the Soviets will not do unto us that which we do not do unto them. Accordingly, an unrelenting search for power is far from the heart of most Americans. On the other hand, there is an unrelenting desire to preserve and protect the values shared at home, whether or not these values prevail elsewhere in the world.

American values and norms, though changing over time, continue to be first and foremost related to fortifying the domestic structure and homogeneity of the United States itself. Contrary to the older states of Europe, the United States does not begin to approximate even that limited measure of ethnic homogeneity and cultural impermeability existing in such states as Japan, France, or even Italy, Germany, the United Kingdom, or China. It must accordingly rely far more on centrally accepted principles of government and on "rules of rule," around which people of extremely diverse origins who have lived in the same territory together for only a very brief historical period can rally. As a result, American foreign policy can never be really divorced from the necessarily continued striving for harmony, cooperation, and preservation of understood principles of governance by Americans at home.

Ultimately, the government of the United States or of any country is not and cannot be seeking a "moral" foreign policy *per se;* what it seeks is a wise policy—a policy which is at the same time "realistic" (in the sense of adapted to existing and, however regrettably, power-oriented realities), "prudential," "rational," and "ethical." A wise policy in that sense will, *ipso facto,* be a moral one, In seeking a wise policy, leaders in world politics deal essentially with analytical problems of measuring ends against means in existing issues and situations, and under prevailing domestic and (to the degree possible) universal norms. Such leaders can no longer employ reifications such as *Staatsräson,* which are increasingly incomprehensible and unacceptable to peoples. They face dealings with human beings, at all levels and in all problems. In seeking a wise foreign policy, they must seek to ensure not the survival of the state *per se* as their highest goal, but as so well and long ago expressed by Santayana,[15] the survival of ends worthy of life. The means of policy must be commensurate with such ends.

The Importance of Human Rights

In present world politics, the development of policy means by states commensurate with the survival and spread of lifeworthy ends is most singularly important in the realm of human rights. Some 350 years after Westphalia and the beginning of the age of states, some 100 years after the beginning of the spread of mass literacy in the world, and some 35 years into the nuclear age, the principal actors who are finally asserting themselves on the world stage are millions upon millions of individual human beings themselves. In every portion of the globe, and even under the most repressive of regimes, individuals are clamoring for and demanding the rights to life, to minimal freedoms, and to the pursuit of the values they prize including—and dominatingly—justice as seen in their own lights. The development of policy means commensurate with the spread of such fundamental human rights can safely be predicted to become in the future an integral component in the conduct of U.S. foreign relations. The present volume was conceived to the furtherance of that end, and it is to the search for means appropriate to its fulfillment that the essays that follow are dedicated.

NOTES

1. Arnold Wolfers, "Statesmanship and Moral Choice," in *Discord and Collaboration* (Balto: Johns Hopkins Univ. Press, 1968). Originally published in *World Politics,* 1948.
2. Hans Morgenthau, *Scientific Man v. Power Politics* (Chicago: University of Chicago Press, 1946).
3. Hans Morgenthau, "To Intervene or Not To Intervene," in *A New Foreign Policy for the United States* (New York: Praeger, 1968). See also Ch. 8.
4. Charles Frankel, *Morality and U.S. Foreign Policy,* Foreign Policy Association Headline Series No. 224 (New York: n.p., February 1975).
5. Ibid.
6. James C. Thomson, "How Could Vietnam Happen? An Autopsy," *Atlantic Monthy,* April 1968.
7. Irving Horowitz, Lecture to Foreign Service Institute, 1971, at U.S. Department of State.
8. Machiavelli, *The Prince,* Trans. Musa (New York: St. Martin's, 1964).
9. Morgenthau, *Scientific Man v. Power Politics.* Also mentioned in other works by Hans Morgenthau.
10. Maurice Cranston, *What Are Human Rights?* (New York: Taplinger, 1973).
11. Eldridge Cleaver, interviewed by Curtice Taylor, *Rolling Stone,* 11 September 1975.
12. Wolfers, *Discord and Collaboration.*
13. Inis Claude, in a lecture to the Foreign Service Institute, 1972.
14. Roger Fisher, *International Conflict for Beginners* (New York: Harper & Row, 1969).
15. "Survival is something impossible; but it is possible to have lived and died well . . . .The function of a civilized government need not be only to preserve itself . . . nor even to preserve the state . . . but rather to redeem human life from vanity and barbarism, even if the agent in this redemption should itself perish." George Santayana, *Dominations and Powers* (New York: Charles Scribner's Sons, 1951), p. 210.

Chapter 2

Ideological Patterns in the United States Human Rights Debate: 1945 – 1978

Richard A. Falk

Assessing the American record on human rights over the period since World War II is problematic on several counts. For one thing, there is no agreement on what is the proper scope of inquiry for such an assessment. Does one consider the broad geopolitical sweep of American foreign policy that includes lending support to a wide variety of repressive governments, provided only that they are anti-Communist? Does one include the goals and effects of covert operations by the CIA? Or, in contrast, does one take account of the linkages that some claim make the cause of world peace depend on not pressing the Soviet Union or its close allies too hard on human rights? Also, to what extent do we base our assessment on the human rights situation in the United States? And, if we do, then do we make our judgments rest upon a comparison between American society and foreign societies at similar levels of economic achievement or by reference to the standards and norms embodied in international law? And, finally, do we conceive of the relevant portion of international law to consist only of validly ratified treaties or do we include authoritative declaratory documents (especially, the Universal Declaration of Human Rights) and widely endorsed treaties (e.g., Genocide Convention) that have not been ratified, but can be regarded as embodying an international consensus that qualifies either as customary international law or an instance of *jus cogens*?

Secondly, the literature on human rights is dominated by naive formalism. For some reason, until very recently, most of those attracted to human rights as a subject of academic concern were bewitched by words and international legal standards. Hence, the American record was judged primarily by how many human rights treaties were supported and ratified at a given time. This sort of formalism rests upon the twin pillars of legalism and moralism, postures that make the pursuit of human rights in the world seem apolitical, involving neither costs nor effects. It also presupposed that issues of human rights were exclusively concerned with what happens in foreign societies, and not at all directed at correcting abuses in America itself.

Thirdly, the promotion of human rights has often served as a propaganda vehicle for a particular foreign policy. The political right has favored emphasis on repression in Communist countries as a way of stirring trouble in those societies and reinforcing a hard-line approach to Soviet-American relations; this emphasis tends to be complemented by a refusal to be troubled by even the most severe violations in anti-Communist countries. On the left the reverse pattern is evident. The emphasis is placed on human rights violations in the capitalist countries (or in America itself) where American responsibility (and leverage) is greatest. By now, most of the left is also disturbed by repression in Communist countries, but is either reluctant to enter terrain dominated by militant reactionaries or believes that it is both futile and dangerous to press the Soviet Union too hard on human rights.

Fourthly, there often appears to be a very opportunistic quality about human rights diplomacy. In the most recent period, it seems obvious that President Jimmy Carter stumbled across the human rights theme on his way to the White House. Once used, it seemed to fit with his temperament, as well as fill an important need to engender domestic support for an activist foreign policy in a period of wide popular depression among the American citizenry after Vietnam and Watergate. Human rights built up some moral enthusiasm for U.S. world leadership without necessarily reviving the tensions of the cold war. In such an analysis, human rights are taken seriously as a concern because of their value in domestic politics, and the international effects of the campaign are incidental, and in certain instances may even be unwanted. In fact, pressing hard on human rights will cause antagonisms abroad with both friends and rivals, and may complicate prospects for economic cooperation, arms control agreements and alliance relations. Such a realization has evidently led President Carter to adopt a more "realistic" and low-profile approach in reaction to the negative aftereffects of his ebullient advocacy of human rights in the first months of his presidency.

Underneath these various factors is the elusiveness of policy in international relations. The reality of the state system, the diversity of social, economic, and political life on a national level, and the importance of fostering international cooperation make it difficult to assess the proper place for human rights in the foreign policy of a state, especially in the foreign policy of a superpower such as the United States. We do not even know with certainty what actions are effective so that we cannot have confidence that a given strategy will promote a desired result. Some argue that support for Soviet dissenters induces a decrease in repression; others feel it results in increased repression; others, a tightening; each view seems persuasive at different time periods.

However, despite all these difficulties, many people feel that indifference to the abuse of rights elsewhere is not the answer, that it would only reinforce the most power-oriented conception of international relations. Besides, even a highly selective pattern of help may still bring relief to a specific group or individual caught in a particular situation. Also, there may be unintended beneficial secondary effects arising from an activist human rights policy, such as stimulating opposition movements in repressive societies, giving dedicated civil servants within the American bureaucracy a mandate to pursue more enlightened policies, encouraging public support for nongovernmental activities in the human rights field, and exposing the gap between the moralistic creed of human rights and the imperialistic logic of geopolitics. Finally, dealing with the dangers and contradictions of the state system ultimately involves moving toward some kind of more integrated form of world order that would presuppose a sense of global community. The most critical foundation for such an evolution is the growth of sentiments and attitudes of human solidarity, which in turn rests upon a concern for the well-being of people as people, regardless of their geographical location or their ethnic, linguistic, religious, cultural, or ideological identity. Such a prospect seems intimately connected with deepening the sensitivity of peoples everywhere to human rights issues.

A Moderate Human Rights Cycle

If a conventional perception of human rights as expressed in formal acts (treaty making, U.S. voting) and official discourse (emphasis in statements by leaders) is accepted, then we notice a rather clear pattern of fluctuation in American behavior. The pattern takes the form of a cycle that seems constrained within certain rather definite boundaries established by mainstream American political attitudes.

Figure 2.1 seeks to portray the U.S. record in a summary form. The vertical axis suggests the level of support for human rights. The trend line from 1940 to 1978 fluctuates between the political center and the right, whereas line B suggests the boundary between the center and the right.

32 THE DYNAMICS OF HUMAN RIGHTS IN U.S. FOREIGN POLICY

The space between A and B represents the political center in which both national parties operate, with the Republican party more consistently in the space between A and C and the Democratic party hovering more consistently around C, or even occasionally straying across the C boundary into the CB space.

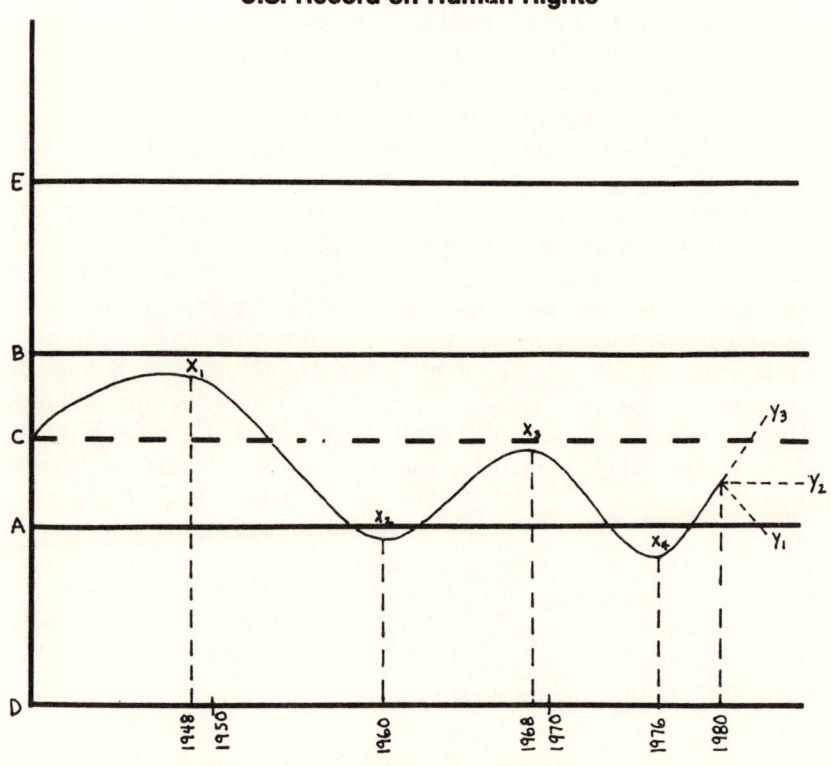

**FIGURE 2.1
U.S. Record on Human Rights**

X_1 = 1948 = Universal Declaration of Human Rights
X_2 = 1960 = Truman Doctrine
X_3 = 1968 = Nixon Presidency Begins
X_4 = 1976 = Carter Presidency Begins

The main trend line takes note of four turning points that mark shifts in the phases of the cycle. From 1940 to 1948 was a waxing phase associated with the presidency of Franklin Roosevelt. This period is identified with the proclamation of the Four Freedoms in 1941. This idealistic mood persisted, in a diminished form, for several years after Roosevelt's death in 1944. X_1 is located at 1948 when the postwar emphasis on human rights reached its culmination with U.S. leadership in the drafting and endorsement of the Universal Declaration of Human Rights. The year 1948 also initiated a waning phase in the human rights cycle as it is the year which most conveniently marks the real beginning of the cold war, epitomized by the proclamation of the Truman Doctrine, which offered economic and military aid to the Greek and Turkish governments to support their struggles against Communist encroachment.

The period from 1948 to 1960, consisting of four Truman years and eight Eisenhower years, was dominated by cold war stridency. John Foster Dulles was the most characteristic figure of the period, devoting his energies to building a global network of anti-Communist treaty arrangements and abandoning any serious effort to promote human rights except in the ideological sense of claiming that the anti-Communist group of states constituted "the free world" in distinction to the totalitarian realm constituted by the Soviet bloc, which was assumed in that period to be a monolithic system orchestrated in Moscow. In such an adversary climate the stress on geopolitics and military approaches to security dominated the foreign policy process.

A second turning point, X_2 1960, marks the beginning of the John F. Kennedy presidency, a period of expansive international liberalism, typified by the Peace Corps, the Alliance for Progress, and global involvement in the internal affairs of foreign societies. The United States under Kennedy was perceived as an idealistic force in international society, despite such contradictory features as anti-Castro interventionary tactics and the escalating involvement in the Vietnam War. After Kennedy's assassination, Lyndon Johnson pressed forward on civil rights for blacks, although such developments as the Dominican intervention of 1965 and government moves to intimidate domestic antiwar activists tarnished the Johnson image. Nevertheless, the Kennedy-Johnson period, 1960-1968, can be viewed as a positive period in terms of support for human rights.

The inauguration of Richard Nixon as president in 1968 brought a reversal of mood in American foreign policy that was also expressed as a downward turningpoint, X_3, in human rights. The Nixon years were premised on intergovernmental relations that generally accepted the legitimacy of territorial sovereignty and exhibited a notable insensitivity to the rights of citizens, whether at home or abroad. The pursuit of human rights in even the Communist countries was largely ignored in this period, exemplified by Nixon's China initiative and coordinated effort to achieve detente in the relations with the Soviet Union. Kissinger, the dominant presence in American foreign policy during the Nixon-Ford years, was openly scornful of introducing human rights concerns into serious diplomacy, treating such concerns as moralistic encumbrances upon the serious business of negotiating stable arrangements of state power. This was evident in the United Nations where the United States, during Daniel Moynihan's tenure, stridently used human rights as an ideological tool against the Third World in an effort to erode the antiapartheid campaign. Of course, some countercurrents were evident even during this time, such as Nixon's support for the ratification of the Genocide Convention, as well as moves to protect individuals and societies from international unofficial terrorism.

At the beginning of the Carter presidency, X_4, a new surge of positive emphasis on human rights commenced. Indeed, the focus on human rights was given unprecedented attention as a dimension of foreign policy during Carter's first year in office. An explicit claim was made that relations with both allies and adversaries would be shaped by human rights considerations. Whether this human rights emphasis has been consequential and will be sustainable is a matter of conjecture. From the outset the tension between human rights aspirations and geopolitical goals was evident, with the latter normally given priority. Administration leaders acknowledged that human rights concerns, however serious, should not be allowed to impair the quality of U.S. relations with strategic countries such as Iran, South Korea, and the Philippines. Similarly, although Soviet dissenters were given some early aid and comfort, later stages in the Carter administration suggest that arms control and trade relations are more significant features of the American relationship with the Soviet Union and cannot be successfully pursued if the stress on human rights is too strong. In effect, Soviet countermoves involve linking human rights attacks on their society with their denial of other forms of cooperation that are important to American leaders, and make it clear that the American hope of separating various aspects of Soviet-American relations is unacceptable to the Soviet Union. Such an interaction has forced American leaders to concede, at least tacitly, the reality of linkage and, then, to rank order their various objectives. In such an ordering economic cooperation and arms control definitely outrank human rights.

As of 1978 it is uncertain how the Carter administration will proceed on the human rights front. Undoubtedly it will seek ideological continuity by maintaining its general concern with human rights and by lending support to mild institutional initiatives at the United Nations. Whether any concrete pressures will be mounted remains obscure. Hence whether the years ahead will be properly interpreted as Y_1, Y_2, or Y_3 is uncertain (see Figure 2.1). Y_2, at this time seems the most probable future course, reflecting the downward pressure exerted by geopolitical developments in a period of economic anxiety and related concern about energy prices and availability. This pressure, however, is likely to be almost neutralized by the bureaucratic momentum created by endorsing human rights as the American anchor in foreign policy, giving bureaucrats and officials more of a mandate, than at any time except in the Roosevelt years, to treat human rights concerns in a serious, positive way. This prospect was reinforced by Andrew Young's presence as chief U.S. representative in the United Nations.

The political assessement offered here suggests that the status of human rights issues is resolved within the American political center, and is most characteristically located below midpoint line C. Nevertheless, from a conservative perspective, that is, below line A, the profession of human rights concern is perceived and attacked as if it were an aspect of left politics, an instance of "creeping socialism" that erodes American sovereign rights and interferes with the pursuit of national interests. In contrast, those who can be associated with the political left, that is, above line B, perceive the progression of human rights as a deliberate mystification by those in or close to power, disguising an imperialistic foreign policy with liberal rhetoric. Figure 2.2 represents, in crude terms, these diverse perceptions of the political identity of the human rights agenda.

FIGURE 2.2
U.S. Record on Human Rights as Perceived

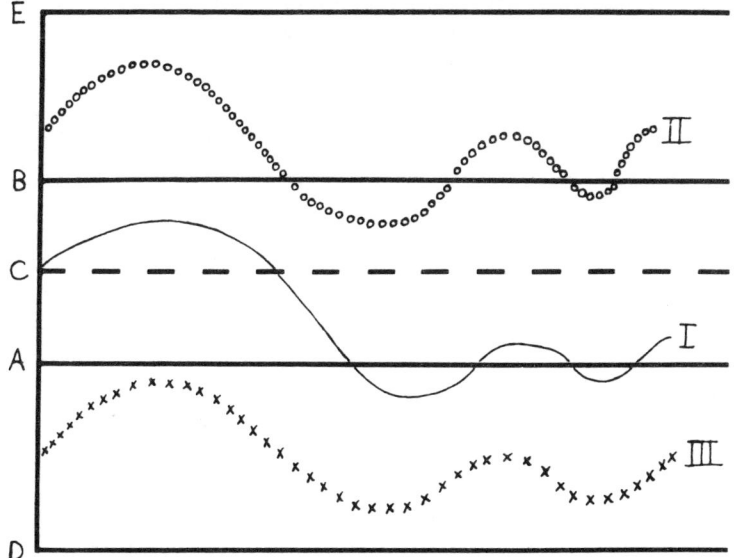

The mainstream perceptions of human rights is indicated by trend line I, the rightist perception by II, the leftist perception by III. ("Rightist" and "leftist" are used here denotatively for the sake of clarity in a manner that corresponds with conventional perceptions of political orientation.) The purpose of Figure 2.2 is to suggest the range of ideological debate pertaining to human rights issues.

There are several observations that can be made about this attempt to graph the United States' record on human rights:

1. It is based on a subjective appreciation of the degree of human rights emphasis generally perceived to exist at a given time; others could challenge the depiction of the trend by projecting a divergent subjective trend or by relying upon some indicators that might objectify the trend line in relation to one or more variables.
2. The United States' record as projected indicates the degree to which human rights policies are rooted in the overall setting of centrist politics, and indeed are mainly a feature of right-leaning centrism, as expressed by the A-C space on the graph. In fact, as portrayed, the waning periods have dipped below line A, indicating a rightist approach, while never penetrating line B, beyond which would indicate a leftist approach.
3. The trend line suggests a cyclical pattern that is generally correlated with presidential and party politics; turning points, except in the case of X_1, associated with the serious initiation of the cold war, coincide with changes in the person and party affiliation of the president. The more waxing phases have been periods when a Democrat was in the White House, and the waning phases were those when the president was a Republican. The cycle is self-generating, the idealistic phases inducing a concern with a foreign policy based on real interests, whereas the realist phases induce an idealistic impulse to vindicate the use of power with an active sense of moral purpose. This alternation in emphasis corresponds to deeply held attitudes embodied in American political culture and diplomatic history. The duration of these phases reflects, in part, the period of time which it normally takes for disillusionment to shift the political mood. If the economic or security situation worsens, then the idealistic strand would probably be eliminated, whereas if it improves it would be strengthened.
4. The perceived reality reflects political orientation; those in the mainstream of American politics would regard the trend line as generally reasonable. Those to the left would shift the line lower, while those to the right would shift it higher.
5. The purpose of this mode of presentation is to offer in concise form an overall image and impression of the United States record on human rights; it attempts to depict general relationships and to regard the controversy about the proper place of human rights in American foreign policy as an intramural concern of centrist politics.

Human Rights in the Domestic Political Arena

Part of the argument of the previous section was that support for human rights oscillates within a relatively rather narrow ideological range. In this section, the implications of these constraints for policy will be explored somewhat further. It is hardly necessary to add qualifiers, especially to underscore the limited utility of such rough and subjective political designations as "left," "right," and "center." The justification for this type of analysis is to reinvest the subject of human rights with political content, thereby challenging lawyers, moralists, as well as cynics, to offer a richer, more relevant type of analysis of the politics of human rights.

**FIGURE 2.3
U.S. Political Spectrum**

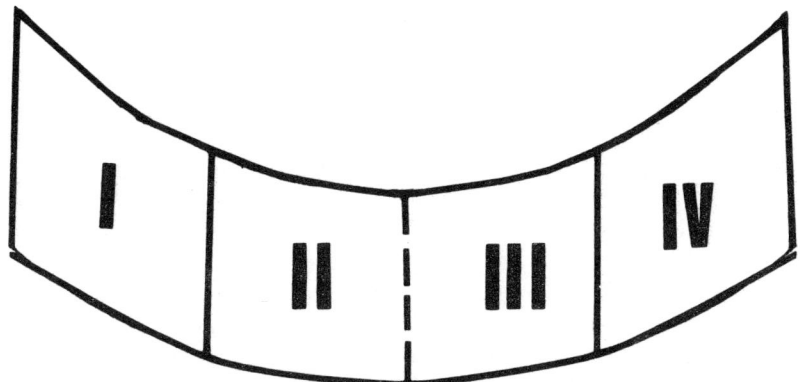

In Figure 2.3, I represents the left, II represents the more liberal portion of the center, III represents the more conservative portion of the center, and IV represents the right. II, III, IV are represented as occupying equivalent political space and as being each twice the size of I. Of course, this representation is crude and static. The relative strengths of these various positions are more elusive and vary from issue to issue and over time. The purpose here is to encourage a way of thinking that is generally in touch with the concrete situation. In a variety of respects, I is far weaker than IV, although IV, while influential, has also been excluded from a commanding position in relation to U.S. policymaking since World War II. The political direction of the United States has been generally positioned in III, the conservative-center space, with periodic enlargements of ideological orientation to embrace the more moderate fringe of II or the more moderate fringe of IV. The coalition-building space in American politics, then, can be extended from mid-II to mid-IV.

To assure the viability of a foreign policy position requires it to have a secure identity within II, and to be genuinely sustainable, it must also have some appeal to the moderate fringe of IV. In crude terms, a supportive coalition needs to be able to command two-thirds of the relevant space, a degree of support that happens to coincide with the constitutional requirements for treaty ratification by the U.S. Senate. The search for a left-leaning coalition based on support for II-III can rarely command a sufficient majority to achieve a two-thirds consensus, whereas a right-leaning one can produce effective results. The strength of IV rests on its influence in Congress, in the Republican party, in business, military, and media circles, in corresponding sectors of the bureaucracy, in grassroots support in the South and West, and in influential national professional and voluntary organizations. In contrast, I has virtually no "presence" in any of these domains, and II has only a shaky, marginal episodic presence, except in some important segments of the media. Political figures such as Robert Taft, Barry Goldwater, and Ronald Reagan are associated with IV, whereas George McGovern, Eugene McCarthy, and Ramsey Clark can be associated with II. Both Goldwater and McGovern won presidential nominations and were decisively defeated at the polls, reinforcing the political dominance in this period of the political center, while II has been only very episodically relevant and really only influential during the short period in the later 1960s and early 1970s when anti-Vietnam sentiments crested.

In 1978 the debate over the Panama Canal treaties illustrated in vivid form the veto power of the American moderate right in the context of coalition-building for foreign policy purposes. Of course, the nostalgic significance of the Panama Canal, its national security role, and the decision by Ronald Reagan to rest his claim for national leadership mainly on a campaign of opposition to the treaties all accentuated the normal circumstances. What is evident, however, is the need of the centrist Carter leadership to move right so as to diminish popular opposition and build sufficient support for the treaties. The support of conservative senators, of the Joint Chiefs of Staff, and of Henry Kissinger, Gerald Ford, and William F. Buckley, rather than that of prominent liberals, is what the Carter administration relied upon in its struggle to build a ratifying coalition. Such a reliance meant making the treaties more attractive to conservatives, and this was done by acquiescing in a series of amendments and reservations. In actuality, the colonial features of the treaties, as well as their ambiguity about the occasion of U.S. intervention, makes them substantively, if not politically, vulnerable to rejection from the left.[1]

The relevance to human rights issues is apparent. No firm national commitments pertaining to human rights can be undertaken if viewed as objectionable by the more conservative fringe of III or the more moderate fringe of IV. For this reason, it is not surprising that the American record on ratification of international human rights instruments lags so far behind the actual standards of domestic observance in the United States. Presidential discretion is not so constrained, especially at the symbolic level. To make presidential initiatives into a durable line of policy, however, eventually requires a normal supportive coalition.

The ideological constraints on human rights derive from several general concerns held by adherents of conservative III, moderate IV outlooks. Broad perceptions of human nature and international relations play some role. These outlooks tend to take a skeptical, Hobbesian view of human nature and regard the world as an anarchic arena of conflict. Such views lead to a stress upon the supposed realities of power, as well as to the conviction that "peace" is promoted by "balance," "stability," and control, rather than by the promotion of decency within and harmony among states. In this regard, the advocacy of human rights, except as an instrument for exposing the moral vulnerability of ideological and geopolitical adversaries, is dismissed as wooly headed, pie-in-the-sky moralism associated with left liberals who inhabit space II.

The strength of this (III-IV) critique of human rights induces compromises with centrist political leaders. For instance, emphasis is upon universal rhetoric coupled with selective application so that the realist worldview prevails, although somewhat disguised by more humanistic pretensions. In turn, left liberals in II seek to be taken seriously by claiming that their more sweeping endorsement of human rights is not only righteous, but efficacious in conventional national interest terms. That is, the right-leaning coalition requirements skew the whole debate on human rights policy in a pragmatic direction, thereby eroding idealistic claims of principled behavior, as well as constraining the policy potential of a human rights emphasis.

The schematic division of approaches can be illustrated by representative voices. On the left, a moderate version of I, is the kind of position set forth by Noam Chomsky and Edward Herman:

> Human rights have tended to stand in the way of the satisfactory pursuit of U.S. economic interests, and they have, accordingly, been brushed aside, systematically. U.S. economic interests in the Third World have dictated a policy of containing revolution, preserving an open door for U.S. investment, and assuring favorable conditions of investment. Reformist efforts to improve the lot of the poor and oppressed including the encouragement of independent trade unions, are not conducive to a favorable climate of investment . . . For most of the sample countries U.S.-controlled aid has been positively related to investment climate and inversely related to the maintenance of a democratic order and human rights.[2]

Characteristic features of position I are illustrated in this Chomsky-Herman passage: a stress on economic (rather than ideological or geopolitical) motivation, no attention at all to formalistic criteria of support for human rights, and a guiding conception of human rights based on humanistic values. This left outlook is antiimperialist and refuses to qualify its endorsement of human rights at all by reference to overriding geopolitical considerations. Indeed, a distinguishing feature of I is to repudiate altogether geopolitical calculations in evaluating the moral content of foreign policy. The position is also critical of Soviet behavior, and more generally, of statism, except in the context of Third World struggles to establish their independent states so as to be free from outside control. The spokespeople for I rarely gain access to mainstream fora and tend to be read mainly by others who share their general orientation.

Position II, the more liberal sector of the political center, is intensely concerned with promoting symbolic, small-scale, gradual gains. Congressman Donald Fraser is an excellent example of this outlook, energetically working to expose human rights abuses and seeking to incorporate into U.S. foreign policy a genuine concern about human rights. Writing in support of the early emphasis by the Carter administration, Fraser said:

> I believe that Carter cannot only make good in his commitment, but that American interests will be advanced by doing so.[3]

Fraser's conviction rests on the view that "societies cannot long be governed peacefully in the absence of mutal respect among citizens and between their citizens and their government."[4] In effect, protection of human rights is a precondition for political stability and a convenient belief for an advocate of human rights to hold, but a difficult argument to sustain with evidence. The empirical record is too mixed; many highly repressive societies seem ultrastable. And, in a broader setting of time and space, Fraser associates American national interests with the "gradual evolution toward a peaceful international system" which he believes requires "the protection of human rights as a foundation for such a system."[5]

To demonstrate that he is not alienated from the political mainstream, Fraser analyses the policy option for the United States in the context of South Korea and the Philippines, two states with whom the United States has a significant security interest. In both instances, Fraser questions the objective character of this interest, and suggests instead that if the observance of human rights standards does not improve, the United States should modify these relationships. In the Korean context, Fraser argues that the "United States must be prepared to disengage from South Korea carefully and in full consultation with Japan on a step-by-step basis," while in the Philippines Fraser hazards the view on the American military bases that "the need for these bases . . . should be studied, because a reasoned argument can be made that they are not important to U.S. security."[6] Note that Fraser's tone is tentative, there is no stress on the economic underpinnings of geopolitics, and the argument is formulated without questioning the security assumptions or framework of the mainstream. Position II does have a minority presence in all significant arenas (government, media, public opinion), but its specific policy recommendations rarely prevail. The tone of position II may exert a genuine influence in periods of Democratic party occupation of the White House and the concerns of its adherents are useful at all times in exposing the realities of human rights abuse. It is important to emphasize the absence of communication between adherents of positions I and II, and the mutual exclusiveness of their respective views of the world. In this regard, II is much closer to III than to I; also IV is much closer to III than I is to II. II tends to be more optimistic about the potential for human nature and global community within the existing world order system than I, III, or IV, although I is more receptive to revolutionary and utopian possibilities.

Position III, the mainstream right-leaning coalition, emphasizes the primacy of geopolitics, although in periods of liberal Democratic presidencies, it seeks to couple this orientation with a moral posture, including the appointment of representative figures associated with II to positions of symbolic leadership. The Carter administration, more than any other, has sought to make the promotion of human rights the moral centerpiece of its foreign policy, which in other respects maintains the priorities and assumptions associated with III. In his major address on foreign policy at Notre Dame University in May of 1977, President Carter said that "we have reaffirmed America's commitment to human rights as a fundamental tenet of our foreign policy."[7]

Carter was careful to emphasize the limited significance of the posture:

> We want the world to know that our nation stands for more than financial prosperity. This does not mean we can conduct our foreign policy by rigid moral maxims. We live in a world that is imperfect, and which will always be imperfect . . . I understand fully the limits of moral suasion. We have no illusion that changes will come easily or soon. But I believe that it is a mistake to undervalue the power of words and the ideas that words embody.[8]

In effect, Carter associates human rights with a posture of moral concern, rather than with the sort of policy and behavioral shifts that are stressed by adherents of position I. And unlike II, Carter's stress on the "imperfection" of the world signals a recognition that conventional American interests will not be jeopardized by the new emphasis on human rights. Geopolitics will continue to be given priority and policy will not be reexamined or reformulated in light of human rights ideals (i.e., the value of military bases in the Philippines or the commitment to uphold, by force if necessary, the status quo in Korea will not be questioned).

Such selective concern for human rights becomes more apparent in the statement of secondary officials responsible for shaping actual policy. When asked about selectivity, Zbigniew Brzezinski, responded:

> I'm sure you must have confronted this same issue in different walks of life . . . If you cannot punish all the criminals, is it fair to punish the one that you can punish? The same thing applies to the international community. If, in fact, you are in a position, without damaging your other relationships, to make progress in the case of country A but not progress in the case of country B, should you therefore abstain from making progress in country A? I would say no.[9]

Selectivity is defended here in general terms of capability, although it is clear from the context that Brzezinski intends that human rights must be subordinated to geopolitics, and that this meaning should be read into the phrase "without damaging our other relationships." The United States' relationship with Iran under the Shah reveals the extent of this selectivity. Here is a country with one of the worst records in human rights, and yet its leader was welcomed at the White House as "strong, stable, and progressive"; it was supplied with the most modern weaponry in great quantities, and an individual with a career that featured counterinsurgency more than diplomacy was appointed as American ambassador.

Since III is prevailing policy it is important to ask whether gains have been recorded. Of course, the basic claim is, in the words of Cyrus Vance, that "we are embarked on a long journey" and, hence, that "we can nourish no illusions that a call to the banner of human rights will bring sudden transformations in authoritarian societies."[10] On occasion, more tangible short-term gains are claimed. For instance, Brzezinski, reacting to the charge that we can do virtually nothing about human rights because almost every important country "has something we want or need" replied with the boast: "Is it really unimportant that we can get 10,000 political prisoners released in Indonesia? Is it really unimportant that, in the case of East European or Latin American countries, with some caution and without fanfare, things may have improved because of our concerns?"[11] Of course, the causal connections are elusive since a target government will never acknowledge that it is acting under pressure. Certainly, the Indonesian government will never acknowledge that their prisoner releases were stimulated by pressure from the Carter administration. Both II and III share the view that idealism and realism must (and can) be reconciled, although the emphasis is somewhat different because II tends to reformulate realism in longer term horizons and, therefore, raises questions about whether the presumed security preoccupations of inherited policy are really warranted.

Of course, the specific content of III shifts through time, partly in response to the growth of external pressures. For instance, minimum human rights credibility in global arenas in the late 1970s requires a much higher level of support for the antiapartheid campaign than was expected a decade earlier. The international consensus on this human rights issue has hardened, and its proponents have escalated their demands, in reaction to the frustration of their inability to achieve their goals.

Similarly, there has been a rise in the global acceptance of expectations that the satisfaction of basic human needs is necessary to any general conception of human rights. Earlier, in the formulation of the Four Freedoms and the Universal Declaration, such economic concerns were acknowledged, but only minimally. The Carter administration has consistently defined human rights as including three main clusters of concerns: (1) rights of the person to be free from government abuse; (2) "right to the fulfillment of such vital needs as food, shelter, health care, and education;" (3) right to enjoy civil and political liberties.[12] Carter went further in accenting this imperative:

> More than 100 years ago Abraham Lincoln said that our nation could not exist half slave and half free. We know a peaceful world cannot long exist one-third rich and two-thirds poor.[13]

At the same time, the human rights initiatives and claims directed at concrete circumstances of foreign societies have all concerned noneconomic violations of human rights, especially abuses of the person. The Carter administration has not been forthcoming with actual plans to restructure the international economy so as to give poor countries a favorable prospect for solving problems of domestic poverty. Thus, the expansion of the conception of human rights to include economic rights has been mostly verbal up to this point and hardly evident in policy settings.

Position IV is rather diverse in composition. Its adherents are not isolated from the mainstream political process as are adherents of I, and its more moderate representatives participate actively in the coalition-forming process. Indeed, even the more extreme adherents of IV, through commanding positions in politics, media, the military, or business exert considerable influence, and in this sense the relations of IV exceed II in their impact on the right-leaning coalition process located mainly in the political space of III. The concerns of IV need to be consistently taken into some account at the level of political action, as they possess an effective veto power over political initiatives proposed by American leaders. As a consequence, for value-sensitive subject matter such as human rights, the capability of III to sustain its policy depends eventually on attracting sufficient support (or at least avoiding active opposition) from IV.

The essence of IV during this period is to invest foreign policy with a heavily ideological character, stressing the fundamental conflict with the Soviet Union and communism, and emphasizing the moral superiority of the United States (and Western allies) in that struggle. Furthermore, that struggle takes precedence over other concerns, and waging it successfully should override by a wide margin all other goals of foreign policy. The more moderate adherents of IV have an affinity with the more conservative adherents of III in their insistence that human rights should be construed in political terms, should emphasize the concrete failings of Communist societies, and should give aid and comfort to opponents of state policy within those societies. The more militant adherents of IV would take any steps in their effort to transform Communist societies, risking even war to do so. In this regard adherents of III tend to be much more cautious in practice, even though they share many of IV's views on what is desirable. Adherents of IV also tend to regard human rights as mainly, if not exclusively, devoted to the failings and struggles associated with Communist societies; with other states they either consider human rights violations subordinate, or they neglect them altogether. Concerns with Communist societies exhaust the legitimate agenda on human rights and adverse pressure should not be placed on governments that are our geopolitical allies.

Daniel Patrick Moynihan is a clear example of a political personality who is in the border region of III-IV. He argues that:

> the Soviets are necessarily singled out by any serious human rights offensive . . . they are the most powerful opponents of liberty on earth today . . . their ideology . . . since the passing of Nazism and the eclipse of fascism as a school of thought . . . remains the only major political doctrine that challenges human rights *in principle*.[14]

Hence, to promote human rights necessarily implies mounting an anti-Communist ideological attack, with all that this portends for deteriorating Soviet-American relations.

It also means repudiating sharply the effort of the General Assembly of the United Nations, acknowledged as valid in the Carter diplomacy, to shift the emphasis of human rights from the defense of liberty to the pursuit of equality. Moynihan explicitly attacks Carter on these grounds and is, particularly, scornful of the view that on North-South issues the United States and U.S.S.R. might cooperate to mitigate the burdens of poverty. Moynihan believes that Carter's conceptual approach to human rights is objectionable to the extent that it diverts "our attention from the central political struggle of our time—that between liberal democracy and totalitarian Communism—and focuses instead on something else."[15] Even more pointedly, Moynihan rehabilitates the justification for Vietnam, acknowledging only that "the enterprise was doomed, because it was misconceived and mismanaged" not because it is "wrong or immoral to resist the advance of totalitarian Communism."[16] Indeed, he argues that the failure in Vietnam, if anything, has "added enormously to the importance of ideological resistance, and this precisely is the role of 'Human Rights in Foreign Policy.'"[17]

Moynihan's outlook is revealingly contrasted with that of Fraser. For Fraser the human rights stress should be mainly associated with the international relationship in which American responsibility exists. While he is quite prepared to condemn Communist abuses of human rights, his main concern is with encouraging liberal democratic values in non-Communist societies, partly on the basis of values, partly as a practical step to assure societal stability. From this perspective, the proper role of human rights is to shape policy that will reduce suffering and produce a more humane world; such a policy objective is not effectively advanced by exposing Soviet failures about which the United States can do little and which may even be counterproductive by creating more tension and less cooperation.

Hard-core adherents of position IV, especially in the 1950s, tended to view the espousal of human rights in general terms, as the province of ultra-liberals associated with position II. The earlier battleground involved sovereign rights, and their alleged compromise by submitting national behavior to international standards, procedures, and scrutiny. These concerns crystalized in a domestic political struggle relating to treaty making, climaxed by the narrow defeat of the Bricker Amendment designed to confine the president's authority to bind the country and to confine treaties within constitutional limits. Even though this initiative associated with position IV was defeated, the closeness and intensity of the struggle has inhibited III and reinforced the perception of IV as a potent blocking force in the human rights area. The poor ratification record of the United States in relation to major human rights instruments has reflected this domestic political situation.

More recently these hard-core adherents of IV dissent from the

Moynihan view that the universal character of human rights standards is an appropriate basis of foreign policy, provided the focus of emphasis is placed on the main danger posed by left authoritarianism associated with the Soviet Union. Their emphasis is upon disentangling geopolitical priorities from liberal moralizing. Such views surface, especially, in relation to criticism of U.S. policy toward South Africa. On the right there is strong resistance to the antiapartheid campaign, to the attitude expressed by Andrew Young, that race is an international issue and to what is regarded as a self-negating policy of American hostility to an economically, strategically, and ideologically useful ally in Pretoria. Underneath this criticism is more general opposition by hard-core IV to taking American foreign policy initiatives in close association with the United Nations. This opposition arises from bedrock nationalism that is threatened by any claims advanced on behalf of humanity or the global community. These anti-U.N. views held by IV are confirmed and inflamed by the tendency in recent years for the main political organs of the United Nations, especially the General Assembly, to take positions opposed by the United States and to be the scene of a rising tide of anti-American rhetoric.

We can draw several conclusions from this analysis of principal political positions in American polity:

1. Human rights policy, to be a sustainable aspect of American foreign policy, must be supported by a right-leaning centrist coalition associated with space III; for formal initiatives such as treaties or legislative actions, this coalition must normally extend across the boundary of III into space IV; for policy-making purposes space I is irrelevant, and virtually "invisible," that is, its adherents lack "weight" except in some limited intellectual circles; space II provides the inspirational leadership for human rights activities, as prod in times of liberal ascendency; as goad in times of conservative ascendency; the influence of space II is to provide data, ideas, rhetoric, and leadership personnel, but its positions are perceived as generally "unrealistic," and receive only diluted endorsement by the actual leadership of the country.
2. The character of mainstream political coalitions means that leaders must reconcile human rights initiatives with significant short- and long-term geopolitical interests of the United States, including especially its role as leader of a global anti-Communist network of alliances; such a requirement also means that the promotion of human rights must not be achieved at the cost of any significant domestic economic interests; these requirements severely constrain policymakers' freedom of action in the human rights field.
3. The United States is one of the few countries in the world in which the left, space I, is neither active nor repressed; as a result, the perception of "balance" in the American system is different from what it is elsewhere, even among the trilateral (or OECD) group of countries; for this reason, the attitudes of the General Assembly are discounted in the United States as "radical" and "extreme" rather than being received as "mainstream" expressions of international public opinion; furthermore, American debate on human rights is

rarely informed by or sensitive to more radical analysis of international developments; consequently there is serious distortion of political discourse in this country, and a genuine difficulty in communicating American official policy abroad; such difficulty is somewhat offset by the relatively high standards of human rights within the United States and by the degree to which idealistic American presidents are taken at their word, rather than their deeds, in many other parts of the world.

A Conjecture on Results

What can we expect to happen, over various periods of time, in relation to a variety of proposed human rights initiatives? What steps would be necessary to attain particular human rights goals? These are enormously complex questions. Policymaking that bears on human rights occurs in a wide variety of arenas. Also, human rights realities can be deeply influenced by a variety of policies that are undertaken for geopolitical reasons, ranging from covert operations in foreign societies to international trade and monetary moves. As a consequence, there is a tendency to fall back on traditional criteria of human rights progress: how many treaties proposed, signed, ratified?; has the number of political prisoners changed?; has the incidence of torture been reduced? Obviously, there is no objection to the consideration of such developments, only to their being used as a sufficient indication of progress.

It seems helpful to adopt a more politically sophisticated framework of assessment. This means, above all else, that the behavioral patterns of U.S. policy will be weighted more heavily than the rhetorical patterns. Hence, if U.S. leadership advocates support for needs-oriented development in Third World countries in public arenas, but uses the CIA to destabilize or overthrow governments so oriented, then that apparent incoherence should be exposed.

Also, if a forward rhetorical stand by the U.S. government on human rights encourages Americans and others to increase their financial support for human rights organizations and thereby gives these organizations a greater opportunity to exert influence, then this result should be noticed and appreciated. In effect, we need to be sensitive to the secondary and tertiary, possibly unintended, effects of a particular human rights policy. A systematic attempt to do this is beyond the scope of this paper, but a schematic outline of what is contemplated is suggested in Table 2.1.

This tentative checklist is designed only to encourage more politically sensitive styles of assessment of human rights activity than have been generally undertaken in the past. Obviously, the checklist can (and should) be refined continually through time.

TABLE 2.1
Checklist for Assessing Human Rights Policy

I. **Diplomatic Settings**
   1. Persuasive diplomacy
      a. Raising awareness
      b. Symbolic actions and omissions (e.g., honoring dissenters, avoiding ports of call, ambassadorial and other appointments)
      c. Private communications (e.g., ambassadorial representations to foreign governments)
   2. Coercive diplomacy
      a. Criticism and censure
      b. Military and economic aid tied to human rights
      c. Boycotts
      d. Sanctions
         i. psychological (e.g., preventing athletic contact), economic, public and private, diplomatic (e.g., breaking relations), and military
         ii. formal, informal
         iii. unilateral, collective

II. **Governmental Settings**
   1. Executive Branch
      a. Upgrading human rights concern via budgetary allocations, machinery, and appointments
      b. Cooperation with other branches of government, with international institutions, with NGOs
      c. Operational support by leadership of active concern by diplomats, bureaucrats
      d. Subordinating goverment programs, including CIA activities, to human rights objectives
      e. Discretionary leadership with respect to refugees, asylum, immigration policy
      f. Information and educational activities associated with United States Information Agency, Voice of America, and so forth
   2. Legislative Branch
      a. Insistence on compliance with legislative initiatives bearing on human rights
      b. Critical scrutiny of Executive Branch country reports on human rights situations
      c. Ratification of international human rights instruments such as Genocide Convention and the two main Covenants, Racial Discrimination

d. Hearings and reports on serious human rights situations identified by the U.N. and respected non-governmental organizations
   e. Support for Presidential initiatives
   f. Initiatives in response to severe deprivations (e.g., boycotts on critical imports and exports from worst violators)
   g. Review of human rights impact of U.S. foreign investment

III. **Policy Domains**
   1. Rights of the Person
   2. Economic rights and duties
      a. Support for new international economic order
      b. Priorities in aid and loans
      c. Trade liberalization for poor countries
      d. Democratization of international economic institutions
   3. Civil and political rights
   4. Reduction of arms sales and defense budget

IV. **Domestic Implementation in United States**
   1. National self-determination for Indian peoples
   2. Satisfaction of basic needs for the poor
   3. Rights of minority peoples
   4. Rights of radical opponents of government
   5. Control of infringement of rights by official agencies (e.g., FBI, CIA, etc.)

A Note on the Carter Approach

Although we have emphasized the Carter approach to human rights as a typical waxing phase of a cyclical pattern, it also has a certain distinctiveness that should be noticed. Unlike earlier moralistic periods in American foreign policy that tended to be oriented around creating conditions for world peace (Wilson, Roosevelt, Kennedy), the Carter initiative is centered on human rights as an end in itself. Never before has concern for the way governments treat their populations been given so much importance in the formulation of foreign policy.

As we have suggested, this embrace of human rights diplomacy by President Carter has weakened since its earliest period, especially in controversial contexts of specific country policies. Nevertheless, in the first retrospective glance at the Carter presidency its emphasis on human rights is its hallmark. Invariably, when critics or supporters of the Carter foreign policy evaluate what has been achieved, their benchmark is human rights. Even a geopolitical hardliner such as Brzezinski rests his defense of Carter's foreign policy, which he is, of course, principal acrobat (architect) on its success in infusing "American foreign policy again with a certain moral content. The human rights issue is very pertinent here."[18] No other American presidency could even claim to be so assessed.

In this respect, the stakes are raised. If the Carter emphasis is abandoned, or leads to his electoral repudiation, then the status and cause of human rights is likely to be set back. If it succeeds, even in part, then the whole cycle of waning and waxing may be shifted slightly to the left, making space II rather than IV the main focus for coalition-building activities. Such an outcome at this writing seems unlikely because of the wider rightward drift of American politics that is likely to erode Carter's broad emphasis on human rights and, more generally, thwart the more liberalizing tendencies evident in the American political mainstream.

In conclusion, the Carter experiment on human rights diplomacy has revealed the basic dynamic of the American political scene, and is unlikely to persist, much less prevail, because of the character of this dynamic. At the same time, the global setting of American policy has its own dynamic that is resulting in more external pressure for human rights implementation and internal pressure to commit violations since governments are relying on increasingly coercive approaches to contain their own populations. For a variety of reasons beyond the scope of this chapter, moderate politics is in decline throughout the globe.[19] The human rights policy likely to emerge from the limited contemporary United States political spectrum may make a positive contribution to the emerging global consensus on human rights but will, at best, have a modest impact on the domestic affairs of regimes which fail to meet this international standard of human rights.

NOTES

1. See R.A. Falk, "Panama Treaty Trap," *Foreign Policy* 30 (1978): 68-82.
2. Noam Chomsky and Edward S. Herman, "The United States Versus Human Rights in the Third World," *Monthly Review* 29 (1977): 22-45, 29-31.
3. Donald M. Fraser, "Freedom and Foreign Policy," *Foreign Policy* 26 (1977): 140-156.
4. Ibid., p. 141. See also Christopher, "The Diplomacy of Human Rights," Department of State Speech, 13 February 1978, p. 2: "Our idealism and our self-interest coincide. Widening the circle of countries which share our human rights values is at the very core of our security interests. Such nations make strong allies. Their commitment to human rights gives them an inner strength and stability which causes them to stand steadfastly with us on the most difficult issues of our time."

5. Fraser, p. 140.
6. Ibid., pp. 148-9.
7. "A Foreign Policy Based on America's Essential Character," *Dept. of State Bulletin* 76 (June 13, 1977): 621-625, 622.
8. Ibid., p. 632.
9. "What's Right with our Foreign Policy," *U.S. News and World Report* 13 (February 1978), pp. 28-32.
10. Cyrus Vance, "Human Rights and Foreign Policy," *Dept of State Bulletin* 76: 505-508, at 508.
11. "What's Right with our Foreign Policy," p. 32.
12. Vance, p. 505.
13. Jimmy Carter, "Humane Purposes in Foreign Policy," *Department of State News Release*, 22 May 1977, p. 4.
14. D.P. Moynihan, "The Politics of Human Rights," *Commentary*, August 1977, pp. 19-26, at 24.
15. Ibid., pp. 24-5.
16. Ibid., p. 25.
17. Ibid., p. 25.
18. "What's Right with our Foreign Policy," p. 28.
19. See R.A. Falk, "Authoritarian Tendencies as a World Order Problem." July 1977, mimeographed.

Chapter 3

Domestic Consequences of United States Human Rights Policies

Robert L. Borosage

When President Jimmy Carter launched his human rights policy, its course was confused and poorly plotted. From its inception, however, it was clear that the human rights stance would have broad implications in the United States, if nowhere else. President Carter committed himself to speak frequently on human rights questions, a commitment he has generally fulfilled. No matter how muddled the remainder of the administration's policy, that commitment alone insured that human rights would become a domestic concern.

The presidency is, as Theodore Roosevelt described it, a "bully pulpit." Presidential statements speak not only to their intended audience, but to the Congress, the bureaucracy, the pundits, and the citizenry at large. In his choice of themes, a president creates a new language for the bureaucracy, structures argument in Congress, provides grist for learned milling, and creates hopes and expectations in the citizenry. Of course, no president can control the uses of his words, and not infrequently presidents have found their own sermons quoted in support of policies they oppose. When Karl Marx announced "I am not a Marxist," he was expressing a plight felt by more than one president. But there is no question that presidents can define the framework for public discussion, and President Carter has done that with his human rights pronouncements.

No policy can be fairly judged after one year. The pinstripes on the political appointees are scarcely rumpled and the struggle with the permanent bureaucracy hardly joined. Yet even with this caveat, it is clear that the administration's human rights policy is aimlessly adrift, caught in a backwater of exceptions, excuses, and limitations. President Carter's bold pledge that human rights would be a "fundamental tenet" of his foreign policy was immediately hedged by his secretary of state, who called for "flexibility" and decried "mechanistic formulas" and "automatic answers," a clear bureaucratic warning that principle would not stand in the way of expediency.[1] The administration has never been willing to apply any human rights principles to the so-called "hard cases," the countries which we deem "important" for one reason or another: Korea, the Philippines, Indonesia, Iran, Zaire, Argentina. Even towards the Soviet Union, the administration has trimmed its human rights concerns to fit the currents of broader policy.

Many are beginning to suspect that the policy has already served its major purposes for the administration, and that those were primarily domestic. However confused in application abroad, the human rights policy has had clear effects in the United States. The rhetoric of human rights, of idealism and principle, has won public purchase of an activist foreign policy which otherwise would have been most difficult to sell. Former Secretary of State Henry Kissinger, among many others, has paid tribute to Carter for tapping "a wellspring of American patriotism, idealism, unity and commitment" by giving the "American people, after the traumas of Vietnam and Watergate, a renewed sense of the basic decency of this country, so that they may continue to . . . remain actively involved in the world."[2]

Equally important, the language of human rights has provided indirect absolution to the managers of the foreign policy establishment, rebuilding the élan, moral certitude, and thirst to govern of the certified national security elite, who were shaken— even a bit abashed— by their follies in Vietnam. Few countries suffer ignominious defeat without banishing its architects from public life, if not worse. Carter has managed to bring back Vance, Brown, and Brzezinski with scarcely a murmur about their hasty return to office.

For these men and their aides, human rights rhetoric has served as both personal and political balm. The haggard look of uncertainty, of self-doubt, of reticence has disappeared. Now Zbigniew Brzezinski, the president's national security adviser, boldly proclaims that the U.S. again "has to set about building a new world system," comparing the task to the effort of the early cold war days of 1945-1950.[3] What Arthur Schlesinger called the "liberal evangelism" of American foreign policy has been reborn, hardly an unmixed blessing for those who hoped the administration would minister to domestic ills rather than expend its zeal on global adventure.

In the past, evangelism contributed much to the cold war, and it is not surprising that a second product of Carter's human rights policy has been renewed ideological conflict between the Soviet Union and the United States. To some extent, this clearly served the administration's domestic political purposes. Carter began his human rights policy by focusing attention on the Soviet Union. Upon first setting foot in the Oval Office, he dispatched a personal letter to Andrei Sakharov, a leading Soviet "dissident." This was followed by stern public criticism of Soviet and Czech treatment of internal critics, by attempts to get the UN Human Rights Commission to investigate the USSR, by a request for vastly increased funding for the Voice of America and Radio Free Europe, and by several other actions bringing a well-deserved public obloquy on the USSR for its human rights violations.

These activities gained the administration early favor among conservative critics, and a start on rebuilding the broad foreign policy consensus at home. The results may have greatly outstripped the president's intentions, however. The renewed ideological attacks fed the hardly latent anticommunism which still exists on the surface of American politics. It emboldened those who saw human rights not as a humanitarian program, but as a political component in American foreign and domestic politics, providing moral purpose for intervention abroad and a logical excuse for military expenditure, secrecy, and repression at home.

For 25 years, anticommunism had provided the ideological glue for the national security apparatus. But after Vietnam and detente, a new rationale was needed. Many business leaders see potential markets rather than implacable foes in the Soviet Union and Eastern Europe. The annual military "red scare" no longer plays to enthusiastic, cowed audiences. "Red baiting" seems the frivolous pastime of foolish fanatics; "Soviet imperialism" did not justify secret gambols in Angola and Zaire. The Carter administration came to office committed to new directions, to putting the cold war to rest. Human rights—which liberals saw as applicable to Banana Republic dictators—was part of this new thrust in foreign policy.

Not surprisingly, the national security bureaucracies and their allies outside of government embraced the human rights argument, using it to regain moral authority for American militarism. Led by outside groups such as the Committee on the Present Danger, the cold war lobby used human rights as the center of its renewed attack on the Soviet Union. The committee, for example, was launched with traditional cold war rhetoric: "The principle threat to our nation, to world peace, and to the cause of human freedom is the Soviet drive for dominance . . . ."[4]

The success of this thrust is apparent after the first year of the Carter administration. Carter now promises to increase the defense budget rather than to trim it. He has allowed his secretary of defense to rail against the Soviet Union. He has been forced to accept interventionist exceptions to the Panama Canal Treaty. The cold war which Carter pronounced dead seems to have been reborn in the first year of his administration.

A Different Course

The administration's vulnerability to the rhetoric of the cold war results from its inability or unwillingness to develop broad popular support for a different foreign policy. The Carter team shares a distaste for public opinion and sees foreign policy as an arena for expertise and managerial ability, not for popular passion and participation.[5] As a result, the administration has been vulnerable to popular appeals to cold war fears and passions, particularly in a period of economic stagnation, with continued unemployment, inflation, and insecurity. What Carter has failed to do is to mobilize human rights concerns as part of a new domestic agenda, gaining in the process a *domestic* constituency for a new foreign policy.

The Carter Approach

In his speech before the United Nations General Assembly, the president recognized the principle that there was a human rights agenda which was applicable to the United States:

> We in the United States accept this responsibility [to foster human rights] in the fullest and most constructive sense . . . I know perhaps as well as anyone that our ideals in the area of human rights have not always been attained in the United States . . . But the American people have an abiding commitment to the full realization of their ideals. We are determined therefore to deal with our deficiencies quickly and openly.[6]

Instead of boldy defining a domestic human rights agenda, however, Carter has hesitantly forwarded a very crabbed view of our responsibility. He has placed before the Congress the international covenants on human rights which the United States has refused to ratify: the International Covenant on Economic, Social, and Cultural Rights; on Civil and Political Rights; and on the Elimination of All Forms of Racial Discrimination; as well as the American Convention. Carter has recognized that the Helsinki Agreements have implications for the travel restrictions the United States places on its own citizens and which the McCarran Act applies to foreign visitors to this country. He has ended most of the remaining travel restrictions on U.S. citizens, and has supported repeal of the McCarran Act (8 USC 1701). (The McCarran-

Walter Act of 1952 defines categories of individuals who are ineligible to receive a tourist or immigrant visa to enter the United States. This list includes maniacs, beggars, prostitutes, drug addicts, people with communicable diseases—and anarchists and communists. The apparent theory is that subversive ideas are communicable diseases and must be quarantined from susceptible ears in this country, otherwise known as the bastion of free expression.)

However laudatory, these commitments hardly offer the basis for building a broad popular constituency on human rights, one which would support a new definition of foreign policy. But that program is readily available for the administration, for domestic human rights offers the opportunity to combine the vocal civil liberties and civil rights constituencies with a broad-based working-class movement for basic human needs. If the president were willing to articulate a domestic human rights program, he could compete with the cold war liberals for their labor base and their popular support. The elements of the program could include the following freedoms.

The Freedom of Political Expression

Of all the rights guaranteed by the international conventions, President Carter has placed the greatest emphasis on the rights of free expression, of peaceful assembly and association, and of freedom from arbitrary interference with individual privacy. These are rights guaranteed also by the U.S. Constitution. They are areas where the administration feels that it can "speak from strength."

But formal legal protection offers no necessary guarantee against abuse. At best, legal guarantees are medicinal, useful only if applied, and they are applied only after the damage is done. The vicious tong which now rules Chile boasts a constitution with one of the best sets of constitutional guarantees in existence, and a savings clause which renders them all irrelevant. The Soviet Union also has extensive legal guarantees of rights which seem honored in the breach.

President Carter has expressed his concern for the fate of the courageous dissidents in the Soviet Union, the small number of intellectuals who challenge the regime and are harrassed, arrested, and sometimes expelled for it. The president should also show some concern for the citizens of another country which has historically used its police agencies to spy on and disrupt the activities of individuals labeled as "dissidents." That country is the United States.

The Senate Committee on the Intelligence Agencies detailed a small part of the abuses of the intelligence agencies in its recent seven-volume report.[7] Domestic "dissidents" were the victims of informers, wiretaps, mail openings, cable interceptions, tax probes, provocations, entrapments, grand jury investigations, conspiracy indictments, and massive surveillance by the Federal Bureau of Investigation (FBI), the Central Intelligence Agency (CIA), the National Security Agency, military intelligence, the Internal Revenue Service (IRS), the Justice Department, and state and local police "intelligence" units.

The government went far beyond mere political voyeurism. The government planted informers to disrupt citizen groups. It aided vigilantes in attacks on innocent citizens. It ordered the burning of private property. It tried to foment riots and violence. It set citizens up for censure and sometimes cruel punishment by planting false information. It wrote anonymous and untrue letters to associates and employers to get citizens in trouble. It broke into homes and ransacked offices. It instituted tax audits and grand jury probes to distract and harass citizens engaged in political activity.

The leading advocate of nonviolence and racial equality was spied on, bugged, and wiretapped, had his name slurred by vicious slanders, and had the government attempt bribery, extortion, and finally a death threat to get him to end his political activities. But what Martin Luther King, Jr. experienced was mild compared to the government program run against Fred Hampton and the Black Panthers in Chicago. The Panthers were infiltrated, their programs were disrupted, their lives endangered by various attempts of the police to spark gang warfare. Hampton himself was finally killed in a hail of police bullets as he slept. The full extent of government responsibility for his death has not yet been finally established, but the evidence indicates that the FBI decided to "get" Fred Hampton. And all of this took place not because he was considered violent—FBI memos dismiss that charge—but because the Bureau feared he was too popular and too charismatic, and that the Panthers might gain a large following in the slums of Chicago.

Only in the past few years have the outlines of illegal political spying and disruption been exposed. To this day, little significant change has taken place. No legislation has been passed to limit the activities of the intelligence agencies by law. The only "reforms" have been a series of executive or bureaucratic directives, which generally reaffirm the justifications used for political spying in the past and legitimate the unlawful for the future. Not surprisingly, the FBI still spies on citizens engaged in political activities. The CIA still runs secret checks on "potential" recruits. Grand juries are still used to harass political "dissidents." Local and state police departments continue to survey political activity that should be protected by the First Amendment.

Those actively opposed to government policy can still find themselves the targets of government lawlessness. Feminist groups in New Haven,

Connecticut and Lexington, Kentucky learned in recent years about the use of the grand jury to imprison political activists without trial. Puerto Rican nationalists are being taught the same lesson in New York. Native Americans at Wounded Knee and elsewhere continue to be the targets of massive governmental disruption. La Raza Unida, a "dissident" political party in Texas and New Mexico, can detail the continuing ties between local, state, and national police in political harassment.

If the Soviet Union is to be censured for its treatment of a thousand "dissident" intellectuals, then surely this country must be similarly judged—not on how it treats the placid majority, but on how it responds to the dissident few. If that is the proper measure of freedom, then the formal protections of the Bill of Rights have failed to cure the abuse of political and civil rights in this country.

What is needed is a strong dose of preventive medicine. Over the next two years, the Congress will legislate new charters for all of the federal intelligence agencies. In addition, a campaign against local and state police spying will take place across the country. Legislation has already been introduced which would get the federal intelligence agencies out of the business of political spying, prohibit political informers, and ban wiretaps.[8] It would also make officials personally responsible for violating the charter provisions of any intelligence agency.

President Carter, however, has chosen not to lead this effort at reform. Instead the administration has joined with the intelligence agencies in seeking new legislated authority, charters which affirm the right of those agencies to investigate Americans for other than criminal activity. Instead of mobilizing the civil liberties activists, the president has already alienated many of them.

Freedom from Want

The centerpiece of a domestic human rights agenda should be a focus on economic and social rights. A bold president could wean organized labor and the lower middle class from support of American militarism by the promise of an economic bill of rights.

The U.N. Covenant on Economic, Social, and Cultural Rights affirms the ideal of free human beings enjoying "freedom from fear and want." The covenant includes a series of rights to achieve that end. Article 7 recognizes "the right of everyone to the enjoyment of just and favorable conditions of work," with fair wages which guarantee a decent living, equal opportunity, and equal pay for equal work among men and women. Article 11 recognizes the right of "everyone to an adequate standard of living for himself and his family, including adequate food, clothing and housing . . . ." It also recognizes the "fundamental right of everyone to be free from hunger." Article 12 safeguards the right of everyone to the enjoyment of the "highest attainable standard of physical and mental health."[9]

These provisions are derived in great part from the objectives announced by Franklin Roosevelt on the eve of World War II. Roosevelt called for the protection of four essential human freedoms: the freedoms of speech and of worship, the freedom from want and from fear. To provide for the third, he detailed an economic bill of rights, which he portrayed as a supplement to our political bill of rights. Roosevelt returned to his theme repeatedly during the war, making it the grand objective for the United States in the postwar years. Roosevelt's vision, and indeed his language, was implanted in the international conventions after the war.

But in the United States, the Roosevelt program was shattered by the cold war. The human rights covenants of the U.N. were ignored, in no small part because of conservative fears of their "socialist" tone. The domestic economic bill of rights was abandoned for "prosperity" based on anticommunism, militarism, and expansion abroad.

On April 29, Secretary of State Cyrus Vance struggled to define the administration's human rights posture and, for the first time, forwarded a formal definition of the rights which the administration felt were encompassed in human rights guarantees. Vance included not only political and civil rights, but also "the right to the fulfillment of such vital needs as food, shelter, health care and education."[10] Vance's statement constitutes the first formal administration recognition of economic and social rights.

The secretary admitted that fulfillment of these rights will depend on the "stage of a nation's economic development . . . ." For the United States, with the most advanced economy in the world, fulfillment of these rights must now become a first priority. These guarantees are also the next objective of the civil rights movement and the women's movement. With the expected passage of the Equal Rights Amendment in the next few years, *de jure* discrimination against minorities and women will be ended, but the stigma of generations of discrimination will still be felt. The guarantees of equal opportunity and equal treatment in fact can be enforced only by the firm guarantee of economic and social rights to all Americans.

President Carter can now return to the promise of Roosevelt more than 30 years after the fact. He will find, however, that its fulfillment will not be easy. Recent trends have moved this country further away from guaranteeing the fundamental economic rights so necessary to human freedom. Unemployment remains at over 7 percent of the work force, which means that some eight million people seek but cannot find work. This figure greatly underestimates the problem of guaranteeing employment at a fair remuneration to all who can work. A 1970 congressional estimate of employment in 51 central cities estimated that an average of 30.5 percent of the labor force was either unemployed, discouraged and no longer seeking work, or part-time employees who could not find full-time work.[11] In 1972, economists calculated that some 40 percent of the population was excluded from "useful paid employment at a decent living wage."[12] By 1975, some 26 million people lived below the officially defined poverty level.[13]

Needless to say, unemployment falls more heavily upon minorities and women. The unemployment rate among blacks is twice that of whites, and has remained the same since World War II. Both black and white women are unemployed at significantly higher rates than black or white men. The guarantee of useful work remains to be reached in this society.

In recent years, unemployment has been accompanied by severe inflation, a cruel tax on all those in lower income brackets or on fixed incomes. Moreover, basic necessities—food, housing, energy, and health care—led the inflationary surge over the past five years.[14] The result is that adequate food, shelter, and heath care are out of the reach of an increasing number of Americans. For example, when a lower-income family faces rising food costs, it finds it cannot "substitute down" to cheaper foods, and must reduce consumption. According to the Select Committee on Nutrition and Human Needs, an estimated 7.6 million people below the poverty level now suffer from malnutrition.[15]

In his first fireside chat, President Carter emphasized that

> inflation has hit us hardest not in the luxuries but in the essentials—food, energy, health and housing. You see it every time you go shopping . . . . I understand that unemployment and inflation . . . have done great harm to many American families . . . .[16]

The administration could now establish the framework for economic and social rights in this country, for a guaranteed level of social justice which can stand as an example to others. Some pledges have already been made in piecemeal fashion, but never guaranteed. The Employment Act of 1946 recognized the value of a job for every able person (although it was explicitly changed from a *Full* Employment Act in the Congress). The Housing Act of 1949 recognized a national obligation to provide "a decent home and a suitable living environment for every American family . . . ." The Social Security Act of 1935 moved towards guaranteeing a minimal standard of living for every American. The administration is pledged to pass universal health care legislation in the near future (although action on the legislation has been postponed for the present).

Now the president should seek to guarantee an enforceable right to work, to eat, to decent shelter, and to health care for all Americans. The administration can provide the framework by accepting this responsibility as part of its domestic agenda on human rights.

Moreover, a domestic human rights agenda offers the only possibility for developing a broad popular constituency freed from the cold war combination of military expenditure, foreign intervention, and economic expansion. Until the president develops popular support for economic rights at home, he cannot hope to develop popular support for a more flexible foreign policy abroad.

NOTES

1. U.S. Congress, House, statement before the House Subcomittee on Foreign Operations, 2 March 1977, *Selected Statements*, 1 May 1977, p. 18.
2. Henry A. Kissinger, "Continuity and Change in American Foreign Policy," *Society* 15 (Nov.-Dec. 1977): 97-103.
3. Interview with Zbigniew Brzezinski, *U.S. News and World Report*, 30 May 1977, p. 35.
4. Committee on the Present Danger, *Common Sense and the Common Danger* (pamphlet), p. 2.
5. See chapter by Samuel Huntington in "The Crisis of Democracy," *Trilateral Commission's Report* (New York: New York University Press, 1975).
6. *Washington Post*, 18 March 1977, p. 1.
7. U.S., Congress, Senate, Select Committee to Study Governmental Operations with Respect to Intelligence Activities (the Church Committee), 94th Congress, 2nd Session, Volumes 1-7.
8. U.S. Congress, House, *Federal Intelligence Agencies Control Act of 1977*, HR 6051.
9. United Nations, General Assembly, *International Covenant on Economic, Cultural, and Social Rights* (see Appendix).
10. *Washington Post*, 30 April 1977, p. 2.
11. W. Spring, et al., "Crisis of Underemployment," *New York Times Magazine*, 5 November 1972, pp. 42-60.
12. "Full Employment at Living Wages," *Annuals of American Academy of Political and Social Science*, March 1975, p. 104.
13. Lester T. Thorough, "Economic Progress of Minority Groups," *Challenge*, March-April 1975.
14. Detailed in studies conducted by The Exploratory Project on Economic Alternatives.
15. U.S. Congress, Senate, Select Committee on Nutrition and Human Needs, *Nutrition and Health* 2 (1976): 81.
16. Quoted in Joan Bannon, *A Working Economy for Americans* (1977), p. 26.

Chapter 4

International Consequences of United States Human Rights Policies

Louis B. Sohn

The issues I will discuss here are rather limited. I do not intend to consider what the United States policy on human rights is in fact today, or to suggest what it will be in the near future. My purpose is to discuss some of the important international implications of various foreign policy options which the United States has already adopted, or which it might contemplate for future execution.

The United States and the United Nations

The first U.S. foreign policy problem to be noted at this time is that it is very difficult for the United States to make up its mind what audience it is addressing when talking about human rights. Obviously, one of the main audiences is the domestic one; and the problems involved there are discussed in the preceding papers in this volume. Secondly, there are audiences in the various countries around the world which need to be considered on both a bilateral and regional basis. Thirdly, and this is probably the weakest part of U.S. policy, is the audience at the United Nations itself, the multinational audience. The United States has been rather uncomfortable most of the time in an international setting, especially when it does not control it. The United States could live with the United Nations in the early 1950s because it could obtain there whatever it wanted; the United Nations was, in most cases, willing to do what the United States wished. Having an independent United Nations controlled by a two-thirds majority of countries which are willing to listen to the United States only on the basis of reason, rather than simply because it is the United States that is speaking, became a little more difficult. U.S. diplomacy always has been geared more to bilateral channels than multilateral ones, to what Jessup calls parliamentary diplomacy. It is not an uncommon occurrence in the State Department, that when one encounters a friend there who is practically in tears and queries him about it, he replies: "They have assigned me to two years at the United Nations; this is going to be a black mark on my record." United Nations service is not considered the proper training for a diplomat-to-be. This situation has personnel implications, of course, but also, in a way, it is a reflection of the general policy. To what extent is the United Nations really at the center of U.S. foreign policy considerations and to what extent is it simply something incidental or accidental that we resort to when we do not know what else to do?

Viewed from the global perspective the latter view of the United Nations is tremendously mistaken because for many countries of the world the United Nations is *it*. They came into being, to a large extent, because of the United Nations. People sometimes discount it, but if it had not been for the United Nations, the revolution in the Third World would not have happened as fast and might not have happened at all except in two or three countries. It would not have spread to all the little places around the world if it had not been for constant United Nations insistence that everyone is entitled to self-determination no matter how weak or poor that country might be. Therefore, these countries started their lives believing in the United Nations as a contributor to their existence. Secondly, often these countries are too poor to have diplomatic relations with very many other countries. They usually maintain a diplomatic mission at the capital of the former mother country, whether France or the United Kingdom; they have two or three missions in some other countries that have special importance to them for one reason or another; but otherwise diplomatic relations are simply conducted in New York, which is the easiest way for them. Also in this setting, functioning jointly, they have much more power than they would have unilaterally. For about two-thirds of the world, the United Nations has become the main focus of diplomacy—for the United States it is still a byway. In thinking about the diplomatic implications of U.S. policy actions, it is always necessary to remember that if they are going to be meaningful to the rest of the world, a major effort has to be concentrated on the UN.

The United States and Human Rights Instruments

To take a few examples: people say, for instance, that it is not very important for the United States to ratify the Convention on Genocide; its government is not going to be committing genocide. It is also said that it would be of no use for the United States to ratify the Convention on Racial Discrimination; it is probably abiding by it more than most countries. As to the covenants on human rights, which in a way were drafted on the basis of the United States' constitutional experience, why should there be any need for the United States to ratify what it has been doing already for two centuries? In fact, since it is a multilateral document, it is argued that it is likely to be much weaker than the U.S. Constitution and, therefore, why should the United States bother? Many were pleased with the Carter administration's decision to sign these documents; but it has taken a long time, and most of the previous administrations simply refused to even think about it. The United States has not signed a number of other human rights instruments and no government agency has investigated in depth what the implications would be for the United States if they were to ratify those documents. In fact several administrations have followed, without any effort at reexamination, the statement of the early 1950s that it is not the policy of the United States to ratify any document concerning human rights. Of course, when that statement was made, there was a good reason for it—the proposed Bricker Amendment to the Constitution and its dangerous implications for the conduct of U.S. foreign policy—but this is exactly the kind of policy that is held against the United States as no longer justified in the new circumstances of the 1970s.

This negative policy has had two immediate implications. In the first place, people say that if you are not going to ratify these documents, you should not participate in drafting them, trying to impose standards which you are not willing to accept for yourselves. And secondly, of course, there are resentments when the United States starts complaining on the basis of these documents that other people are misbehaving. U.S. spokesmen sometimes glibly suggest that the Soviet Union in a particular instance has violated an article of the Covenant on Civil and Political Rights. The Soviet Union easily replies, "Who are you to talk, you have not even ratified the document!" Therefore, it is quite obvious that one of the basic policy actions which would have a very important United Nations, and therefore global, implication is for the United States to ratify the basic international instruments on human rights: the four documents that have been mentioned, as well as the inter-American Convention which presents a parallel regional method of dealing with this problem.

But these should not be the only steps. There are many other human rights documents; the United Nations has prepared a nice blue volume containing all the human rights texts it has adopted and those adopted by the specialized agencies. There are many other conventions which the

U.S. has never ratified on the pseudo-excuse that its legal system is based on a federal-state dichotomy and that it is, therefore, very difficult for it to ratify documents dealing with issues which to some extent are within the jurisdiction of the component states. It was thus claimed that the federal government has nothing to do with the labor relations in this country. This attitude was adopted in the early 1930s and it has never changed. Though everybody knows how the situation has changed domestically as far as labor relations are concerned, the United States has ratified just a few minor documents and the only ratifications of some importance are those relating to maritime labor. Among those which the United States has not ratified are some which were the result of a U.S. initiative. To this group belongs, for instance, the Convention on the Freedom of Association. The United States originally proposed it in 1947 as a means to put the Soviet Union on the spot, but the Soviet Union ratified it finally after objecting to it very strongly for the first few years, while the United States never took this step. When President Kennedy presented it to the Senate in the 1960s, that was one of the conventions to which the American Bar Association immediately objected, arguing that it would interefere in the domestic affairs of the United States. And this, of course, is the basic problem: there are two sides to each coin. If one wants to apply a certain standard to other nations, one has to be ready to apply the same standard to oneself. Part of the game is that, in order to do so, to take the first step in that direction, one must ratify the basic documents. It does not mean that the United States cannot have a few reservations here and there on particular provisions which do not agree with its constitutional doctrines and about which the people and the Congress feel very strongly. Other states have been doing the same, and even the Scandinavian countries have made some reservations; so nobody would consider this to be wrong. But the crucial point is for the U.S. to join the rest of the world in ratifying at least some of the most important documents.

Once the United States has done so, it will be in a better position at the United Nations to insist that further actions are necessary. In the first place, the United States would then have the moral basis to ask others to do more; at present, the U.S. in the eyes of other countries has no such basis. Secondly, the United States would thus acquire the legal basis for enforcing the standards of the covenants, namely through the Human Rights Committee of the United Nations to which only parties to the Covenant on Civil and Political Rights can be elected. As long as the United States is not a party, this important channel is closed to it. Almost 50 countries now have ratified the covenants and if the United States should ratify them, very quickly another 30 or 40 would also ratify them, as many countries have simply been saying: "The United States has not ratified them, why should we?" If that should happen, then it would become possible to have those standards enforced through an international channel with respect to a majority of the world's nations. The very important factor here is that whatever one does, it is much better psychologically, politically, and diplomatically, to do it through a multilateral rather than a unilateral channel. The United States is a very big country, very strong both militarily and economically; if it tries to do something on a bilateral basis, even that which may sound very gentle, it is always considered bullying. On the other hand, if the United States could proceed through the United Nations, if it could present to a UN committee its grievance against a country and submit the evidence that this country is violating the covenant, and if that committee then would investigate and chastise that particular country, then everybody would accept the action as legitimate. When the United States government acts unilaterally, as when the administration presents to congress a detailed report about country X's violations of human rights, it is considered unilateral interference in someone else's domestic jurisdiction. Such intervention for most countries, because of their unhappy experience in the past, is taboo; and, consequently, however gentle the United States tries to be about it, it is resented. Acting under the United Nations Charter is quite different. Even in making a statement the difference is clear: if the United States makes a statement in Washington about some human rights violations elsewhere, we are viewed as interfering. If it makes exactly the same statement in a debate in the United Nations, everybody accepts our doing so as a legitimate act. This kind of psychological difference, to many countries, is of great importance.

If one accepts this approach, one can no longer entertain the acceptability of one set of options: United States' unilateral actions. The United States can never achieve a climate of acceptability for such acts. The only thing one can hope for is acceptance of multilateral actions, once the United States learns how properly to use multilateral channels. In the present world of interdependence where small nations are sensitive about their equality, only intervention through multilateral channels has some chance of success. Other countries can never accept unilateral intervention, however well intended.

The Relationship Between Human Rights and Economic Measures

Another point which needs to be mentioned relates to the relationship between political and economic measures. In many respects, it is a fact of present international relations that economics are considered more important than politics. It is likely that the late 1970s, and even more so the 1980s, are going to be known as the Economic Era of international relations. In the last 30 years most political issues have been solved; most of those which still remain, like the Middle East and Southern Africa, have human rights implications. Once these issues are resolved, what remains are the basic grievances of the rest of the world against the major Western powers and they are fundamentally economic. Therefore, it is necessary to pay very close attention to the interrelationship between economic rights and political rights. Unless it can be proven to particular countries that their economic development will not be jeopardized by their compliance with various human rights standards, it will be very difficult to persuade them to abide by these standards. The only way to encourage countries to provide civil and political rights as well as economic rights is to help them economically to such an extent that they are able to develop without having to impinge on civil and political human rights. It seems that trade rather than aid is probably the better way to achieve this result; and aid, if at all, has to be, again, multilateral. It is encouraging that the Carter administration has put strong emphasis on the multilateral approach after many years of tough insistence on the alleged political advantages of a unilateral doling out of favors.

It is much easier for the World Bank to insist on a link between human rights and economic assistance. For instance, it can tell somebody: "We are not going to give you that particular loan because we feel that it may be to the great detriment of the Indians living in the Amazon jungle if you build new roads there. You must provide us with some guarantees of those Indians' rights." It is all right for the World Bank to do it; but if the United States had tried to do it, it would have quickly landed in real trouble. On the one hand, it is necessary to pay close attention to the economic factors; on the other hand, it is as important to find a way in which human rights are not jeopardized by economic developments. Again, in order to strengthen the United States bargaining hand, it is very important for the United States to ratify the Covenant on Economic, Social, and Cultural Rights, and not to limit its ratification to the civil rights one. If Congress should be worried about the implementation of these rights, it might be reminded that, like everybody else, the United States can use the loophole in the Economic, Social, and Cultural Covenant which allows a state to say that it is really trying, and that it will do its best as soon as it can. There are certain things even the United States cannot do yet though it is the economically strongest country. The covenant is a reasonable document; it allows a progressive approach to its implementation.

Human Rights Impact Statements

There is another relationship between economics and human rights which should be taken into account. Whenever the United Nations or the

United States contemplates an action which might affect human rights in a country, a human rights impact statement should be required. One might even require such a statement for certain private activities. If somebody plans to invest more than X number of dollars in a foreign country, before doing this he should be obliged to present to a proper authority a human rights impact statement with respect to that investment. Sometimes it is rather obvious; for instance, when the Volta Dam was being built in West Africa, one result was that one of the African tribes had to be dispossessed and sent to some other place. They were, of course, very unhappy about it but somebody simply decided that the dam had to be in that place and the tribe's being dispossessed was just too bad for them. Nobody ever considered that their human rights were involved.

That something can be done about this is shown by the situation which arose during World War II. At that time a clause was developed for government supply contracts which provided that any corporation which, in connection with the war effort, supplied materials from abroad—for instance, by producing copper in Chile—should, in producing those materials, follow to the greatest possible extent the American labor standards. There were a few complaints from some corporations about it but the profits were so high that they did not mind it. And, as a result, there was suddenly tremendous improvement in labor standards in those countries as far as American corporations' operations there were concerned. Of course, the local governments did not object to this; they did not mind their people earning more money. This kind of approach is much more feasible than trying to persuade foreign governments to enforce similar rules. The United States can impose conditions on American corporations and under U.S. law a corporation has a duty to comply with them. If necessary, the United States could sugar the pill by saying: "If you do this, then you will be entitled to an extra foreign investment credit, and if you do not do it, you will lose all such credits." In such a case everybody calculates the pluses and minuses and is likely to decide that it is much better business to comply and get the tax credit.

Need for Cooperation in the Economic and Human Rights Field

Another problem in the economic field is that it is very difficult for one country to try to enforce human rights standards by unilateral action. If the United States should refuse military or economic assistance to, for instance, Chile or Argentina the very next day, the United Kingdom or France is likely to come and provide whatever is wanted. When the United States was trying to enforce some slight sanction on Brazil, Germany opened its door and agreed to give them even nuclear reactors. Something that has not been done sufficiently and is perhaps easier to do than some other things, would be to have in addition to summit meetings on economy, energy, etc., a meeting on human rights attended by the influential leaders of the United States, Canada, Japan, Europe, and a few others, including such countries as Costa Rica in Latin America and similar more liberal countries in Africa and Asia. The Indian leaders might love to be invited to something like this. Once they have assembled, they might agree to take action on human rights in concert. Of course, while the United States has a lot of influence, the United States, Europe, Japan, and a few others together can double or even triple that influence. And this approach would also take out the stigma of unilateral actions which is the strongest criticism of action by the United States alone. So, in addition to acting through United Nations channels, as emphasized previously, much more can be done by simply getting the democracies of the world to unite in common action and announce to the world that they are going to stay united and other countries will no longer be able to play games, getting from one major power what they cannot get from another. If the United States should, on human rights grounds, refuse to do something for a country, that country should not be able to get it somehow from France or other nations. If one can create a united front on this subject, the impact might be much more important, especially if the united front is not interventionist in the negative but interventionist in the positive sense.

Human Rights and Security Issues

The third point which needs to be considered is security. In a way this is probably the most difficult one, because to many governments security is the issue which overrides anything else — economics or human rights. Even the United States will never trade issues of security for human rights. One cannot forget what happened to the Japanese-Americans in World War II, nor what happened during the McCarthy period when human rights violations were deemed necessary for fighting the cold war in the 1950s; and it can reoccur very quickly if again the people feel that the country's security is in danger. And the same is true about other countries. One should not blame the British that in Northern Ireland they had to establish emergency rules and one cannot blame a number of other governments which have suspended civil and political rights when they felt that they were under siege by elements that were working to overthrow them. The basic rule of each government is self-preservation, even if it finds it necessary to do things that normally are not permitted. The only thing that one can hope is that the rules which states are willing to apply internationally, they would be willing to apply internally; and one must try to establish some kind of basic regulations through the Red

Cross conventions that are being redrafted for this purpose or other such means.

Another issue to be considered is the attitude to take with respect to revolutionary regimes. Simply saying that one should not accept certain types of regimes in some countries as being legitimate is not very helpful. If one looks around the world, one finds quickly that no regime ever has been really completely legitimate, including the government that was established in the United States in 1776. And in fact this is a problem that American diplomats have to face very often when dealing with foreign revolutionary governments. People in other countries say: "You represent a government that was established by fighting against colonialism, by a violent revolution. However, you do not seem to understand just 200 years later that we are going through the same process and that our actions during that process may be as necessary as yours were in the 1770s." It is generally forgotten how the Tories were treated in the United States in the 1770s and 1780s, how some other unpopular minorities were treated later, and how various "sedition" acts were enforced. It is easy to forget the "intertemporal element," namely that one should not compare the situation in developing countries with the situation in the United States or Western Europe today. One should compare it with the United States or Western Europe at the same stage of development, whether it was 1776, or Cromwell's revolution in Britain, or whatever. One should only compare periods which are truly comparable.

Need for Regional Approaches

It is also necessary to remember that the United States' influence is different in various regions, and that one might have to pay a different price — in terms of the willingness of others to accept United States activities as humanitarian rather than self-serving — depending on the ideology of a particular region. In particular, one needs to separate clearly anything the United States may try to do with respect to the Soviet bloc from what it may try to do in other parts of the world, especially the noncommitted nations. At the beginning one might want to stay out of both areas. It may be easier, for instance, to be effective in the rest of the Western world, to make sure that certain things do not happen in Greece, Turkey, Portugal, Spain, etc. The United States action can have a positive impact in these places as opposed to a negative impact, or no impact at all, elsewhere. At present, action in the West should have top priority. One should start with the relatively easy cases. Somehow there is a tendency to start with the hardest cases, and then one is unpleasantly surprised when no success is achieved. It seems preferable to start always with the easiest case, and only when one finishes there, to then move to the next, more difficult level. There will be fewer complaints then about intervention since one needs to do less in the easier cases before achieving a measure of improvement in the situation.

The other element which is often neglected is the transferability of standards from region to region. Can one expect the United Nations to apply Western standards to other parts of the world? Is it not self-righteous to say that only the Western ideas of human rights should be applied? It would seem more appropriate for President Carter, after having gone to Europe, to arrange for a meeting of such African leaders as Kenyatta, Nyerere, Kaunda, Senghor, and Houphouet-Boigny, who are considered as the elder statesmen of Africa. After getting them together, he might ask them: "If you were in my shoes, and you wanted to promote human rights in Africa, what would you do? Assuming the southern African problem is solved, what other issues in Africa need to be solved and how?" The best advice that one can get on that subject would be from the elder statesmen of Africa; it would be the same way for any other part of the world. This technique would be far better than telling them to apply Anglo-American standards.

Combining the various approaches suggested previously one might wish to start with a Western-African summit: three Western leaders — the United Kingdom, the United States, and France would talk to five or seven African leaders. Both France and the United Kingdom have special interests in Africa, which everybody recognizes. The United States' interests are everywhere. While Germany and Italy have some inchoate interests in Africa because they were once colonial powers, it might be easier to start with a limited meeting. Otherwise the Scandinavians and other countries active in Africa would also want to participate and the situation might become unmanageable. As far as substance is concerned one should try to get from this meeting suggestions by the Africans as to what they think the West could do to improve the human rights situation in Africa. And then all the Western nations could get together and try to do something with and for the Africans. If this method works, it would be a tremendous success. If it does not work, then one would have to try something else.

If the method works one would try it in other regions. For instance, several major powers would meet with a few leaders of Latin America to obtain their advice about steps which might be taken to improve the human rights situation in Latin America, and so on. What is important is to rely on regional wisdom for the solution of regional problems. One should not ask Africans what to do with Latin America, nor vice versa. But once the needed steps are discovered, they should be taken in concert by as many countries as possible. If the African or Latin American leaders make it clear that they no not want any unilateral action by any country or group of countries, then the matter would have to be reconsidered in the U.N. framework. In any case it is imperative that the United Nations be kept informed about each initiative and each step taken, and its advice on the modalities of any action proposed or taken should not be lightly disregarded.

If the United States (or the West) does not find it possible to act through the U.N., it should at least follow the precedent set in the so-called Truman Doctrine, when aid agreements were first concluded with Greece and Turkey. On Senator Vandenberg's insistence a provision was added to these agreements that any action taken under them will cease if the Security Council or the General Assembly of the United Nations should decide that further unilateral assistance is unnecessary or undesirable. The United States even agreed at that time to waive its right to a veto in the Security Council with respect to any such decision. Similar provisions with respect to any future human rights action would seem desirable. They might diminish any apprehension about the proposed action, as the Third World majority will be able to stop it whenever it should deem such action undesirable.

Conclusions

In conclusion, it seems important to emphasize again that United States policy on human rights in the rest of the world should not be unilateral but should be based on cooperation with other likeminded countries and, to the maximum extent possible, should utilize truly international channels, both regional organizations and the United Nations. Since the United States is not really accustomed to operating through the U.N., special effort must be made to strengthen the human rights element of the United States policy in the United Nations. Whatever the United States does in the United Nations is likely to have a direct or indirect impact on human rights in other parts of the world. That impact should be considered before an action is taken; at present, too often the United States is surprised when an impact occurs some time after an action is taken.

The United Nations machinery for dealing with various human rights issues is available, and the specialized agencies are also constantly increasing their capability for dealing with human rights issues. The United States häs to learn how to use it better for the common advantage of the people of the world. However, the United States cannot do that effectively as long as it refuses to share the obligations which many other members have already accepted. Thus, the ratification by the United States of several basic human rights instruments is a precondition for its effective participation in the international human rights system. The Carter administration has started the ratification process. If it succeeds in accomplishing this goal, an important step in the right direction will have been taken.

Part II

United States Participation in the Identification and Definition of International Human Rights

Chapter 5

The United States and International Codification of Human Rights: A Case of Split Personality

Bruno V. Bitker

The idea that man acquires individual rights solely by reason of his birth is not an original philosophical or political belief expounded, practiced, and honored principally by Americans. It was something known, though not always expressed, in the classical period of history and in the earliest of religious doctrines. It would be difficult to fix a date or cite a specific document during the current era in man's history, in which the idea was first proclaimed that rights of the individual were superior to those of the state, the nation, the monarch, or whatever form of sovereignty existed. It is generally asserted, however, that for us in the United States, the first influential document was the Magna Carta issued by King John of England in 1215. Though this instrument was of a limited nature, it helped bring into force the British Habeas Corpus Act in 1679 and the English Bill of Rights in 1689. And before our own written statements of individual rights, philosophers such as Locke, Montesquieu, Voltaire, and Burke were writing about the birthright of man.

In America, expressions of liberty and of individual freedom and rights were appearing in colonial charters and in statements of political leaders as early as the 17th century, and well into the pre-Revolutionary period. Then, in 1776, three weeks prior to our Declaration of Independence, Virginia adopted its Declaration of Rights. The effect of that act was to further inspire those attending the Continental Congress in Philadelphia to adopt the Declaration of Independence on July 4, 1776. The Declaration was short: but in one sentence it pronounced the basic philosophy regarding individual rights which has been the basic philosophy of the United States ever since. That sentence bears repeating: "We hold these truths to be self-evident, that all men are created equal, that they are endowed by their Creator with certain inalienable Rights, that among these are Life, Liberty and the pursuit of Happiness . . . ."

It is uncertain what effect the issuance of the Declaration of Independence may have had abroad. Certainly the liberals in England and elsewhere in Europe were inclined to view the revolutionists more sympathetically thereafter than might otherwise have been the case. Surely the American Revolution had its influence upon the French Revolution in 1789, and the French Declaration of the Rights of Man adopted in 1791. With this historical commitment to individual human rights it is not easy to understand the reluctance of the United States, since World War II, to become a party to international human rights treaties.

The Union Preserved

Whatever part human rights may have played in U.S. foreign policy between 1776 and 1861, it became a significant factor in the preservation of the Union during the American Civil War. From the beginning of the war President Abraham Lincoln had taken the position that, although he personally was opposed to the institution of slavery, the war was being fought to preserve the union, not to emancipate the slaves. Considerable pressure was being exerted upon him to take some action which would confer a different and more idealistic purpose upon the sacrifices which the North was suffering. The war had not gone well for the Union in 1861 and 1862: in fact, it was going badly.

A serious problem lay in the attitude of England, and its direct and indirect assistance to the Confederacy. Economically its trade with the South, particularly in cotton, appeared of greater significance to the English than the preservation of the Union. Undoubtedly there were English politicians who might have welcomed the United States as two small nations rather than the single, rich, strong, expansive nation into which it was obviously developing. There was even the suggestion that England might officially recognize the Confederate states as an independent, sovereign nation. This could have proved disastrous to the North for various reasons, one of them being the right of a nation to enjoy the freedom of the sea.

By the end of the summer of 1862 it was obvious to President Lincoln that the stated objectives of the war must be broadened, not only because the antislavery supporters in the North had to be persuaded that abolition was a purpose of the war, but because the rest of the world needed to be assured that the war was more than a family fight over a federal power versus states rights. A large segment of Englishmen were philosophically opposed to slavery and generally sympathetic to the North because there was hope for the slaves if the North prevailed, and none if the South won the war. But concerned Englishmen could arouse little enthusiasm for the Union unless it was also considered as an antislavery cause. Either the United States believed in and was willing to fight for man's "inalienable rights" or it was fighting a war merely for political domination over real estate.

President Lincoln finally concluded that some kind of pronouncement expressing the humanitarian objective of the war was necessary to serve military, political, and especially, diplomatic ends. On January 1, 1863, he issued the Emancipation Proclamation. Although acclaimed nationally and internationally, the proclamation was in fact of limited effect, freeing only those slaves within such states as were still in rebellion against the United States on the date of its issuance. Despite what seems like a questionable basis for gaining historical fame as the Great Emancipator, by this proclamation, Lincoln had given a spiritual direction and a new meaning to the war. He had made what was generally interpreted as a commitment to the nation and to the world at large, that slavery would be abolished. Historians may differ as to when the turning point in the war was reached: Was it a certain battle, was it the naming of a particular general, was it something else? But January 1, 1863 must be considered as the critical point. Thereafter the idea that England might recognize the Confederate states as an independent nation lost momentum. In France and elsewhere in Europe the liberals favoring the North were increasingly supported.[1] Human rights as an element of U.S. foreign policy had not only reestablished its place in our national policy, but also proved a significant factor in preserving the Union. Thus Lincoln had not only made possible the achievement of his objective, but had dramatically reasserted America's basic philosophy "that all men are created equal."

Early U.S. Treaties and Diplomatic Actions on Human Rights

It should not be thought that between the Declaration of Independence in 1776 and the Emancipation Proclamation in 1863 the United States was indifferent to human rights in its foreign relations. Quite the contrary. Time after time it evinced its belief in the protection of the individual. Thus, in the Paris Treaty of Peace with Great Britain in 1783 it provided (Article VI) that "no person shall, on that account (participation in the War of the Revolution) suffer any future loss or damage, either in his person, liberty or property...."[2] The final, formal treaty of 1794 ending the war with England contained other detailed provisions protecting individuals.[3] Shortly thereafter (1795), in a treaty with

Algiers, the right of the U.S. consul "to exercise his religion in his own house" was protected.[4] These early treaties indicate that, perhaps in what might now be considered a minor way, the U.S. and nations with which it was concluding treaties had always considered individual rights proper subjects for inclusion in international treaties.

Similar references can be made to other treaties in the 19th century prior to the U.S. Civil War. Thus, in 1808 in the treaty with France by which we acquired Louisiana, the United States agreed to incorporate the inhabitants of the territory as soon as possible but "in the meantime they shall be maintained in the free enjoyment of their liberty, property and the religion which they profess."[5] In a treaty with Brazil (1828) the parties appear to have included a principle (basic to the Nuremberg judgment more than a century later) recognizing individual responsibility for acts of individuals.[6] A similar provision appears in a treaty of 1831 with Mexico which provided that citizens of that country residing in the U.S. "shall be allowed the free exercise of their religion in public or in private."[7]

The ratification of these treaties may not have been as dramatic as proclaiming the Declaration of Independence; nor as directly effective as the Emancipation Proclamation in 1863; but it was a continuing recognition of the U.S. position on individual rights. In the period between the Civil War and World War I, the United States on various occasions further supported its ideals through diplomatic humanitarian intervention even though it had no formal treaties within the particular countries involved. This diplomatic activity was especially noteworthy respecting the treatment of Jews by Russia and by Rumania, and of the Armenians by Turkey.[8]

Although the Versailles Treaty ending World War I made no provisions for protection of individual rights, a number of so-called minorities treaties entered into at the time did exactly this. Their coverage was limited, but they did assure some recognition to minorities in certain countries.[9] But the United States was not a party to these treaties, nor did it ratify the articles establishing the League of Nations after World War I. Between World Wars I and II, the United States was not a leader in the international community in support of human rights. It did, however, ratify the Slavery Convention of 1926[10] which was aimed at the international traffic in slavery.[11] It obviously is a human rights convention.

With the coming into power of Hitler and the Nazi advocacy of the superior race theory, accompanied by the shocking and brutal treatment of its Jewish citizens, including the use of mass murder (subsequently identified as genocide), the United States renewed its interest in supporting the rights of the individual against the acts of the sovereign state.

Prior to our entry into World War II, President Roosevelt in his State of the Union message in January 1941 called for a world founded upon four essential human freedoms.

> The first is freedom of speech and expression—everywhere in the world. The second is freedom of every person to worship God in his own way—everywhere in the world. The third is freedom from want—which translated into world terms, means economic understandings which will secure to every nation a healthy peacetime life for its inhabitants—everywhere in the world.
> The fourth is freedom from fear—which, translated into world terms, means a world-wide reduction of armaments to such a point and in such a thorough fashion that no nation will be in a position to commit an act of physical aggression against any neighbor—anywhere in the world.[12]

The Four Freedoms were constantly referred to thereafter and when we entered the war in December 1941, they were generally accepted as our war objectives. But in the back of the minds of leaders in the democracies was the idea of a postwar world organization. The steps that led to the creation of the United Nations Organization (as it was initially referred to) are set out in considerable detail in the "History of the United Nations Charter: the Role of the United States," 1940-1945, by Ruth B. Russell.[13] Within the Department of State, several committees worked on proposals for a worldwide organization of states.[14]

The Initial Proposal for an International Bill of Rights

Although the United States proposed an international bill of rights to the other governments at Dumbarton Oaks, where preparations were being made for the projected United Nations Conference, the actual proposals when presented at San Francisco contained no international bill of rights.[15] Provisions regarding human rights appear to have been compressed to merely empower the Economic and Social Council "to make recommendations on its own initiative, with respect to international economic, social, and other humanitarian matters."[16]

This failure to include provisions for a bill of rights did not go unnoticed at the San Francisco Conference. It was at this point that the so-called "Consultants to the U.S. Delegation" made their influence felt. These included representatives of 42 nationally recognized, nongovernmental organizations, constituting a wide variety of private institutions which included professional, religious, labor, business, women's, and community groups. Joining with these consultants were representatives of smaller nations. The direct result is described by Vera Micheles Dean in her foreign policy report, made immediately after the close of the San Francisco Conference:

> The preamble (to the Charter), the work of many hands, as finally adopted, lists matters that had been left out of the Dumbarton Oaks Proposals—human rights, the dignity and worth of the human person, the equal rights of men and women and of nations large and small...the promotion of social progress and better standard of living in larger freedom.[17]

As expressed by Senator Arthur H. Vandenberg, then the ranking minority member of the Senate Foreign Relations Committee: "Dumbarton Oaks has been given a new soul—the Charter names justice as the prime criterion of peace."[18]

Despite efforts to include in the Charter an international bill of rights, it became apparent to the supporters that there was neither the time then available [19] nor perhaps the will to draft such an instrument. But the activities of those who favored including a bill of rights in the Charter resulted in incorporating provisions concerning human rights in the preamble of the Charter and in its stated purposes and principles (Articles 1, 3). In addition, Articles 13, 55, 56, 62, 68, and 76 deal with human rights. Article 13 (h) requires the General Assembly to initiate studies "assisting in the realization of human rights and fundamental freedoms for all without restriction as to race, sex, language or religion." Article 56 provides that "all members pledge themselves to take joint and separate action in cooperation with the organization for the achievement of the purposes set forth in Article 55." Article 62 empowers the Economic and Social Council to "make recommendations for the purpose of promoting respect for and observance of human rights and fundamental freedoms for all." And Article 68 requires the Economic and Social Council to set up commissions "for the promotion of human rights...." This is the only separate commission required under the Charter. Under the Chapter (XII) on the International Trusteeship System, Article 76 (c), a basic objective of the trusteeship system is "to encourage respect for human rights and for fundamental freedoms for all without distinction as to race, sex, language, or religion..." and, under subdivision (d), "to ensure...equal treatment for the latter (members of the United Nations and their nationals) in the administration of justice...."

Although he was not referring specifically to an international bill of rights, it is no wonder that Phillip C. Jessup, a former member of the International Court of Justice, comments that, "It is already law at least for members of the United Nations, that respect for human dignity and fundamental rights is obligatory. The duty is imposed by the Charter, a treaty to which they are parties."[20]

By way of emphasizing the U.S. position, President Truman in his closing address to the San Francisco Conference asserted that, under the Charter,

> we have good reason to expect the framing of an international bill of rights, acceptable to all the nations involved. That bill of rights will be as much a part of international life as our own Bill of Rights is a part of our Constitution. The Charter is dedicated to the achievement and observance of human rights and fundamental freedoms. Unless we can attain those objectives for all men and women everywhere—without regard to race, language, or religion—we cannot have permanent peace and security.[23]

Although a detailed bill of rights was not adopted at San Francisco, "The idea of establishing an International Bill of Rights was, however, treated as inherent in the Charter."[22]

Drafting the Bill in the United Nations

The ink was hardly dry on the Charter when work began on a draft of the bill. The new Commission on Human Rights, created under Article 68, was directed to prepare an appropriate recommendation. When the commission began its work, there developed sharp differences between the members as to the form that the bill should take. There was strong support for issuing a declaration only, and also support for producing a treaty which would constitute legally binding obligations on the ratifiers. Finally, after some two years of discussion, the Commission on Human Rights resolved the problem by applying the term "international bill of rights" to a combination of instruments: one would be a general Universal Declaration of Human Rights and the other would be a specific treaty plus measures of implementation. This program was subsequently approved by the General Assembly. Eventually the treaty was divided into two separate covenants with an optional protocol to one of the covenants. These are the Covenant on Civil and Political Rights with an Optional Protocol and the Covenant on Economic, Social, and Cultural Rights.[23] (See Appendix for texts)

In light of the many years required before the two covenants were drafted and adopted by the United Nations, it is interesting to note the comparative speed with which the Universal Declaration was drafted and approved. The vote in the General Assembly meeting in Paris on December 10, 1948, was unanimous in favor, no votes against, though eight nations (the Soviet bloc) abstained. The fact that it was a declaration rather than a binding treaty may account for its overwhelming endorsement by the assembled nations. This nonbinding fact was enunciated by Eleanor Roosevelt, the U.S. representative on the Human Rights Commission, in her statement prior to the meeting of the General Assembly that the declaration "is not a treaty; it is not an international agreement. It is not and does not purport to be a statement of law or of legal obligation."[24] In the same statement, Mrs. Roosevelt reaffirmed the intention to eventually produce an international bill of human rights in asserting that "the Declaration of Human Rights is of course only the first step in the implementation of the human rights program called for by the Charter of the United Nations...(it) forms only part of the International Bill of Rights...(by) the completion of a Covenant on Human Rights in the form of a treaty with measures of implementation...."[25]

Despite the early assertions that the declaration was not a legally enforceable document, it soon came to have a unique status of its own. It was constantly cited as the basis for claims against states alleged to be violating the human rights of its own citizens. It was cited in a General Assembly resolution adopted within five months of the approval of the declaration in the so-called Russian Wives Case. The charge against the Soviet Union was based on its refusal to allow Soviet wives of citizens of other nationalities to leave the Soviet Union to join their husbands in other countries. That resolution[26] cited Articles 13 and 16 of the declaration, the first of which protected the right of everyone to leave his own country, and the second of which accorded men and women of full age the right to marry without any limitation as to race, nationality, or religion. Thus, though only the first instrument of the International Bill of Rights had come into existence, the declaration was already considered an authority in asserting charges of violations of human rights.

The influence of the declaration is thus summarized in Sohn and Buergenthal:

> The Universal Declaration of Human Rights has, since its adoption, exercised a powerful influence throughout the world, both internationally and nationally. Its provisions have been cited as the justification for various actions taken by the United Nations, and have inspired a number of international conventions both within and outside the United Nations. They have also exercised a significant influence on national constitutions and on municipal legislation and, in several cases, on court decisions. In some instances, the text of provisions of the Declaration has been used in international instruments or national legislation, and there are many instances of the use of the Declaration as a code of conduct and as a yardstick to measure the degree of respect for and compliance with the international standard of human rights.[27]

Although not specifically identified as a bill of rights, the declaration has in fact become "international custom, as evidence of a general practice accepted as law" and thus international law which, under the Statute of the International Court of Justice, (Article 38, b) the court could apply.²⁸

The Teheran Proclamation

The obligations under the declaration may not have been considered binding on those states that abstained from voting in favor on December 10, 1948, when it was adopted. But over the years, these states also cited the declaration as authoritative. This was evidenced by the unanimous vote on the Final Act of the International Conference on Human Rights,²⁹ convened under the auspices of the United Nations at Teheran, April 22 to May 13, 1968, to observe the 20th anniversary of the adoption of the Universal Declaration of Human Rights. The participants included the Soviet Union and members of the Soviet block that had abstained in the General Assembly on December 10, 1948.

In the Proclamation of Teheran, the parties solemnly declared that "the Universal Declaration of Human Rights states a common understanding of the people of the world concerning the inalienable and inviolable rights of all members of the human family and constitutes an obligation for the members of the international community."³⁰ The Universal Declaration is again cited in paragraphs 4, 14, and 15 of the proclamation. The formal resolutions adopted at the Teheran Conference are replete with references to the Universal Declaration of Human Rights.

The Helsinki Final Act

The more recent Conference on Security and Cooperation in Europe, usually referred to as the Helsinki Conference, adopted its Final Act on August 1, 1975.³¹ The main participants were members of the Warsaw Pact and of NATO. In its Declaration of Principles, it not only includes respect for human rights and fundamental freedoms, ³² but specifically calls upon the participants to act in conformity with the Universal Declaration of Human Rights.³³

With all of these proclamations and all of the citations to the declaration, domestically and internationally, it can be assumed that, by itself, the Universal Declaration may be considered a common law bill of rights. Based upon the Teheran Proclamation, Professor Louis B. Sohn asserts that it is a binding instrument:

> thus, (citing the proclamation) the Declaration not only constitutes an authoritative interpretation of the Chapter obligations, but also a binding instrument in its own right, representing the consensus of the international community on the human rights which each of its members must respect, promote and observe.³⁴

The Two International Covenants

This now brings us to the next step in the final formulation of the International Bill of Rights, which was the adoption by the U.N. General Assembly on December 16, 1966, of the two international covenants on human rights. One covenant is on economic, social and cultural rights and the other is on civil and political rights, to which is appended an optional protocol. This step was not completed until 21 years after the adoption of the United Nations Charter in 1945, and 18 years after the adoption of the Universal Declaration of Human Rights. Considering the recognition eventually accorded to the declaration although it is not designated as a treaty, it might be claimed that the covenants are superfluous. But, in fact, they add to and make more precise the provisions of the declaration and put them in a form, the legal application of which cannot be denied by ratifying states. The covenants were to enter into force after ratification by 35 members and the optional protocol when ratified by 10 nations who had become parties to the civil rights covenant. The economic covenant did come into force on January 3, 1976, and the civil rights plus the optional protocol came into force on March 23, 1976.

The Universal Declaration itself is divided between articles relating to civil and political rights and those relating to economic, social, and cultural rights. The two covenants are divided along similar lines. The civil rights covenant imposes restraints upon the states in exercising power which affects the liberties and rights of its own people. The economic covenant, on the other hand, sets forth goals and the expectation that member states acting in a positive manner would move to achieve the objectives set forth in the covenant. (See Appendix for text.)

Differences Between Declaration and Covenants

There are some obvious differences between the declaration and the covenants. For example, the economic covenant specifies a number of economic, social, and cultural rights not spelled out in the declaration. These are, however, goals and not necessarily obligations, as indicated in Article 2, 1 which provides that:

> Each State Party to the present Covenant undertakes to take steps, individually and through international assistance and cooperation, especially economic and technical, to the maximum of its available resources, with a view to achieving progressively the full realization of the rights recognized in the present Covenant by all appropriate means, including particularly the adoption of legislative measures.

It may be said that the obligations imposed by the economic covenant are relative rather than absolute. Still, they are clearly more expressive and definite than under the declaration.[35]

Similar differences exist between the declaration and the civil rights covenant. The former is general in nature, while the latter is not only specific but is specific in what it expects of the states. It also expands upon some of the articles in the declaration.[36] Thus, while the declaration bars torture, the covenant also protects the individual from being subjected to medical or scientific experimentation without his consent (Civil Rights Covenant, Article 7). The covenant also requires (Article 20, 1) member states to prohibit propaganda for war, a provision of doubtful validity under the U.S. Constitution free speech clause. This same comment applies to the second provision of Article 20 requiring statutory prohibition for "advocacy of national, racial or religious hatred that constitutes incitement to discrimination, hostility or violence...."

In the declaration, Article 29, rights and freedoms are subject "to such limitations as are determined by law for the purpose...of meeting the just requirements of morality, public order and the general welfare in a democratic society." Under the civil rights covenant (Article 19.3 b.), freedom of expression may be subject to certain restrictions, provided by law, "for the protection of national security or of public order, or of public health or morals." This article, too, raises doubt as to the extent of protection that might be asserted by an individual expressing sharp and perhaps provocative attacks upon the current government of his country.

It should be noted, too, that another possible inapplicability under the U.S. Constitution of the civil rights covenant is Part II, Article 4.1, which provides that "in time of emergency which threatens the life of the nation and the existence of which is officially proclaimed, the States Parties to the present Covenant may take measures derogating from their obligations...to the extent strictly required by the exigencies of the situation, provided that such measures are not inconsistent with their other obligations under international law, and do not involve discrimination solely on the ground of race, colour, sex, language, religion or social origin." However, Section 2 of Article 4 prohibits derogation from Article 6 (right to life, genocide); from Article 7 (torture or cruel and inhuman punishment); from paragraphs 1 and 2 of Article 8 (slavery); from Article 11 (imprisonment for debt); Article 15 (ex post facto laws); from Article 16 (recognition at law); and from Article 18 (freedom of thought, conscience, and religion).

Thus, while the derogation provision, which does not appear in the declaration, appears broad in the covenant, the limiting provisions of paragraph 2 do not take too much away from the protections granted individuals.

The United States Record on Ratification

The history of the United States on ratifications of human rights treaties reflects a classic case of schizophrenia. The leader in support of all the treaties within the United Nations, frequently the principal drafter of the documents, the proposer before the San Francisco U.N. Conference of an international bill of rights, the United States has been the outstanding laggard when it comes to signing on the dotted line. Since the founding of the United Nations in 1945, the United States has ratified only one new human rights treaty, i.e., the Convention on the Political Rights of Women.

The most shocking example of the failure of the United States to honor its announced policies on human rights is that of the Genocide Convention. Adopted by the United Nations in 1948 under the leadership of the United States, submitted by the president to the U.S. Senate in 1949 for its advice and consent, reviewed extensively and favorably for ratification by the Foreign Relations Committee of the Senate, the treaty has yet to be finally voted on by the Senate.

In a spirit of chauvinism, it is not difficult to understand how Americans take so much credit for instituting and supporting human rights on the international scale. Americans did in fact take leadership in drafting and sponsoring the human rights documents in the UN. It is therefore difficult to understand the stone wall that has prevented the United States from ratifying these treaties.

When President Truman sent the Genocide Convention to the Senate for its advice and consent, it was generally assumed that Senate approval would be routine. But to the administration's surprise, and to the shock of interested Americans, opposition began to be asserted and political clout felt.

Whatever can be said, or has since been said on the constitutionality and desirability of the Genocide Convention, was made a part of the extensive hearings conducted by the subcommittee of the Senate Foreign Relations Committee in 1950.[37] What becomes clear in these hearings is that the opposition was moved more by fears of threats to states rights within the United States rather than by any basic constitutional problems. It was even asserted that, in effect, if a citizen of a state were accused of the crime of lynching that he could be seized by some foreign secret police agency, flown to an unknown destination, and tried before a communist court. Human rights treaties were considered by many opponents as an indirect method of enacting civil rights legislation within the United States, a result to be opposed by them at all costs. The continued sectional opposition to these treaties at this late date gives emphasis to the idea that opponents equate international human rights treaties with domestic civil rights against which there continues to be deep emotional opposition.

The American Bar Association (ABA) in the early days of the United Nations announced its full support of the new organization. It opposed the Connally Reservation which sought to restrict the jurisdiction of the International Court of Justice. It condemned genocide and resolved that it "should have the constant opposition of the United States and all of its people." But at the same time it declined to support ratification of the Genocide Convention on the ground "that the proposed convention raises important fundamental questions but does not resolve them in a manner consistent with our form of government."[38] Although no formal international covenant on human rights had been adopted by the U.N. nor was one up for a vote in the U.S. Senate, the ABA's early opposition as expressed on genocide was reaffirmed in February 1970[40] by a close vote in its House of Delegates. However, on February 17, 1976, by an overwhelming vote, the ABA finally reversed its previous negative position and endorsed ratification of the Genocide Convention with three understandings previously approved by the Senate Committee.

These three understandings construe: (1) "intent to destroy, in whole or in part" to mean to destroy "in effect a substantial part of the group concerned"; (2) "mental harm...to mean permanent impairment of mental facilities"; and (3) Article VI of the convention (place of trial) to mean "that nothing in Article VI shall affect the right of any state to bring to trial before its own tribunals any of its nationals for acts committed outside the state." There was also a declaration that the United States "will not deposit its instrument of ratification until after the implementary legislation referred to in Article V has been enacted." [41]

Stalemate in the U.S. Senate

The effectiveness of the ABA's previous opposition to genocide was noted by Senator Paul Sarbanes, when he said: "One of the things that has always been used very effectively by the opponents of ratifying the convention has been the position of the American Bar Association."[42] But, despite the change in the ABA's position, despite the special message from President Carter,[43] despite several favorable reports by the Senate Foreign Relations Committee prior to the 1977 hearings, no further action by the Senate has been taken on the convention. As of March 1, 1980, it is still pending in the committee and nothing indicates that it will be brought out soon. It continues to be kept in cold storage.

It is suggested that threat of a Senate filibuster has kept the Senate leadership from bringing the matter on to the floor for a vote. Whatever the reason, the failure to act favorably on this convention bodes nothing hopeful either for the two international human rights covenants or the related protocol. President Carter signed the two covenants on October 5, 1977, at a special ceremony at the UN.

The United States — A Split Personality

It is difficult to explain the split personality of the United States on human rights treaties. The previous negative attitude of the American Bar Association cannot be proffered as the main factor against ratification. The Senate failed to act favorably despite the association's changed position in 1976. In another instance, the ABA in 1967 went on record opposed to the Convention on the Political Rights of Women. The Senate Foreign Relations Committee took note of the association's opposition in its report of December 18, 1975, but reported it out favorably, [44] and in January 1976 the Senate gave its advice and consent to ratification.

The Block from the Bricker Amendment

Another factor, at least in the Eisenhower days, resulted from the attempt to enact the so-called Bricker Amendment to the U.S. Constitution. This amendment was intended to limit the authority of the president in foreign affairs. The pending human rights treaties were frequently cited as examples of threats to the sovereignty of the United States. To avoid this argument, specious though it may have been, the then secretary of state, John Foster Dulles, announced that the administration did not then intend to seek ratification of any human rights treaties. [45] In 1953, Dulles specifically stated that: "We (the Eisenhower administration) do not intend to become a party to any such covenant (on international human rights) or present it as a treaty for consideration by the Senate" (parentheses supplied).[46]

Although the Bricker Amendment did not prevail, the effect of the debate was to cut off serious consideration of human rights treaties for several years. Occasionally a congressman would make reference to the failure of the United States to act. Congressman Henry S. Reuss of Wisconsin spoke out, deploring the fact that this country "stands almost alone in opposing in principle treaties relating to human rights."[47] On the opening day of the Senate in January 1967, Senator William Proxmire of Wisconsin began a series of statements for the Congressional Record in support of ratification of the Genocide Convention. He has continued to do so on every regular business day of the Senate since that time, including the session of the Senate which convened in January 1978.[48]

The Two Covenants Go to the Senate

On February 23, 1978, President Carter transmitted to the U.S. Senate the two international covenants on human rights: i.e., the Covenant on Economic, Social, and Cultural Rights and the Covenant on Civil and Political Rights (signed for the United States on October 5, 1977) seeking the Senate's advice and consent to their ratification subject to certain reservations, understandings, and declarations. The letter of transmittal also sought the Senate's advice and consent to ratification of the Convention on the Elimination of All Forms of Racial Discrimination (signed for the United States September 28, 1966) and the American Convention on Human Rights (signed for the United States on June 1, 1977).

The president's letter[49] is accompanied by a letter from the Department of State, dated December 17, 1977, which summarizes the four treaties and sets forth in detail suggested reservations, understandings, and declarations which the state asserts are desired to avoid conflict with United States law. The Department of Justice is quoted as being of the view that "with these reservations, declarations, and understandings, there are no constitutional or other legal objections to United States ratification of these treaties".

This paper has not attempted to fully analyze the suggested declarations or understandings on the four treaties. Limitations of time permit only a general reference in this paper to the suggested limitations as to the two international human rights covenants, in which this paper is primarily interested, because they are two of the three legs of the International Bill of Rights. The optional protocol has not been signed for the United States and is not included in the President's letter.

The State Department's letter states that the economic covenant provisions, "while for the most part in accord with U.S. law and practice, are nevertheless formulated as statements of goals to be achieved progressively rather than implemented immediately." It then suggests an understanding that the goals of Articles 1 through 15 "be achieved progressively rather than through immediate implementation". This understanding appears superfluous in face of the language of Article 2 (1) that merely requires states "to take steps...to the maximum of its available resources with a view to achieving progressively the full realization of the rights recognized...."

Although the covenant does not ban the right of private ownership of property, it does not specifically mention it. Hence, the proposal that there be a declaration that according to the United States:

> Under the Covenant everyone has the right to own property alone as well as in association with others, and that no one shall be arbitrarily deprived of his property.

Another recommended statement relates to Article 5 (1) which does not allow any activity aimed at the destruction of the rights recognized in the covenant. This raises a freedom of speech problem and would support a recommendation to include a statement that "nothing in this covenant shall be deemed to require...action by the United States which would restrict the rights of free speech protected by the Constitution, laws, and practices of the United States."

The State Department letter refers to the federal system of the U.S. and proposes a reservation requiring the U.S. to "progressively implement all the provisions of the Covenant over whose subject matter the Federal Government exercises legislative and judicial jurisdiction...." With respect to matters over which constituent units exercise jurisdiction, the federal government is merely required to "take appropriate measures, to the end that the competent...constituent units may take appropriate measures for the fulfillment of this Covenant." Whether this reservation is in derogation of the recognized Constitutional principle that a treaty is the law of the land, is a question too basic to discuss here. It obviously, however, raises a serious question as to the soundness of its inclusion as a reservation.

A final recommendation on the economic covenant is a declaration that the provisions of Articles 1 through 15 are not self-executing. If these articles are merely goals, then this declaration appears superfluous and may only raise questions.

With respect to the Covenant on Civil and Political Rights there are additional suggestions for reservations, declarations, and understandings. The free speech problem, implicit in the economic covenant, is again presented in the civil rights covenant (Article 5). A proposed reservation would provide that "nothing in this Covenant shall...require...action by the United States which would restrict the right of free speech protected by the Constitution, laws and practice of the United States." Presumably this would apply without any further enunciation, but adding the reservation resolves all possible controversy.

The covenant (Article 6) forbids execution of persons under the age of 18 or of pregnant women. This is not the law in the U.S. and a proposed reservation would allow capital punishment in such instances of any person convicted under laws permitting it. This reservation implies that the U.S. would authorize execution of minors and pregnant women. This is most objectionable.

Paragraph 5 of Article 9 authorizes compensation for an unlawful arrest or detention, and Paragraph 1 of Article 15 provides that if after a crime is committed, the law is changed for the imposition of a lighter sentence, the offender is to benefit thereby. This is not law in the United

States and a reservation is proposed making these provisions inapplicable in the United States.

The Covenant (Article 10 (2) and (3)) requires persons criminally accused to be segregated from commited prisoners, and that juveniles be separated from adults and tried speedily. It also provides that the aim of the penitentiary system is to reform and rehabilitate prisoners. The State Department suggests that ratification include a statement that these objectives are "goals to be achieved progressively rather than through immediate implementation."

Certain standards for the conduct of trials are set out in Article 14. The State Department indicates that these may all be consistent with U.S. law, policy, and practice. Nevertheless, it suggests an understanding on some specifics, such as not requiring a court-appointed counsel for a defendant financially able to retain counsel. The other understandings on Article 14 appear less consequential.

A Human Rights Committee is authorized, under Article 25, consisting of 18 members. They shall be nationals of states parties to the covenant but "shall serve in their personal capacity." Article 41 authorizes that committee to receive complaints from a state party against another state party. No state party is required to recognize the competence of the committee. But the Department of State's letter of December 17, 1977, indicates that if the covenant is ratified, the United States will elect to recognize the competence of the committee. The president's letter of February 23, 1978 states his intention to make the declaration regarding the committee's competence, if the Senate gives its advice and consent to ratification. This is desirable although not as effective as the optional protocol to the covenant which would permit the committee to receive complaints from individuals. It is interesting to note that the State Department, in its letter of transmittal, refers to the optional protocol, describes it briefly, but makes no recommendation in respect to it. It merely states that it "is not being submitted to the Senate at this time." As of March 1, 1980, it had not been signed by the U.S. The department characterizes the protocol as "a related instrument of significance." It certainly is that and one that should be ratified by the United States.

Under Article 47 nothing in the covenant shall impair the "inherent right of all peoples to enjoy and utilize fully and freely their natural wealth and resources." A declaration is suggested so that this right "may be exercised only in accordance with international law." Because of the breadth of Article 47, this declaration may be desirable.

As it does with respect to the economic covenant, the State Department recommends a reservation by which the civil rights covenant shall be implemented by the federal government only over subjects on which it exercises legislative and judicial jurisdiction. As to provisions whose subject matter constituent units (presumably states and local governments) exercise jurisdiction, the federal government is required merely to "take appropriate measures, to the end that the competent authorities of the constituent units may take appropriate measures for the fulfillment of this Covenant." This suggestion could emasculate some of the objectives sought to be obtained under the covenant and appears of dubious value. It opens the door to all sorts of questions including the applicability of Article VI of the United States Constitution making treaties "the supreme law of the land."

A final recommendation of the department is for a declaration that Articles 1 through 27 be deemed non-self-executing. This might be appropriate with respect to the economic covenant because the latter is essentially a statement of goals. But it seems inappropriate to the civil rights covenant which is mainly a restatement of ideals long held by the United States and imbedded in its Constitution, its laws, its practices, and its customs.

Congressional Support

Beginning in the 1970s there appeared to be a thawing out in the Congress of the cold war on human rights matters produced in part by the Bricker battle. In 1971 Congressman Reuss introduced an amendment to the Foreign Military Sales Act of 1971, which was adopted. It barred military sales and guarantees which "would have the effect of arming military dictators who are denying the growth of fundamental rights or social progress to their own people," unless the limitation was waived by the president for security reasons.[50]

Subsequently, Congress in 1975 enacted Section 116 of the Foreign Assistance Act of 1961 as amended whereby no assistance was to be provided "to the government of any country which engages in a consistent pattern of gross violations of internationally recognized human rights...unless such assistance will directly benefit the needy people of such country."[51] A further amendment to Section 116 in 1977 (Subsection (c)) provides that the administrator of AID is required to consult with the assistant secretary of state for human rights and humanitarian affairs (a newly created post, Section 109, Public Law 95-105), on the extent of cooperation of a country seeking development assistance, on actions taken by the president and Congress regarding multilateral and security assistance because of human rights considerations, and investigations of alleged violations of human rights in such country. Further, under Sections 116 (d) and 502B (b) of the Foreign Assistance Act (see Appendix) annual reports are to be submitted by the secretary of state on the status of human rights in countries receiving U.S. foreign assistance.[52]

Under the International Financial Institutions Act[53] U.S. executive directors to various agencies are required to vote to promote human rights and to seek to channel assistance to countries which do not violate human rights unless that assistance is directed specifically to programs which serve the "basic human needs" of the citizens of such countries. Similarly an amendment to the Agriculture Trade Act of July 10, 1954[54] prohibits sales of agricultural commodities to governments engaging in consistent patterns of gross violations of human rights unless the commodities or proceeds from their sale benefit needy people (Section 112, Public Law 480). The Export-Import Bank Act of 1945 has also been amended to discourage exports to countries not observing human rights.[55]

It is significant that under Section 113 of the Fiscal Year 1978 Appropriations[56] October 31, 1977, Congress specifically prohibits the obligating of security assistance funds to any country "for the purpose of aiding directly the efforts of the government of such country to repress the legitimate rights of the population of such country contrary to the Universal Declaration of Human Rights." This is another example of how the Universal Declaration has come to be recognized by the United States as international custom.

The Jackson-Vanick Amendment to the Trade Act of 1974, as amended, is a well-publicized restriction denying to nonmarket countries who deny their citizens a right to emigrate or impose more than a nominal tax fee for emigration, eligibility for most favored-nations trade treatment, and are excluded by the Stevenson Amendment from direct and indirect U.S. credit and guarantees. Such countries may not enter into commercial agreements with the U.S.[57]

The attitude of Congress is expressed in a number of statutes. But it could be stated no more clearly than in Section 502 B of the Foreign Assistance Act, as amended. It reads in part as follows:

> a) (1) It is the policy of the United States in accordance with its international obligations as set forth in the Charter of the United Nations and in keeping with the Constitutional heritage and traditions of the United States, to promote and encourage increased respect for human rights and fundamental freedoms for all without distinction as to race, sex, language, or religion. To this end, a principal goal of the foreign policy of the United States is to promote the increased observance of internationally recognized human rights by all countries.
> (2) It is further the policy of the United States that, except under circumstances specified in this section, no security assistance may be provided

to any country the government of which engages in a consistent pattern of gross violations of internationally recognized human rights.

(3) In furtherance of the foregoing policy the President is directed to formulate and conduct international security assistance programs of the United States in a manner which will promote and advance human rights and avoid identification of the United States, through such programs, with governments which deny to their people internationally recognized human rights and fundamental freedoms, in violation of international law or in contravention of the policy of the United States as expressed in this section or otherwise.

By this legislation, Congress has made clear its support of human rights in foreign countries. It must be emphasized that these statutes are congressional mandates in response to the U.N. Declaration of Human Rights, and the growing awareness of policymakers to the role of human rights in U.S. foreign policy.

Presidential Support

Every president of the United States since World War II has, at the least, pronounced his support of international human rights by this country. This was done by presidents Roosevelt, Truman, Eisenhower, Kennedy, Johnson, Nixon, Ford, and Carter.

The Carter administration has been most direct and explicit in its pronouncements, and has made concern for human rights throughout the world a central part of U.S. foreign policy. This is certainly a fair statement. But what has, in fact, been done to implement this policy in the ratification process of the various human rights treaties adopted by the U.N. and the specialized agencies and regional organizations? President Carter stated most succinctly his philosophy in Paris at the Palais des Congress on January 4, 1978:

> There is one belief above all others that has made us what we are. This is the belief that the rights of the individual inherently stand higher than the claims or demands of the State.[58]

Certainly there can be no more explicit an exposition of what this country stands for than the president's statement.

Conclusions

Perhaps the time for the attainment of an enforceable International Bill of Rights was passed in June 1945 when what was a unique gathering of representatives of the world community met in San Francisco. Perhaps it was then that sovereignty should have been so defined as to permit no nation to hide behind its cloak in denying rights to any human being regardless of citizenship or residence. But whether or not the key opportunity was missed when the U.N. Charter was approved, its provisions not only emphasize but also require member states to achieve "universal respect for, and observance of, human rights and fundamental freedoms."

It has been said that "nothing reflects more accurately or expresses more forcefully the true aspirations of man than the enjoyment of the rights and freedoms set forth in the Universal Declaration of Human Rights and reduced to law in the International Covenants on Human Rights....International protection of human rights brings into international relations those dreams and hopes by which humanity moves from one epoch to another."[59]

In this historical move from the philosophy that the state is absolute to the recognition that the rights of individuals are supreme, the United States must take an active leadership. It is not sufficient to constantly proclaim our support of human rights in the international community. We must formally, by treaty, commit ourselves to protecting these rights not only within our own geographical borders but within the whole wide world.

NOTES

1. See Carl Sandburg, *Abraham Lincoln, The Prairie Years and the War Years,* pp. 337, 347, 454, 455.
2. See W. Malloy, *U.S. Treaties, Conventions, International Acts, Protocols, and Agreements between the United States of America and Other Powers 1776-1909* (Washington: Government Printing Office, 1919).
3. Ibid., p. 590.
4. Ibid., p. 4.
5. Ibid., Art. III., at p. 509.
6. Ibid., note 4, p. 143.
7. 1 Malloy, Art. XV, 2nd. para., p. 1089.
8. See Sohn-Buerganthal, *International Protection of Human Rights* (Indianapolis: Bobbs-Merrill Co., 1973), pp. 182 et seq. and at p. 916.
9. Ibid., pp. 213 et seq.
10. 46 Stat. 2183, T.S. #778.
11. See Tuttle, *International Lawyer* 3 (#2): 389.
12. *Public Papers and Addresses of Franklin D. Roosevelt: War and Aid to Democracies* (New York: Random House, 1938), p. 672.
13. Ruth B. Russell, *History of the United Nations Chapter; The Role of the United States* (Washington: The Brookings Institution, 1940-1945).
14. Ibid., p. 221.
15. See Appendix I of Russell, p. 1019.

16. Ibid., p. 1027.
17. See Clark M. Eichelberger, *Organizing for Peace* (New York: Harper & Row, 1977), p. 226.
18. Ibid., p. 267.
19. Russell, p. 780.
20. Jessup, *Modern Law of Nations,* p. 91. See, too, Bitker, "The Constitutionality of International Agreements on Human Rights," *Santa Clara Lawyer* 12 (1972): 279.
21. U.S. *Department of State Bulletin* 13 (26 June 1945): 5.
22. Egon Schwelb, *Human Rights and the International Community* (Chicago, Quadrangle Books, 1959), p. 31.
23. Schwelb, *American Journal of International Law*, 70 (July 1976): 511.
24. U.S. Department of State Publication 3643 (October 1949), p. 14.
25. Ibid.
26. U.N., General Assembly, GA #285, III, 25 April 1949.
27. Sohn and Buerganthal, p. 516.
28. See Sohn and Buerganthal, p. 518, et seq. on the legal effect of the declaration. For a summary of the application of the Declaration in the United States, see Bitker, *DePaul Law Review* 21 (1971): 337.
29. U.N. Publication, No.E.68.XLV. 2, 1968.
30. P.4. Par. #2.
31. Department of State Publication #8826, General Foreign Policy Series 298.
32. Article VII, p. 80.
33. Ibid., p. 81.
34. Louis B. Sohn, "The Human Rights Law of the Charter,"paper presented for the American Society of International Law Panel at Wingspread Conference Center, 10 October 1974.
35. See *International Legal Protections for Human Rights* (World Peace Through Law Center, 1977), p. 30.
36. Ibid., p. 34.
37. Executive Order, Jan.-Feb. 1950.
38. U.S. Senate Hearings on Genocide, Executive O, Jan.-Feb. 1950, p. 158.
39. Ibid., p. 152.
40. *Journal of the American Bar Association,* April 1970, p. 370.
41. Report of Senate Foreign Relations Committee on Executive O, April 29, 1976, p. 1 as to understanding and p. 33 as to proposed implementary legislation. For ABA resolution of support see Senate Committee Hearings on Executive O, 25 May 1977, p. 48.
42. Ibid., p. 53
43. Ibid., p. 54.
44. Executive Report #94-20, 94th Congress, 1st Session.
45. Bitker, *Human Rights Journal* 2 (#4, 1969): U.S. Policy on Ratification of International Human Rights Conventions.
46. Foreign Relations Subcommittee Hearings on Treaties and Executive Agreements, April 1953, p. 825.
47. Congressional Record 102 (5 March 1957): 3167.

48. The statements are too numerous to permit citations: a recent one is in the Congressional Record for 19 January 1978, pp. 580-82.
49. Executive C.D.E. and F., Senate Foreign Relations Committee, 28 February 1978.
50. 22 U.S.C.A. Section 2751, Public Law 91-672.
51. 22 U.S.C.A. 2151, Public Law 94-161.
52. The latest report, Country Reports on Human Rights Practices Joint Committee Report, 95th Cong. 2nd Session, was issued on 3 February 1978.
53. Public Law 95-118 of 3 October 1977.
54. Public Law 480.
55. Public Law 95-143, 26 October 1977.
56. Public Law 95-148.
57. 19 U.S.C.A. 2434 Sec. 402, Public Law #93-618, Trade Act of 1974, as amended.
58. *U.S. Department of State News Release* (New York: Bureau of Public Affairs, 4 January 1978).
59. Moskowitz, *The Politics and Dynamics of Human Rights* (Oceana Publications, 1968), p. 211.

Chapter 6

The United States and the Right of Self-Determination

Walker F. Connor

Upon first reflection, the issue of the place of self-determination in American foreign policy may appear to be a sterile or (at best) a relatively insignificant one. Several factors lend themselves to such an assessment: (1) When so many momentous issues are vying for attention, the question of self-determination hardly seems worthy of holding center stage. Given such foreign policy priorities as control over the production and deployment of non-conventional weaponry or the highly complex quadrangular interactions of Chinese, Soviet, Western European, and American relations, does the subject of self-determination really merit our serious consideration? (2) In the immediate post-World War II period, national self-determination was associated with the colonial question, and many may feel that its significance therefore waned with the political emancipation of most of Asia and Africa from European control. (3) Over-exposure to the expression *national self-determination* is also involved: when leading figures as diverse in their political philosophies as Stalin, Charles de Gaulle, and Mohandas Gandhi pay lip service to it, one is tempted to conclude that self-determination is little more today than an empty platitude. (4) To the degree that national self-determination is possessed of substance, the United States's commitment to support the doctrine has ostensibly been so steadfast that the question of its role in American foreign policy should not arise. Indeed, the origin of the doctrine of self-determination is popularly most closely identified with a former U.S. president, Woodrow Wilson. And, as school children, Americans have been taught that the United States, throughout its history, has been an ardent and unswerving champion of the philosophical assumptions underlying the doctrine.[1] Presidents and foreign policy spokesmen regularly reaffirm the American commitment to the principle.[2]

All such considerations to the contrary, it is the conviction of this writer that self-determination is of greater significance today than ever before and that it would be difficult to exaggerate its remaining revolutionary potential. Indeed, it represents the single most serious threat to the stability of political borders and the balance of power within states as presently delineated. Given the emotion it evokes both among members and adversaries, ethnonational struggle fought in the name of self-determination is apt to remain the principal form of warfare. If such an assessment be even approximately correct, it follows that the self-determination doctrine and movements conducted or apt to be conducted in its name should indeed be assigned a high priority by the formulators of American foreign policy. Yet, despite the paeans to self-determination periodically made by U.S. officials, American foreign policy in practice indicates the absence of such a priority. In many instances, it discloses a lack of comprehension of both the nature and the fullness of the implications of the self-determination phenomenon.

The Meaning of Self-Determination

In order to reconcile the seemingly irreconcilable positions set forth in the two preceding paragraphs, it is necessary to reflect upon the meaning and the history of self-determination. That doctrine postulates that any people, solely because it considers itself to constitute a separate people, has the *right,* if it so desires, to create its own state. As such, it makes ethnicity the ultimate criterion of political legitimacy.[3]

Considering its broad-scale acceptance today as a self-evident truth, it is curious that the discovery of this essential linkage between ethnicity and political legitimacy is a relatively recent development. From antiquity to the 19th century, the political borders of empires and states had been drawn with little or no regard for the distribution of ethnic groups. Nor did it occur to the masses to protest political incorporation, simply on the ground that the rulers(s) was(were) of a different ethnic stock.[4] The popular linking of ethnicity and legitimacy awaited the coming of the doctrine of popular sovereignty. Prior to the emergence of this doctrine, the basis of political legitimacy was found in such diverse elements as a gift from the gods (divine right), a prerogative of royal blood, a hereditary legacy, a fidelity owed because of protection and/or other services rendered (feudalism), the spoils of conquest, an ancillary right flowing from the ownership of the land inhabited by the people, or any combination of the foregoing. What all such claims to legitimacy shared was the negative presumption that the right to rule had nothing whatsoever to do with the ruled. The people were the object, not the source of political authority. In such a climate, the ethnicity of the subjects was simply not an issue. But with the coming of popular sovereignty—the notion that the right to rule is somehow vested in the people themselves — it was only a short step to the notion that one's people should not be ruled by "outsiders," by aliens. All that was necessary was for a group to interpret the abstract notion of *the people* in whom sovereignty was said to be vested into *my people,* that is to say, into the French, German, Greek, Irish, Japanese, or other nation. For if the right to rule was somehow vested in the national group, it followed that the group was endowed with the right to determine its own political destiny, free of alien domination.

In a very real sense, then, national self-determination is a special application of the theory of popular sovereignty. The rather bloodless and remote notion of *the people* did little to make the political philosophers' theory of popular sovereignty comprehensible to the masses. But linking this notion with the intuitive sense of identity inherent in the idea of *my people* infused the concept with such life that national self-determination might well be termed "popular, popular sovereignty."

The almost imperceptible manner in which *the people* becomes in practice *my people* has been unintentionally captured by a reviewer of a book on the French Revolution:

> Popular sovereignty is an awesome idea precisely because it means nothing less than the existential freedom of a people to be responsible for its own fate, without recourse to any "father." The regicides created this terrible and magnificent freedom, the only one commensurate with the fullness of human potential. With the execution of Louis, they could solemnly declare to the nation: "From this moment, one will no longer write the history of France, but rather the history of the French."[5]

It was in fact at the time of the French Revolution that we first clearly find popular sovereignty linked to a specific ethnonational people.[6] As Article 2 of the Declaration of Rights of Man and Citizen would intone: "The source of all sovereignty resides essentially in the nation; no group, no individual, may exercise authority not emanating expressly therefrom." *"L'etat c'est moi!"* had been transformed into *"L'etat c'est nous!"* and the *nous* was identified as my nation (i.e., *my* people).

The French Revolution did not, of course, involve the drawing of a new state but the internal reordering of an old one. Nonetheless, the precedent had been established for a national group to assert the right, in its own name, to create its own state and to declare that state to be the political expression of the nation, its servant and the principal protector of its destiny. Statehood was henceforth to be the handmaiden of nationhood. As emperor, Napoleon was a major factor in spreading the new message wherever his forces went; his appeals to the political aspirations of the people, *qua* particular national groups, constituted a key element of his propaganda.[7] Nor did the message evaporate with the emperor's downfall. Beginning with the Greek national war of liberation, Europe was rocked by a series of both successful and abortive movements, each aimed at establishing a state that would be essentially coterminous with one or another ethnic homeland.

At first both unrecognized and untitled, the common underlying force behind these movements became known as "the principle of nationalities" about the time of Louis Napoleon, who, just as his more illustrious namesake, thought it strategically advantageous to appeal to the growing national consciousness of politically subservient or divided national groups.[8] Contrary to popular opinion, it was not Woodrow Wilson who coined the expression "national self-determination." This was done more than a half century before Wilson used the expression, so far as can be ascertained, by Karl Marx.[9] It may appear somewhat perplexing that the most famous rallying cry of ethnonationalism should be the invention of the most famous internationalist, who addressed his credo to the "working men of all countries" and who insisted that it was precisely their nonnational outlook that differentiated communists from noncommunists.[10] The explanation is that Marx in his later years came to appreciate both the growing influence of ethnonational aspirations, the strategic value of seemingly supporting the notion of national liberation in *abstracto,* and in very selectively supporting those national movements whose success would further the goals of global scientific socialism.[14] But despite this earlier publicity generated by Marxists, it was unquestionably Woodrow Wilson who, through his many public endorsements of national self-determination during the World War I era, played the major role in first assuring the phrase global fame.

The Revolutionary Potential of Self-Determination

When discussing self-determination, care must be taken not to confuse the slogan which the phrase has become with the historic content of the idea. We have seen that the idea of national self-determination surfaced long before it was given its present sloganized form (or, for that matter, long before its earlier christening as "the principle of nationalities"). Marx and later Wilson were each describing a force already well underway and gaining adherents.[12]

Beginning, as we have noted, with the French Revolution and given impetus by the Napoleonic Wars, the idea of self-determination has subsequently spread rapidly. In the century and a quarter separating the Napoleonic Wars from World War II, all but three of Europe's states had either lost significant territory as a result of ethnically inspired aspirations or were themselves the result of successful self-determination movements.[13] Its spread outside of Europe was much slower, although it had surfaced in Japan, China, and the Levant prior to World War I. It spread much more rapidly thereafter, and the growing conviction that alien rule was illegal rule was the driving force behind the anticolonial movement that saw the retreat of European control from Africa, Asia, Oceania, and the West Indies.[14]

Though the campaigns for their independence were conducted under the banner of national self-determination, the newest states are themselves multinational entities. However, as we are reminded by the abortive Biafra and the successful Bangladesh movements, as well as by a host of lesser known separatist movements throughout the Third World, national groups are now insisting that the self-determination principle be carried a further step toward its logical conclusion. Nor are the Third World states alone in this regard. Such older states as Belgium, Canada, Denmark, France, Italy, Romania, the Soviet Union, Spain, Switzerland, and the United Kingdom have also been afflicted in the post-World War II era.

Indeed, during the 1960s and 1970s, nearly one-half of all states suffered from such *fissiparous* ethnic pressures.[15] Moreover, the number of self-determination movements can be expected to grow. A survey of the ethnic composition of 132 states produced the following breakdown.[16]

1. Only 12 states (9.1%) could be described as essentially homogeneous.
2. Twenty-five states (18.9%) contained a nation or potential nation[17] accounting for more than 90% of the state's total population but also contained an important minority.
3. In another 25 states (18.9%), the largest nation or potential nation accounted for between 75% and 89% of the total population.
4. In 31 states (23.5%), the largest ethnic element accounted for only 50% to 74% of the population.
5. In 39 states (29.5%), the largest nation or potential nation accounted for less than half of the entire population.

Moreover, this portrait of ethnic diversity becomes more vivid when the number of distinct ethnic groups within states is considered. In some instances, the number of groups within a state runs into the hundreds, and in 53 states (40.2% of those surveyed), the population is divided into more than *five* significant groups. In a world inhabited by thousands of ethnic groups but divided into only some 145 states, the revolutionary potential inherent in the doctrine that each nation has the right to its own status is quite obvious. As we noted at the outset, the urge for national self-determination did not wane with the end of the colonial era. An intelligent foreign policy must therefore anticipate the likelihood of its occurrence throughout the globe on an accelerating basis.

The Opposition to Self-Determination by Existing Nation-States

At this point one might question why, if self-determination has proven to be such a powerful group imperative, has its record been so dismal? Why in fact are there so few ethnically homogeneous states? Elsewhere, a number of reasons have been examined.[18] But the single most fundamental reason for the great discrepancy between the theory of self-determination and the reality of multinational states is the adamant opposition of governments to any plan calling for a shrinkage in their state's territory. There is a seemingly universal tendency on the part of those in authority to base all decisions upon the implicit or explicit assumption that the political integrity of the sovereign territory—no matter how acquired and no matter how many national groups inhabit it—is sacrosanct and must be maintained. Statesmen may be willing to endorse the principle of self-determination in the abstract or to commend its application to a rival state, but they are hardly likely to countenance its application to their own country. Preservation of state dominates their thinking. As noted elsewhere:

> Against a right of self-determination, the authorities raise the right and duty to preserve the union, to stamp out rebellion, to insure domestic tranquility, and to defend the state's political and territorial integrity. What is self-evident truth to those desiring separation is treason to those in authority. In this dichotomic atmosphere, "the God-bestowed inalienable right of the nation to determine its own destiny" is deprecated as "parochialism," "tribalism," "communalism," "particularism," "splittism," "primordialism," "Fascism" or worse. The presumption that the state is a *given* and must not be compromised therefore causes governments to resist, if need be with force, any attempt to dismember the state in the name of self-determination.[19]

With emotion-laden phrases such as "self-determination," "homeland," and "freedom fighters" pitted against others such as "treason," "flag and country," and "traitors," once underway, a self-determination movement will be conducted in an atmosphere of suspicion, hatred, and a spirit of give-no-quarter. The advantages that are normally at the disposal of a government in such a competition are enormously one-sided. Industry (particularly the weapons industry), the armed forces, internal security agencies, the communications network, and legal access to external sources of supplies are all responsive to the government's demands. In the typical (and, therefore, nondemocratic) state, the government will attempt to employ its monopoly of communications to silence the message of the self-determination movement. The movement itself is apt to be described by governmental press releases as nothing more than "hoodlum elements" or the nefarious actions of a few malcontents or *agents provocateurs*. Perceived as traitors, and therefore something worse than criminals, arrested leaders will be decimated or incarcerated for lengthy periods of time.[20]

As against all of these advantages, the principal offsetting asset of the movement is the empathy of the local populace in whose name they struggle. This empathy, however, is of great significance, for it makes it possible for the leadership of the movement to contemplate, with some hope of success, the undertaking of a guerilla war. This type of struggle was perspicaciously identified by Giuseppe Mazzini more than one hundred years ago as the logical form for a people's struggle for national liberation to assume: "Insurrection — by means of guerrilla bands — is the true method of warfare for all nations desirous of emancipating themselves from a foreign yoke."[21] Mazzini indeed proved prophetic, for guerrilla war has in fact become a principal type of warfare, particularly in the post-World War II era. And, given the ethnic complexity of the world's states to which we earlier alluded, far more guerrilla wars of national liberation can be expected.

This outlook is a particularly grim one because of the passions with which such crusades and anticrusades are waged. Not even the roughest assessment of the fatalities due to such conflicts since World War II can be made, but it is known that the figure runs to several millions.[22] And even if such an enormous figure could be ascertained, it would not reflect the large-scale atrocities and other forms of mass suffering that quite commonly characterize ethnic struggles.[23]

Self-Determination as a Human Right

Since governments are therefore not disposed to extend the right of self-determination to groups within their own state, how are we to reconcile their general tendency to support self-determination in the abstract? This tendency is reflected in the charters of interstate organizations and in multistate treaties or resolutions. A reference to self-determination has become almost *de rigueur* in such documents. But even more *de rigueur*, because it more truly reflects the policies of the signatories, is the inclusion of a reference to the quite antithetical notion of the sanctity of present borders. Thus, while the United Nations Charter (Article I, paragraph 2) promises "respect for the principal of equal rights and self-determination of peoples," it elsewhere (Article II, paragraph 7) denies the right "to intervene in matters which are essentially within the domestic jurisdiction of any state." Similarly, the Charter of the Organization of African Unity, after opening with the assertion "that it is the inalienable right of all people to control their own destiny," notes that the member states are "DETERMINED to safeguard and consolidate. . . the sovereignty and territorial integrity of our States" and further adds that among the purposes of the organization with regard to the member states is "to defend their sovereignty, their territorial integrity and independence." Still another illustration of this same practice of combining praise for self-determination with commitments to the concept of territorial integrity is offered by the Final Act of the Conference on Security and Cooperation in Europe, the so-called Helsinki Accords, the primary purpose of which was to gain recognition of the immutability of the political borders demarcating the states of Eastern Europe. Pursuant to that end, the signatories promised to respect each other's "territorial integrity," to recognize "as inviolable all one another's frontiers as well as all frontiers of all states in Europe" and to refrain from any activity "against the territorial integrity, political independence, or unity of any particular state." Having thus guaranteed the permanence of borders, thereby disavowing the right of the region's numerous minorities to their own state, the document then proceeded to a eulogistic affirmation of the right of national self-determination, that read in part:

> By virtue of the principle of equal rights and self-determination of peoples, all peoples always have the right, in full freedom, to determine, when and as they wish, their internal and external political status, without external interference, and to pursue as they wish their political, economic, social and cultural development.

As habitual in such documents, no attempt was made to explain how a commitment to self-determination was to be reconciled with what went before in the document. But it was clear to all the signatories which of these sets of contradictory standards was to be respected in practice.

The inclusion of references to self-determination in so many documents has in part been due to the high regard in which the doctrine is generally held by public opinion. But the inclusion has been too broadly practiced to be dismissed simply as the product of cynicism or duplicity. Paradoxical though it may appear, when they speak of self-determination of nations, governmental spokesmen, heavily influenced by popular slipshod terminology in which the terms *nation* and *state* are regularly interchanged despite their vitally different meanings (witness the obvious misnomers, the League of *Nations* and the United *Nations*), customarily do not have in mind self-determination for self-differentiating groups of people, but rather are referring to self-determination for states or for colonial territories.[24] Thus, throughout the 1970s, members of the U.N. consistently castigated the attempts of the Republic of South Africa to create independent homelands (bantustans) for its diverse ethnonational groups, maintaining rather that national self-determination required that South West Africa (Namibia) be granted independence as a territorial unit and that the remainder of South Africa also be maintained as a single territorial-political unit, despite the multinational composition of both units. Similarly, the member states refused to recognize the new state of the Xhosa people, when independence was conferred upon it by the South African government, on the ground that separate independence for this group did not constitute a valid exercise of self-determination, even though no one contested the popularity of the decision on the part of the Xhosa.

The tendency to refer to states or to territories rather than to national groups badly beclouds the entire issue of national self-determination. Self-determination of states is obviously a redundancy since independence, along with territory, population, and a government are the definitional prerequisites of a state. More to the point, the fact that national self-determination is sometimes used in reference to ethnonational groups and at other times to refer to states has permitted a single expression to cloak two principles that must contradict one another in all but a handful of situations involving homogeneous states. The former meaning is revolutionary, the latter is pro-*status quo*. Therefore, the cloaking of the latter in self-determination garb has precluded statesmen (and scholars) from appreciating the revolutionary potential that the *idea* of self-determination still possesses.

States and interstate organizations such as the United Nations can be expected to view most self-determination movements distastefully. Moreover, states can be expected to be particularly hostile toward any self-determination movement that threatens its own territorial integrity. Furthermore, statesmen can be expected to continue to employ the slogan of national self-determination in confusing and often contradictory fashion. But all of this will have little dampening effect upon national self-determination. As earlier noted, self-determination preceded and is not dependent for its dynamism upon its sloganization. The host of current ethnopolitical struggles makes abundantly evident that the imperative term self-determination operates quite independently of the wishes, perceptions, and pronouncements of statesmen. The resistance of governments, with all their advantages, is a major reason for the poor record of self-determination to date, but the prospect is nevertheless for an escalation in the number of challenges to this posture.

The United States and Self-Determination

The American experience with the doctrine and practice of self-determination shows many parallels to that of other states. We noted, for example, the inconsistency of those who, having achieved independence under the banner of self-determination, subsequently denied the same right to secessionist-minded groups within the new state's borders. Similarly, Americans revere the note of self-determination enshrined in the Declaration of Independence:

> When in the Course of human Events, it becomes necessary for one People to dissolve the Political Bands which have connected them with another, and to assume among the Powers of the Earth, the separate and equal Station to which the Laws of Nature and of Nature's God entitle them....

But, quite inconsistently, Americans are also taught to accept unreservedly the American government's denial of a right to secession less than a century later. The government adopted Daniel Webster's view, expressed as early as 1830, of "Liberty and Union, now and forever, one and inseparable."[25] This view of a state in perpetuity subsequently received the country's highest legal sanction when the Supreme Court denied that the southern states had in fact seceded from the United States, on the ground that secession was impossible under the Constitution, which, "in all its provisions, looks to an indestructible Union."[26]

Neither the successful secession of the thirteen American colonies from Britain nor the aborted secession of the American South involved distinct ethnonational groups. Neither should therefore be employed to substantiate an American tradition either pro or con national self-determination. Nevertheless, American spokesmen have often invoked the former as proof of historic U.S. respect for self-determination, while conveniently ignoring the Civil War experience. For example, in a television interview on May 1, 1976, President Gerald Ford, in the course of explaining a U.S. decision to support black majority rule in Rhodesia, announced that this position was consistent with the traditional American commitment to self-determination, dating back to the American Revolution. Similarly, a State Department publication under the heading, *Right of Self-Determination,* asserts: "That right is enshrined in the U.N. Charter and is strongly reaffirmed in the General Assembly's Friendly Relations Declaration. The United States, *in line with its own historic experience,* is a strong supporter of that right."[27]

Both national self-determination and the American Declaration of Independence involve a right of secession, and to that degree are related. But if American spokesmen feel constrained to point out this precedent for secession in American history, they should also acknowledge the antisecessionist precedent of the 1860s.

Others have found evidence of a traditional American commitment to self-determination in an implacable aversion to colonialism dating back to their own preindependence, colonial period. This hostility to colonialism is said to have manifested itself quite early in American foreign policy. As secretary of state, John Quincy Adams asserted that "the whole system of modern colonization is an abuse and it is time it should come to an end."[28] This attitude formally became part of American foreign policy two years later, when the Monroe Doctrine announced that attempts to recolonize any of the new republics in the Americas would be viewed by the United States as an unfriendly act. Woodrow Wilson would later explicitly link the principle underlying the Monroe Doctrine to that of national self-determination:

> I am proposing, as it were, that the nations should with one accord adopt the doctrine of President Monroe as the doctrine of the world: that no nation should seek to extend its polity over any other or people, but *that every people should be free to determine its own polity,* its own way of development, unhindered, unthreatened, unafraid, the little along with the great and powerful.[29]

Still later, the well-known scholar of international law, Quincy Wright, would similarly perceive an uninterrupted commitment to principle extending from the Monroe Doctrine to U.S. support for national self-determination in the post-World War II period.

> The United States...denied the claim of the autocratic monarchs of Europe after the Napoleonic period to assist each other by military aid when menaced by popular revolt, and proclaimed the Monroe Doctrine to prevent such intervention in the Western Hemisphere. It refused to ask for aid, and denied the right of the Confederacy to do so, during the Civil War. It has often asserted the right of revolution against the tyrannical governments. It has supported the principle of "self-determination of peoples" during World Wars I and II, and in the United Nations.[30]

As in the matter of secession, an assertion of an American anticolonialist tradition ignores a great deal of contradictory history. The concept of Manifest Destiny that so captivated the American imagination in the decades preceding the Civil War was certainly neither anticolonialist nor pro-self-determination in spirit. Its more visionary disciples in the Congress prophesied a single United States extending from the Arctic to the Pampas.[31] And surely the sorry history surrounding the acquisition of the Indian lands cannot be reconciled with an altruistic regard for the ethnopolitical aspirations of other peoples. But the most devastating challenge to the claim of a traditional anticolonial animus must be seen in the U.S.'s own fling with overseas imperialism during the 1890s, when it acquired Hawaii, Puerto Rico, the Philippines and several lesser islands in the Pacific.

On the other hand, it must be acknowledged that the twentieth century American record for granting self-determination to *overseas* peoples under its control has been a relatively excellent one. The voluntary promise to free the Philippines in ten years time was made in 1934, long before the high-tide mark of anticolonialism. The people of Alaska (not technically an overseas territory), the Hawaiian Islands, Puerto Rico, and the Northern Marianas were all granted the plebiscitary right to determine their political allegiance. The voluntary return to Japan after World War II of the Volcano, Bonin, and Ryuku Islands (including the important island of Okinawa) followed the pattern of the application of the principle of self-determination to American overseas territories.

In marked contrast is America's record with regard to supporting self-determination for peoples under the authority of other states. At best the Monroe Doctrine was a statement that independence, once achieved by Western Hemispheric peoples, should subsequently be respected by European powers. It was not a statement, for example, that Britain, France, and the Netherlands should relinquish their control over peoples of the hemisphere.[32] Elsewhere, the prevailing American attitude toward national movements was characterized more by disinterest than by support.[33] The wave of ethnonationalism that swept Europe during the 19th century did not evoke any noteworthy American sympathy. Wilson's claim to the contrary, then, a U.S. commitment to national self-determination would have represented a departure from, rather than an extension of, American foreign policy. Moreover, although he publicly espoused the doctrine in the most universal of terms, Wilson envisaged at best its application to the defeated powers.[34] Subsequently, with but very few exceptions, the United States has opted for the status quo, the safety of stability, good relations with other state governments, and avoidance of charges of intervention in matters which were "essentially within the domestic jurisdiction of any state,"[35] rather than to proffer moral or other support to self-determination movements. We have noted the proliferation of such movements in the post-World War II era.[36] In its relations with the overwhelming number of such afflicted states, the United States chose to ignore the existence of the separatist groups. Thus, relations with Burma were not perceptibly affected by any U.S. concern for the Karen, Shan, Kachin, Chin, and other non-Burmese peoples who had been conducting national wars of liberation against Rangoon since the state's inception. Although the United States was sufficiently ambiguous in its attitude toward the Kashmiri right to self-determination to convince both India and Pakistan of its nonneutrality, the struggle of the Mizos and Nagas never became a major issue in Indian-American relations, nor did the Baluchi and Pushtun independence movements become an issue in Pakistani-American relations. Similarly, the Basque and Catalan movements have not become a cause for strain between Spain and the United States. Nor has the United States in any way supported the Irish movement within Northern Ireland (an ethnonational movement regularly but erroneously referred to in the American press as religious). The list could be extended to cover American relations with scores of other states. To be sure, the United States, following the customary practice of holding enemies to a higher standard than friends, often, particularly during the more frigid period of the so-called "cold war," berated communist states for their treatment of "captive nations."[37] And often, while ostensibly maintaining an official hands-off policy, the United States employed a "benevolent neutrality," as it did toward the Ibos of Nigeria in the late 1960s. On the other hand, it was also known to have been "benevolently neutral" toward the Pakistani government during the Bengali secession. And in the case of the attempted Katangan secession from what is now known as Zaire, the United States openly abetted the government with material and diplomatic support.

Indeed, since American financial and military assistance to a foreign government has usually been curtailed only when a self-determination struggle has reached a scale at which its existence cannot be denied or played down (e.g., the above cases of Biafra and Bangladesh, as well as the Eritrean movement in the late 1970s), and since even such a belated curtailment left the government with a substantial America-supplied arsenal, it could well be argued that the United States has been a major, though unintended, force in countering self-determination movements.

Whether out of confusion or the desire to cloak one's policies in the most attractive attire, U.S. spokesmen have also applied the expression "self-determination" to inappropriate situations. Thus, the American ambassador to the UN, in explaining his government's support for a Security Council resolution on multiethnic Namibia, spoke of the hope "that the people of the territory may exercise their right to self-determination;" yet, the resolution *demanded* that South Africa recognize "the territorial integrity and unity of Namibia as a nation [sic]."[38] A unilateral and much more significant illustration relates to American policy toward southeast Asia in the late 1960s and early 1970s.

The American military involvement therein was regularly described as motivated by the self-determination principle.[39] But regardless of the sincerity of such statements, it is evident that this proposition ignored the fact that the Vietnamese, both from north and south, constituted a single people. More significantly, it overlooked the desire of the non-Vietnamese Montagnards within both northern and southern Vietnam to be free of Vietnamese rule.[40] Moreover, having determined to leave the South Vietnamese to their fate, the Nixon administration unblushingly continued to drape American policy in self-determination garb. The 1973 agreement between Hanoi and Washington, which explicitly recognized the inevitability of the coming forcible "reunification of Vietnam," still spoke of "the South Vietnamese people's right to self-determination," describing it as "sacred" and "inalienable."[41]

In summary, then, while U.S. domestic policy has been better than most in the honoring of self-determination, its foreign policy has not diverged significantly in this respect from that of other states. Both the global chaos that would ensue if all national groups actively pursued a right of secession, and the animosity that could be expected to be directed at Washington by the heads of multinational states should the United States openly encourage the separatist aspirations of their minorities, have dampened any inclination to support actively a universal right of national self-determination. *Raison d'etat* remains the ultimate standard of foreign policy. True, in a related field, the late 1970s found the Carter administration supporting what it termed "human rights" in a number of states, despite the obvious displeasure of the leaders of those states. However, as critics of the administration pointed out, the choice of states said to be violating human rights was highly selective, and the vigor with which the campaign was conducted also varied greatly from state to state depending upon its overall relationship with the United States. (Similarly, we noted with regard to respect for national self-determination, that the United States has tended to judge adversaries by a more demanding standard than it has allies and neutrals.) But, in any case, the Carter administration's concern for human rights should not be confused with national self-determination. The former involves individual rights; the latter, collective rights. Even in the case of the right of Jews and members of other national groups to leave the Soviet Union, the administration was speaking of the right of individuals to depart and not of a people to secede. Indeed, it is both ironic and informative that the administration's campaign for human rights should crystallize most conspicuously with regard to the Helsinki Accords. As earlier noted, the principal original purpose behind the Accords had been to gain recognition of the inviolability of the borders of the states of Eastern Europe. In signing the Accords, the United States had in effect denied any validity to a right of national self-determination to all peoples within the region, no matter what rights they might retain as individuals.

In sharp contrast to its highly publicized support for human rights was the Carter administration's hesitancy to lend its name to national self-determination in the Middle East. In early 1978, under pressure from the Arabs to endorse self-determination for the Palestinians and under reciprocal pressure from Israel and its supporters, the administration issued the following statement:

> There must be a resolution of the Palestinian problem in all its aspects. [The resolution of] the problem must recognize the legitimate rights of the Palestinians and enable the Palestinians to participate in the determination of their own future.

The statement immediately gave rise to broad conjecture concerning the president's endorsement of self-determination. Had he or hadn't he? One reporter noted that "his stress on solving 'all aspects' of the Palestinian question implicitly was at odds with the standard Israeli thesis that only a refugee problem is involved—not the Palestinian right to self-determination as insisted on by the Arabs." Further, the reporter read great significance into the fact that the phrase "legitimate rights" had been linked to having the Palestinians "participate in the determination of their own future." He countered: "A U.S. diplomat said privately, 'Carter's just a hairsbreadth away from [accepting] self-determination,' which hitherto had been taboo in official U.S. pronouncements because of Israeli opposition."[42] Whatever the merits of recognizing or not recognizing a Palestinian right to self-determination, this entire Alice-in-Wonderland scenario gave the lie to any claim of a universal American commitment to national self-determination.

The Future of Self-Determination in U.S. Foreign Policy

Regardless of past practice, should the United States be dedicated to the support of self-determination? Faced with this question, authorities usually point out that the principle of self-determination raises more questions than answers. Abstractions are more easily articulated than applied. Some sample problems follow:

1. The question of constituency. Who is the "self" in self-determination? If the British had conducted a plebiscite to determine the fate of all of Ireland in 1920, Ireland would be united and the non-Irish of Ulster would be a minority. Would a plebiscite today that is limited to Northern Ireland be fair to the Irish minority therein? A second example: Should the fate of Quebec be decided by the Franco-Canadians therein without recourse to the sentiments of the local Anglo-Canadians? Should Franco-Canadian separatists

be expected to honor a vote for independence that had the support of a majority of the Franco-Canadians but fell short of a majority of the total vote?
2. The preceding presupposes an open society. How does one determine group opinion in the more typical nondemocratic society? As noted, the government will deny the movement has broad support. If it holds a plebiscite, it is apt to be farcical, as was that conducted by Indonesia in West Irian in the late 1960s. On the other side, the voice of the self-determination movement is apt to be only that of a handful of articulate individuals. The inability of outsiders to know who spoke for whom in the cases of Angola and Rhodesia in the mid 1970s exemplifies the problem.
3. Is *raison d'etat* an even greater right than a self-determination claim? Should a concentrated Puerto Rican community in New York City be granted independence if it indicates a desire to secede?
4. Does a self-determined people have the right to expel minorities in the name of the will of the people to purify the homeland and to avoid future secessionist movements?
5. Considering that anthropologists have identified some three thousand distinct ethnic elements in the world, should self-determination be unconditionally supported without regard for the impact that such a development would exert upon world order?
6. Given the tiny size of some ethnonational groups, should there be a minimum size with regard to population and territory, so as to insure economic viability?
7. Should a state be guaranteed access to the sea, even though no members of the ethnic group presently dwell on a seacoast?
8. How is one to draw the borders of an ethnic state when the group is distributed, as is commonly the case, throughout a number of noncontiguous pockets?
9. Is self-determination the ultimate principle of human affairs? Can it be countered by others, such as that of domestic tranquility, the right to stamp out rebellion, the avoidance of bloodshed?
10. Are good relations with the current state more important than our meddling in an issue of self-determination?

Some of the above belong to a higher order of consideration than others, but *in toto* they suggest some of the complexities that are involved when one raises the banner of self-determination as a universal right. However, the most important consideration to this writer is whether encouraging self-determination movements does not risk bringing on the greater evil. Knowing that states will resist such movement and knowing the hatreds and inhumanity that ethnic strife unleash, dare anyone encourage participation in such a *horrida bella*?

There will, of course, be movements that once underway, the U.S. should support. Liberation from a situation characterized by genocide, pogroms, and the like is a case in point. More commonly, the U.S. should use its good offices or other devices to help minimize the suffering that accompanies a self-determination effort. But particularly in cases where the United States has no plans to proffer assistance, it should carefully eschew encouraging the national aspirations of peoples. Should, for example, the United States do anything to encourage the anti-Moscow attitudes of the Soviet peoples, knowing that it will do nothing should an insurrection occur? The American role both before and during the Hungarian uprising of 1956 (when talk of an American "rollback" proved to be empty phraseology) still haunts a number of United States citizens. The road to hell is not only paved with one's own good intentions but is also paved with the high-sounding encouragement of others. Since the United States quite obviously is not prepared to wage a global struggle for self-determination movements, phrases such as "dedication to a universal right of national self-determination" should be avoided by American spokesmen.

Beyond this, one particularly unwholesome temptation should be eschewed by all concerned with American policy. As the number of cases of ethnic dissonance has spread, there has also grown an increased appreciation on the part of governments of the strategic value of such groups. With little or no regard for the cause of such peoples, governments have perceived them as trojan horses residing within the gates of their enemies. During the 1970s, for example, the Shah of Iran encouraged and supported the self-determination cause of the Kurds living within Iraq. When in 1975 relations between the two states suddenly altered for the better, the Shah quite cynically closed the border, leaving the Iraqi Kurds to the mopping up operations of the Iraqi forces. Despite vigorous U.S. State Department denials of complicity, a columnist for the *New York Times* produced documentation showing that the United States had quite knowingly and purposefully long cooperated with Iran in a program aimed at keeping the Kurdish war of liberation alive but short of victory. At the time of the Shah's about-face, Secretary of State Henry Kissinger refused to respond to the desperate appeals of the Kurdish leaders, including one which referred to the "moral and political responsibility towards our people who have committed themselves to your country's policy."[43] The doctrine that a people has the right to determine its own political destiny may indeed be a pernicious abstraction, impossible of attainment. But if of the stuff that dreams are made, it is even more certainly of the stuff for which those wrapped up in its mystique will make any sacrifice, including that of their lives. To manipulate such a grail is beyond any justification grounded in statecraft.

NOTES

1. See below, pp. 15 et seq.
2. For a series of statements concerning American traditional support for self-

determination, made by United States officials over the years, see the section entitled "Self-Determination" in Marjorie Whiteman, *Digest of International Law*, 5 (Washington, D.C.: U.S. Government Printing Office, 1973): 38-87.
3. Legitimacy here refers to state legitimacy and not to lower forms of governmental and/or regime legitimacy. See Walker Conner, "Nationalism and the Political Legitimacy of States," paper presented at the Conference on Minority Nationalism, New York University, Toronto, Canada, March 1977.
4. One of the more interesting examples is offered by Britain. In 1714, the Parliament quite willingly conferred the right to rule Englishmen upon George I, a German by birth, residence, language, and preference. (During his lifetime George I disdained learning the language of his subjects.) Significantly, the masses did not question his legitimacy nor that of his son and successor, George II, who like his father, was German both by birth and inclination. However, with the spread of popular sovereignty, only a century later the Parliament refused Queen Victoria's repeated requests to have the essentially empty title of King Consort conferred upon her husband, because of the latter's foreign background.
5. Richard Andrews in a review of Michael Walzes, *Regicide and Revolution: Speeches at the Trial of Louis XVI* in *The New York Times Book Review*, 9 June 1974, p. 3.
6. The earlier American Revolution, though a manifestation of popular sovereignty, did not involve identification of *the people* with a particular ethnonation.
7. See Felix Markham, *Napoleon and the Awakening of Europe* (London: English Universities Press, 1968).
8. This term remained popular in French circles long after "national self-determination" became popular elsewhere. See, for example, Rene Johannet, *Le Principe Des Nationalites*, Nouvelle Edition (Paris: Nouvelle Librairie Nationale, 1923), and Robert Redslob, *Le Principe Des Nationalites* (Paris: Libraire Du Recueil Sirey, 1930).
9. The term appeared in the Party's *Proclamation on the Polish Question* (1865) and thereafter increasingly in the programs and declarations of the First, Second, and Third International.
10. As set forth in the *Communist Manifesto:* "The Communists are distinguished from the other working-class parties by this only: (1) In the national struggles of the proletarians of the different countries, they point out and bring to the front the common interest of the entire proletariat, independently of all nationality."
11. For further details, see Walker Connor, *The National Question in Marxist Theory and Strategy*, forthcoming.
12. Thus, 1848, the year in which the Communist Manifesto was published was also a year of intense national unrest throughout Germany, Italy, and Eastern Europe.
13. For details, see Walker Connor, "Ethnonationalism in the First World: The President in Historical Perspective" in Milton Esman (ed.), *Ethnic Conflict in the Western World* (Ithaca: Cornell University Press, 1977), pp. 19-45.
14. The impact that this same conviction among certain elements within the mother countries exerted upon colonialism should also not be overlooked. Particularly in Britain, there was an increasing tendency to question the "oughtness" of rule over foreign peoples.

15. For a list of the afflicted states, Walker Connor, "The Politics of Ethnonationalism," *Journal of International Affairs*, 27 (1973): 2.
16. The survey was conducted January 1, 1971. For more details, see ibid., p. 1.
17. By a potential nation is meant a distinctive ethnic group but one in which national consciousness has not yet coalesced. In the case of such prenational people, primary group identity does not yet go beyond clan or locale.
18. "Nationalism and the Political Legitimacy of States," pp. 12-24.
19. "The Politics of Ethnonationalism," p. 12.
20. For some specific illustrations, see Walker Connor, "Self-Discrimination: The New Phase," *World Politics* (October 1967): 30-52.
21. Life and Writings, (n.p., 1890): 109.
22. For some tentative estimates by a long-time scholar of self-determination movements, see Rupert Emerson, "The Fate of Human Rights in Third World, " *World Politics* (January 1975): 201-226.
23. For example, newspaper photographs and television coverage of starving, stomach-bloated, eyes-protruding Ibo children were quite common fare for the American public during the Biafran affair. Similarly, the independence movement leading to Bangladesh provided photographs of decapitated Punjabi soldiers and confirmed accounts of the mass murder and burial of unarmed Bengali academicians.
24. For agreement on this point by two of the most perspicacious analyzers of self-determination, see Rupert Emerson "Self-Determination," *The American Journal of International Law* 65 (July 1971), particularly 463, and his earlier *Self-Determination Revisited in the Era of Decolonization* (Cambridge: Harvard University Center for International Affairs, 1964); and Vernon Van Dykes's "Self-Determination and Minority Rights," *International Studies Quarterly* 13 (September 1969): 223-253, and "The Individual, the State, and Ethnic Communities in Political Theory," *World Politics* (April 1977): particularly 357 et seq. For further comments on the problem of language, see W. Connor, "Nation-Building or Nation-Destroying?" *World Politics,* (April 1972): particularly 332-336.

    In a most unusual acknowledgement of the tendency of statesmen to misemploy *state* and *nation,* a former Canadian prime minister and secretary of state has commented:

    > What is meant by "nationalism"? Few words have come to mean more different things to more people. Nationalism doesn't necessarily mean sovereignty. The word "nation" does not mean state in that sense, though this is the way it is most often used. Indeed, I often use it in that sense, thereby adding to the confusion that I now want to clear up. A nation can, of course, coincide with a state, and often does. But there can be more than one nation inside a sovereign state, and often is.

    Lester Pearson, "Beyond the Nation-State," *Saturday Review,* 15 February 1969.
25. From Webster, "Second Speech on Foote's Resolution" (January 26, 1830).
26. *Texas v. White* (1869).
27. *A Current Foreign Policy: The Role of International Law in Combating Terrorism* (Department of State Publication 8689, January 1973), p. 6, emphasis added.

28. *Memoirs of John Quincy Adams*, ed. Charles Adams Francis, 6 volumes (Philadelphia: J.B. Lippincott, 1874-1877), 6: 104.
29. From an address of January 22, 1917. Reprinted in Green Haywood Hackworth, *Digest of International Law,* Vol. V (Washington, D.C.: U.S. Government Printing Office, 1943), p. 442, emphasis added.
30. "United States Intervention in the Lebanon," *American Journal of International Law* 53 (1959): 122.
31. For details, see Walker Connor, "Myths of Hemispheric, Continental, Regional, and State Unity," *Political Science Quarterly* 84 (December 1969): 555-582.
32. In essence, the doctrine was a unilateral claim to a sphere of influence, whose character became more clear with the affixing of the "Roosevelt Corollary" in 1904.
33. The principal exception might have been America's turn-of-the-century policy of discouraging European annexation of China, the so-called "Open Door Policy." However, as R.R. Palmer has cogently noted, "the Open Door was a program not so much of leaving China to the Chinese, as of assuring that all outsiders should find it literally 'open'." [R.R. Palmer and Joel Colton, *A History of the Modern World,* 4th ed. (New York: Alfred A. Knopf, 1971), p. 704].
34. See Alfred Cobban, *The Nation State and National Self-Determination* (New York: Thomas Y. Crowell Company, 1970), pp. 62-66; Michla Pomerance, "The United States and Self-Determination: Perspectives on the Wilsonian Conception," *The American Journal of International Law* 70 (January 1976): 1-27; and Connor, "Self-Determination: The New Phrase."
35. U.N. Charter, Article 2, paragraph 7.
36. Our estimate may be conservative. While our data show that nearly 50% of all states were bothered by ethnic unrest, then U.N. Secretary General U Thant asserted in 1969 that *more* than half of the organization's members were troubled by secessionist movements. See the *Washington Post,* 29 January 1969, p. A14.
37. For an eloquent criticism of Soviet practice towards self-determination by American U.N. Ambassador Adlai Stevenson, see Whiteman, pp. 82-83.
38. Arthur Rovine, *Digest of United States Practice in International Law, 1974* (Washington, D.C.: United States Government Printing Office, 1975), p. 10.
39. President Lyndon Johnson noted that self-determination was "the very principle for which we are engaged in South Vietnam."
40. Despite earlier promises by Hanoi to grant the non-Vietnamese people autonomy and/or independence once they had consolidated their control over the entire territory, the Vietnamese leaders almost immediately upon victory began a rigorous campaign of integration.
41. For the pertinent sections of the agreement, see Arthur Rovine, *Digest of the United States Practice in International Law, 1973* (Washington, D.C.: United States Government Printing Office, 1974), pp. 6-7. In a subsequent defense of the agreement, Henry Kissinger made much of "the fact that the South Vietnamese people's right of self-determination is recognized both by the DRV [Democratic Republic of Vietman] and by the United States," ibid., p.8.
42. Jonathan Randel in the *Washington Post,* 5 January 1978. All brackets in original.

43. William Safire, "Son of Secret Sellout," *New York Times,* 12 February 1976. The secretary's refusal to respond also ignored the warning by subordinates of an impending massacre. A similar cynical viewpoint of ethnonationalism was evident in a statement by a close State Department associate of Kissinger, in a speech that became known as the "Sonnefeldt Doctrine," which reduced the historic Polish struggle for their own state to the following words: "The Poles have been able to overcome their *romantic political inclinations* which led to their disasters in the past." The speech became famous for its reference to the desirability of making "the relationship between Eastern Europeans and the Soviet Union an organic one." For an official State Department summary of the speech, see the *New York Times,* 6 April 1976, p. 14.

Chapter 7

The United States and Recognition of New Human Rights: Economic and Social Needs

Peter Weiss

Since the term "human rights" was moved to the center of our political stage by candidate Jimmy Carter during the 1976 presidential campaign, it has lost some of its nobility and gained a measure of tawdriness. Two questions will illustrate this shift: How could the same man who wrote the letter to Sacharov sit down to break bread—or, in this case, lobster—with Pinochet? How can the same president and administration exhibit both a positive devotion to the dignity of the individual as thinker, speaker, or writer and a virtual indifference to the dignity or the individual as worker, patient, consumer, or unwilling mother?

In exploring these questions, and the more fundamental problems which they symbolize, I will make two assumptions: (1) In contrast with the hypocrisy of the Nixon-Kissinger era, the concern for human rights voiced by President Carter and other spokesmen of his administration is genuine, as far as it goes; (2) the concern does not go nearly far enough, either in implementing those human rights which are perceived to be important, or in defining the full array of human rights entitled to our concern.

Administration Recognition of Economic and Social Rights

It is probably fair to say that, in line with our time-honored anti-intellectual tradition, Washington's approach to human rights is pragmatic, inductive, free-floating, and unencumbered by philosophical underpinnings.

It dispenses with the search for original justice, the derivation of rights from the political compact, the theory of natural law, or the relationship between the First Amendment and the labor theory of value.

So be it; better a set of acceptable propositions tendered on a take-it-or-leave-it basis than a set of unacceptable ones carefully erected upon a theoretical infrastructure. And, from a legal point of view, there is at least one great advance: while Henry Kissinger and Richard Nixon were contemptuous of international law, Carter and Cyrus Vance have gone on record more than once as accepting, at least in the area of human rights, not only the moral guidance, but also the binding force of international law. As the president said in his speech to the United Nations on March 17, 1977:

> All the signatories of the United Nations Charter have pledged themselves to observe and to respect basic human rights. Thus, no member of the United Nations can claim that mistreatment of its citizens is solely its own business. Equally, no member can avoid its responsibilities to review and to speak when torture or unwarranted deprivation occurs in any part of the world....[1]

And the secretary of state in his Law Day address at Georgia Law School on April 30, 1977, added the following important technical note:

> Since 1945 international practice has confirmed that a nation's obligations to respect human rights is a matter of concern in international law.[2]

What are these rights that the United States recognizes, both as binding upon itself and as entitling it to meddle, as some call it, in the affairs of other nations, or, to use the president's more courteous phrase, "to review and to speak" when another state violates them?

When the question is asked, the screen begins to flicker and the reception grows faint. Clearly there are today, on the international scene, two distinct but related bundles of rights: one economic, social, and cultural, the other political and civil.

The first, which we may call the ECOSOC bundle, is sketched in Articles 22 through 27 of the Universal Declaration of Human Rights and detailed in the International Covenant of Economic, Social, and Cultural Rights. It includes the rights to social security, to work, to rest and leisure, to an adequate standard of living (including food, clothing, housing, medical care and necessary social services), to education, and to culture and the arts.

The second, which could be called the Bill of Rights bundle, is enunciated in Articles 4 through 21 of the Universal Declaration and spelled out in the International Covenant on Civil and Political Rights. It includes the so-called negative rights to freedom from slavery, torture or degrading treatment, arbitrary arrest, detention or exile, ex post facto legislation, or punishment and invasion of privacy, as well as the positive rights to recognition and equality before the law, due process, freedom of movement, asylum, nationality, marriage, property, freedom of thought and expression, peaceful assembly, participation in government and public service, and secret and universal suffrage.

It is a tenet of the current conventional wisdom that the socialist countries and most of the developing countries regard the ECOSOC bundle as the important one of the two and view the Bill of Rights bundle as either a "bourgeois illusion" or a luxury they can ill afford at this stage of their development. The United States and the other Western countries, on the other hand, are perceived as stressing political and civil rights to the virtual exclusion of economic, social, and cultural one.

What, in fact, is the U.S. position? It would not be correct to say that the United States recognizes only the Bill of Rights bundle. President Carter, in his speech to the Permanent Council of the Organization of American States on April 15, 1977, said, "Our values and yours require us to combat abuses of individual social and economic injustice."[3] In his Georgia Law Day address, Cyrus Vance defined human rights as falling into three categories: first, the right to be free from governmental violation of the integrity of the person; second, the right to the fulfillment of such vital needs as food, shelter, health care, and education; and third, the right to enjoy civil and political liberties. The same triad, in identical language, appears in Deputy Secretary Christopher's address to the American Bar Association on August 9, 1977,[4] confirming that it is now part of the official liturgy.

U.S. Implementation of Economic and Social Rights

In practice, however, there is a vast difference in the United States between the importance attached to those rights concerned with the fulfillment of vital needs and those concerned with the integrity of the person and political and civil liberties. This is true not only for the administration, but for the Congress, which has done such pioneering work in recent years in building a human rights component into American foreign policy. And it is true for such nongovernmental organizations as Amnesty International, the International League for Human Rights, and the International Commission of Jurists, whose fact-finding and publicizing activities provide much of the impetus for the human rights movement.

Congress, in striking a balance between the desirable and the feasible, has reduced its definition of a country which should not receive U.S. aid to one "which engages in a consistent pattern of gross violations of internationally recognized human rights, including torture or cruel, inhumane, or degrading treatment or punishment, prolonged detention without charges or other flagrant denials of the right to life, liberty, and the security of Person."[5]

The reports of the human rights NGOs, with rare and inadequate exceptions (such as the 1977 ICJ Report on the Philippines),[6] are strong on political and civil rights, but virtually silent on "vital human needs."

I suggest that there are three fatal flaws in this approach. The first is the failure to recognize that an infinitely larger number of the world's people are suffering—actually suffering—from "consistent patterns of gross violations" of their fundamental rights to work, food, health, shelter and education—their rights, in short, to *live* their lives instead of struggling for their existence—than from violations of their rights to freedom from torture, arbitrary detention, and censorship of the press. The second flaw is the failure to admit—since it is hardly possible not to recognize—that the economic policies and activities of the rich countries, in their relations with the poor countries, are playing a major role in perpetuating, if not deepening, their poverty. And the third flaw is the failure to understand the complex relationship between economic and political rights. One consequence of this is an assumption which is wholly unsupported, and, indeed, controverted by historical evidence: that the securing of political and civil rights, which is sometimes referred to as Western-style democracy, will somehow, as if by magic, lead the Third World out of underdevelopment.

Examples of this narrowly focused human rights policy are so numerous as to make meaningful selection difficult. Our government takes a stand for majority rule in South Africa, but lifts not one finger to dissuade American companies from allowing their South African subsidiaries to practice the most absolute form of racial discrimination found anywhere on the face of the globe. Bribery in foreign countries, which distorts and delays the process of economic development, is condemned, but the bribegivers in their New York corporate headquarters are penalized, if at all, not for their acts but only for their failure to disclose them. Most-favored-nation treatment is denied to countries which violate the right to emigrate, but is accorded to others which produce goods for the American market under the most sickening sweatshop conditions. The imposition of martial law in the Philippines and the putsch by the Junta in Chile—two countries which prior to these events were meeting unusually high standards of political and civil rights observance—were followed, in short order, by vast inflows of American capital through private as well as official channels. By contrast, the maintenance of trade embargoes against Cuba and Vietnam, wholly indefensible in the present context under recognized principles of international law, and carrying serious consequences for the health and wellbeing of millions of Cubans and Vietnamese, is lamely justified, at least in part, by references to the less than perfect human rights records of both countries.

No one understood these contradictions better than Orlando Letelier. In the last work published before his death, "Economic 'Freedom' and Political Repression,"[7] he graphically demonstrated the devastating effects of the Junta's fanatical devotion to free enterprise on both the political and the economic conditions of his ravished country. Speaking of Treasury Secretary William Simon's visit to Chile in May 1976, when Simon expressed concern about the human rights situation while congratulating Pinochet for bringing "economic freedom" to the Chilean people, Letelier said:

> This particularly convenient concept of a social system in which "economic freedom" and political terror exist without touching each other, allows these financial spokesmen to support their concept of "freedom" while exercising their verbal muscles in defense of human rights.

Pinochet's charade in "abolishing" DINA, the Chilean secret police, would not have surprised Letelier, but the Carter administration's readiness to accept this cruel hoax at face value would have saddened him. Nor would he have been surprised to read in the *New York Times* that "Chile has become a bazaar filled with foreign goods that are snapped up by the well-to-do while millions of workers and their families are living hand to mouth."[8]

It is important in all this to remember why Pinochet and his goons decreed Letelier's death. Had he merely "flexed his verbal muscles," it would not have been enough for the Junta to risk the consequences of an assassination on American soil. Had he merely been one of the most effective leaders of the Chilean exile community, it would not have been enough. What sealed his fate was his partial success in persuading governments—ours and that of the Netherlands in particular—that as long as money flowed into Chile from the financial capitals of the world, the Junta was prepared to deal with criticisms of its human rights violations as a minor annoyance. What Pinochet could not afford—what no dictator can afford—is to have the outside world translate human rights politics into financial and economic action.

Private U.S. Economic Activity and Human Rights

Human rights advocates have long deplored financial assistance to dictators on the ground that such assistance provides both the material and the moral support without which repressive regimes cannot function.[9] But the connection is not always made between the closed nature of such societies at home and their openness to foreign capital, between mass killings in Soweto and a 23% return on capital invested in South Africa, between the death squads of Brazil and that country's "economic miracle," between American-financed sweat shops and the jailing of political dissidents in South Korea.[10] The liberal community in this country has tended to see the fight for human rights in American client states as a fight against a paranoid conception of national security which sees a "red" under every bed and no alternatives to either fascist dictators or communist puppets. It has failed to face up to the fact that, quite apart from cold war politics, the suppression of political and civil rights is the essential condition for the suppression of economic and social rights and that vital American economic interests—markets, investments, cheap raw materials, and unorganized labor—are, indeed, threatened by "liberal" regimes.

It seems imperative, in this connection, that we dispense, once and for all, with the utterly foolish notion that capitalism can bring about economic and social justice in the Third World. It is doubtful whether it ever could; it is absolutely certain that it cannot do so in its present confused, hysterical, and morbid stage. The Chilean example has demonstrated for all but a handful of functional illiterates, including the committee which awards the Nobel Prize in economics, the brutal consequences of the Chicago School approach. But the Chicago School is only a special case of generalized folly. The "benign," or "enlightened" capitalism of a Eugene Rostow or a Robert McNamara produces results which for the mass of the people are little different from those found in Chile. This is clearly shown by unemployment, malnutrition, and income distribution figures in such World Bank favorites as Brazil, Iran, and the Philippines.[11]

In a remarkable opinion editorial piece in the *New York Times* of September 4, 1977, poetically entitled "The Rights of Cogs," Sylvia Ann Hewlett, a Columbia economist, points out that a recent study of growth and social equity in 74 developing countries found that most people are worse off after several decades of economic development. Hewlett states that the multinational firms, "utilizing large amounts of capital and small numbers of people," produce, for the top 25% of the population of the developing countries, a "vicious circle of wealth," which rigidifies and exacerbates the inequalities of the colonial period and completely bypasses the vast mass of the people who remain in a state of miserable poverty.

None of this should lead one to conclude that there is on anyone's drawing board a simple blueprint which will reverse the vicious cycle of repression and poverty. In fact, there are dozens, and of those which are given a chance to be put into practice, some will work and some will not. All we in the First World can do, if we are serious about the whole gamut of human rights and not just those which cost us nothing, is to restrain our mad impulse to throw our weight around in every corner of the globe, whether it be for base reasons of financial gain or "national security," or because of our propensity, in Stringfellow Barr's classic phrase, "to do good against people."

The time is propitious for such a turn. In the past three decades, American intervention to save the Third World for free enterprise—more often than not for a model long since discarded in this country—has been swift, brutal, open or barely concealed, and usually effective. Today, post-Vietnam, post-Watergate, post-CIA scandals, with an administration not entirely devoid of moral principles and with a Congress and a people focused on our mounting domestic problems, it is just barely possible that a halt can be put to this wholesale aggression. But it will take hard work, staunch resolve, and unflagging vigilance.

Another hopeful sign is that the multinationals are having second thoughts over whether their global reach may not have been global overreach. For most of them, according to the August 1977 issue of *Fortune*, "the party's nearly over." One reason for this agonizing reappraisal is the enormity of the Third World's debt structure, with its built-in potential for a collapse in the world money market and its depressing effect on the creditworthiness of developing countries.[12] Another is the new look which Congress and the administration are taking, in the context of tax reform, at how long the multinational corporations should be allowed to keep their bacon abroad before they bring it home.

Rethinking the Means and Ends of a Genuine Human Rights Policy

If we are, in Ronald Dworkin's phrase, to "take rights seriously,"[13] and to do so with respect to the entire gamut of rights now recognized by the world community as being legally and morally valid, this will require a conceptual breakthrough going far beyond the ritualistic recitals which now emanate occasionally from the White House and the State Department. Such a leap forward would have enormous implications, not only for our foreign policy, but on the domestic front as well.

Think of it: Is the right to strike[14] compatible with Taft-Hartley? Does OSHA ever worry about Article 7(b) of the International Covenant on Economic, Social, and Cultural Rights?[15] What does the right to work[16] mean to the 60% of black teenagers who are unemployed in our central cities? Can the patent system be squared with "the right of everyone ... to enjoy the benefits of scientific progress and its applications"?[17] How many of our citizens enjoy "the highest attainable standard of physical and mental health"?[18] Is "higher education equally accessible to all on the basis of merit"?[19] Does each resident of the United States have the right "to an adequate standard of living for himself and his family, including adequate food, clothing, and housing"?[20]

The questions are rhetorical, and the answers obvious. But if only political and civil rights are real, what was going through Deputy Secretary of State Warren Christopher's mind when he told the American Bar Association that "the efforts we are making ... to overhaul our outmoded and unfair welfare system are also important contributions to the cause of human rights"?[21] Perhaps we are seeing, in statements such as this one, the first stirrings of a new, more comprehensive human rights philosophy. Perhaps we shall discover, one of these days, that our tradeoff was too clever by half. Just as Eastern Europeans accepted some political and civil rights language in the Helsinki Declaration in exchange for secure borders, only to see that language assume a wholly unexpected reality within those borders, so our lipservice to economic and social rights, in exchange for the acceptance by other states of political and civil ones, may, with surprising rapidity, find expression in movements, in popular pressures, and eventually in governmental policy.

There would be irony in such a development, but much good would come from it as well. It will not happen, however, without a fusing of traditional human rights action and traditional economic and social action.

When Orlando Letelier was assassinated, he was, as director of the Transnational Institute, working on this problem in the most fundamental and most intelligent way: by concentrating on the inequities inherent in the current international economic order and laying the groundwork for a new order in which *all* the human rights which are now recognized for the first time by the international community could be implemented for all of the world's people.

An ambitious program? Yes, but nothing short of it will do. This is not the place to lay out a grand plan for the realization of such a program. But we can make a modest beginning in one respect. We need, in the area of economic and social rights, the same kind of unbiased, comprehensive information which is available, at least partially, in the area of political and civil rights. Some of this information can be obtained from official organizations like WGO, UNESCO, ILO, UNICEF, OECD, etc. But these are intergovernmental agencies, largely dependent for their sources on data supplied by member governments, and governments, particularly repressive ones, are not famous for their candor in releasing to the world bad news about the condition of their people. What is needed, it seems to me, is one or several competent, unbiased, and authoritative organizations which will do for food, housing, health, education, culture, and all the other components of the right to life what Amnesty International and similar organizations do for torture, arbitrary arrest, and other violations of political and civil rights. We need doctors, educators, nutritionists, artists, economists, and housing experts who will undertake serious research and fact-finding missions and bring back and publicize the kind of reports which will move the discussion of economic and social rights away from vacuous generalities into the arena of concern and implementation.

One of the major achievements of the 32nd Regular Session of the United Nations General Assembly was the adoption, by a vote of 123 to 0, with 15 abstentions (including the United States and most European countries) of Resolution 32-130, somewhat awkwardly entitled "Alternative Approaches and Ways and Means within the United Nations System for Improving the Effective Enjoyment of Human Rights and Fundamental Freedoms." The principal operative provisions of this resolution, which give the lie to the belief common in the West that the developing countries accord a higher priority to economic and social than to political and civil rights, read as follows:

a. All human rights and fundamental freedoms are indivisible and interdependent; equal attention and urgent consideration should be given to the implementation, promotion, and protection of both civil and political, and economic, social and cultural rights;
b. The full realization of civil and political rights without the enjoyment of economic, social and cultural rights is impossible; the achievement of lasting progress in the implementation of human rights is dependent upon sound and effective national and international policies of economic and social development, as recognized by the Proclamation of Teheran (1968);
c. All human rights and fundamental freedoms of the human person and of peoples are inalienable;
d. Consequently, human rights questions should be examined globally, taking into account both the over-all context of the various societies in which they present themselves as well as the need for the promotion of the full dignity of the human person and the development and well-being of the society . . . .
f. The realization of the new international economic order is an essential element for the effective promotion of human rights and fundamental freedoms and should also be accorded priority . . . .

The time has come to erase the dividing line between first- and second-class human rights. The electrode to the nipple is an affront to human dignity; so is the nipple that has no milk for the suckling infant. The use of psychiatric institutions to harbor political dissidents is a perversion of professional responsibility; so is the failure of hospitals to care for the sick. Arbitrary arrests and detention violate the integrity of the person; so does the impersonal system of triage which, under a regime of enforced scarcity, decides who is to live and who is to die.

Let us begin to act as if these equivalences had meaning. And as we lecture others on human rights, let us make certain that what our government, our corporations, and our culture[22] do unto others does not result in a more serious deprivation of human rights than what they do unto themselves.

Conclusion

Although this contribution has discussed "human rights and vital needs," it has tried to suggest that the dichotomy implied is a false one. Vital needs are, in fact, human rights; derived, as all rights are, from the concensus of human aspirations and from the increasingly common cultural and philosophical heritage of humankind. This administration has taken a giant, if bumbling, step forward in recognizing this fact, without, for the time being, facing up to its implications or translating them into a working policy. It is up to the human rights community, both academic and activist, to help make the administration the prisoner of its own rhetoric.

NOTES

*This chapter is adapted from a speech delivered at the first annual Letelier-Moffit Human Rights Award Ceremony on September 19, 1977, in Washington, D.C.

1. *U.S. Department of State News Release* (New York: Bureau of Public Affairs, 17 March 1977).
2. *The Secretary of State Speech* (Athens, Georgia: Bureau of Public Affairs, 30 April 1977).
3. *U.S. Department of State Statement* (Philadelphia: Bureau of Public Affairs, 15 April 1977).
4. *U.S. Department of State Speech* (Chicago: Bureau of Public Affairs, 9 August 1977).
5. U.S. Congress, House, *Foreign Assistance Act of 1977*, Secs. 116(a), 502(b)(2), and 502(d) (1). See Appendix E.
6. "The Decline of Democracy in the Philippines" (Geneva: International Commission of Jurists, August 1977).
7. Orlando Letelier, "Economic 'Freedom' and Political Repression," *TNI Pamphlet* 1 (Transnational Institute, Washington, 1977).
8. *New York Times*, 10 September 1977. Cf. "Chile: Recycling the Capitalist Crisis," *NACLA Latin America & Empire Report* 10 (November 1976); and Michael Moffit, "Chicago Economics in Chile," *Challenge: The Magazine of Economic Affairs* (September-October 1977), p. 34.

9. During the three-year reign of the Allende regime, from 1971 to 1973, Chile received $159,300,000 in aid and credits from the United States and multilateral agencies dominated by the United States. For the first three years of the junta's reign of terror, from 1974 to 1976, this figure amounted to nearly 10 times as much, $1,454,300,000. "Human Rights and the U.S. Foreign Assistance Program," Part 1 (Washington: Center for International Policy, 1977), p. 46. Exxon and Goodyear have announced investments of $107,000,000 and $34,000,000 in Chile, respectively. International Bulletin, *Internews* 5 (27 February 1978): p. 7.
10. President Geisel of Brazil must have felt reassured by the following exchange which occurred in President Carter's press conference in Brasilia on 30 March 1978:

    Q. Mr. President, the American commercial banks are the main Brazilian source of external credit. It seems to some people in Washington that sooner or later, a congressman may try to establish a link between the commercial banking loans and the human rights policy. I'd like your opinion about this subject.
    A. Brazil is a major trading partner of the United States in commercial goods and also in loans ... It would be inconceivable to me that any act of Congress would try to restrict the lending of money by American private banks to Brazil under any circumstances. This would violate the principles of our own free enterprise system. And if such an act was passed by Congress, I would not approve it.

11. The following two statements from Leonard Silk's interview with McNamara, the *New York Times*, 2 April 1978, p. E3 typify the contradiction between what may be assumed to be McNamara's genuine commitment to the eradication of poverty and his failure to understand that this goal cannot be achieved under fascist regimes:

    Among the most fundamental of human rights are the rights to minimum acceptable levels of nutrition, health and education.
    We do not, we have not in this institution allowed our lending policy to be determined by civil rights considerations, whether they be civil rights considerations in leftist or rightist governments. And our lending policies to Chile have been dictated, both under Allende and under Pinochet, entirely by economic considerations.

12. Cf. Howard Wachtel, "Multinational Banks in the Third World," *TNI Pamphlet* (Washington: Transnational Institute, 1977).
13. Ronald Dworkin, *Taking Rights Seriously* (Cambridge, Mass.: Harvard University Press, 1977).
14. U.N., *International Covenant on Economic, Social, and Cultural Rights*, Art. 8 (1) (d). See Appendix B.
15. "The States Parties to this Covenant recognize the right of everyone to . . . safe and healthy working conditions." For a rare discussion of occupational safety and other socioeconomic desiderata as human rights, see Vicente

Navarro, "Occupational Safety and Health vs. the Right of Capital Accumulation," in *These Times*, 6-12 December 1977, p. 17.
16. U.N., *Universal Declaration of Human Rights*, Art. 23 (1); *Economic and Social Rights Covenant*, Art. 6 (1). See Appendix A for the *Universal Declaration*.
17. *Economic and Social Rights Covenant*, Art. 15 (1) (6).
18. *Economic and Social Rights Covenant*, Art. 12 (1); *Universal Declaration*, Art. 25 (1).
19. *Economic and Social Rights Covenant*, Art. 13 (1) (c); *Universal Declaration*, Art. 26 (1).
20. *Economic and Social Rights Covenant*, Art. 11 (1); *Universal Declaration*, Art. 25 (1).
21. *U.S. Department of State Speech* (Chicago: Bureau of Public Affairs, 9 August 1977).
22. For a remarkable discussion of cultural imperialism, see John Leonard, "American Visitor," *The New York Times Book Review*, 12 March 1978, p. 3.

Chapter 8

The United States, International War, and the Preservation of Human Rights: The Control of Arms

Marcus G. Raskin and Ann Wilcox

We begin this chapter with the premise that practical concern with human rights is the life instinct of civilization. Without a shared consciousness and means for the application of human rights standards, there is little chance that humanity and civilization will be able to survive the next 50 years without horrifying and devastating tragedies. It goes without saying that any *progress* which human civilization might make is utterly tied to the meaning that human rights is given in the daily practice of nations and peoples.

This volume examines the development of human rights standards with their interrelated parts—national and international economic arrangements, the problem of meeting basic human needs of people around the world, the protection of human dignity and security, and the enhancement of civil and political rights. We will here argue that the arms race is a critical element of this process, and that a combined conscious and unconscious spirit in arms negotiations is moving toward the protection of victims' fundamental human rights. The post-World War II Nuremberg and Asian war crimes trials confirmed the principle of official responsibility in war and that precedent is now being linked to nuclear weapons policies and the intended use of such armaments on captive populations. We will examine the development of this relationship and the role of the United States in defining and implementing an end to the arms race which is critical to any framework for the fulfillment of basic human rights.

There is no way for any of us to escape the political ground of the twentieth century sagging with a humanity that cries out for something other than concentration camps, nuclear wars and arming for them, torture, ecological disaster caused by the drive for profit, domination, or *hubris*. And people cry out silently or in their dreams to find ways that they can confront and overcome institutions and states which seek to stop the mass of humanity from realizing themselves as subjects with their own collective hopes and personal histories.

Some will say that there is nothing "new" in the collective horror of the century where reason is detached from personal feeling and subjective understanding. But they would be wrong. Our sophisticated, calculative intelligence is translated into military technologies of violence in being, like missiles, thermonuclear weapons, smart bombs, prisons, torture chambers. Others will say that there is nothing new in huge bureaucratic structures where people are reduced to roles of processor and processed, joined together in a Kafkaesque embrace waiting for each to exchange roles. But there is a difference between this and other times. By virtue of what technology allows there does not have to be limits to behavior. And that is what has happened. No limits are known either in peace or war, no quarter is given, fascism reigns supreme often flying under false banners of socialism or democracy. The half-awakened consciousness of the mass of humanity is caught in the vise of impersonal violence, hidden by bureaucratic shields of secrecy. Fascism, in the sense of the worship of personal and now more frightening impersonal bureaucratic violence, defines the very nature of our daily lives. Ideological hopes fall in the face of systemic cruelty and power drives of officials.

There is another side. Silently people cry out "enough," in a world gone morally and legally mad, where few either speak for humankind or with a human face. Is it too much to say that a half-awakened consciousness of people is slowly becoming aware of a membrane which holds civilization together?

This membrane is human rights and it is our task to bring intellectual and political sustenance to those rights. This is not easy because the very nature and definition of human rights is ambiguous. In our time the concept of "human rights" emerged from the second world war where cruelty and abomination had reached stunning proportions. It emerged from a period in which human beings had been the "objects" of great powers with virtually no standing in international law and where the individual person's life was open to intrusion and destruction by states or the games which statesmen play with each other. The League of Nations took no notice of the internal affairs of states, no matter how brutal the result. And leaders were not thought to be responsible for their actions under international law. As one of the lawyers for the German defendants at Nuremberg put it, there is no individual responsibility for war "as long as the sovereignty of states is the organizational basic principle of interstate order."[1] Some scholars in international law like Hans Kelsen argued that the United Nations Charter itself, which partially grew out of the experience of the League of Nations and the hopes left behind by the second world war, did not recognize human rights or the rights given individuals in international law as formal obligations of states.[2]

Yet other scholars, and with them we would agree, stated that it took the second world war to recognize that "there is a link between respect for freedom within the State and the maintenance of peace between states."[3]

The Development of International Standards

It is important to remember the historical, moral, legal, and even psychological relationship between the Charter of Nuremberg, which attempted to develop a definition of personal responsibility, the United Nations Charter, and later the Universal Declaration of Human Rights. Even though narrowly interpreted by judges, the Charter of Nuremberg had sweeping and high purposes. The articles themselves either overlap or deal with those questions which *in practice* are human rights questions: questions which determine whether a state is something other than the means to organize people into submission or violence. The Tribunal sought individual responsibility in the following areas:

a. Crimes Against Peace: namely, planning, preparation, initiation or waging of a war of aggression, or a war in violation of international treaties, agreements, or assurances, or participation in a common plan or conspiracy for the accomplishment of any of the foregoing.
b. War Crimes: namely, violations of the laws or customs of war. Such violations shall include, but not be limited to, murder, ill-treatment or deportation to slave labor or for any other purpose of civilian population of prisoners of war or persons on the seas, killing of hostages, plunder of public property, wanton destruction of cities, towns or villages, or devastation not justified by military necessity.
c. Crimes Against Humanity: namely, murder, extermination, enslavement, deportation, and other inhuman acts committed against any civilian population, before or during the war, or persecutions on political, racial or religious grounds in execution of or in connection with any crime within the jurisdiction of the Tribunal, whether or not in violation of the domestic law of the country where perpetrated.[4]

As Wasserstrom pointed out, the principle of vicarious liability was also introduced, holding members of a conspiracy responsible whether or not they had committed a particular act. Thousands of people were brought to justice under the Charter of Nuremberg and a similar one in Japan. Nuremberg is a stubborn fact of international affairs. It is a precedent that will not go away. Indeed, as will be suggested, it is critical to our present understanding of international politics and human rights.

Simultaneous with the emergence of the cold war and the breakup of old empires, the need has remained to forge some other, more positive direction which would limit the destruction of man's institutions upon people themselves. The Nuremberg Charter and the U.N. Charter were such imperfect instruments. The objective of the United Nations as laid out in the Charter did not consist of a list of formal human rights obligations which were a condition precedent to membership in the United Nations. Nevertheless even without an explicit provision dealing with formal obligations it would be absurd to think that the members of the United Nations did not formally accept the principles of respect for human rights. As Lauterpacht has said:

> It would be contrary both to these requirements (of treaty interpretation) and to the principle of effectiveness if the repeated and solemn provisions of the Charter in the matter of human rights and fundamental freedoms, conflict with the clear obligations to promote respect for them by joint and separate action, were interpreted as devoid of the obligation to respect them.[5]

Respect is, of course, not the same as legal commitment.

The question of how to promote human rights in practice floundered on the rock of political sovereignty, legal imprecision and bureaucratic fear, and the cold war. With the passage of the Universal Declaration of Human Rights in 1948, the world's people learned how limited—if any existed at all—were the obligations of the states to either apply or sign and implement by treaty the declaration's provisions. Mrs. Eleanor Roosevelt, chairperson of the Commission on Human Rights, stated prior to its passage that the declaration was not a treaty or agreement: "It is a Declaration of basic principles to serve as a common standard of *achievement,* for all peoples and all nations" (emphasis added).[6] Yet the declaration carried moral weight with the mass of people; it made clear that human rights were more than a "luxury." The miracle of that document was that people with opposed ideologies had agreed on a basic list of rights although they could not state *why* they favored those rights as basic, or how the definition of those rights would operate in practice or a common philosophical understanding of the world.

The rights of the declaration as they came to be spelled out in the Covenants embody a range of rights discussed in earlier chapters.

Serious questions can be raised about some of these as "fundamental rights." For example, do scientists have an "unlimited" right to use the resources of the community to make weapons of mass destruction, or undertake experiments which may point to a change in the species of man? We doubt that they have such an unlimited right. It should be noted, however, that Article 29 of the declaration also sets forth obligations of the person to the "community," which suggests the linked nature of these rights, and therefore, of the person to the group.

> 1. Everyone has duties to the community in which alone the free and full development of his personality is possible.
> 2. In the exercise of his rights and freedoms, everyone shall be subject only to such limitations as are determined solely for the purpose of securing due recognition and respect for the rights and freedoms of others and of meeting the just requirements of morality, public order and the general welfare in a democratic society.

Disagreement about first principles made it very difficult to forge a series of practices which would cause the enforcement of the Universal Declaration. While the document was predicated on many American notions, such as those laid out in the American Declaration of the Rights and Duties of Man (Bogota Conference of American States, 1948) and the thoughts of President Franklin Roosevelt's New Deal, and while diligent efforts caused the declaration to be quickly adopted, the United States did not accede to the document as a legally binding one, claiming that it had no such force. The document was seen by nations as an exercise in moral *oughtness*.

The United States faced a hornet's nest early on with the effect of the declaration on the thinking of national leaders around the world. In its 1952 constitution, Puerto Rico "forwarded to the United States Congress for approval, detailed provisions concerning economic and social rights." Congress strongly objected to such provisions, but nevertheless passed the Puerto Rican Constitution in 1952. Likewise, members of the Senate criticized the Japanese Peace Treaty because "its preamble stated the intention of Japan to realize objectives of the Universal Declaration of Human Rights."[7] By the time Dwight Eisenhower and John Dulles came to power in 1953, the stage was set for the United States to withdraw any sort of support for effective human rights treaties. Dulles made clear in the spring of 1953 that the U.S. did not "intend to become a party to any such covenant or present it as a treaty for consideration by the Senate."[8]

The reason the United States took this position during the time of Eisenhower is a complex one. In part, it reflected the fears of conservatives in Congress and the Republican party that the "socialistic" ideas of the United Nations and other countries as well, would upset the internal social system of the United States. U.S. courts were taking notice of the U.N. Charter in various of their decisions.[9] There was also a more complicated foreign policy reason. Dulles had enunciated the doctrine of liberation for East Europe in the 1950-54 period. Except for covert operations, this reflected cold war rhetoric more than the actualities of military intervention. Dulles feared that those to his political right as well as liberal interventionists would use the human rights covenants and declarations to insist that the U.S. use these treaties as legal justification for military action in East Europe. In fact, Dulles did not intend to implement such a policy, as shown during the 1956 Hungarian Revolution.

But a generation is a long time in the history of international affairs. Friends become enemies, disputes which are thought of as settled flare up, ideas and goals thought of as too difficult to achieve become important questions to discuss and negotiate. The Helsinki Conference on Security and Cooperation in Europe set the diplomatic terms of reference for future U.S. diplomatic policy regarding East Europe and human rights in Europe. Politically this agreement is seen as a fine line between disengagement and liberation and a means to reintegrate Europe. On the Western side, what could not be done by the spice of "rollback" was to be accomplished by the sugar of detente. For our purposes, however, the human rights aspects of the Helsinki Accords are critical. The same secretary of state who objected to the American ambassador giving "political science lessons" to the Chilean junta when he complained about Chilean torture, accepted the human rights sections of the Helsinki Accords. The language of this agreement is similar in purpose and intent to the Universal Declaration. "In the field of human rights and fundamental freedoms the participating States will act in conformity with the purposes and principles of the Charter of the United Nations and with the Universal Declaration of Human Rights. They will also fulfill their obligations as set forth in the international declarations and agreements in this field, including *inter alia* the International Covenants on Human Rights, by which they may be bound."

The participating states, according to principle seven of the accords, are meant to "respect human rights and fundamental freedoms, including the freedom of thought, conscience, religion or belief for all, without distinction as to race, sex, language, or religion. They will promote and encourage the effective exercise of civil, political, economic, social, cultural, and other rights and freedoms, all of which derive from the inherent dignity of the human person and are essential for his free and full development."[10] The Helsinki Accords do nothing to point up the criminal nature of the arms race, calling instead for "confidence-building measures" such as "prior notification of major military maneuvers, exchange of observers" which "by their nature constitute steps towards the ultimate achievement of general and complete disarmament under strict and effective international control, and which should result in strengthening peace and security throughout the world."

What can we conclude from this litany of new good intentions? Moral pretension plays an important role in the statements, if not in the actions of states, and while such a view may be cynical, it is also true that governmental energy is often spent explaining how the action of the particular state is in the path of moral righteousness and decency. This is understandable since most statesmen recognize, consciously or unconsciously, that both a state and the law which it uses and lives under, require a moral basis if either the particular law or the state is to have any lasting significance—especially during a period of great transformation and turbulence. *Without a moral basis which can be recognized as such by those who are not part of that particular system of beliefs one may be sure that such laws or that state will become casualties of social transformation and world opinion.* We see this phenomenon operating in Southern Africa and we saw it as well in the 35-year struggle against outside domination waged by the Vietnamese people.

Certain rights have stood the test of time and the test of modern revolution as the basis upon which the people's freedom, and their own hopes, are to be staked. These freedoms can be added to and deepened in meaning as people discover more clearly the means necessary to help them in their active subject role in history. The human rights of any particular period are rights necessary for people to exist and thrive in that particular historical period. But rights also are cumulative. Free speech or assembly is no less important because economic security is guaranteed in a society. Nor is it the case that the rights of economic security cease to exist because there is free speech and assembly. Rights in this sense are additive, not contradictory. In this regard Article 3, "Everyone has the right to life, liberty and security of person," Article 4, "No one shall be subjected to torture, or to cruel, inhuman, or degrading treatment or punishments," are statements or rights won in another century, but which are critical conditions precedent to any sort of life in a body politic.

Preparing for Genocide

These rights, critical as they are, and central to our present dilemma, are merely the beginning of understanding the problem of human rights as we should now come to consider it. In this sense we are confronted with an irony. The declaration which should have been translated from "oughtness" to legally binding treaties a generation ago is not adequate to face the present turbulent world because of the generally limited or ambiguous definition of human rights which is seen as applying to individuals, but not to individuals as part of a collective or class that can seek relief *prior* to an action of states. Thus, it would seem that genocide has to be completed before there is acknowledgment that genocide has occurred.

The U.S. is in an even more troubling situation conceptually and morally. The Genocide Treaty has yet to be ratified by the U.S. Senate. Nor is the arms race and arms preparation recognized as part of the way that human rights are violated, or a crime nationally or internationally committed. Instead, nations see arming only as "defense." As one commentator has noted, "The very condemnation of aggression as illegitimate has, in effect, increased the dignity and legitimacy of self-defense, with the concomitant danger that nations may abuse the concepts of individual and collective self-defense. The preparations for ever more destructive and catastrophic wars have actually never been as relentless as in this era of war prohibition."[11]

In fact, the military policies and trappings of this country do not constitute a defense policy at all. We define defense to mean ensuring the independence and security of the American people as they seek to reconstruct the social, political, and economic fabric of the nation. Instead, the U.S. maintains a stance of imperial offense and U.S. foreign policy continues to revolve around armaments and especially nuclear weapons. Weapons are seen as the primary means of asserting the will of the state in the international arena. Policymakers do not take seriously, except in an abstract way, the criminal aspects of aggressive war and nuclear bomb use. It is not only nuclear war which has lost its forbidden quality: flexible brushfire war concepts tested in Vietnam add a variant to conventional war fighting capabilities, making the latter all the more conceivable. Indeed, such capabilities are seen as necessary so that nuclear weapons do not have to be used.

While lip service is given to the dangers of the arms race, arms control negotiations act as a spur to arming. The problem of current leadership is the classic twentieth century question of brinksmanship—how to threaten with nuclear weapons, or armaments generally, sanctioning the buildup in them, while codifying a system of war and negotiations which will guarantee that weaponry will be used in a controlled and "rational" way.

The question of human rights must be linked to issues concerning the arms race and war. As one commentator has pointed out, the direct nexus between the idea of human rights and the existing law of war was not envisaged until the second world war was over. In Article 1 of the U.N. Charter the framers contend that the unleashing of aggressive war occurred at the hands of those states in which the denial of the value and dignity of the individual human being, of whatever race, color, or creed, was most evident. The nexus that the Charter framers saw between the criminality of state aggression by armed forces and the denial of human worth within the frontiers of such states—which was repeated and increased in areas occupied through military adventures—rammed home in a way that mankind was not likely to forget the connection between aggressive war, the way it is waged, and the total disregard of the individual.[12] In the modern technological context this formulation gives rise to the question of genocide, defined as "the structural and systematic destruction of innocent people by a state bureaucratic apparatus."[13]

Cataclysmic social and political events serve as a catalyst to ideas which are "in the air" but have not crystallized because the events have not forced the reconsideration of basic conceptual frameworks which set the terms of debate. It is only now that we begin to see the direct relationship between the work of the Nuremberg judgments and a new understanding of human rights. The Nuremberg trials and judgments grew out of principles of accountability and responsibility from the laws of agency, democratic, and socialist theory. However, this conception of personal accountability and individual human rights has consistently avoided the relationship of the powers of national leaders to make war either on their own people or on people of other lands. Consequently, international law has been silent on the importance of human rights as a *line of defense* by the individual person, the family, or the community against the state's activities as they relate to war preparations, or the more specific question of participation in warlike acts.[14]

In this sense human rights should be seen as a condition precedent to the penumbra of policies which states follow that shade into war, cold war, arming, and covert war. It is a conceptual and moral error to assert that humanitarian rules should be found in the context of armed conflict. Instead the "human rights" rules should be seen as governing actions of governments *precedent* to any particular policies which they intend to pursue. They are required to ask the question, what is the effect that the government's foreign and defense policies have on innocent populations? This question goes to the very nature of the arms acquisition and arms race process, a more euphemistic phrase for the preparation for mass murder and genocide.

The legal formulations and judgments to emerge from Nuremberg and the Asian war crimes trials, as well as the moral suasion of the Universal Declaration, the Charter, and later resolutions of the General Assembly on war and disarmament, are in direct conflict with the types of weapons (nuclear, thermonuclear, chemical, and biological, plus missiles) which states acquire or make. Besides being a horrifying tragedy, their use sets the stage for considering those who prepare, acquire, and use such weapons as criminals. After all, there is nothing in the laws of war which would justify the types of armaments used or contemplated for use at this time by the great powers. In this sense, if the killing cannot be legitimated by the laws of war, then surely the actions of leaderships fall more within the context of domestic and international criminal concern than high policy. The international community has before renounced the use of war in the conduct of national policy, through declarations and treaties such as the Kellogg-Briand Pact of 1928. Moreover, Article 22 of the Hague Regulations (1907) makes clear that, "Belligerents have not got an unlimited right as to the choice of injuring the enemy." The illegality of reprisals is undisputed in international law, as seen in the Geneva Conventions of 1949 and the U.N. Charter. Municipal law becomes the means of bringing leaderships to justice for denying the security of the person through the choice of weapons used to defend the nation. Indeed, under Justice Jackson's stricture, such is the major way to hold leaderships accountable to their citizenry.[15]

Obviously, the question of bringing such actions against governments falls in the psychological area of political will coupled with the existence of appropriate legislation. Will is usually exercised where there is an aroused and organized citizenry which sees a means to bring such pressure to bear against its government by championing already existent principles. Thus, during the Indo-China war many young people refused to be drafted on the grounds that they would be in violation of the U.N. Charter and the Nuremberg judgment, just as other people within the Soviet Union staged civil disobedience on the ground that they could do no other because of the Universal Declaration of Human Rights.

Such a stance, which uses an emerging consensus of international legal doctrine against the excesses of states, needs to find a double constituency. One is among diplomats and international civil servants. The other is among groups in other countries who see that their own liberties are directly tied to those people who are prepared to challenge state law that has no basis in universally accepted principles, while their challenge is legitimated and codified in the U.N. Charter, covenants, provisions, resolutions, and international law generally. In some cases municipal legislation may not exist, and policymakers may think that because there is no law which abjures their action, they are not covered by the domestic criminal law.

In this regard, the Kastenmeier bill (H.R. 8688, U.S. House of Representatives) is a significant piece of legislation which would commence the tedious but necessary process of holding government officials in the foreign and national security policy areas personally accountable for their plans and practices.[16] Kastenmeier's bill uses as a standard the norms laid on Germany and Japan at the end of the second world war and states that such legislation should be internalized in U.S. law. It also calls for internalizing the Charter as well as other international legal strictures against war crimes. Kastenmeier and his group in Congress held that the person's security is robbed in the case of war, and fundamental human rights are therefore violated in the process. In an earlier model draft version there were provisions for the citizen to legally refrain from tax payment or from being drafted where the courts determined that all or a part of the government had acted to make or prepare an aggressive war, or use weapons or mass destruction in derogation of Charter obligations and judgments made at the Nuremberg trials.

The nature of war preparation should now come under direct scrutiny. There is little doubt that a person's security and, therefore, human rights are directly violated by the nature of weaponry adopted. In modern states, huge organizations enter into a series of activities on a daily basis which may not appear to be crimes or violations of anyone's rights. But once we are able to remove the conceptual blinders from our eyes, the reality is that those actions are crimes *in situ*, crimes in being. The armaments race, given the nature of the arms made and the war plans fashioned, is criminal when compared to laws of war or peace, the criminal laws of individual nations, and the Nuremberg and Asian trial standards.

The arms strategists' plans of "taking out" millions of people either in first strike or second strike reprisal are surely not contemplated by any internationally lawful system of defense. That we see nations and their leaders thoughtlessly reducing their actions to criminal activity hardly means that laws do not exist which directly contradict such behaviour. As the judges at Nuremberg said, "after the policy to initiate and wage aggressive wars was formulated, a defendant came into possession of knowledge that the invasions and war to be waged were aggressive and unlawful (against international law and treaty), then he will be criminally responsible if he, being on the policy level, could have influenced such policy and failed to do so."[17] Thus, since such actions once contemplated are war crimes *in situ*, because of their genocidal or illegal nature, we are seized of a complicated conceptual problem. The final "frame" or act in a process which leads to a culminating event, in this case the "go" signal for nuclear war or aggressive war, does not have to be completed for us to realize that the event is already underway. One needs only to look at arms budgets and strategic doctrine to comprehend the criminal nature of the arms enterprise. Government officials descend to the level of bureaucratic gangsterism as their political lives and practices fly directly in the face of Article 1 of the Charter and Declaration.

Once we begin our understanding that we are living in an event of genocide which has not, thankfully, played out the final notes of civilization's Gottedammerung, we are able to evaluate an entire spectrum of negotiations and talks on arms control and disarmament from a somewhat different perspective than we usually use. The participants in the Strategic Arms Limitation Treaty (SALT) talks, favoring great secrecy, eschew necessary moral, legal, and criminal questions when discussing armaments. There is a necrophilic quality to the type of technical expertise which calculates one missile against another, as diplomats become brokers in charred bodies. When these talks are divorced from the fundamentally criminal nature of the weaponry or strategies under discussion, arms control talks are reduced to a narrow exercise between state representatives on the character and size of genocidal forces. Unfortunately, the SALT talks give the appearance of legitimacy to the entire field of weapons of mass destruction because they create the mind-set among elites in the media and the universities, as well as the people as a whole, that such weapons are "needed" and that they should be considered in the card catalogs of libraries and treasury accounts under the heading of "Policy and Diplomacy" rather than "Crime and Criminal Behavior." To repeat the point, there can be no successful discussion which is meant to comprehend the character and gravity of the weapons, and to limit and eliminate them, without the discussion beginning from accepted international legal principles about genocide, population safety, and the Nuremberg judgment of personal accountability of public officials to either municipal or international tribunals.

Arms strategists, scientists, governments, civil servants, defense ministries, and diplomats should be acutely aware of the legally and morally exposed situation in which they now find themselves. They have caused to be developed the type of weaponry and military technology which breaches every law and fundamental human right. We are required to change our theories of arms control and disarmament discussions from the type of epicycle reasoning which has gripped those interested in these questions and political leaderships to a far more basic and clearheaded understanding of what is going on. We cannot accept the sort of analysis of a leading "epicyclist," Henry Kissinger, who says that the SALT II agreement means "that a cap has been put on the arms race for a period of 10 years."[18]

Beginning the Disarmament Process

It is clear that the global conventional arms race and nuclear buildup, masked by an arms control discussion, can be reversed only by a commitment to a comprehensive disarmament plan. This includes unilateral and multilateral moves, completed within a definite time frame. Such plans have in the past been ignored or abandoned for various reasons. The McCloy-Zorin Eight Points and the general and complete disarmament proposals of 1959-1961 were bound by the principle of interlocking stages "for reducing or eliminating weapons and armed forces, and with precise stipulated timing to assure that the process of disarming would not leave any nation's security weakened." These principles were never translated into actual policy, but were eclipsed by U.S. efforts to counter national liberation forces in Indo-China and around the world, as well as by Soviet attempts to achieve parity with the U.S.

Present disarmament discussions are fragmented. MBFR, SALT, and test ban discussions are conducted as separate activities and do not contain an interlinked time boundary. Each is *not* meant to be a challenge to the overall direction of the arms race and to the overall defense purposes or strategic posture of the United States. Indeed, policies formulated during the Kissinger-Schlesinger period at the national security wheel encouraged preparation of counterforce—like strategies without surrendering countervalue strategies. Meanwhile, more sophisticated missiles were developed along with new conventional war options. There is nothing to suggest that the Carter administration has changed the counterforce/countervalue imperative.

Any disarmament proposal judged as an alternative must, therfore, be an interlinked and *comprehensive* national security system for the United States and, indeed, for other nations to judge in their own terms for themselves. In this regard our political task is to encourage other nations and their representatives, including action groups, to adopt strategies or proposals which are in the same frame of reference as the one we propose.

Any serious comprehensive agreement must be *time* bound. The document should state what has to be accomplished within a limited period of time, what can wait or be deferred, and what needs to be strengthened. It must bring into play not only state or governmental factors but societal pressures within one's own state, as well as those nongovernmental contacts which enhance the success of the agreement. The document should also use fairly mechanical ways of judging whether certain nations are carrying out their pledges. The use of quantitative measurements, however, or arguments about them should not be a cover for continuing the arms race. The purpose of comprehensive disarmament negotiations is not to justify the arms acquisition or sales system of nations, nor is it to set up a control system which merely legitimates that process.

A second consideration is the length of time it would take to reach general and complete disarmament. The road is no doubt a long one, but it has to be built, for its purpose is to change the direction and value system of nations and peoples. Important questions of intervention, responsibility, defense, and use of armed forces and technology must be confronted. But by saying that the road is long we should make clear that within this framework there are goals to be achieved which can be qualitatively or quantitatively measured through technical inspection systems controlled by an international disarmament organization of the United Nations. In terms of length of time, we would urge that a coordinated and comprehensive strategy include goals of disarmament which are to be unilaterally and multilaterally achieved within *10 years*. It should begin in the following way:

1. Announcement of a 10-year disarmament plan. The nature of the plan should be discussed for one year in the Security Council with the leaders of the various great powers, and a similar debate should continue in the General Assembly, weighing and studying the sort of proposals presented by the great powers. These proposals would set out definite reduction requirements; i.e., eliminating weapons systems from particular categories, accompanied by cuts in defense budgets. The plan would be lobbied through the U.S. government and discussed publicly at local and national levels.
2. Present structures and processes for disarmament discussion in the General Assembly and its First Committee should be strengthened. We should also propose that the military committee of the U.N. reconvene to work on the world disarmament plan from the perspective of military security.
3. Nonproliferation agreements of a vertical and horizontal nature and pledges of no-first-use are essential first steps for the General and Complete Disarmament Plan.
4. Each nation would examine its domestic economy as well as international economic arrangements in terms of replacing arms manufacturing processes with productive work designed to meet basic human needs.

Any meaningful disarmament plan must also recognize the relationship between political interests as represented by the stationing of troops and the alliance system, and arms control and surveillance methods. The process of balanced reductions is a subjective one in which individual nations decide whether a political activity is equal to a change in weapons posture. Thus, for example, the U.S. may feel that it cannot give up hegemony of South Korea, and therefore it needs certain armaments to assure itself of hegemony. On the other hand, if it sees no interest in hegemony or believes that there is another way to maintain U.S. interest in a so-called independent Korea, it may be prepared to give up certain sorts of armaments. Thus, *political* plans are required for each area of the world; these would start from the assumption that essentially the same distribution of power in terms of the world's pyramid will continue during the disarmament plan. This is not as terrifying or silly as it appears *just because* there is a greater tendency to polycentrism across the world and the costs of the arms race are so great.

Worldwide meetings horizontally between city, neighborhood, and nongovernmental representatives of different nations should be arranged to consider the substantive meaning of human rights in the context of the problems which humanity now faces. The purpose of such a reconsideration is not to undo the painstaking work already accomplished. The intent is exactly the opposite: it is to make clear that human rights are the inescapable ground upon which international relations exist, not in the sense that human rights become a cloak for busybody intervention and imperialism. Instead, they are to be the ground upon which nations, diplomats, statesmen, and people come to understand the essential need of rights in practice in questions concerning the international economic order, the arms race, the relations of their states to other states, and the internal rights of their own citizenry. We would propose an international, nongovernmental monitoring agency which permanently reported on the question of human rights violations, as defined according to the covenants and the Universal Declaration, the Nuremberg Charter, and the U.N. Charter.[19] It would seek and receive information from governments, nongovernmental organizations, and individuals. It would also fashion economic standards and comment on major technological and military systems, their effect on human rights, individual, and group security. It would aid groups in various countries. Human rights in this framework would assert that international economic actions must be in furtherance of aspirations which are stated in treaties and General Assembly Resolutions that seek to set out a framework in such matters as disarmament and apartheid.

We should note that the United States signs human rights declarations and other multilateral statements of principle in terms of their being goals. They are not meant as rules of behavior. In the case of disarmament, we are not talking about *goals* but new rules of behavior and institutions which internally support an alternative national and international security strategy. It is therefore critical to pass legislation which creates a mechanism for holding officials responsible for their actions. Major treaties in other areas of international affairs as well should affirm *personal* standards and accountability for government officials as well as a standard of behavior to which they and their states repair. The language of an international document should reiterate how the intent of the Charter is carried out in the document and the foreign policy pursued by the state.

There is an overriding need to develop transnational institutions which support each other and are used as transnational links for shared purposes. In this regard it is time to form a transnational grouping of parliamentarians, representatives of organizations, scholars and publicists, leaders of labor and consumer groups that would forge a series of legislative proposals to be presented for consideration in the world's parliaments. Such model legislation would aim at standards of personal responsibility of government officials in the areas of economics, the environment, and defense. Professional, military, labor, and consumer organizations would be called upon to fashion Hippocratic oaths for government officials, diplomats, natural and social scientists, and others so that an ethical and moral base could be asserted in government and civil society. Scholarship and public action would be expected to parallel the fundamental aspirations of the Charter and Declaration. Perhaps we will then be able to escape the tawdry sight of a leading economist receiving a Nobel prize while giving advice to a terror state which seeks to implement the "economic doctor's" policies.

Protecting the Rights of Civilian Populations

An important impetus to the disarmament effort and the broader human rights movement will be found in the recently negotiated Protocols Additional to the 1949 Geneva Conventions on War and relating to the protection of victims of international armed conflict.[20] Negotiators, meeting under the sponsorship of the International Red Cross, have excluded weapons of mass destruction from their talks on the ground that such questions are being dealt with in another forum. The critical question remains whether all weapons will be subjected to the standards laid down in this treaty. It appears that the U.S. will take reservation on the question of nuclear weapons of mass destruction, but this is a serious mistake. It is ludicrous to develop laws of war which neither touch the nature of arms acquisition nor the existence of major weapons arsenals which are criminal by nature and harmful to any basic human rights.

We argue that the United States should take no reservation to the protocols, but rather should accept the full significance of this instrument. The over 115 nations that have signed or initialled the treaty should "bite the bullet" and consider that language as binding their own conduct in national defense and arms policy. It should also be binding on negotiations for SALT or any comprehensive disarmament arrangement—whether negotiated in the UN Special Session on Disarmament or other forums. The articles of the protocol define conduct in such areas as care of sick and wounded civilians and military personnel, use of medical transportation, civil defense arrangements, and "methods and means of warfare combatant and prisoner-of-war status." We draw particular attention to those articles defining the terms of protection of civilian populations; these are of great significance in judging the accumulation of weapons and the preparation for their use as a human rights problem. These articles define civilians and civilian populations and prohibit indiscriminate attacks on them. According to Article 51, indiscriminate attacks are:

a. those which are not directed at a specific military objective;
b. those which employ a method or means of combat which cannot be directed at a specific military objective; or
c. those which employ a method or means of combat the effects of which cannot be limited as required by this Protocol; and consequently, in each such case, are of a nature to strike military objectives and civilians or civilian objects without distinction.

Paragraph 5 continues, stating that an indiscriminate attack is one which treats as one military objective distinctly separate cities or towns; it is also

> an attack which may be expected to cause incidental loss of civilian life, injury to civilians, damage to civilian objects, or a combination thereof, which would be excessive in relation to the concrete and direct military advantage anticipated.

The terms of the treaty also protect civilians and civilian populations from attacks of reprisal and from being used as shields for military objectives. Other articles protect cultural objects and places of worship and "objects indispensable to the survival of the civilian population"—i.e., foodstuffs, agricultural areas, crops, drinking water, etc. Article 55 prohibits the use of methods and means of warfare which cause "widespread, long-term and severe damage" to the environment.

"Works and installations" (dams, electrical generating stations, etc.) are protected—even if they are military objectives—if attacks on them would endanger civilian lives (Article 56). Subsequent articles require those planning military operations to take precautions ensuring that civilian populations will not be attacked in the course of the operation. Furthermore, precautions must be taken against harmful *effects* on civilian populations during attacks (Articles 57 and 58).

This protocol can be conceptually linked with the various U.N. resolutions on comprehensive disarmament and with the terms of the Nuremberg and Tokyo war crimes proceedings. Together, the instruments create a strong framework for denouncing the accumulation of nuclear weapons of mass destruction which are held like a threatening sword over innocent populations. Such a framework must inform and be the basis of any international disarmament discussions because we are in mortal danger of turning defense policy into elements of crime.

Conclusion

Humankind will not begin to confront the massive and complex problem of promoting human rights without a will to do so on the part of governments and peoples. The legal instruments outlined in this discussion are mechanisms for beginning this process. Since Nuremberg the question of accountability of officials has been on the political agenda. For Americans, passage of an Official Accountability Act became more urgent as the result of three events: the Cuban Missile Crisis, in which millions of lives were risked; the Vietnam War, which was a criminal war; and Watergate, in which official power was abused. The United Nations Covenants on Human Rights, while being a "laundry list" of economic, social, political, and civil rights standards, help to shape conceptions of rights in the thinking of citizens and leaders. Through such instruments we may begin to codify the principles embodied in the Universal Declaration of Human Rights, the Nuremberg Charter, and similar statements.

Citizens must continually seek to sustain and enhance the moral basis of their society. We have argued that human rights are *precedent* to state power. But the people of a nation must define the substance and meaning of those rights, which when implemented will protect them against abuses of that power. The creation of legally binding instruments such as those outlined above is an important step in forming the structure of respect for human rights.

Indeed, the language of such instruments must not be seen as the language of foolish idealism. Rather the language should reflect an operational belief. Negotiations for the protocol to the 1949 Geneva conventions, disarmament, and SALT negotiations must be conducted on this basis. National and transnational public-interest groups can reinforce this process as they hold leaders responsible for the development and acquisition of both nuclear and conventional weapons systems. In this way people will assert their collective rights against their own and other governments, thus ensuring that they may live their lives in genuine security.

Human rights are an increasingly important element in the currents of world politics. Millions around the world are denied basic nutritional and medical needs and heavy-handed regimes, many of them supported by U.S. corporate power, crush the spirits and lives of countless more. We have argued that the threat to destroy civilization through the use of nuclear weapons overshadows the existence of all of us. That reality must now be seen as a human rights problem. Only through concerted action within and between groups of citizens can we hope to stop the last toll of the bell for humankind.

NOTES

1. Quoted in "The Relevance of Nuremberg," Richard Wasserstrom, in *War and Moral Responsibility*, ed. Thomas Nagel (Princeton: Princeton University Press, 1974), p. 139.
2. Hans Kelsen, *The Law of the United Nations* (London: Stevens, 1951), p. 29.
3. Quoted in Heribert Golsong, "Implementation of International Protection of Human Rights," in Hague Academy of International Law, *Receuil des Cours*, 110 (1963): 7.
4. Wasserstrom, p. 136.
5. Sir Hersh Lauterpacht, *International Law and Human Rights* (Oxford: Oxford University Press, 1963).
6. U.S. Department of State Bulletin 14 (December 19, 1948), p. 751. Cited by James Frederick Green in *The United Nations and Human Rights* (Washington: The Brookings Institution, 1958).
7. Ibid., pp. 700-770.
8. Ibid., p. 703.
9. Namba v. McCourt: 204 p. (2d) 569.
10. *Final Act of the Conference on Security and Cooperation in Europe* (CSCE) in Helsinki, Volume 73 Department of State Bulletin 323, 1975, or 14 ILM 1293 1975, of the American Society of International Law.
11. John Fried, "War-Exclusive or War Inclusive Style in International Conduct," *Texas International Law Forum*, 2: 11.
12. G.I.A.D. Draper, "Human Rights and Armed Conflicts," *Israel Yearbook on Human Rights* (Tel Aviv: Faculty of Law, Tel Aviv University, 1971), p. 103.
13. Irving Louis Horowitz, *Genocide* (New Brunswick, New Jersey: Transaction, Inc., 1976), p. 18.
14. Compare Article 15 of the European Convention on Human Rights: (1) In time of war or other public emergency threatening the life of the nation, any High Contracting party may take measures derogating from its obligations under the convention to the extent strictly required by the exigencies of the situation, provided that such measures are not inconsistent with its other obligations under international law. (2) No derogation from Article 2 (right to life) except in respect of deaths resulting from lawful acts of war, or from Article 3 (No torture or inhuman punishments), 4 paragraph 1 (No slavery or servitude), and Article 7 (No crime without a law, international or municipal, existing at the time of commission) shall be made under this provision.
15. Note also in Re. Yamashita 327, U.S. 1 (1946).
16. The same bill was introduced into the House of Representatives by various cosponsors, in the following forms: HR 8388 on July 8, 1975; HR 9761 on September 22, 1975; and HR 10800 on November 18, 1975.
17. *Trials of War Criminals Before the Nuremberg Military Tribunals Under Control Council Law 11* (Washington: Government Printing Office, 1950), p. 488-489. Quoted by Sanford Levinson, "Responsibility for Crimes of

War," *War and Moral Responsibility*, ed. Thomas Nagel. This is the lesson that we can draw from the trials of over 10,000 Germans found guilty of war crimes. Where policies were undertaken which by their nature were breaches of laws of wars or international law, and the official was in a position to stop or veto such policies but failed to do so, that person could be held criminally responsible.

18. The Stockholm International Peace Research Institute comments on Kissinger's point in the following way: "But just what is it that is being 'capped'? Only, it seems, the number of strategic delivery vehicles and MIRVed missiles. Under such an agreement, the actual number of nuclear warheads carried by the bombers, missiles and submarines (and it is, after all, this number that really counts) could without any effective limitation, increase to the maximum carrying capacity of these vehicles—an increase which is very considerable indeed. The Soviet Union is only now beginning to put MIRVs on its missiles. But once begun, the MIRVing program is likely to continue rapidly.

    Most serious of all—and this is the crux of the matter—the qualitative arms race is not 'capped' in any way at all.... We can therefore look forward, even with SALT II, to strategic nuclear arsenals containing tens of thousands of thermonuclear weapons.

    Even the most enthusiastic Soviet or U.S. military planner must find it difficult to discover targets for so many warheads." *World Armaments and Disarmament Yearbook* of the Stockholm International Peace Research Institute (SIPRI) (Cambridge: MIT Press, 1975), p. 12.

19. This idea has been suggested by Peter Weiss in Chapter VII of this work.
20. *Protocol Additional to the Geneva Conventions of 12 August 1949, and relating to the Protection of Victims of International Armed Conflicts (Protocols I and II)*, International Red Cross, Geneva, July 1977.

Part III

Human Rights Policies of the United States in International Organizations

Chapter 9

The United States and International Protection of Minorities

Robert G. Wirsing

Racial, linguistic, and religious minorities — what we shall here refer to simply as ethnic minorities — rank consistently among the most common and brutalized victims of human rights violations.* Often defenseless, they have a wholly natural and understandable wish to be protected. Historically, they have had to seek protection on many occasions by "vanishing," either through cultural conversion or simply flight. Only infrequently was there an impartial tribunal to which they could turn for effective relief. They were the objects of persecution in ancient city-states, in feudal principalities, in tribal kingdoms, and in sprawling empires; and their situation has not improved markedly since the advent of the age of nation-states. In fact, the chauvinistic urges characteristic of this age have upon occasion inspired outbursts of demoniacal nationalism unexcelled in any earlier age in the ferocity of intolerance displayed for minority communities. Nonetheless, the nation-state system has clearly given rise to a novel opportunity for minorities. In our own century it spawned the most devastating wars in history and these wars led directly to the creation of supranational institutions equipped with unprecedented potential for preventing the persecution and destruction of minority groups. At least the framework of an impartial and permanent system of justice now exists. The over-arching and as yet unresolved question is whether these new institutions, the far from independent offspring of states, can develop and enforce rules of behavior that effectively protect minorities when protection is unobtainable from the states themselves.

The question is more complicated than that, of course. Majorities are occasionally the victims. Ethnic minorities dominate in some countries and in others they have been blatantly responsible for the weakening or subversion of the state. Minority rights sometimes parallel but not infrequently compete with majority rights. And it is not at all certain, when they are cast as the rights of groups, that minority rights are entirely compatible with the rights of individuals. Indeed, depending upon the breadth of one's definition of minority rights (or of a minority), it is conceivable that reasonably humane people might not wish to protect them at all.

In the shadow of the problem of minority protection lurk equally intractable issues of sovereignty, of the nature of the political contract between man and the state, and of the meaning of justice within and among states. These assure the continuity of the problem and the towering complexity of its resolution.

A pronounced characteristic of the subject is its neglect by contemporary statesmen. It has been made clear in other analyses of the problem that this neglect is not fortuitous, the chance result of historical events.[1] It seems entirely consistent, in fact, with the behavioral norms of the nation-state system which structurally inhibit the international protection of anything, including minorities. Harsh realities shaped whatever institutions now exist for the international protection of minorities; these institutions will not easily be improved or replaced. There most definitely are no easy solutions. It is conceivable that there are none. And yet, there is not a more dynamic element in the world today — nor a greater threat to the peace of nations — than the unsatisfied aspirations of ethnic communities. Of one thing we may be certain: minorities will not soon cease demanding rights and wanting protection from those who deny them.

The problem of protecting minorities is an old one. This chapter explores it from a contemporary perspective, seeking to define the issues which now crowd in upon statesmen everywhere — American statesmen not least among them. We begin by identifying some of the basic issues and more prominent milestones in the development of international protection of minorities under both the systems of the League of Nations and the United Nations. The highly influential historical role of United States policy in regard to minority protection is reviewed. This we follow with an examination of the case for and the case against international protection of minorities, in which we take cognizance of the urgent need for, as well as enormous hazards inherent in, a universalist approach to minority protection. We then consider several existing and less comprehensive approaches to minority protection (kin-state, transnational, and self protection), measuring their adequacy as alternatives to international protection. The discussion concludes with an assessment of options available to American policymakers in regard to international protection.

The Development of International Protection

Viewing minority rights from a global historical perspective, one cannot fail to be impressed by the amount of human energy that has been expended in the long effort to obtain international guarantees for their protection.[2] What began many centuries ago as occasional agreements among ruling princes extending protection to dissident and persecuted coreligionists in neighboring kingdoms has swelled since the turn of the twentieth century into a voluminous outpouring of resolutions, declarations, treaties, and covenants, many of them endorsed by virtually the entire international community, honoring the rights not only of religious but of linguistic, national, and racial minorities as well. Spurred on by the mammoth catastrophes inflicted on minorities in two world wars, the dissolution of polyglot empires, and the arousal of explosive political self-consciousness among minorities everywhere, contemporary statesmen have repeatedly avowed their belief in the interconnectedness of pacific international relations and the just treatment of minorities. Acutely aware of the frailty of good intentions, they have attempted to armor the conviction with the collective moral and political authority of international organization and law. While there is thus little doubt that violations of minority rights have been given more international attention in this century than ever before, the existence of an unequivocal and categorical international obligation to extend protection to minorities cannot yet be claimed. In fact, there has never been much unanimity among states as to which minority rights deserved protection, much less how, or even whether, rights were to be enforced. Indeed, precisely what constitutes a bona fide "minority" has not yet been internationally agreed.[3]

The development of minority rights has paralleled and, in significant respects, inspired the centuries-long evolution of human rights. But the two sets of rights, while in some ways indistinguishable, have not always, in fact, had a perfectly symmetrical or harmonious relationship. The rights of minorities have sometimes been seen simply as a subcategory of, at other times as a category independent of, human rights. The two have sometimes worked in tandem, the one reinforcing the other; at other times, they have been in conflict, the one seeming to retard the progress of the other. International protection has never been fully extended to either—or extended equally to both. Indeed, contemporary statesmen have occasionally felt compelled to choose between the two. The particular choices they have made deserve close inspection.

Fundamental Questions

The assertion that minorities have rights has itself been seriously questioned in the twentieth century. No one denied it more emphatically than Nazi theorists. While not above loud proclamations of sympathy for persecuted minorities, they carried nineteenth century nationalist thinking to its logical conclusion with the insistence that the boundaries of each state coincide with one biologically descended cultural group. Ethnically alien minorities remaining within these boundaries, they reasoned, had no natural right to elect citizenship of the state of birth and/or residence. Ethnically related minorities resident beyond these boundaries, on the other hand, retained a spiritual bond with their primordial homeland no matter how much time or space had intervened. When possible, they should be physically reunited with the homeland; but in any event they owed it political loyalty. In practice, this fanciful doctrine rationalized German aggression and cruelly victimized non-German minorities—especially those who had no homeland available with which to reunite. Their only right, it seemed, was to flee. And even that was ultimately foreclosed.[4]

Nazism was obviously extreme. But even when minority rights have been recognized under international law, protection has almost always been extended to individual members of minorities, not to minority groups as such. Moreover, the international community has been much more inclined to recognize "negative" rights of nondiscrimination (requiring no more than equal treatment for all citizens) than the "positive" rights of cultural preservation (requiring special treatment of minorities). Positive rights were granted to specified groups in the Versailles settlement following World War I. But those concessions, which have not been extensively repeated, were identified mainly as the rights of individuals and were not meant as an endorsement of group rights. These are the bane of all modern statesmen, who are naturally covetous of the rights of states. Negative rights, if enforced, do protect minorities, but not from loss of their culture. Positive rights, expressed as the rights of individuals, may help sustain minority culture, but without explicitly conferring authority on the minority group itself. Positive group rights presumably best protect minority culture, since they offer collective defense against the authority of the majority at least in the realm of cultural affairs. This explains, no doubt, why most majorities have strenuously avoided them. These distinctions are crucial and need to be understood.

Liberal political theory is saturated with individualism. One of its foremost claims is that individuals author the social contract and are thus endowed with inalienable rights. Accordingly, only individuals have a distinct moral right to limit the authority of the state. Groups intermediate between man and the state are essentially ruled out. Groups may hold derivative rights (rights that are reducible to individual moral claims), but individuals are the basic right-and-duty-bearing units.[5]

The implication for ethnic minority groups is plain: members of them shall not be denied the rights guaranteed to all individuals, including the right to maintain distinct cultural and linguistic traditions—or voluntarily to depart from them. Groups do not possess a moral right to survive culturally, except as that which may be assured through the protection of their individual members. States do not have any moral obligations to ethnic groups as such; survival depends on the group's own resources.

Western practice has never been as rigidly individualist as its theory, of course, and ethnic minorities have often been the beneficiaries of the exceptions. Indeed, a convincing case can be made that there is abundant precedent in recent history to reinforce moral justification for a concept of right-bearing units large enough to house ethnic communities.[6]

Here we need not argue the question whether ethnic groups have or ought to have irreducible rights reflecting moral claims. But there is no doubt that denial of such rights in liberal thought has widely influenced practice in much of the world for most of the twentieth century, with profound implications for the preservation and development of minority languages, religions, and cultures. Against this most powerful individualist credo is arrayed a near endless procession of minority claims, whose central tenet—that groups have rights—clearly challenges the fundamental liberal conception of the political contract. For it does not unduly stretch logic to claim that a group having rights to education in its own tongue, to unrestricted observance of its religious beliefs, or to recognition of any other cultural practice, also deserves the right to some form of group political recognition, be it in the form simply of self-governing cultural institutions or complete territorial independence.

Nothing has been more apparent to contemporary statesmen than the dangers to the nation-state system inherent in minority claims to moral rights. On occasion they have made concessions. But they have not made them often. Nor have they always made them permanent. They made them most copiously following World War I. That war, in whose outbreak and conclusion minorities played especially prominent roles, forced the issue of minority rights for the first time to the level of global politics. Urged along by Woodrow Wilson's unshakable faith in liberal internationalism, European statesmen decided on that occasion that the negative rights of at least some minorities should be protected. To a considerable extent they even consented to the need for protection of positive cultural rights. Furthermore, they agreed to create a system which would supply unprecedented international protection of minorities. But the League of Nations machinery they invented had barely been set in motion when issues unresolved in World War I again plunged the planet into total war, wrecking the League and leaving essentially unanswered the question how to successfully institutionalize enforcement of minority rights in a world of independent nation-states.

The League System

Decisions made by the victorious Allies at Versailles in 1919 materialized in an extensive series of minority-related international agreements signed both during and after the peace conference. Concluded not only with the defeated powers but with the new or refashioned states that emerged from the war, these agreements constituted what came to be called the League system of minority protection.[7] Under this system, minority rights were stipulated as fundamental legal obligations of the treaty-bound states, their observance guaranteed by the new League of Nations organization.

Minority rights were given unusual breadth of definition in the treaties. The Polish Minorities Treaty, the first drafted and hence the model for subsequent undertakings, was well stocked with negative guarantees of nondiscrimination and equal treatment of individuals. But it also provided for positive protection by supplying assurances for the survival and development of linguistic, religious, educational, and other minority cultural activities.[8] These latter provisions came close to giving at least implicit international sanction to group rights, since they clearly could not be realized apart from the group. But the statesmen at Versailles strenuously avoided terminology explicitly recognizing minorities as collective legal entities. Wanting to protect minority groups without giving unacceptable offense to the host states, they settled for an ambiguous and inherently troublesome formula. It inevitably aroused the political expectations of minorities, but carried the unmistakable message that nothing done at Versailles was meant to impair the concept of sovereignty or retard social integration.[9]

The protection which the League system supplied was far from unlimited. While its authors deliberately universalized the mode of enforcement by lodging it in the Council of the League of Nations, they did not lay down protective principles of universal application to minorities everywhere. The system was constructed of highly concrete cases, and treaty provisions relating to minorities were both very detailed and tailored to specific minority situations persisting in Eastern and Central

Europe.¹⁰ Even in these treaty-designated cases, intervention by the League was considerably less than automatic. Among other provisions built into the system to safeguard the prerogatives of League members was the restriction of minorities themselves to the lowly rank of informant. The League's guarantee of international sanctions was thus highly imperfect. Its effective mandate extended no further than specific treaties allowed, and these subjected League supervision to a variety of procedural restraints. ¹¹

The League system of minority protection was far too feeble to function successfully in the menacing environment that prevailed in Europe in the interwar years. This fact has tarnished the League model, perhaps irrevocably, with the stigma of failure. It is highly doubtful, however, that any other conceivable system could have withstood any better the belligerent statesmanship of that epoch. The League system was, in fact, a bold experiment, especially noteworthy in three respects: (1) it formally recognized the denial of *minority* rights as a principal cause of international conflicts; (2) it extended the mantle of international protection to the *positive* as well as negative rights of minorities (while remaining ambiguous, however, as to the group basis of positive rights); and (3) it was without precedent in the extent to which it bound the protection of minorities to the authority of an *international* institution. The League system was thus innovative in the attention paid to minorities, in the sanction given to the protection of minority cultures, and in the appointment of a universal international agency as impartial watchdog of their treaty-protected rights.

The United Nations System

The League's concept of international responsibility for the protection of minorities did not survive World War II. The statesmen who shaped the peace following that war had not forgotten the League system; but they were obviously most impressed by the League's frequent inability either to safeguard minority rights or to prevent the exploitation of minorities for subversive purposes. Consequently, when the opportunity arose to revise the League system, they unceremoniously abandoned it. In its place they built the foundations of an alternative system providing for the protection of general human rights. In so doing, they deliberately deemphasized the distinction between minority rights and ordinary individual rights, turning their backs on minority claims to special treatment. "The hard fact," observed Inis Claude, "was that statesmen, generally backed by a public opinion which was deeply impressed by the perfidy of irredentist and disloyal minorities, were disposed to curtail, rather than to expand, the rights of minorities."¹² The architects of the

United Nations system did emphasize, as had the advocates of the League system, the connection between the violation of rights and international conflict, and the urgent requirement of international concern for the prevention of such violations. And they urged the prevention of discrimination.[13] But they were conspicuously silent in regard to the positive rights of minorities. Moreover, in sharp contrast to the League model, the design of the United Nations system minimizes the international community's authority to protect rights in general and minority rights in particular. At least so far as minorities are concerned, the United Nations system amounts to a studied retreat from the limited internationalism of the League system.[14]

The United Nations human rights system admittedly far surpasses the League system in enumerating, codifying, and universalizing rights. There are today at least 40 major United Nations and regional human rights treaties in force; and they supply international endorsement for an unprecedented number of rights reaching well beyond those conventionally protected in the Western civil libertarian tradition.[15]

Many of these treaties prohibit depredations most commonly inflicted upon minorities. Prominent among these are the International Convention on the Prevention and Punishment of the Crime of Genocide, adopted in 1948, which makes criminal "acts committed with intent to destroy, in whole or in part, a national, ethnical, racial or religious group as such," and the International Convention on the Elimination of All Forms of Racial Discrimination, adopted in 1965, which bars any invidious "distinctions, exclusion, restriction or preference based on race, colour, descent, or national or ethnic origin...." Equal treatment and nondiscrimination clauses such as this last are conspicuous, in fact, are in a large number of the declarations and conventions adopted or proposed since the founding of the United Nations.[16]

But apart from the Genocide Convention's guarantee of group rights to *physical* existence, these agreements stop well short of assuming any burden for the protection of the positive rights of minorities. *None* of the human rights treaties authored in the post-World War II era provides for the differential treatment of minorities in order to preserve the particular cultural characteristics which distinguish them from other cultural groups inhabiting the state.

The reluctance to give even nominal international guarantees to positive minority rights is transparent in the lengthy discussions which preceded the final adoption of Article 27 of the International Covenant on Civil and Political Rights. This article, the only item in this basic human rights treaty to give explicit recognition to minority rights, reads as follows: "In those States in which ethnic, religious or linguistic minorities exist, persons belonging to such minorities shall not be denied the right, in community with the other members of their group, to enjoy their own culture, to profess and practice their own religion, or to use their own language." Its careful wording encumbers signatory states with no positive obligations of any kind, defines the right in terms of individual persons rather than groups, and — in its reflection of the demand by some states that the question of the existence of minorities be left to their discretion — leaves plenty of room for denying their claims. States are enjoined to foster tolerance: i.e., to protect individuals from discrimination. They are called upon neither to support cultural diversity nor to abandon assimilation. Without doubt, Article 27 was intended to protect individual members of ethnic, religious, and linguistic minorities rather than to guarantee the collective interests of minority groups. [17]

Very little institutional machinery for the effective protection of minority rights has been forthcoming under the United Nations system. The sole explicit institutional recognition of minority problems within this system is the Sub-Commission on Prevention of Discrimination and Protection of Minorities, a body created in 1947 and tucked away amongst the responsibilities of the Human Rights Commission — hardly the most prestigious, powerful, or aggressive agency of the Economic and Social Council.[18] In spite of its dual responsibilities, very little of the agenda of the subcommission has been given over to the problem of protecting minority rights. "It was only in the period 1947-1954 and again after 1971," according to a recent and authoritative report, "that the problem of minorities was included among the subjects dealt with in depth by the subcommission. From 1955 to 1971, the subcommission concentrated its activities almost entirely on questions of discrimination."[19]

In comparison with the League prototype, the United Nations system considerably enlarges the scope of individual rights, including the negative rights of minorities. But in the insistence on equal rather than exceptional rights for minorities, the United Nations system represents a substantial reduction in international commitment to minority rights. Additionally, in refusing to assert a prominent role for international authority in the settlement of disputes involving minorities, the United Nations system restores to states whatever modest responsibility for the fate of minorities had earlier been transferred to the League of Nations. On the other hand, the architects of the human rights system of the United Nations have in common with those who designed the minority system of the League profound reluctance and/or inability to invent durable devices for the effective enforcement of obligations to minorities of any kind.

Minority Protection in United States Policy

The United States launched its post-World War I international minorities policy with an inconsistency of historic proportions. On the one hand, the United States supplied much of the moral inspiration and leadership that lay behind the creation of the League system. President Woodrow Wilson was a forceful advocate of the view that minority problems were a root cause of war, and he was a dogged protagonist of the internationalist philosophy that inspired the minorities treaties. His influence, profound though it was, proved to be shortlived, however. Congressional rejection of American membership in the League of Nations and refusal to ratify the minorities treaties repudiated Wilsonian premises of international collaboration and abruptly foreclosed any U.S. participation in the enforcement of League obligations to minorities. There is little question that American abandonment considerably abridged the system's chances for success.[20]

Anticosmopolitan convictions were fashionable in the United States in the interwar years, which witnessed, among other things, passage of the most restrictive immigration laws in the country's history and growing irritation with the uncertain patriotism of certain hyphenate Americans—conspicuous among them Italians, Germans, and Japanese. The 1930s culminated in near hysteria over the reported "fifth column" activities of immigrant Fascists and Nazis, whose real or alleged disloyalty did much to sully the reputation of minorities in general.[21] When the second world war was over, Americans were no better disposed towards the international protection of minorities than anyone else. Coddling encouraged meddling, or so it was thought. Hence, it is not surprising that the United States, vigorously backed by those states which had suffered at the hands of disloyal minorities, took the lead in dismantling the League's discredited system of international protection. There were other ways to deal with the minorities problem, or so it seemed in the immediate postwar period.

One war was through assimilation, of which the United States was probably the world's most renowned practitioner. America's ethnic melting pot was yet an unimpeachable idea in those years, and to many it must have seemed admirably suited for export. For whatever losses it entailed for cultural diversity were felt more than made up for by gains to national unity. Another way to deal with the minorities problem, less attractive but with ample precedents in the American tradition, was through mass population transfer. This too had its advocates. At the Potsdam Conference in mid-summer 1945, for example, President Harry Truman readily consented to the forced removal of minority groups (mainly Germans) from their Eastern European homelands. Many millions were uprooted in this involuntary exodus, one of the harshest and most massive in modern times.[22].

Having broken with the League model, the United States should have found much to applaud in the system of minority protection developed by the United Nations over the next several decades. But even the United Nations' minimalist approach failed to receive more than the slenderest American endorsement. Not until 1977—over a decade since their adoption by the General Assembly—did the United States government even sign the two principal human rights covenants. Not until February 1978 did it transmit to the Senate for its consideration the International Convention on the Elimination of All Forms of Racial Discrimination, which is of special interest to minority groups, in spite of the fact that over 90 states had already ratified the Convention in the 13 years since its adoption by the General Assembly in 1965. And the United States Senate refuses yet to ratify what is for minorities the most elementary of all protective agreements—the Genocide Convention adopted in 1948.

I do not mean to suggest that the United States, in proving so reluctant to participate in the formal elaboration of the new system, has a worse overall record with regard to minority protection than most other states. Ratifying treaties, as we all know, is no assurance of good will toward men. Nor do I wish to imply that the aloofness of the United States betokens extraordinary hostility for the idea of minority rights. America's political leaders have rejected virtually the entire accumulation of human rights instruments produced by the United Nations, regardless of content. But the fact remains that the United States has maintained for decades an Olympian detachment from the problem of international minority protection that is without parallel among the major states of the world.

The reasons for America's detachment are not entirely obvious, but their relationship to East-West and North-South controversies in the United Nations is unquestionable.[23] America's test of wills with the Soviet Union and, more recently, with the less developed countries has pervaded all the work of the United Nations—including the protection of minorities.[24] It was naturally impossible to proceed with the definition of their rights uninfluenced by the strategic and ideological interests inevitably at stake in deliberations of such sensitivity. Whether mistaken or not, American interests were rarely seen to coincide with those of the world's minorities.

We have entered, rather awkwardly, upon an era of detente with the Soviet Union; and there are signs that mutual understanding may not be impossible between the wealthy industrial states and at least parts of the Third World. With these changes—perhaps to some extent because of them—has come renewed interest in the international protection of minorities. In fact, a new debate over international protection has already begun.[25] There are thus compelling reasons for Americans to reconsider the arguments on both sides of international protection. We proceed now to an examination of them.

The Debate over International Protection

The word "minority" may convey a misleading sense of the importance of minority groups. They are, by definition, smaller than the majority.[26] But nothing could be more inaccurate than to think that they therefore constitute—singly or in batches—a small force on the global stage. While it would be extraordinarily difficult to state with any precision what percentage of the world's inhabitants consists of racial, linguistic, and religious minorities, the percentage is certainly large. Minorities, by whatever criteria of definition, include many hundreds of millions of people. Consider, for example, the Soviet Union. Even if we count as minorities only the non-Slavic (rather than non-Russian) nationalities, we are still reckoning with roughly 26% of its 1970 population, or over 62 million people.[27] India is an even richer storehouse of minorities. While its Hindus vastly outnumber the Muslim *religious* minority, its non-Hindi-speaking *linguistic* minorities are collectively—in this land of 650 million—a mammoth, albeit polyglot, majority.[28] Much the same story is told in Nigeria, Yugoslavia, Ethiopia, Lebanon, Switzerland, Zaire, Burma, and scores of other countries.

The source of all these minorities is, of course, ethnic heterogeneity, which is the rule in practically all states. There are homogeneous or nearly homogeneous societies—Japan, both Koreas, and some of the Scandinavian states are among them. But they are relatively rare. States with minorities are unquestionably in the majority.[29]

Neither the abundance nor the near ubiquity of ethnic minorities would justify, by itself, their international protection. But it is essential that we proceed with examination of the arguments entirely disabused of the notion that minorities are mainly folkloric curiousities, costumed dancers brought out of cultural storage on special occasions. Minorities are residuals, but not anachronisms, of the historical process. An endangered species, they are yet far from extinction.

The following arguments do not exhaust either the case for or the case against international protection of minorities. I have selected for discussion only those which seem to me the stronger arguments.

The Case For Protection

1. *The minorities problem is permanent.* For a while after World War

II, it was fashionable among statesmen and scholars to assume the imminent disappearance of many or even most ethnic minorities. The war itself had hastened the departure of some: most of Europe's Jews had been physically liquidated and many of those remaining sought refuge in Israel, where Jews themselves were in the majority; German minorities were in large part forcibly repatriated to Germany, cleansing Eastern Europe of a particularly nettlesome problem; and numerous other minorities were likewise eliminated or at least reduced in size through a succession of population transfers and border rectifications at the war's end.[30] Of course, many minorities remained, in and out of Europe. But these, it was apparently believed, would succumb more or less gracefully to the inexorable forces of assimilation. Urbanization, industrialization, mass education, and the secularizing influences of science and technology would surely finish what violence had so well begun.

The assumption of minority impermanence proved to be profoundly mistaken.[31] There are more politically aroused minorities today than when the war ended; and they are noisier than ever. Minorities whose existence was a short time ago known only to ethnographers and perhaps a handful of civil servants are today assassinating statesmen, hijacking jets and railway trains, planting bombs, threatening secession, waging guerrilla war, and occasionally toppling governments. The French, who did not think they had any minorities, have banned four autonomist movements.[32] Few of us can think of any minority problems that have been amicably resolved.[33] All of us can name a dozen which have not been. Minorities we thought had long since accommodated themselves to genteel forms of domination (Scots, Welsh, French Canadians) suddenly reemerge with immodest demands for independence. Writers search for metaphors to describe the widening circle of minority turbulence in the contemporary era. One calls it "a convulsive ingathering of people"; another, "the universalization of ethnicity."[34]

Obviously, not every minority is retreating from social ecumenicism, or stands poised on the edge of open rebellion. Assimilation has taken a substantial toll of ethnic identities, in some cases virtually obliterating them and in many other cases at least nibbling away at the edges. Boundary changes, population transfers, jurisdictional concessions, and various "consociational" arrangements have been often and usefully employed to keep minority problems within manageable limits without resort to coercion.[35]

But it requires an unusual exertion of faith to believe that the average government of a multiethnic state—usually poor, ethnically hodgepodge, and lacking in talented leaders—can or will keep up in *these* ways with the astonishingly rapid and explosive political mobilization of minorities.[36]. *The minorities problem is permanent not only because most of the world's minorities have refused to disappear, but because they are asking more and more for what most governments are quite unable or unwilling to deliver.*

Almost everywhere minorities are inundating governments with demands for change. What they demand varies with circumstances: claims for change in territorial jurisdiction are emphasized by some groups; for equalization of social, economic, or political opportunity by others; and for less restrictive controls on internal or external population movements by still others. Minorities are not monolithic entities, uniformly agreed on the kinds of rights which minorities ought to have; there is not consensus among them, in fact, that they ought to have any rights at all apart from the majority.[37] While there are groups, or parts of groups, therefore, which would settle happily for cultural integration, there is clearly a strong accent on claims for positive rights—those which would help assure cultural survival. The sentiment is widely shared that minorities are right-bearing units, legal selves in at least certain respects equal to the quantitative majorities. Frequent declarations of at least cultural independence have resulted, challenging well-established notions of majority rule.[38] Minorities are not now demanding merely equal rights, but equality of separate rights.[39] It is a revolutionary development. The popular justification for it, of course, is the allegedly primordial right of self-determination.

The concept of self-determination has certain obvious virtues and a number of equally obvious faults.[40] Its cardinal fault is its ambiguity, which has been apparent from the concept's birth.[41] Statesmen have freely attached various meanings to it, some having found such a principle very useful in their own endeavors first to liberate from colonial rule and then to secure the independence of the new states.[42] But statesmen of every hue—rabid revolutionaries and the most bloated colonialists—have generally stood shoulder to shoulder denying its pertinence to minorities. Few would have found anything objectionable in a remark made by the late Secretary General U Thant in 1970. "So, as far as the question of secession of a particular section of a Member State is concerned," he said,

> the United Nations' attitude is unequivocable [sic]. As an international organization, the United Nations has never accepted and does not accept and I do not believe it will ever accept the principle of secession of a part of its Member State.[43]

As contemporary statesmen tend to see it, self-determination was clearly not meant to serve as an absolute principle, available to discontented citizens of independent states on the same terms as to the subject peoples of crumbling European empires. What was good for the colonized goose was not necessarily right for the minority gander.

It is easier, however, to chastize minorities for exaggerating their claims than to hold them back from realizing them. With the world's bemused statesmen looking on, self-determination has grown from a principle of limited application into a much-invoked right with universal implications. A milestone in its progress was the adoption by the United Nations in 1966 of the two human rights covenants, both of which unequivocally endorsed self-determination as a fundamental right in their first article. In identical words, the right to "freely determine their political status and freely pursue their economic, social, and cultural development" was pledged to *all peoples*. Although it is certain that the covenants' authors did not intend to indulge the separatist tendencies of minorities in existing states, or to give credence to the radical notion of "internal colonialism," the wording adopted does precisely that.[44] Semanticists continue to dispute the meaning of "peoples," but for minorities the issue is essentially closed: they have a right of self-determination equal to that of all other ethnic communities with whom they share the state.

By insisting that the principle of self-determination sanctions some degree of cultural separation, minorities are obviously demanding rights that preclude easy compromise with political leaders nurtured on the absolute nature of state sovereignty and intent upon cultural absorption. These often sharply antithetic objectives introduce at least the shadow of secession into virtually every ethnic conflict, and supply the primary explanation for the permanence of the minorities problem. They also compel reconsideration of international protective devices. International protection may not itself contain the liberated genie of self-determination; and it is hardly a foolproof remedy for the destructive impulses of the nation-state system. But it is one of few apparent alternatives to endless and savage civil strife. It need no longer be feared that international protection will itself encourage the political alienation of minorities, and is therefore to be avoided. We know now that the spirit of secession flourishes without any protection at all.

2. *Government treatment of minorities is commonly intolerable.* This is an innocuous statement in the abstract, since there is near universal agreement that minorities are generally mishandled. Imagine, however, trying to obtain consensus as to which governments were administering intolerable treatment—or as to precisely which kinds of treatment were intolerable! In regard to such matters, judgment is inevitably torn between the rival desiderata of majorities and minorities, and is naturally colored by legitimate discrepancies in societal objectives. Unfortunately,

it is often difficult, if not impossible, to maximize minority interests at no expense to other groups and other goals; mistreatment is not born exclusively of illwill and stupidity, nor are minorities wholly innocent of responsibility. Minorities, furthermore, are often on the frontline of ideological warfare, where dispassionate analysis of their treatment is highly improbable. In this Orwellian age, repression masquerades as liberation with confusing regularity. Information, when not entirely lacking, is frequently vague, contrived, or exaggerated. Let us forthrightly acknowledge, therefore, that there is no common standard of tolerable treatment, and that, even if there were, it would still be extremely difficult to fix responsibility for some misdeeds. It is fully possible, even likely, under such circumstances, that two astute observers of an encounter between government and minority will arrive at diametrically opposed conclusions.[45]

Granted, then, that we have here a statement simply infested with ambiguities, unacceptable except as generalization. Applied to particular cases, it is easy prey to subjectivity and partisanship.

But the statement, as generalization, would be difficult to contest. Virtually every government on earth has affixed its signature to one or more international legal instruments inspired in large measure by frequent and harsh victimization of minorities. Nothing could more forcefully make the point than their overwhelming endorsement of it. The human tragedy of forcible mass dispersion and expulsion; of political, economic, and social discrimination; and of wholesale liquidation is more than amply documented.[46]. Members of minorities have died violently in the twentieth century far out of proportion to their numbers. Estimates of global carnage seem agreed on that.[47] The London-based Minority Rights Group has completed over 35 studies of abused minorities; and it has a long way to go before the subject will have been exhausted.

Governments certainly differ enormously in their regard for minority welfare. Systematic, unrelenting, and pitiless persecution of minorities, of the sort waged by Nazi Germany against the Jewish people of Central and Eastern Europe, is rare on this planet. Few governments are ruled by genocidal maniacs. On the other hand, it seems that few, if any, are entirely immune from occasional fits of barbarism. In recent decades, ghastly atrocities against innocent civilian members of minority groups have been officially inspired or at least tacitly approved by governments as far removed from one another in ideology, political structure, and record of humane observance of human rights as Israel and Burundi.[48] The well-being of ethnic minorities is nowhere automatically and irreversibly secured.

There is not much hope, either, for the early abatement of mistreatment. Minorities are not only vociferously demanding their rights. As pointed out above, they are busily extending the list of rights—and, by implication, of the kinds of treatment that they consider intolerable. Even if governments grow no more heavy-handed in their management of minorities, the range of what is considered intolerable treatment is almost bound to lengthen. And with that, so too will grow minority resentments, government efforts to contain them and, thus, the probability of mistreatment. Eighty-three governments have thus far ratified the Genocide Convention of 1948 which guards minorities against government-inflicted mental and bodily injuries. But it does not protect minority interests in *cultural* survival.[49] Since progressive cultural integration is at least the implied objective of most contemporary multiethnic states, including all of the largest and most powerful of them, the basis for claims of intolerable treatment seems firmly established.

While reluctant to supply effective international protection, governments have, in principle, long since conceded that the treatment of minorities has generally been poor and that *some* form of protection for *some* of the rights of their *individual* members is desirable. But government treatment can hardly avoid being intolerable where minorities claim what governments uniformly believe has no right to protection of any kind.

3. *The minorities problem is inescapably international.* "Nothing," observed Woodrow Wilson at the Versailles Peace Conference in May 1919, "is more likely to disturb the peace of the world than the treatment which might in certain circumstances be meted out to minorities."[50] In November 1977, almost 60 years later, the Security Council of the United Nations unanimously imposed a mandatory arms embargo on the Republic of South Africa on the grounds that arms exports to that racially troubled state constituted a threat to the peace.[51] In between these two events nothing occurred to diminish the almost universal conviction that minority problems (including those in which the minority happens to be dominant) rank high among the sources of violent international conflict. Minority problems figured prominently in the events precipitating both world wars; and they have been central issues in a great many of the lesser violent struggles of this century.

The "trigger" effect of minority problems has almost certainly been exaggerated. What Suhrke and Noble call the "Wilsonian postulate"—the belief "that internal ethnic conflict constitutes a major source of international conflict"—neglects the restraining effect which the ethnic dimension often exercises in international conflict, and fails to give adequate attention to the international collaborative endeavors which internal ethnic disputes frequently inspire.⁵² So far as international relations are concerned, minority problems are not inevitably poisonous.

Nevertheless, they are exceedingly difficult to contain within domestic boundaries. One reason for this, obviously, is that outsiders often have enormous motivation to become involved. They have made good use of minorities, for example, to influence or subvert host governments. Adolf Hitler was a master manipulator of ethnic "fifth columns"; and his techniques, applied liberally to dozens of ethnic German minority settlements in Europe and abroad in the 1930s, have been emulated on numerous occasions since.⁵³ In some regions of the globe, the rush to intervene presents an amazing spectacle. Take the African Horn, for example. In that ethnically polyglot and politically tumultuous area, writes Walker Connor, there has been an almost irresistible temptation "to ride Trojan horses that graze within another's gates. In the early 1970s," he says,

> the Libyan government was furnishing assistance to a separatist movement across its southern border in Chad. While deploring this intervention, the Chad government was offering aid and sanctuary to black insurrectionists in the southern Sudan. While trying to suppress this movement, the authorities at Khartoum were simultaneously supporting a separatist movement within the Eritrean sector of Ethiopia. Ethiopia, which was fighting a number of separatist movements in addition to that of the Eritreans, was countering by joining Chad (as well as Uganda) in aiding the blacks of the southern Sudan.⁵⁴

The poisonous agent, all of this would imply, is often extraterritorial.

Minorities are not always innocent bystanders, let me hasten to add, for external interference occurs often at their behest. Minorities have natural disabilities: they are always smaller, usually weaker, than the majorities. One way to offset these disadvantages is to invite the collaboration of outsiders. I have in front of me, for example, a recent newspaper report revealingly headlined: "Remote Karens Wonder Why World Ignores Them."⁵⁵ The Karens are a mainly Christian minority occupying the east-central portion of Burma adjacent to Thailand. At present virtually independent of Burmese control, they seek to guarantee their long-term survival with outside assistance. Pleas for international attention similar to theirs have been heard from scores of other minorities in the same straits.⁵⁶ Without adequate resources of their own, and with little reason in most cases to expect much generosity from their internal enemies, minorities naturally go hunting for external allies. The record suggests that they usually find them.⁵⁷

The full story of the Palestine Liberation Organization's (PLO) colossal efforts to obtain international assistance in the struggle against

Israel has yet to be told. When it is, there will be revealed an unparalleled attempt to win the support of outsiders for goals absolutely beyond the reach of Palestinian Arabs acting alone. The PLO sought and won recognition of its political legitimacy from individual states, ceremonial honors and observer status from the global United Nations organization, full membership in the regional League of Arab States, and confirmation by Arab states of its claim to be sole negotiating representative of the Palestinian Arab people. It secured vast sums of money, combat training, arms, and indispensable sanctuary from Arab and other states. It obtained countless endorsements in support of its claims from public and private, governmental and intergovernmental organizations of every description. Success (in late 1978) was still eluding the PLO. But it had already supplied the world—and how many other minorities?—with a matchless model of internationalized minority struggle.[58]

The repeated insistence that minority problems are domestic problems, and that their control is therefore exclusively or mainly a domestic affair, pays tribute to the powerful shibboleth of state sovereignty. But it entirely ignores the facts. Minorities are major international actors.[59] They persist in their efforts to escalate local into international conflicts because they cannot win them otherwise. And outsiders, often for reasons having little or nothing to do with ethnicity, not infrequently welcome their efforts. The minorities problem is inescapably international because, to a very substantial degree, the minorities problem is an internationally *caused* problem. Foreign governments instigate, intensify, and prolong ethnic disputes, manipulating minority grievances for their own ends. Noninterference is a rule observed consistently by very few. International protection would help to safeguard the rule, while supplying alternative and impartial means for the settlement of minority disputes.

The Case Against Protection

1. *Minority identities resist internationally acceptable definition.* There have been many scholarly efforts to define precise criteria of ethnic group membership. None has succeeded so far and one suspects that the mission may be impossible.[60] Tidy-looking definitions may be concocted for textbooks but they rapidly disintegrate in the field. There, as many social scientists have warned us, ethnic identities cannot be sorted out and counted like colored beads. "Identity," one recent analyst points out, "is a subjective self-concept; cultural self-definitions are among the social roles individuals may assume in a given situation."[61] Situations change; so do identities. And there is more than one kind of ethnic identity (racial, linguistic, religious) in the ordinary in-

dividual's repertory of social roles. In their collective state, these identities often overlap and intermingle, so that in all but the most polarized societies even the boundaries between majority and minority become obscured. Ethnic identities are not infinitely elastic but they are sufficiently pliant to keep ethnographers baffled.

Under any circumstances, it would be very difficult to reconcile all such ambiguities sufficiently to universalize the definition of ethnic minorities. And some definition would be imperative in a regime of international protection: it is clearly impossible to protect what cannot be identified. But one suspects that there are shrewd diplomats who could find the right words to make the venture practicable were the problem merely lexical.

Unfortunately, it is not. Ethnic identities are tightly interlinked with political struggles, some of them stretching back to antiquity, most of them with high stakes. Ethnic identities (majority and minority) inspire conflicts and are major weapons in them. One cannot apply inflexible definitions of ethnicity to them without describing—and perhaps influencing—an inherently political situation.

A particularly good illustration of this is found in contemporary Turkey. The Kurdish population of Turkey, settled mainly in eastern Anatolia and numbering over four million (or roughly 10% of the population), poses a potentially severe security problem for the Turkish government. Turkish leaders have been understandably concerned for much of the 20th century with the loyalties of their frontier minorities—especially the Kurds, who are susceptible to the appeals of the pan-Kurdish movement. Ever since Ataturk launched Turkey on its modernizing mission in the 1920s, the Turkish response to Kurdish nationalism has consistently been to accelerate "turkification" and thereby, through cultural integration, to eliminate the threat of minority dissidence or secession. To this end, the Turkish government has banned the use of Kurdish on radio and television, and has forbidden study of written Kurdish in the schools; it has denied Kurds separate political recognition of any kind, promoted their resettlement in non-Kurdish areas, and in other ways discouraged Kurdish self-determination. The assertion that Kurds even exist in Turkey is blankly rejected: in Turkey Kurds are officially classified as "mountain Turks."[62]

One may or may not sympathize with the Turkish government in its efforts to strengthen Turkish nationalism at the expense of ethnic minorities. But there can be no doubt that any effort by the international community to define minority identities could help to "define" the existence—and hence dignify the rights—of the Turkish Kurds, and thus contribute to the outcome of a long struggle which the Turks believe, no doubt, is theirs to decide. In an early draft of a study on minority rights prepared in 1972 by a special rapporteur of the Subcommission on Prevention of Discrimination and Protection of Minorities, a working definition of minority was proposed, as follows: "an ethnic, religious or linguistic minority is a group numerically smaller than the rest of the population of the State to which it belongs and possessing cultural, physical or historical characteristics, a religion or a language different from those of the rest of the population. A group may constitute a minority *even if it has never been mentioned as such in the legislation or by the public of the country to which it belongs.*"[63] Although the rapporteur took special care to disavow any intent to foster interference in internal affairs, his definition, for obvious reasons, would not have had much appeal for the Turks.[64]

Internationally agreed definitions both reflect and may alter the political balance.[65]. Accordingly, no reasonable international definition of ethnic minorities could consistently escape the appearance of political intervention. Indeed, there would be little point to the definitional exercise were intervention to assure observance of minority rights not contemplated under any circumstances. It is by no means established, however, that such intervention—even if unintentional—would be wholly desirable in every case. A definition meant to resolve may instead fuel disputes involving minorities. It may encourage governments to retreat from culturally accommodative strategies in order not to hinder natural processes of cultural integration and assimilation. Or it may inspire political oppositions to accent cultural cleavages where only the thinnest veneer of cultural difference actually exists.

Minority rights can be and often have been *declared*, of course, without the existence of an internationally agreed definition of an ethnic minority.[66] But minority rights will not be universally and successfully *defended* until there is a consensual and actionable international definition of a minority. Since this development is neither very likely nor in every respect desirable, the most prudent course for the international community is to concentrate on securing for minorities the same rights which it seeks to secure for majorities—general human rights. These rights, like the rights of minorities, are troubled with definitional ambiguities. But there is no difficulty at all in defining the subject of protection—the individual.

2. *Protection of minorities conflicts with alternative societal goals.* The international protection of minorities does imply the imposition of limitations upon the sovereignty of states. In effect, minorities become clients of the international community in a manner somewhat reminiscent of the way in which native Indians became wards of the American

federal government in the last century. And they become such for essentially the same reason: the failure of "local" governments to adequately protect them. The limitations on local authority may not amount to much in practice: but the *principle* of international protection, once established, clearly works against the "marked inertial propensity" of the nation-state system to preserve itself against all challengers—humanitarian-minded international organizations and secession-minded minorities included.[67] Most of the European states upon which the minority treaties of the League system were urged never ceased to view them with distaste. They recognized, as we must, that minority protection, to the extent that it encourages separate cultural self-consciousness, may interfere with national unity.

Now there is nothing especially sacrosanct about existing states, their governmental systems or boundaries; nor is there any good reason why every minority group should wish to preserve them or remain within them. There are compelling reasons, in fact, for many minorities to feel no loyalty to the state at all. Let us in fairness admit, however, that states do have legitimate reasons to be concerned about national unity. Some minorities are receptive to the blandishments of foreign powers, whose manipulation of discontented elements within minority groups is not uniformly in the interests either of political stability or of greater social justice. Minorities concentrated in frontier districts are particularly attractive targets of subversion—and particularly menacing to state security. The Peoples Republic of China is concerned about the loyalties of its Tibetan, Mongol, and other minorities for good reason.[68] There is far less reason, in fact, to expect the fragile and ethnically heterogeneous states of the Third World to enthusiastically embrace a legal regime which might threaten their territorial integrity and newly won independence. In spite of the fact that Indian minorities abroad have often been subject to discrimination and sometimes to cruel persecution, India has displayed little interest in universalizing the protection of minorities. Charged with governing one of the most ethnically fragmented of all modern states, India's leaders might be excused for their extraordinary sensitivity on the subject of minority rights.[69]

The urge to preserve is not the sole reason for state objections to international protection, nor is it the sole societal goal with which minority expectations may conflict. One must realize that governmental efforts to pursue the broad public interest in the *economic* sector might not be well served by respecting minority interests. The highly uneven pace of modernization and economic development, and the far from equal distribution of resources from one ethnic community to another are realities widely recognized in such countries as Zaire, Nigeria, Malaysia,

India, and Pakistan. Emphasis on minority rights in such societies can disguise ulterior motives and help to perpetuate gross socioeconomic inequalities.[70]

Political leaders are not the only ones to worry about the divided loyalty of minorities. Such fear is not uncommon among minorities themselves. The ambivalence of American Jews, for example, on the subject of minority rights is well known. While in the forefront of those demanding international protection against discrimination (i.e., negative minority rights), they have in recent decades shown little interest in a regime incorporating positive rights which would accent their alien origins by singling them out for special treatment. Jewish integration into American society has progressed very rapidly since World War II, promising an end to the plague of antisemitism. While cultural extinction must seem to many a severe penalty to avoid the charge of tepid loyalty, at present most American Jews seem disposed to safeguard corporate communal interests without aid of international guarantees for their cultural survival.[71]

On a more philosophical plane, societies may object to international protection of minorities on the grounds that it encourages entrenchment of regressive inegalitarian and illiberal values. In his discussion of Canada's French-Canadian dilemma, sociologist John Porter argues that the contemporary revival of ethnicity and increasing "saliency of ethnic differences is a retreat from the liberal notions of the unity of mankind." He suggests that

> citizenship rights are essentially universalistic whereas group rights are essentially particularistic. One of the reasons why many developing societies cannot be compared with modern societies is that they have not yet embodied some, or indeed any, of these citizenship rights in either their value systems or their social organization. They remain essentially premodern, emphasizing tribalism and localism and resolving their ethnic conflicts, sometimes even to the point of genocide, with the particularistic focus. In modern western nations that have established democratic procedures and, albeit inadequately, but nonetheless perceptively, have developed the social rights of citizenship, ethnic conflict is about equality of condition and full participation in a modernizing opportunity structure as well as the political community. To resort to the group basis of settling claims, if necessary, is regrettable.[72]

It is difficult enough, in other words, to defend universalistic individual rights against tyranny. Societies should not be burdened with having to contend, also, against the particularistic rights of groups.[73]

3. *Equal and impartial enforcement of minority rights is improbable.* In retrospect it may seem rather quaint that the leaders of the Allied Powers in World War I felt no compunction in excusing their own coun-

tries from the rules drafted for the protection of ethnic minorities in Eastern and Central Europe. Obviously these same countries have subsequently not proven immune to minority problems or to the allegations of discrimination and oppression that stem from them. Under the circumstances, charges of hypocrisy and double standards were unavoidable. The League system was bluntly imposed by the powerful on the weak, presumably for the good of all. The weak did not like it; but there was nothing much they could do about it.

Allied statesmen were uninterested in applying the rules equally; and they were apparently unable or unwilling to apply them impartially. The French, preoccupied in the interwar years with their own security, were far less interested in supervising Poland's observance of its obligations to minorities than in strengthening Poland's resolve against Germany. Britain pursued peace much more avidly than social justice, and seemed powerless to prevent Germany and other revisionist states from flagrant interference in disputes involving client minorities. The demise of Czechoslovakia stands as an unpleasant reminder of this. [74] On very few occasions, in fact, did *realpolitik* defer to the juridical authority of the League system. Regarding impartiality, the record of that experiment is relatively disillusioning.

Strong states are no more interested today in subjecting themselves to international scrutiny than they were a half century ago. But since the weak have a much larger voice today in drafting the rules than they did in 1919, treaties as unequal as were the Minorities Treaties have small chance of adoption. Neither do less discriminatory treaties, however, since the weak are agreed with the strong that the less international meddling in minority affairs the better for everyone.

We need not dwell long on this argument. We live in an era of violent creeds, of deceit and distrust, of gigantic inequalities, and of feeble international peace-keeping institutions. These are terribly inhospitable conditions for the impartial adjudication of disputes involving ethnic minorities. They are not an absolute bar to a new system of international protection. But they guarantee that for most contemporary states, participation, as in the past, would be reluctant at best.

The Alternatives to International Protection

The preceding discussion suggests that we are in a quandary with regard to international protection, for the merits of arguments on either side are considerable. The international community is wrong to deny minorities its protection, it seems, but for good reasons! Before we take up the question whether there is any way out of this impasse, we should pause briefly to consider the alternatives to international protection. The world has had opportunity to experiment with a number of them and knows well their uses and limitations. The alternatives fall somewhere between total neglect and complete international protection. They are unlikely to solve the minorities problem on their own; but they have supplied minorities with protection in the past, and presumably will continue to do so, regardless of whether an internationally fabricated system is reintroduced.

Kin-State Protection

Inis Claude defined a kin-state as "a state which regards itself as standing in a special relationship to a national minority in another state, by reason of ethnic affinity, ..."[75] This "special relationship" has always been a troublesome factor in bilateral relations. The multilaterally guaranteed Minorities Treaties after World War I were intended to neutralize it; but their failure to prevent Nazi Germany's grotesque abuse of its ties to German-speaking minorities abroad in the 1930s cast a dark shadow over *avant garde* solutions. Bilateral and multilateral agreements on minorities problems were not entirely abandoned by any means. There have been many international treaties and similar measures since World War II which at least implicitly recognize the dangers and the responsibilities that continue to inhere in the kin-state connection.[76] Nonetheless, the disillusioned statesmen of the 1940s essentially restored responsibility for minorities problems to the level of the state, where it remains today a standing invitation to the ad hoc activation of the special relationship.

The relationship has been activated many times, in fact, since World War II — by India (on behalf of the Indian minority of South Africa), by Ireland (on behalf of the Catholic minority of Northern Ireland), by Mexico (on behalf of the Mexican minority in the United States), by Turkey (on behalf of the Turkish Cypriots), by Somalia (on behalf of the Somali minority of Ethiopia), by both Chinas (on behalf of overseas Chinese minorities in Southeast Asia), by Israel (on behalf of Jewish minorities in many Arab countries and in the Soviet Union), and by any number of Arab states (on behalf of the Arab minority under Israeli control). The Arabs—and the Islamic states in general—have been particularly active in the kin-state role. Apart from the Palestinians, the Muslim minorities of the Philippines, Ethiopia, Chad, France, and Thailand have all been the recipients of bilateral or multilateral assistance from their Islamic brothers in recent years. [77]

One does not have to linger very long over these illustrations to recognize that kin-state protection yields very mixed results. The predominantly Muslim Eritreans of Ethiopia's Red Sea coast clearly owe much of the success they have had in recent years to Arab (or Muslim) kin-states of the region; but with regard to the Palestinian Arabs, there is some question whether the Arab states have done more to help or to handicap them over the past several decades.[78] The Peoples Republic of China could not prevent the massacre of thousands of Chinese in Indonesia in 1965 or the mass expulsion of Chinese from Vietnam in 1978; and, while the entire 36-nation Islamic Conference lined up against him in late 1976, President Marcos of the Philippines has by no means completely foresworn the use of military force to settle the Moro question in the southern part of his country.[79] Even where the application of kin-state pressures might be judged at least temporarily successful, as in Eritrea, the criteria of success would necessarily have to exclude avoidance of extensive bloodshed.

There are several reasons (apart from its bloodiness) for the general inadequacy of the kin-state approach to minority protection: (1) Many ethnic minority groups do not have any kin-state from which they could even theoretically expect support. Some of these (e.g., Tibetans, Navajos, Nagas, Sikhs, Australian aborigines, Basques, Bashkirs) are located entirely or almost entirely within the borders of one state; others (e.g., Kurds, Gypsies, Baluchis, Meos, Berbers, Armenians) are distributed in substantial numbers over two or more states, but are minorities wherever they dwell. (2) Other minority groups (e.g., Chinese Mongols, Yugoslavian Albanians, Vietnamese Christians, Soviet Rumanians) have a nominal kin-state (or states), but their putative defenders are too weak, too remote, or too disinterested to intercede effectively. There are plenty of question marks in this category, since the solidarity of many potentially forceful kin-states with their wandering kinsmen (France and the French-Canadians? Britain and the British South Africans?) has not yet been put to the test. (3) The protection of minorities must compete with the kin-state's other interests, many of which often take priority. The 13 million or so overseas Chinese of Southeast Asia should be able to relax in their adopted lands secure in the knowledge that there are 900 million mainlanders to lend them a hand whenever necessary. While China's "sojourners" abroad may at some future point enjoy this happy condition, it is very apparent that they do not now do so. The overseas Chinese have been a valuable asset to China—Nationalist and Communist. But they have not been enough of an asset, it seems, to offset the costs of their protection to competing diplomatic objectives. There is good evidence that Peking in recent decades has been abandoning China's historically highly protective posture towards the overseas Chinese in favor of a diplomatically far more attractive policy of "decolonization."[80] (4) There is a very fine line between kin-state protection and subversion; and that line has often been crossed. Adolf Hitler pressed irredentist claims in the guise of humanitarianism. Others have done so since, though rarely with so little concern for appearances.[81] (5) Kin-state protection, especially if it is urged by a stronger upon a weaker state, commonly has the appearance of bullying. Bullying might not in every case be entirely devoid of merit (Turkish military intervention on Cyprus may fall in this category); but it is hardly an ideal way to assure the impartial adjudication of disputes, or goodwill among nations.

Transnational Protection

Governments are not the only agencies which can supply protection to minorities. Minorities can draw upon the resources of many kinds of nongovernmental organizations (NGOs)—multinational business and financial; racial and ethnic; professional and trade union; religious and humanitarian; political and ideological—whose activities cut across the boundaries of states, and which are, at least in part, concerned with the well-being of particular ethnic groups or of minorities in general. The importance of these so-called "transnational actors" is now widely recognized.[82] They carry on their own "foreign policies," sometimes in collusion with, other times in spite of, the policies of their own governments. They forge alliances with other NGOs, or with sympathetic governmental and intergovernmental agencies. They have wide-ranging capabilities to assist minorities with information gathering and publicity, foreign policy lobbying of friendly governments, fund raising, economic sanctions, and even weapons supply. They are extremely diverse and numerous; and their talents, motives, and resources vary enormously. Some of them (e.g., Amnesty International, International Commission of Jurists, World Council of Churches) have a major and sustained role in the global protection of minorities. Others (e.g., Irish-American groups protesting British treatment of Irish Catholics in Northern Ireland) are activated by their interest in particular situations or events. The transnationals can be surprisingly effective. At no time in the twentieth century, for example, have the rights of a minority been more widely or vociferously defended than in the present decade over the right to emigrate of the Soviet Union's Jewish minority.

Soviet reluctance to lift restrictions on Jewish emigration provoked a transnational organizational effort in the late 1960s which, when it peaked in 1973, must have looked in Soviet eyes like a Jewish Armada. There are hundreds of local, state, and national Jewish organizations in the United States alone, and many of the more powerful and prestigious of them—Hadassah, B'nai B'rith, Zionist Organization of America, Synagogue Council of America, American Jewish Committee—contributed to the campaign to pressure the Soviets into a more liberal view of emigration rights. The movement spawned many of its own local and national organizations; and in many other countries, Jewish groups (such as the French League Against Antisemitism) were similarly mobilized. A series of international Jewish conferences—the Conference on Problems of Soviet Jewry (Paris 1960), the World Conference of Jewish Communities on Soviet Jewry (convened in Brussels in 1971)—forged transnational solidarity and gave the effort global visibility. In the space of little more than a month at one point in the campaign, rallies, teach-ins, sit-ins, protest marches, torchlight parades, and other kinds of demonstrations in support of Jewish emigration occurred in places as distant from one another as Buenos Aires, Copenhagen, Cape Town, Rome, Mexico City, Amsterdam, New Zealand, and New York.[83]

The Jewish assault on Soviet policy was joined by many non-Jewish individuals and groups in the United States, many of them responding to the larger human rights issues symbolized by the Jewish protest. And abroad, at one time or another the Socialist International and the Communist and Socialist parties of France, Holland, Austria, Britain, and Australia were aroused to protest Soviet treatment of Jews.[84] Obviously, governments—including that of the United States and the Israeli kin-state—also played a highly significant role in the course of events.[85]

The Jewish emigration issue provoked a storm of controversy, especially in the United States, over the compatibility of minority interests with the national interest. It recalled many earlier debates in this country over the role of the "ethnic lobby," and dramatized a major handicap of the transnational alternative. Most transnational organizations are exceedingly weak and cannot really compete successfully against governments. Without the collaboration of the U.S. government, the congressional branch in particular, it is virtually certain that the Jewish emigration campaign against the Soviet Union would not have succeeded in facilitating the emigration of well over 100,000 Jews.[86]

There are other factors, of course, which undermine confidence in the protective capabilities of transnationalism. Many transnational organizations make no pretense to universality, leaving large numbers of minorities unprotected. Admittedly, an organization like Amnesty International does give attention to offenses against minorities in all parts of the globe; but its concerns do not extend much beyond abuses against the individual rights of political prisoners, whether or not they happen to be members of minority groups. Amnesty International deserves its excellent reputation; but its work hardly begins to satisfy the aspirations of the world's minorities.

In an especially well-informed and revealing study of the transnational antiapartheid movement, Shepherd argues that foreign (Western) governments have chiefly been obstacles to progress in South Africa and that transnational organizations are the best, perhaps the only, alternative available.[87] He may be right, in this case at least, about both the governments and the transnationals. But the extraordinarily large, active, and highly motivated antiapartheid movement (which concerns the plight of a very conspicuous and widely supported black *majority*) is not to be compared with transnational activities, if any, undertaken to relieve the plight of those scores of minorities (including many in black African states) whose situation does not hold the same fascination for the transnational human rights community.[88]

Transnational protection has been greatly facilitated by contemporary developments in communications and transportation technology; there *is* something new under the sun when American Jewish leaders can speak directly via telephone with Soviet Jewish dissidents, or stand beside them after a short flight by supersonic jet.[89] But the "magic" of transnationalism, like the occasional "might" of kin-states, is a limited alternative at best.

Self Protection

On December 20, 1973, a powerful explosive buried just beneath the surface of a boulevard in Madrid exploded, sending a government limousine hurtling dozens of feet in the air and Spain's Prime Minister Admiral Carrero Blanco to an especially violent death. The radical wing of the Basque nationalist movement, the Basque Nation and Liberty (Euzkadi Ta Askatasuna), claimed responsibility for the deed.[90] The assassination illustrated in an unusually sensational way the most basic and common means for the protection of minorities—that which they provide for themselves.

Minority self-protection, as all know who follow world news, is frequently violent. The violence may be modest—an occasional Puerto Rican or Basque bombing, for instance. But the case histories of the Northern Irish Catholics, the Naga and Mizo tribal groups of northeastern India, the Ibos of Nigeria, the Philippino Moros, and other minorities too numerous to mention testify to the fact that dissident minorities, with or without outside assistance, are capable of violence on a grand scale. No ethnic minority group resorts exclusively to violence; and there are many, in fact, who have made significant gains with mainly pacific measures. One thinks of the French-Canadians in this context, or of black Americans. Violence has severe limitations; it has not secured the right of secession from an established state for a single ethnic minority since World War II.[91] On the other hand, it has certainly won minorities plenty of recognition and, in some cases, significant concessions.[92]

Self-protection could not carry minorities very far without the development of fairly widespread group political consciousness and talented leaders with the capacity and will to mobilize group resources and to command their use against larger and more powerful political adversaries. These would appear to be essential assets in a minority's protective arsenal. It is hard to believe, in fact, that any kind of protection would work in the absence of a minority's determined defense of itself. Palestinian Arab dependence, especially on the Arab states adjacent to Israel, is a notorious fact. But no Arab statesman of the 1970s would accuse the Palestinians of any lack of independent will!

Self-protection is indispensable. But self-protection is what most ethnic minorities have always had to survive on. This was well enough for those with size, wealth, talent, location, cohesion, or other advantages (including, in some cases, a benign adversary) in their favor. It was never enough for all, as we know from the dreary history of minority massacres.

Even those minorities which can muster a credible self-defense will often resort to dangerous weapons and desperate measures to achieve their objectives. Self-protection is by no means the most responsible form of protection. One wonders whether, in an era in which incredibly destructive forces have been released, it can any longer be left to its own devices.

The United States and the Future of International Protection

The minorities problem is something of a pariah among the great global issues of the day. Unlike the food, population, or environmental problems, it is not a "fashionable" issue with statesmen and cannot be added to the agenda of collective international concerns without causing considerable unease among them. Minorities do not fit well in a system of states committed simultaneously to the principles of cultural homogeneity and territorial integrity. They are important enough to be generally tolerated, but not popular enough to be widely accommodated. Judging from the past half century or so, one cannot have much confidence in the capacity or even will of governments to do much for them.

In addressing the United States in particular, one is forced to reflect upon the disillusioning fact that this country has been peculiarly erratic in the twentieth century with respect to its foreign policy goals. Subject to wild fluctuations in mood, it has been quick to appropriate quixotic ideals, quicker still to abandon them. Idealism (for the moment) seems back in vogue; but the question is still there whether it is genuine enough, or will it survive long enough to overcome the deadening inertial properties of our governmental system. Consider the Genocide Convention. With hardly a voice raised against it in the entire country, with the endorsement of the prestigious American Bar Association and the ratifications of 83 other nations behind it, and in spite of the passage of 28 years since its first transmittal to Congress by Harry Truman in 1949, the Genocide Convention failed once again in 1977 to obtain the consent of the U.S. Senate![93]

The American record in these matters is thus not one to inspire an optimistic forecast. I believe, however, that its record is neither entirely dreadful nor utterly beyond redemption. And there are good reasons, I think, to wish for the early occurrence of the latter.

Several compelling reasons (permanence of the problem, intolerable treatment, inexorable internationalization) have already been discussed in surveying the general case for protection. To these we could add a number of others with alleged traditional appeal to Americans (disdain for tyranny, sympathy with the oppressed), none of them likely to move the government. Instead, let us briefly note three *practical* reasons why the United States in particular should give serious attention to minorities and to measures that might contribute to their protection.

The American Interest

The first reason for increased attention to minorities and their protection is that the United States is already extensively involved, officially or unofficially, in minorities problems in many countries of the world. In one way or another, American action has been a significant factor in the development of the Northern Irish, Kurdish, Moro, Palestinian Arab, Soviet Jewish, Eritrean, Biafran, and Indochinese tribal struggles. The list could easily be extended. In some parts of the world, it is very difficult for the United States *not* to be involved. Our involvement, even when relatively minor, has raised serious moral issues. The version of the Pike Committee report on U.S. intelligence agencies released to the *Village Voice* in mid-February 1976 referred to America's covert Kurdish operation as a "cynical enterprise"—a judgment with which it is hard to disagree.[94] Those Vietnamese and Laotian tribal groups (such as the Meo) known to have given some support to American armed forces during the Vietnam war reportedly have suffered severe retribution at the hands of the victorious Vietnamese. Their fate was certainly foreseeable.[95] Moral questions aside, the inescapable fact remains that virtually *any* action the United States takes in some disputes (the Palestinian Arab, Soviet Jewish, and Eritrean, for example) is laden with consequences.[96] Greater attention to the minorities problem in general (which we now neglect) might facilitate more enlightened and less dangerous strategies in regard to these particular situations (which we cannot always avoid).

The second is that the minorities problem, occasionally with a distinctly secessionist pallor many thought was a congenital defect of the postcolonial Afro-Asian societies, is emigrating westward and has ceased to be an academic subject for the North Atlantic states. France, Belgium, Spain, Great Britain, and even Switzerland have experienced relatively severe ethnic disturbances in recent years; and since René Levesque's *Parti Québécois* won a surprise victory in Canada's French-speaking province in the elections of November 1976, the idiom of secessionist struggle has been heard with increasing regularity on America's northern border.[97] The minorities problem, never absent but long thought domesticated, is now a major issue for North Americans as it is for some of their West European allies. The vexatious idea of national self-determination, until now dealt with at arm's length, has come back to haunt the land which first gave it international respectability.

A third very practical reason for reappraising American policies relating to the international minorities problem is that the United States is in a unique position to supply leadership. It is virtually the only sizable multiethnic state whose frame of reference on the international minorities issue is not entirely cluttered with domestic considerations. One should not expect the Soviet Union, the Peoples Republic of China, Indonesia, India, Great Britain, or Nigeria—major states all of them—to take the lead in reassessing the problem; for all of them the question of minority rights extends well beyond school busing. Of course, America has deeply discontented ethnic minorities—black, Native American, and Hispanic mainly. But they have never seriously threatened the authority of the state nor made a secessionist bid of any substance. And there is not much likelihood that they will in the near future. American has not by any means secured ethnic equality for all its citizens; but it has ethnic security—i.e., the apparent political loyalty of its ethnic minorities—to an extent that must be the envy of its multiethnic friends and adversaries. Most American minority groups appear to be hopelessly, even if unhappily, Americanized—even, says Andrew Greeley, the Irish![98]

Policy Options

In spite of all these reasons for being concerned with the world's ethnic minority communities, it must be acknowledged that America's options are sharply limited. Some of the limitations are of its own making. When it comes to minorities (domestic *or* foreign), this country's hands are obviously not entirely clean nor are its pontifical inclinations everywhere appreciated. Others stem from the inherently intractable character of the minorities problem itself. Minority rights have the ring of conspiracy about them; and no government—friend or foe of the United States— is going to risk the security and integrity of the state (or its own permanence) merely to satisfy an abstract conception of social justice. Very few voices have been raised in recent decades on behalf of the restoration of an international protective authority even remotely resembling the League system. International protection of *that* sort, for all its wants, seems utterly beyond the imagination of contemporary statesmen. It is as important to recognize this adamantine fact as it is to understand the necessity for taking steps, no matter how modest, to prevent the oppression of ethnic minorities.

But what steps? What can the United States—with great but hardly unlimited influence—realistically accomplish?

I believe that the essential first step for the United States is to revive its role in the United Nations human rights system. Some of the responsibility for accomplishing the revival is in the hands of the president, whose interest or lack of interest in that system will help to determine the quality and quantity of American participation in it. But a considerable share is in the hands of the Senate, whose capability for influencing American participation was vastly enlarged with the transmission to it by President Carter in February 1978 of four basic human rights treaties.[99] Senate consent to these treaties will hardly satisfy every minority aspiration. Positive minority rights are only weakly affirmed in these documents, if at all; and, in any event, their enforceability is far from assured. On the other hand, U.S. ratification will certainly help to revalidate America's qualifications to participate more fully in the international human rights rule-making process. American leaders cannot speak with any moral authority on the subject of minority rights if they have not first committed themselves unequivocally to the global quest for human rights. That is an essential commitment. And they have clearly not yet made it.

Lest I be misunderstood, I do not mean to convey the impression that the revival will have been accomplished with ratification of the treaties pending in the Senate. Other human rights agreements, including the two protocols on humanitarian law opened for signature in December 1977, await their turn.[100] The revival will not have meant very much either if it is not followed by this country's sustained involvement in the redefinition, amplification, and enforcement of human rights law.

Still within the framework of the United Nations system, the United States can take an additional useful step. It can help to rescue the international minorities problem from the near oblivion into which it has fallen since World War II. Minorities deserve a fair hearing. They have not been given one before a significant international forum since the peace settlement concluding World War I. Indeed, they often perish, physically and culturally, with less publicity than attends the rapid extinction of the ocean-going whale or its land-dwelling brother the elephant. These unfortunate creatures urgently require attention, and so do minorities.

There are innumerable ways to get them some attention. In the conclusion to a recently completed study prepared for the Subcommission on Prevention of Discrimination and Protection of Minorities, Francesco Capotorti recommended a number of measures for international action which seem worthy of consideration. Acknowledging that positive rights of cultural preservation are not clearly defined in Article 27 of the International Covenant on Civil and Political Rights, Capotorti proposed, for example, that the United Nations consider "preparation of a draft declaration on the rights of members of minority groups, within the framework of the principles set forth in article 27 of the Covenant." Such an effort, he argued, would illuminate the cultural implications of the article and supply guidelines for the achievement of its objectives.[101] This is a proposal to which the United States should give serious thought.[102]

One much-tested attention-getting device—also mentioned by Capotorti—is the regional or global conference. Minority rights have been the subject of two internationally sponsored seminars, both held in Yugoslavia, first in 1965 and again in 1974. But these were very minor events in comparison with the elaborately staged United Nations meetings on the environment, population, food, habitat, oceans, natural resources, new economic order, and women which we have observed in recent years. Is there not sufficient justification for a plenary meeting of the nations, on the same scale as these others, on the minorities problem?

Realistically, the minorities problem would not be instantly dissipated by such a gathering. The Third United Nations Conference on the Law of the Sea, first convened in Caracas, Venezuela, in June 1974, proceeded into 1980 without agreement on a new regime of the seas, held up, it seems, by a dispute over rights to mine manganese nodules blanketing parts of the seabed. But the Law of the Sea Conference has without doubt generated tremendous interest in the oceans, inspired profoundly far-reaching research on them, identified negotiable subjects, and narrowed the nonnegotiable ones to manageable—even if irreconcilable—proportions. That is not an insignificant achievement.[103]

There would be unusual risks in urging a global or even regional conference on the international minorities problem. Minorities are not as innocent as the blue whale; nor are the difficulties which would arise in attempting to meet their demands comparable to those encountered in the effort to apportion fairly the vast mineral wealth of the deep seas. But the risks are far greater, I suspect, in acquiescing to a collective global policy of indifference.

In considering such steps as these, we run up against some very stubborn problems. It would be pointless, for example, to encourage foreign governments to reconsider the rights of ethnic minorities if our own government could not decide what those rights were or, indeed, whether minority rights required further articulation independent of general human rights. The question of minority rights, especially of positive group rights, is extraordinarily complicated and sensitive; let no one be unmindful of that. But this question touches upon issues so fundamental to the liberal democratic tradition that we dare not neglect it. The neglect of the rights of minorities surely threatens to contaminate the rights of majorities.

We have all grown up in a system of nation-states whose historic rationale anchors our minds to obsolete and potentially injurious concepts. The system may be irreplaceable.[104] But the concepts we retain only at considerable expense to ourselves. Our fright of minorities and of "their" right of self-determination may be among these. As Lung-Chu Chen advises in an especially thoughtful essay, the sources of our fright are not altogether rational. "The essence of self-determination," he writes,

> is human dignity and human rights. Underlying the concept of human dignity is the insistent demand of the individual to form groups and to identify with groups that can best promote and maximize his pursuit of values both in individual and aggregate terms. The formation and reformation of groups are ongoing processes.[105]

Apparently, self-determination is also "our" right. It is questionable whether majorities can deny it to minorities without denying it to themselves. It is at least a worthy subject for American political leaders to debate.

Conclusion

Woodrow Wilson believed that to make the world safe for democracy, it had also to be made safe for ethnic minorities. In 1919 he and the other Allied statesmen launched us, therefore, on a bold cooperative experiment in the protection of minorities. The mechanisms they crafted ultimately failed. But the forces of nationalism which had compelled their creation in the first place continued to gather momentum. In World War II, those forces proved so destructive that a new generation of statesmen decided that the world could only be made safe for majorities. Self-determination, the exalted ideal of international protection after the first war, seemed now in constant danger of becoming a dreaded fetish of minority insurrection. Minorities did not disappear, nor did the apparently inexorable forces that steadily mobilized them. Statesmen increasingly thought less of protecting minorities, however, more of protecting against them.

Protecting against minorities is a costly exercise. Long-standing cultural cleavages are not quickly or cheaply bridged, regardless of whether the instruments employed are accommodative or coercive. Minorities are often as truculent as governments, and as firmly wed to their own separatist dogma as governments are to theirs of domestic jurisdiction and territorial integrity. The costs fall heavily on both sides. They are both material and spiritual. And they are likely to grow.

Unfortunately, protecting minorities is not an easily adopted alternative. In practical as well as philosophical terms, it raises issues whose entangled fibres the most cunning sophistry can neither disguise nor unravel. Governments shy away from proposals that would seem to undermine the integrity of the state, and many individuals of undoubted commitment to human rights are extremely reluctant to lend support to minority claims which might jeopardize universalist values many hold dearer than the survival of minority cultures.

In the final analysis, however, the international protection of minorities is an inescapable alternative. The fulfillment of human rights demands it, for their fulfillment is plainly impossible so long as majorities have the right of cultural tyranny over ethnic minorities. What is anachronistic on this planet is not the existence of minorities or their claims for cultural survival. By far the greater anachronism is the frequent claim of majorities to exclusive cultural dominion within the precincts of the territorial state. This claim neither will nor should much longer be sustained by history. We are approaching the day, I believe, when the self-assertions of ethnic minorities will seem far less premodern—and the sovereign rights of states now invoked to suppress them far more unacceptable—than is currently the case.

Until such time, however, we are compelled to continue the search for protective measures acceptable to both majorities and minorities, unduly offensive neither to those who wish to preserve and promote minority cultures nor to those who labor to enlarge the domain of humanist values. That is an enormously difficult assignment, the broad outlines of which have been only faintly traced in the course of the 20th century. The work must proceed with very uncertain guidance from history.

The League system was based upon expectations of interstate behavior which many have called idealistic or utopian. The United Nations system is based upon behavioral premises most have called realistic. Insofar as minorities are concerned, the League system was a failure. And the United Nations system has yet to prove itself any better. The historical record of the minorities problem in the twentieth century counsels, in fact, neither idealism nor realism, but a workable legal and institutional formula—regardless of the blend—that discourages the heedless victimization of ethnic minorities. It is a formula which Americans, for good reasons of their own, should earnestly help to discover.

NOTES

* I wish to thank my colleagues Paul Kattenburg and Natalie Hevener for their very helpful comments on a draft version of this essay. For the sabbatical leave which enabled me to write it, I am very indebted to the University of South Carolina.
1. The subject of minority protection has inspired a considerable number of studies. One of the most recent and comprehensive of them is the culmination of an exhaustive investigation by Professor Francesco Capotorti, special rapporteur of the Subcommission on Prevention of Discrimination and Protection of Minorities of the United Nations Commission on Human Rights, *Study on the Rights of Persons Belonging to Ethnic, Religious and Linguistic Minorities* (E/CN.4/Sub.2/384 and Add.1-7) (Geneva, June 30, 1977). Other recent and informative discussions include J. W. Bruegel, "A Neglected Field: The Protection of Minorities," *Revue des Droits de l'Homme* 4 (1971): 431-452; Mary Francis Lowe, "International Organization and the Protection of Minorities: Alternatives, Approaches, Prospects for the Future," unpublished thesis, Geneva, Graduate Institute of International Studies, 1976; and J. Claydon, "The Transnational Protection of Ethnic Minorities: A Tentative Framework for Inquiry," *The Canadian Yearbook of International Law* 13 (1975): 25-60. Less recent but in some ways still one of the most illuminating analyses is Inis L. Claude, Jr., *National Minorities: An International Problem* (Cambridge: Harvard University Press, 1955). For additional perspectives consult J. A. Laponce, *The Protection of Minorities* (Berkeley: University of California Press, 1960); J. Josef Lador-Lederer, *International Group Protection: Aims and Methods in Human Rights* (Leyden: A. W. Sijthoff, 1968); Rodolfo de Nova, "The International Protection of National Minorities and Human Rights," *Howard Law Journal* 11, (Spring 1965): 275-290; and Moses Moskowitz, *The Politics and Dynamics of Human Rights* (Dobbs Ferry: Oceana Publications, Inc., 1968), pp. 155-173.
2. For lucid expositions of the historical background, see Carlile A. Macartney, *National States and National Minorities* (London: Oxford University Press, 1934); Oscar I. Janowsky, *Nationalities and National Minorities* (New York: The Macmillan Company, 1945); and Claude, *National Minorities*.
3. For a concise statement of the difficulties, see Capotorti, Section I: "The Concept of a Minority" (E/CN.4/Sub.2/384/Add.1).

4. Nazi cultural doctrine is ably discussed by Ralph F. Bischoff, *Nazi Conquest Through German Culture* (Cambridge: Harvard University Press, 1942); and Franz Neumann, *Behemoth: The Structure and Practice of National Socialism 1933-1944* (New York: Octagon Books, Inc., 1963 reprint), especially pp. 98-218.
5. Vernon Van Dyke, "The Individual, the State, and Ethnic Communities in Political Theory," *World Politics*, 29 (April 1977): 343-369.
6. Vernon Van Dyke, "Human Rights and the Rights of Groups," *American Journal of Political Science*, 18 (November 1974): 725-741; and Yoram Dinstein, "Collective Human Rights of Peoples and Minorities," *The International and Comparative Law Quarterly*, 25 (January 1976): 102-120.
7. League-guaranteed international instruments containing stipulations for the protection of minorities (in force in 1929) are listed in Louis B. Sohn and Thomas Buergenthal, compilers, *International Protection of Human Rights* (Indianapolis: Bobbs-Merrill, 1973), pp. 213-214.
8. For the text of the Polish Minorities Treaty, see Louis B. Sohn and Thomas Buergenthal, editors, *Basic Documents on International Protection of Human Rights* (Indianapolis: Bobbs-Merrill, 1973), pp. 238-242.
9. Cf. Janowsky, pp. 129-134; and Claude, pp. 17-20.
10. "What the [Versailles] Conference had to deal with," according to a report on the protection of minorities prepared for the League Council in 1929, "was a number of problems which were purely local, which arose only in certain specified districts of Europe, but which at the same time, in view of the political conditions of the moment, were serious, urgent and could not be neglected." Sohn and Buergenthal, *International Protection of Human Rights,* 219.
11. Judicious appraisals of the League system are made by Janowsky, op. cit., pp. 122-134; and Claude, pp. 31-50.
12. Ibid., p. 69.
13. This is reflected in many of the articles of the Universal Declaration of Human Rights, adopted by the General Assembly in 1948 without a dissenting vote.
14. "Perhaps the most striking and significant feature of the proceedings at Paris," according to one account of the Peace Conference of 1946, "was the de-internationalization of the minority problem." Claude, p. 143.
15. For a convenient tabulation of international human rights documents, including recent figures on ratification, see U.S. House of Representatives, Subcommittee on International Organizations of the Committee on International Relations, *Human Rights in the International Community and in U.S. Foreign Policy, 1945-76*, 95th Cong., 1st Sess., July 24, 1977, pp. 41-46.
16. Many of these are collected in Sohn and Buergenthal, *Basic Documents.*
17. For an illuminating discussion of Article 27, see Capotorti, Section II(C): "Background to Article 27 of the International Covenant on Civil and Political Rights," and II(D): "Scope of Article 27 of the International Covenant on Civil and Political Rights" (E/CN.4/Sub.2/384/Add.2), pp. 60-95.
18. Cf. Bruegel, pp. 424-433.

19. Capotorti, Section II(B): "The Question of Protection Since the Second World War" (E/CN.4/Sub.2/384/Add.2), p. 49. For the most comprehensive assessment of the work of the subcommission, see Lowe, "Protection of Minorities," For an earlier discussion see John P. Humphrey, "The United Nations Subcommission on the Prevention of Discrimination and the Protection of Minorities," *American Journal of International Law*, 62 (October 1968): 869-888.
20. On this fateful period, see the two major works by Thomas A. Bailey, *Woodrow Wilson and the Lost Peace* (Chicago: Quadrangle Books, 1944) and *Woodrow Wilson and the Great Betrayal* (New York: The Macmillan Company, 1945).
21. For some contemporary perspectives, see Frank C. Hanighen, "Foreign Political Movements in the United States," *Foreign Affairs,* 16 (October 1937): 1-20; Martin Dies, *The Trojan Horse in America* (New York: Dodd, Mead, 1940); and Marcus Duffield, "Mussolini's American Empire: The Fascist Invasion of the United States," *Harpers,* 159 (November 1929), 661-672.
22. Joseph B. Schechtman, *The Refugee in the World* (New York: A.S. Barnes and Company, 1963), p. 13.
23. The relationship of global political controversies to the pursuit of human rights is explored in Moskowitz, *Human Rights.*
24. Particularly instructive on this point is Humphrey, "Prevention of Discrimination."
25. See infra n. 102.
26. But a great many writers confuse the situation by using the word in reference to subordinate social groups (women, South African blacks), regardless of numerical ratios. For a defense of such usage, see Norman R. Yetman and C. Hoy Steele, editors, *Majority and Minority* (Boston: Allyn and Bacon, Inc., 1971), pp. 3-4.
27. For recent commentaries on the Soviet nationalities problem, see George W. Simmonds, editor, *Nationalism in the USSR & Eastern Europe in the Era of Brezhnev & Kosygin* (Detroit: University of Detroit Press, 1977); Teresa Rakowska-Harmstone, "Ethnicity in the Soviet Union," *The Annals* 433 (September 1977): 73-87; and Carl A. Linden and Dimitri K. Simes, editors, *Nationalities and Nationalism in the USSR: A Soviet Dilemma* (Washington: Center for Strategic and International Studies, Georgetown University, 1977).
28. On Indian ethnicity, see Jyotirindra Das Gupta, *Language Conflict and National Development: Group Politics and National Language Policy in India* (Berkeley: University of California Press, 1970); Paul R. Brass, *Language, Religion and Politics in North India* (London: Cambridge University Press, 1974); and Richard A. Schermerhorn, *Ethnic Plurality in India* (Tucson: University of Arizona Press, 1977).
29. Even when minorities represent but a tiny fraction of a country's total population, as in Communist China, they may be both large in numbers and strategically significant. For an excellent discussion of China's minorities

problem, see June T. Dreyer, *China's Forty Millions* (Cambridge: Harvard University Press, 1976).
30. On German repatriation, see G. C. Paikert, *The German Exodus* (The Hague: Nijhoff, 1962). Nicholas Bethell, *The Last Secret* (New York: Basic Books, 1974), supplies a revealing account of forcible repatriations of Russian and Ukrainian POWs to the USSR. The best general survey of postwar European population movements is Joseph B. Schechtman, *Post War Population Transfers in Europe* (Philadelphia: University of Pennsylvania Press, 1962). See also Claude, pp. 114-144.
31. For an astute analysis of the reasons for the wide gap between theory and reality in postwar discussions of ethnicity, see Walker Connor, "Nation-Building or Nation-Destroying?" *World Politics* 24 (April 1972): 319-355.
32. One Corsican, one Basque, and two Breton liberationist movements were banned in early 1974. *Christian Science Monitor*, February 12, 1974. One excellent recent study of Breton nationalism is Jack E. Reece, *The Bretons Against France: Ethnic Minority Nationalism in Twentieth-Century Brittany* (Chapel Hill: University of North Carolina Press, 1977). For a brief treatment of France's ethnic problems, see Walker Connor, "The Political Significance of Ethnonationalism within Western Europe," in *Ethnicity in an International Context,* ed. Abdul Said and Luiz R. Simmons (New Brunswick: Transaction, Inc., 1976), pp. 119-122.
33. The South Tyrolean problem is one. For a discussion of how it was accomplished, see Peter J. Katzenstein, "Ethnic Political Conflict in South Tyrol," in *Ethnic Conflict in the Western World,* ed. Milton J. Esman (Ithaca: Cornell University Press, 1977), pp. 159-178.
34. The first quote is from Harold R. Issacs, *Idols of the Tribe* (New York: Harper & Row, Publishers, 1975), p. 1; the second is the title of Nathan Glazer's article, "The Universalization of Ethnicity: Peoples in the Boiling Pot," *Encounter* 44 (February 1975): 8-17.
35. For an excellent discussion of the application of accommodative or consociational methods in culturally divided societies, see Arend Lijphart, *Democracy in Plural Societies: A Comparative Exploration* (New Haven: Yale University Press, 1977).
36. Even relatively rich societies may have severe problems. Scholars sharply dispute the capability of Soviet leadership, for example, to pacifically contain the country's minority nationalities. For some opposed views, see Linden and Simes, *Nationalities and Nationalism.*
37. Cf. Claude, p. 82.
38. Cf. Arend Lijphart, "Political Theories and the Explanation of Ethnic Conflict in the Western World: Falsified Predictions and Plausible Postdictions," in Esman, *Ethnic Conflict,* pp. 61-62. Opposition to unrestricted majority rule is probably the sole matter upon which dominant white South Africans agree with the rest of the world's minorities. For an interesting argument against majority rule as a solution for South Africa's problems, see Howard Brotz, *The Politics of South Africa* (Oxford: Oxford University Press, 1977).

39. Cf. Bruegel, 436.
40. Among innumerable commentaries on self-determination, see Alfred Cobban's classic study, *The Nation State and National Self-Determination*, revised edition (New York: Crowell, 1970); W. Ofuatey-Kodjoe, *The Principle of Self-Determination in International Law* (New York: Nellen Publishing Company, Inc., 1977); Lee C. Buchheit, *Secession: The Legitimacy of Self-Determination* (New Haven: Yale University Press, 1978); Lung-Chu Chen, "Self-Determination as a Human Right," in *Toward World Order and Human Dignity: Essays in Honor of Myres S. McDougal*, ed. W. Michael Reisman and Burns H. Weston (New York: The Free Press, 1976), pp. 198-261; Yonah Alexander and Robert Friedlander, editors, *Self-Determination: National, Regional, and Global Dimensions* (Boulder: Westview Press, 1978); Walker Connor, "Self-Determination: The New Phase," *World Politics* 20 (October 1967): 30-53; and Rupert Emerson, "Self-Determination," *The American Journal of International Law* 65 (July 1971): 459-475.
41. Woodrow Wilson's second thoughts on its burgeoning popularity, foreshadowing the reservations of practically every statesman since, have been frequently quoted. "When I gave utterance to those words [right of self-determination]," he stated, "I said them without the knowledge that nationalities existed, which are coming to us day after day.... You do not know and cannot appreciate the anxieties I have experienced as the result of these many millions of peoples having their hopes raised by what I have said." Quoted in Louis L. Gerson, *The Hyphenate in Recent American Politics and Diplomacy* (Lawrence: The University of Kansas Press, 1964), p. 82. Wilson's secretary of state, Robert Lansing, had even earlier entered in his diary a prophetic warning about the principle of self-determination, a phrase, he said, "simply loaded with dynamite," that would "certainly come home to roost and cause much vexation." Lansing is quoted in Alan J. Ward, *Ireland and Anglo-American Relations 1899-1921* (London: Weidenfeld and Nicolson, 1969), pp. 170-171. Wilson's view of self-determination is considered in detail in Michla Pomerance, "The United States and Self-Determination: Perspectives on the Wilsonian Conception," *The American Journal of International Law* 70 (January 1976): 1-27.
42. For an excellent discussion of varying interpretations of the concept, see Vernon Van Dyke, *Human Rights, the United States, and World Community* (New York: Oxford University Press, 1970), pp. 77-102.
43. Quoted in Chen, p. 199.
44. Michael Hechter applies the concept of internal colonialism to British ethnic history in *Internal Colonialism: The Celtic Fringe in British National Development, 1536-1966* (Berkeley: University of California Press, 1974).
45. For a good illustration of this extremely common phenomenon see Neville Maxwell, *India and the Nagas*, Report No.17 (London: Minority Rights Group, 1973); and Onkar Marwah, "Northeastern India: New Delhi Confronts the Insurgents," *Orbis* 21 (Summer 1977): 353-373.
46. An excellent theoretical analysis of genocidal violence in parts of Africa is

Leo Kuper, *The Pity of It All: Polarisation of Racial and Ethnic Relations* (Minneapolis: University of Minnesota Press, 1977).
47. For one estimate see Isaacs, p. 3. Christopher Hewitt makes an interesting effort to trace patterns of ethnic violence in "Majorities and Minorities: A Comparative Survey of Ethnic Violence," *The Annals* 433 (September 1977): 150-160.
48. An account of the tragic slaughter of 49 Arabs in the Arab village of Kfar Kassim in Israel in October 1956 is given in Sabri Jiryis, *The Arabs in Israel* (New York: Monthly Review Press, 1976), pp. 140-153. On genocidal violence in Burundi and other areas of Africa see Kuper, *The Pity of It All*.
49. Claude, pp. 154-157.
50. Quoted in Macartney, p. 232.
51. *New York Times*, November 5, 1977, p. 1.
52. Astri Suhrke and Lela Garner Noble, "Spread or Containment: The Ethnic Factor," in *Ethnic Conflict in International Relations*, ed. Suhrke and Noble (New York: Praeger, 1977), pp. 230-231.
53. The classic study of the Hitlerian "fifth column" is Louis De Jong, *The German Fifth Column in the Second World War* (London: Routledge & Kegan Paul, 1956). See also Bischoff, *Nazi Conquest*.
54. Walker Connor, "The Politics of Ethnonationalism," *Journal of International Affairs* 27 (1973): 15.
55. *The State* (Columbia, South Carolina), December 29, 1977.
56. Kurdish pleas, for example, reiterated over many decades, are reviewed in Charles Benjamin, "The Kurdish Nonstate Nation," in *Nonstate Nations in International Politics*, ed. Judy S. Bertelsen (New York: Praeger, 1977), pp. 87-90.
57. Admittedly, much of the assistance that has been rendered has not been very effective. And sometimes it has not been forthcoming at all. Katangan envoys reportedly offered Costa Rica $2.5 million in a desperate and utterly unsuccessful attempt to find even one state that would offer their rebel movement diplomatic recognition. Crawford Young, *The Politics of Cultural Pluralism* (Madison: University of Wisconsin Press, 1976), p. 81.
58. For an analysis of one dimension of the PLO's external linkages, see Galia Golan, *The Soviet Union and the PLO*, Adelphi Papers Number 131 (London: The International Institute for Strategic Studies, 1977).
59. This is the theme of a number of recent publications, including Bertelsen, *Non-State Nations*.
60. This may account for Wsevolod W. Isajiw's finding that "very few researchers of ethnic relations ever define the meaning of ethnicity." "Definitions of Ethnicity," *Ethnicity* 1 (July 1974):111.
61. Young, p. 41.
62. For recent commentaries on the Kurdish predicament in Turkey and elsewhere in the Middle East, see George S. Harris, "Ethnic Conflict and the Kurds," *The Annals* 433 (September 1977): 112-124; and Martin Short and Anthony McDermott, *The Kurds*, Report No. 23 (London: Minority Rights Group, 1977). See also Majeed R. Jafar, *Under-Underdevelopment: A*

Regional Case Study of the Kurdish Area in Turkey (Helsinki: Social Policy Association in Finland, 1976); and Jane Cousins, *Turkey: Torture and Political Persecution* (London: Pluto Press, 1973), especially pp. 92-93.

63. Francesco Capotorti, "Study on the Rights of Persons Belonging to Ethnic, Religious and Linguistic Minorities," in Sohn and Buergenthal, *International Protection of Human Rights,* p.327 (italics added).
64. In his final report, Capotorti defines the term minority (after emphasizing that it was drawn up specifically for use in application of Article 27) as "a group numerically inferior to the rest of the population of a State, in a nondominant position, whose members—being nationals of the State—possess ethnic, religious or linguistic characteristics differing from those of the rest of the population and show, if only implicitly, a sense of solidarity, directed towards preserving their culture, traditions, religion or language." Section V: "Conclusions and Recommendations" (E/CN.4/Sub.2/384/Add.5), p. 7. While this definition permits varying interpretations, Capotorti emphatically denies in his report that states should have any discretionary power to decide the existence or nonexistence of ethnic minorities within their borders. Section II(D): "Scope of Article 27 of the International Covenant on Civil and Political Rights" (E/CN.4/Sub.2/384/384/Add.2), p. 72.
65. The lengthy effort to define international "aggression" is a good example of the definitional pitfalls. For an unusually competent treatment of this subject, see Julius Stone, *Conflict Through Consensus: United Nations Approaches to Aggression* (Baltimore: Johns Hopkins University Press, 1977).
66. Cf. Capotorti, Section V: "Conclusions and Recommendations" (E/CN.4/Sub2/384/Add.5), pp. 3-5.
67. The quoted words are from Young, p. 81.
68. Cf. Lowell Tillett, "The National Minorities Factor in the Sino-Soviet Dispute," *Orbis* 21 (Summer 1977): 241-260.
69. Their sensitivity—shared with most Third World leaders—has often provoked the allegation that Third World enthusiasm for human rights terminates with decolonization. On this see Rupert Emerson, "The Fate of Human Rights in the Third World," *World Politics 27* (January 1975): 201-226.
70. On this subject see the recent analysis by Jyotirindra Das Gupta, "Nation, Region, and Welfare: Ethnicity, Regionalism, and Development Politics in South Asia," *The Annals* 433 (September 1977): 125-136.
71. By far the best informed and most carefully reasoned recent discussion of organized American Jewry's political perspectives is Daniel J. Elazar, *Community and Polity: The Organizational Dynamics of American Jewry* (Philadelphia: The Jewish Publication Society of America, 1976).
72. "Ethnic Pluralism in Canadian Perspective," in *Ethnicity: Theory and Experience,* ed. Nathan Glazer and Daniel P. Moynihan (Cambridge: Harvard University Press, 1975), pp. 298, 303.
73. The antiethnicity position is forcefully argued by Orlando Patterson, *Ethnic Chauvinism: The Reactionary Impulse* (New York: Stein and Day, 1977).
74. For a recent and highly competent reappraisal, see J. W. Bruegel,

Czechoslovakia Before Munich, The German Minority Problem and British Appeasement Policy (Cambridge: Cambridge University Press, 1973).
75. Claude, p. 5.
76. These include the peace treaties with Bulgaria, Finland, Hungary, Italy and Romania (1947); the Austrian State Treaty (1955); the agreement concerning minorities between India and Pakistan (1950); the Trieste Settlement signed by Great Britain, The United States, Italy and Yugoslavia (1954); the agreement of minorities between Denmark and West Germany (1955); and the Treaty of Friendship and Mutual Aid between Poland and Czechoslovakia (1947). For a more complete compilation see the United Nations publication, *Protection of Minorities: Special Protective Measures of an International Character for Ethnic, Religious or Linguistic Groups* (Sale No. 67.XIV.3) (1967). See also de Nova, 286-288.
77. Assistance has sometimes been more symbolic than material. For an effort to classify internationally rendered forms of assistance to ethnic minorities, see Wirsing, "The International Politics of Cultural Pluralism: Preliminary Observations on the Role of External Actors in the Regulation of Cultural Conflict," paper presented at the 18th Annual Convention of the International Studies Association, March 1977, St. Louis.
78. The kin-state handicap is a constant lament in Fawaz Turki, *The Disinherited: Journal of a Palestinian Exile* (New York: Monthly Review Press, 1972).
79. Correspondent Frederic A. Moritz reported in late 1977 that the Conference-arranged cease-fire was being only nominally observed. *Christian Science Monitor*, December 7, 1977. According to an earlier report in the same newspaper (November 8, 1977), President Marcos has disclosed that civilian deaths in five years of secessionist fighting may total as high as 50,000.
80. This thesis is capably argued by Stephen Fitzgerald, *China and the Overseas Chinese: A Study of Peking's Changing Policy, 1949-1970* (Cambridge: Cambridge University Press, 1972).
81. Even the Somali Republic, whose militant irredentism is overtly displayed in the design of its flag (which has stars representing ethnic Somalis of Kenya and Ethiopia), strove to maintain the fiction that the temporary capture of the Ogaden desert from Ethiopia in 1977 was accomplished entirely by the Somali minority *within* Ethiopia. *Christian Science Monitor*, July 26, 1977.
82. Among others see Robert O. Keohane and Joseph S. Nye, Jr., editors, *Transnational Relations and World Politics* (Cambridge: Harvard University Press, 1970); and Werner Held, *Non-Governmental Forces and World Politics: A Study of Business, Labor, and Political Groups* (New York: Praeger, 1972).
83. Rebecca Rass and Morris Brafman, *From Moscow to Jerusalem* (New York: Shengold Publishers, Inc., 1976), pp. 160-161.
84. Boris Smolar, *Soviet Jewry, Today and Tomorrow* (New York: The Macmillan Company, 1971), p. 202.
85. So did intergovernmental organizations. For example, see Ronald I. Rubin "The Soviet Jewish Problem at the United Nations," in *American Jewish*

Yearbook, 1970 (Philadelphia: American Jewish Committee and The Jewish Publication Society of America, 1970), pp. 141-159.

86. The Jackson-Mills-Vanik Amendment to the Trade Reform Act of 1973, linking trade benefits to the Soviet Union with the question of the right to emigrate, pushed the dispute to the level of detente diplomacy. Among many discussions of the Jackson Amendment see, for example, William Korey, "The Struggle Over Jackson-Mills-Vanik," *American Jewish Yearbook, 1974-75* (Philadelphia: American Jewish Committee and the Jewish Publication Society of America, 1975), pp. 199-234; Morris Brafman and David Schimel, *Trade for Freedom: Detente, Trade and Soviet Jews* (New York: Sengold Publishers, Inc., 1975); and Theodore Sorensen, "Most-Favored-Nation and Less Favorite Nations," *Foreign Affairs* 52 (January 1974): 273-286. For wide-ranging discussions of the ethnic lobbies in general, see Abdul Aziz Said, editor, *Ethnicity and U.S. Foreign Policy* (New York: Praeger, 1977); Gerson, *The Hyphenate*; Lawrence H. Fuchs, "Minority Groups and Foreign Policy," *Political Science Quarterly* 74 (June 1959), 161-175; and Russell Warren Howe and Sarah Hays Trott, *The Power Peddlers: How Lobbyists Mold America's Foreign Policy* (New York: Doubleday, 1977).

87. George W. Shepherd, Jr., *Anti-Apartheid: Transnational Conflict and Western Policy in the Liberation of South Africa* (Westport: Greenwood Press, 1977).

88. There are those who question whether that community can achieve much more even in regard to South Africa. Richard E. Bissell, *Apartheid and International Organizations* (Boulder: Westview Press, 1977), concludes (p. 170) that "within the arena of international organizations, the antiapartheid campaign is largely burned out."

89. Cf. Elazar, p. 96.

90. For an introduction to the Basque problem in Spain consult Pedro González Blasco, "Modern Nationalism in Old Nations as a Consequence of Earlier State-Building: The Case of Basque-Spain," in *Ethnicity and Nation-Building*, ed. Wendell Bell and Walter E. Freeman (Beverly Hills: Sage Publications, 1974), pp. 341-373; and Kenneth Medhurst, *The Basques* (London: Minority Rights Groups, 1972).

91. Bangladesh represents the sole secessionist movement to have won independence from one of the new postcolonial countries. But the Bengalis were a majority, in fact, of Pakistan's population.

92. On this last point see Onkar Marwah's "Northeastern India" on the progress of India's Nagas.

93. U.S. Senate, Committee on Foreign Relations, *Genocide Convention*, 95th Cong., 1st Sess., May 24 and 26, 1977.

94. The report was published by the *Village Voice* (New York) as a special supplement, "The Pike Papers: House Select Committee on Intelligence CIA Report," in September 1976. The reference to cynicism falls on p. 27.

95. And of course it was foreseen. See the contributions, for example, in Nina S.

Adams and Alfred W. McCoy, editors, *Laos: War and Revolution* (New York: Harper & Row, Publishers, 1970).

96. Note, for example, Jonathan Harsch's comments on President Carter's Ulster statement in late Summer 1977. *Christian Science Monitor*, September 1, 1977.
97. For background on the French-Canadian struggle see John Saywell, *The Rise of the Parti Québécois, 1967-1976* (Toronto: University of Toronto Press, 1977); Kenneth McRoberts, "Quebec and the Canadian Political Crisis," *The Annals*, Vol. 433 (September 1977), 19-31; and Leon Dion, *Quebec: the Unfinished Revolution* (Montreal: McGill-Queen's University Press, 1976).
98. *That Most Distressful Nation: The Taming of the American Irish* (Chicago: Quadrangle Books, 1972).
99. The International Covenant on Economic, Social, and Cultural Rights; the International Covenant on Civil and Political Rights; the International Convention on the Elimination of All Forms of Racial Discrimination; and the American Convention on Human Rights.
100. The protocols are the product of a four-year Diplomatic Conference on Reaffirmation and Development of International Humanitarian Law Applicable in Armed Conflict, concluded in 1977, which substantially updated and augmented the Geneva Conventions of 1949. Provisions on internal war are particularly pertinent to ethnic minorities. For full text of the protocols see *International Legal Materials* 16 (November 1977): 1391-1449. For background consult David P. Forsythe, "The 1974 Diplomatic Conference on Humanitarian Law: Some Observations," *American Journal of International Law* 69 (January 1975): 77-91.
101. Capotorti, Section V: "Conclusions and Recommendations" (E/CN.4/Sub.2/384/Add.5), p. 27.
102. In fact, it has already been granted an opportunity to do so. At its 13th session in late Summer 1977, the Subcommission on Prevention of Discrimination and Protection of Minorities adopted Capotorti's proposal, an action which was subsequently approved by the Commission on Human Rights. In May 1978 that body, in soliciting the views of all member states of the United Nations on the proposal of a minority rights declaration, set in motion worldwide deliberations with potentially far-reaching implications. On these developments see Commission on Human Rights, *Report on the Thirty-Fourth Session*, Official Records, 1978 (E/CN.4/1292) (New York, April 1978). See also Wirsing, "Cultural Minorities: Is the World Ready to Protect Them?" *Canadian Review of Studies in Nationalism*, in press.
103. It is not a monumental achievement, on the other hand, considering that postwar deliberations on a new regime of the seas actually began over 20 years ago (1958) in Geneva.
104. So argues Professor Hedley Bull in *The Anarchical Society: A Study of Order in World Politics* (New York: Columbia University Press, 1977).
105. Chen, "Self-Determination," p. 242.

Chapter 10

The United States, The United Nations and the Struggle Against Racial Apartheid

C. Clyde Ferguson

No more persistent and intractable issue has engaged the United Nations, almost from its founding, than that of South Africa and the policy of apartheid. United Nations responses to this issue have had a profound effect not only upon international politics as practiced in the United Nations and other international organizations, but also on the very fabric of international law itself. Moreover, the presence of the issue of apartheid in South Africa has created almost intolerable tensions and contradictions in the conception, formulation, and execution of American foreign policy not only in the United Nations and its constituent organizations but also in non-United Nations international organizations (such as NATO). More than any other single factor, the U.S. position on issues of South African racial policies has been a proximate cause of the decline of U.S. prestige, and hence influence, in international organizations. Understanding this extraordinary phenomenon in foreign affairs requires a tridimensional inquiry. For Americans, and indeed for most of the world seized with the issue of apartheid, the first inquiry is that of the substantive content of the "South African situation." A second foci of the tridimensional inquiry is that of the development of the policy of the United States. Lastly, inquiry must be directed towards identifying those elements of the political and economic environment which dictate the parameters of possible future policy, both of the United States and of the United Nations.

The Situation in South Africa

The maintenance of a rigid system of racial discrimination in South

Africa is not a recent development. Rather, an ideology of white supremacy and a policy of racial segregation has marked both the English-speaking and Afrikaner regimes in South Africa.

From 1912 to 1948 the English-speaking South African governments presided over a political system that not only enforced laws and customs based on racial discrimination as the core of domestic policy but also pursued a foreign policy designed to shield its domestic situation from international inquiry and concern. While the white English-speaking governments for the most part relied upon custom and conventional behavior to enforce its segregationalist policy, these governments did not hesitate to resort to legislation when custom and convention appeared to be inadequate. The 1911 Color Bar Act prohibited employment of skilled black labor in extractive industries. Two years later the Natives Land Act established the policy, still in force, of restricting freehold ownership of land to whites. Thus in a period prior to 1948, when South Africa was free of international pressures against its domestic policies, it went about the entrenchment of racial discrimination as a cardinal element of its social structure.

The unexpected victory of the predominately Afrikaner Nationalist party in 1948 marked a quickening in the pace of entrenchment of racial segregation and an intensification of racial repression directed not only toward blacks but also towards "coloureds" and Asians. The new Afrikaner government unleashed a flood of racially repressive regulations. The Natives Land Act of 1913 took on a much harsher form in the 1950 Group Areas Act which established not only separate residential areas for each racial group but also prescribed areas of employment and recreation for each of South Africa's races. There followed an array of statutes, ordinances, and regulations applicable to every aspect of daily life—mixed marriage bans, immorality acts, job reservation laws, and pass and permit legislation. The domestic policy at the same time acquired a new name—*apartheid*—a word now needing no translation into any language of the world. In the name of apartheid from 1950 to the present day, the South African government has progressively dismantled the rule of law as an organizing principle of social and political organization through such legislation as the "General Laws Amendment Acts" granting unlimited executive powers to arrest and detain without such traditional due process safeguards as court approval and supervision. To the same repressive ends the Suppression of Communism Act granted unchecked powers of restriction and banning of members of suspect organizations. Finally, the Terrorism Act broadened the definition of terrorism to encompass mere dissent and authorized indefinite detention without trial.

Three quarters of a century of a consistent policy of racial segregation based on conceptions of white surpremacy—even Afrikaner supremacy—has now culminated in the Bantustan policy. At once the justification and the main bulwark of apartheid, this policy seeks to create separate tribal "independent" homelands for each ethnic group. The homelands conception represents the ultimate embodiment of "separate but equal" according to its South African architects. But, after years of efforts to consolidate the homelands, only 13% of South Africa's territory has been allocated to 18.5 million blacks while 87% is reserved to 4.2 million whites.

South Africa's internal racist policies of segregation, discrimination, exploitation, and repression did not escape the attention of the international community. Prior to the founding of the United Nations, however, governmental policies worldwide founded on racist doctrines were the rule rather than the exception. Thus, international concern with South Africa's internal situation was restricted to the small hardy band of "do gooders." In official eyes in the United States, for example, it was cause for derision if a few individuals were concerned with "milk for the Hottentots."

The Policy of the United Nations and the United States

It is the United Nations and its associated international organizations which provide the fora for expressions of the international community's concern with South Africa and its now unique racist policy—apartheid.

Almost literally at the birth of the United Nations, the racial practices and policies of South Africa were placed upon the international agenda. Charging a violation of a treaty obligation, the Indian delegation to the 1946 General Assembly asserted that since 1885 Indian settlers in South Africa had been subjected to increasingly harsh racial discrimination. There was no dispute as to the accuracy of the Indian allegation. But the South African government took the position that since the matter was solely within its domestic jurisdiction it was immune from United Nations inquiry under Article 2 (7) of the Charter of the United Nations. The United States gave tacit support to South Africa's contention. Of course, in 1946 the United States was equally vulnerable to the same charge in regard both to blacks and to native American Indians.

In the 1952 General Assembly 13 countries were able to inscribe an agenda item entitled "The question of race conflict in South Africa resulting from the policies of apartheid of the government of the Union of South Africa." The group of 13 based its action on the argument that the massive violation of human rights in South Africa not only constituted a breach of charter obligations, but also constituted a threat to international peace and security within the meaning of Chapter 7 of the charter. This charge against South Africa, first made in 1952, remains to this day the central focus of concern in the international community. The reaction of the UN in 1952 was to create a commission to study the situation in South Africa and report back to the General Assembly. South Africa, however, clung to its position that the United Nations had no power to concern itself with an internal matter of a member state.

In 1954, the U.N. Commission on the Racial Situation in South Africa reported: "Although the Commission appreciates the importance of securing equal economic opportunities for all, regardless of differences of race, color or belief, it feels bound to state its conviction that *steps to achieve political equality among ethnic groups are of prime importance and cannot be continually deferred without serious danger...*"[1] (commission's emphasis). The reaction of South Africa to the request was again to insist that the United Nations was incompetent to consider the matter. In the U.N. General Assembly debate South Africa's representative, relying on statements made by John Foster Dulles in the course of drafting Article 2 of the charter, asserted that under international law the relationship between a state and its nationals, "including the treatment of these nationals," is a matter of domestic jurisdiction "which allows no interference either by another state or by any organization."[2]

During the 1950s South Africa was consistently supported by the United States and the United Kingdom in this position. The issue of whether South Africa's treatment of its nonwhite population is a matter of "international concern" or is solely within "domestic jurisdiction" has been a divisive issue for the world community throughout the intervening period.

It is fair to conclude in 1978 that the overwhelming weight of legal opinion as expressed in the opinions of the International Court of Justice and writings of academic authorities is that massive violations of human rights within any particular country are a matter of international concern and not a matter within the exclusive domestic jurisdiction of the nation-state.

The first reaction to the ever increasing concern of the international community with apartheid came from South Africa itself. In response to the United Nations Economic, Social, and Cultural Organization's (UNESCO) program adopted in 1956 which *inter alia* would launch studies of race and race discrimination, South Africa withdrew from the organization. The United States and the United Kingdom inspired a resolution of UNESCO's General Conference urging South Africa to reconsider its withdrawal and rejoin the organization. In 1963, South Africa ceased to pay its assessment to the World Health Organization (WHO) despite the fact that WHO has no constitutional or procedural provisions for the expulsion of members. In 1964 the Universal Postal Union became the first international governmental organization to expel South Africa from membership for maintaining its policy of apartheid. From 1964 to date the Postal Union has adopted an annual resolution excluding South African participation in deliberations of the Union. In the absence of a Security Council determination, however, South Africa's nonmembership has no effect on international mail interchanges. International actions against *apartheid*—and hence South Africa—have centered, however, in the General Assembly and the Security Council of the United Nations.

From 1946 to 1978 in the General Assembly alone there have been more than 400 resolutions concerning the racial policy of South Africa. This compilation does not include the resolutions and decisions of subsidiary organizations of the U.N. or the specialized agencies; nor does it include literally thousands of condemnations which have emanated from international organizations in every conceivable form.

There is little question then but that South African apartheid and its associated racial policies have become one of the predominant issues in the U.N. and its family of international organizations. Increasingly, the focus of concern has centered on two fundamental issues: (1) South Africa's formal membership in international organizations, and (2) sanctions against South Africa on the grounds that its internal situation represents a threat to international peace and security.

South Africa's membership in the U.N. was first discussed by the Security Council between October 21-30, 1974.[3]

The issue of South Africa's membership originated in the Credentials Committee of the General Assembly when the committee rejected South Africa's credentials on the ground that the white minority regime, because of its policy of apartheid, could not represent the 80% of the country's population which was black.

The General Assembly endorsed the decision of the Credentials Committee and referred the matter to the Security Council to review the relationship between the U.N. and South Africa. In the Security Council a draft resolution was introduced by Kenya on behalf of Iraq, Cameroon, and Mauritania. The resolution reaffirmed that "the policies of apartheid are contrary to the principles and purposes of the Charter of the United Nations and inconsistent with the provisions of the Universal Declaration of Human Rights, as well as South Africa's obligations under the Charter" and urged the Security Council to recommend to the General Assembly the immediate expulsion of South Africa from the United Nations in compliance with Article 6 of the Charter. During the debate in the Security Council, arguments in favor of and against the resolution centered on the three main issues: namely, the nature of U.N.

membership, the meaning of universality of U.N. membership, and the effect of expulsion.

Nature of United Nations Membership

The representative from Madagascar argued that no meaningful international cooperation is possible without a minimum of good faith. Such a standard of good faith had been breached by South Africa by persistent violations of the principles of the Charter to which South Africa is a signatory. Similarly, the representatives from Egypt argued that the state of membership is valid only if there is adherence to the aims and principles of the Charter. "Once those principles have been violated purposely and repeatedly, it goes without saying that such membership would be nonexistent, null and void."

The Kenyan representative argued that at the time of the founding of the U.N., South Africa's internal policies on racial discrimination were mild. However, after 1948 the regime took a sharp turn which in effect would have made South Africa ineligible for membership in the U.N. in 1945. Since 1948 the U.N. has pointed out the incompatibility of apartheid with the principles of the Charter but South Africa has behaved contemptuously. Moreover, he maintained, initial admission to the U.N. does not confer a right to permanent membership since any member may subsequently become ineligible if it fails to conform to the general principles of the Charter or the rules and regulations relating to rights and obligations of the members.

Those opposed to the resolution took a different view. The U.S. representative contended that the U.N. was not founded to be simply "a league of the just" but is "a unique international forum for exchanging ideas, where those practicing obnoxious doctrines and policies may be made to feel the full weight of the world opinion."

Universality of Membership

Many arguments for and against the resolution centered on the concept of the universality of U.N. membership. The main issue was whether universality of the U.N. is "a function of community, of objectives and principles, of readiness of members to recognize that community and of the determination of the organization to ensure that it is respected."

The French representative characterized the United Nations as one of the centers of universal policy. Because of this it should retain within its ranks those who, for better or for worse, have public power. It is in this sense, he stated, "that the argument drawn from universality seems to me the most pertinent." The representative of the United Kingdom described the U.N. as a universal organization which reflects the "realities of the world of 1974 and it is the stronger and healthier for this fact." In his view Article 6 was intended for use only in the "most hopeless circumstances" against members "beyond redemption, when the influence of the organization to remedy the situation is totally exhausted."

Representatives in favor of the resolution disagreed. They did not see expulsion as a contradiction of universality "since universality in essence means that all members of international organizations abide by the same Charter principles which imply brotherhood and interdependence" (Egypt).

The representative of Indonesia argued that expulsion does not weaken the principle of the universality of membership. In this case, "it is not so much the organization which wants to expel South Africa but in fact it is South Africa itself which, by its persistent defiance of the United Nations has disassociated itself from the organization." The Nigerian representative interpreted universality as conditional. It can only be pursued in accordance with the principles of the Charter; otherwise Articles 5 and 6 would become inoperative.

Effect of Expulsion

Many representatives in favor of the resolution expressed opinions as to the effect of expulsion and the purposes of Article 6. Those against the resolution pointed out the unfortunate consequence of a precedent under that article. The United States, the United Kingdom, and France, the three permanent members of the Security Council who vetoed the resolution, strongly argued against a precedent that might set off a chain reaction. While not at issue, Israel's membership in the U. N. clearly was the ghost at the banquet.

The representative of the United Kingdom, for example, was of the opinion that use of Article 6 to expel a member in other than "hopeless circumstances" would be a counsel of despair and a dangerous precedent. "I doubt whether any Israeli student of the records of our meetings over the past 12 days would so readily exclude the possibility." Similarly, the U.S. representative had grave concern about expelling South Africa. "Even if this would help thwart the crime of apartheid, expulsion would set a shattering precedent which would gravely damage the United Nations structure." As for the French representative, the main worry was the subjective manner in which Article 6 of the Charter might be applied or interpreted in the future:

> We ... mention the very serious dangers which such a precedent could create for our organization. There are, as you know, many degrees in the

definition of evil, many differences of opinion in the assessment of errors and distortions of which each country—or even a majority of countries may accuse another. A drastic measure can call for others in an endless chain reaction which we shall not encourage.

In addition to setting an unfortunate precedent, those against the resolution did not think that it would substantially improve the situation. The British representative thought that expulsion would solve nothing because it would not encourage the South African government to alter its policies. On the contrary it might encourage "illiberal elements" to intensify apartheid. The U.S. representative argued on the same lines that expulsion may make the "most hardened racist elements" indifferent to world opinion.

The representatives in favor of expulsion strongly felt that it would be better to have a precedent of expulsion of an obstinate member than to establish a precedent of perpetual breach of the Charter. "The same morality which justifies a national authority to deprive an offending citizen of his or her rights compels a body like this to enforce the rules and regulations of the organization (Nigeria)." On the whole, those who supported the resolution thought that expulsion would have a deterrent effect on other members of the United Nations.

Procedure and Article 27

During the debates some countries, especially Cuba, Algeria, Mauritius, and Madagascar, raised a procedural question. Article 27 disqualifies parties to the dispute from participating in the proceedings. This argument was raised against the three Western permanent members on the ground that they were allies of South Africa and had diplomatic, political, and military relations with South Africa. No decision was taken on this issue but it is likely to arise again.

For the first time in the history of the U.N. three vetoes were cast and the resolution to expel South Africa was defeated. As a political matter no member of the U.N. can be expelled if one of the permanent members of the Security Council is ready to use the veto. It follows that ultimately the decision is governed more by political factors than by the technical applicability of the Charter or the culprit's violation of binding legal obligations. Many of the arguments in favor of expulsion were in fact superfluous and those against fallacious. For example, the fear of a precedent that would set off a chain reaction makes no sense since a precedent does not mean that the right to veto by the permanent members is *subsequently* forfeited. Indeed the function of the veto would be to prevent just such a chain reaction. Similarly, the argument that expulsion would isolate South Africa from world opinion is unfounded as

South Africa's membership has not made world opinion effective either. In the end South Africa finds itself excluded from the General Assembly—a body in which its influence was nil and its presence an embarrassment to the United States, the United Kingdom, and France. It is even arguable that the results of the membership contretemps made the U.S. position in international organizations more credible.

The Possibility of Effective Sanctions

Of much more consequence is the matter of sanctions against South Africa. Only the Security Council can impose such sanctions and only after a finding by the Council that there is a threat to the international peace and security within the meaning of Chapter 7 of the Charter.

Clearly the next issue on the agenda of the United Nations is whether to declare that South Africa's internal situation—not merely the supply of arms to South Africa—constitutes a threat to the peace. Imposition of sanctions hinges upon such a finding. While the U.N. Security Council Resolution of November 4, 1977, terming export of arms to South Africa a threat to the peace and invoking a mandatory arms embargo, represented a forward step in its potential for changing South African policy, the immediate effect is generally recognized as nil. The adoption of the resolution does, however, mark the demise of the "domestic jurisdiction" defense against international action.

There are at least two grounds upon which the Security Council might well find that South Africa presents a threat to international peace. The first ground relates to South Africa's role in assisting Rhodesia to break sanctions imposed upon Rhodesia pursuant to Chapter 7. Here the argument is fairly simple: South Africa is an accessory to Rhodesia's violation. The second ground is much more difficult to demonstrate: that is, South Africa's racial policies are in themselves a threat to peace and security.

The rising tide of militant nationalism within South Africa, combined with the reactions of black African nations, the Soviet Union, and others to the Vorster government's use of force to suppress all black attempts at political organization, have created a tinderbox similar to Rhodesia. Increasing violence by the Vorster government against black consciousness groups is bound to generate increased counterviolence. Transborder guerrilla movements are already occurring, and this threat to international peace will certainly grow unless the Vorster government changes its policies.

Such a finding would not require the United States or any other Western power to support the immediate application of sanctions. There is no legal requirement that recognition of a "threat to peace" requires coterminous economic or military sanctions. The two issues are entirely separable. Indeed, it might well be more effective first to recognize that the situation is a threat to the peace, leaving to the future the imposition of appropriate sanctions.

It is not altogether clear that imposition of mandatory economic sanctions would guarantee change in either South Africa's policy or conduct. One basis for this uncertainty rests upon the assertion that sanctions "just don't work." The example given is Rhodesia. But the Rhodesian situation is not comparable to that of South Africa. Rhodesia had a sympathetic neighbor on its border—South Africa. South Africa itself would enjoy no such good fortune. Thus the ultimate question is: does the international community in 1980 exhibit the political will to impose *effective* sanctions on South Africa? The evidence suggests that the answer to this query is "no."

There is clearly a lack of will on the part of the United Kingdom, a permanent member of the Security Council, to impose a condition of economic isolation on South Africa. The United Kingdom's volume of trade with South Africa and the level of investment in the South African economy is such that effective isolation of South Africa would threaten the viability of the British economy itself. Of course the Charter of the United Nations provides that a country injured by imposition of economic sanctions on a third country is entitled to compensation. But there is no evidence that the international community or any part of it is willing to undertake the task of underwriting the British economy. Thus, in the present international economic political context it is highly unlikely that the United Kingdom would refrain from exercising a veto against effective economic sanctions.

The position of the United States regarding sanctions is at once both distinguishable from that of the United Kingdom and comparable to it. The level of U.S. trade and investment is such that the economy of the United States would not be threatened by a complete elimination of South African trade and investment. At the same time, however, the profitability of American investment is so attractive that the very presence of the investment in South Africa becomes a constraint on imposition of *effective* sanctions. This being so, the position of the United States is not surprising. President Carter is reported to have stated that the United States could not support imposition of economic sanctions on South Africa. This position is a clear reflection of the constraint on American policy arising out of American economic interests in South Africa.

This constraint on Western policy arising out of Western economic interests in South Africa has long been recognized by the non-Western international community. Since 1963 the non-Western international community has called for the elimination of foreign investment in South Africa and a cessation of trade. However, so long as the three Western permanent members of the Security Council maintain substantial economic interests in South Africa these calls are likely to go unheeded. Thus, the U.S. position on this single issue will result in a continued deterioration of U.S. prestige and effectiveness at the United Nations and in the international community at large.

NOTES

1. Louis B. Sohn and Thomas Buergenthal, *International Protection of Human Rights* (New York: Bobbs-Merrill Co., Inc., 1973), p. 667.
2. Ibid., p. 638.
3. All of the quotations in these sections are taken from the Security Council discussion of the four power draft resolution recommending expulsion of South Africa from the organization. The discussions were held at the Security Council Sessions of October 18, 21, 24, 25, 28 and 29 and the resolution was defeated on October 30, 1974. *United Nations Monthly Chronicle* 11 (November 1974): 9-40.

Chapter 11

The United States, The Organization of American States, and Political Repression in the Western Hemisphere

Martin Weinstein

Shortly after taking office, the Carter administration made human rights a major theme in American foreign policy. The "new morality" in foreign affairs proclaimed by the administration was a breath of fresh air in comparison with the amoral *realpolitik* of the Kissinger years. However, the question that is yet to be answered is whether human rights is going to be seen as "a problem to be solved or an issue to be used," i.e., will human rights "be treated as a political problem or a propaganda exercise?"[1] Complicating the issue even further is the fact that even those individuals who see human rights as an important political problem are far from convinced as to the best way to implement an effective policy. In this essay I will examine the problems and prospects, the reality and rhetoric, of a hemispheric foreign policy concerned with the promotion and protection of human rights.

Human Rights Within a Hemispheric Policy

Our intimate involvement with Latin America coupled with the human rights violations of many of its governments—governments with which we have been closely identified through our aid, investment, trade, and diplomatic efforts—make this region a particularly important test of any administration's will on this issue and an excellent example of the dangers, pitfalls, and benefits of a high profile human rights approach to foreign policy. Whether this administration and its human rights advocates can routinize a human rights policy that has to be implemented by a "business as usual" State Department and a Congress under heavy crosspressures is far from clear. After all, the "national security state" has dominated the perception and implementation of U.S. policy during the past three decades, and no one can be so presumptuous as to assume that it will not again prevail as the glow of human rights policy confronts the animosity of our traditional allies in Latin America and the testing and testiness of Moscow.

Fortunately, the era of "pathological realism" in the conduct of U.S. foreign policy may be coming to an end. This approach to our international politics has been neither "realistic" nor rational. It helped create the cold war, led us to brinksmanship and potential nuclear disaster, brought us Vietnam, involved us in the destruction of constitutional government in Chile, and spawned Watergate by providing the moral and political climate conducive to that sad affair. In no area of the world was the product of this policy more obvious than in Latin America, where the results included aiding and abetting brutal military dictatorships whose record on human rights has been abysmal and whose vision of man, his society, and politics is anathema to all of our professed ideals.

As the Spanish filmmaker Luis Buñuel has observed, "When power feels itself totally justified and approved, it immediately destroys whatever freedom we have left...." With regard to our Latin American policy the word "approved" deserves special emphasis. In spite of the rhetoric emanating from the Nixon and Ford administrations, we continued to swim in a cesspool partly of our own creation. Fortunately, we now appear to be using our power and influence to help clean it up or at least extricate ourselves from it so that we will not suffer from contamination. We have begun to recognize the truth that our foreign policy cannot be conveniently divorced from domestic policy—with the moral (or amoral) considerations of one carefully kept from influencing the other—despite the attempts of so many to do so.

To argue that human rights is just one more interest to be considered in the panoply of interests that go into the foreign policy decision-making matrix is to exhibit a fundamental misunderstanding of the concept and nature of human rights. Two classical interests that have influenced our post-World War II foreign policy have been private American investments abroad and cold war ideology. Human rights has been relegated to a lesser order of importance than these two interests which have so often been the excuse for the manipulation of our policy and the failure of that policy.

In Latin America these two "interests" (U.S. commercial and financial activity and anticommunist ideology) have been predominant and frequently determinative factors in our policy. Teddy Roosevelt's Big

Stick, the Marines in Central America and the Caribbean in the 1920s, the CIA in Guatemala in 1954, the Bay of Pigs invasion in 1961, the 1965 intervention in the Dominican Republic, and the more recent destabilization efforts in Chile are evidence of a clear pattern. This pattern involves the promotion and protection of U.S. business interests in Latin America and active hostility toward any political movement, labor organization, or, in the instances in which it has occurred, any government which exhibits a leftward tilt or even hints of "communism." In this context, human rights becomes a "soft" subject, rarely if ever meaningfully factored into policy formulation.

Human Rights and Democracy

I see human rights as an integral aspect of democracy and the democratic process, not merely as an issue or one interest among many in the foreign policy process. As a colleague and I have expressed it:

> Effective citizenship requires the existence of human rights. It is not an extrinsic factor which one decides ought or ought not to be included in making policy decisions (domestic or international). However, without the context of democratic theory, human rights is set among a number of factors to be tossed up and analyzed to see where the clusters lie. If it survives the rotation and looks well, then it can be part of the policy. If not, well....[2]

Tragically, it has been established beyond the doubts of even a hardened skeptic that state-directed terror in Latin America has reached epidemic proportions. Reports from individual witnesses and victims, journalists and diplomats, and from such internationally recognized agencies and bodies as Amnesty International, the International Commission of Jurists, the International League for Human Rights, the United Nations Human Rights Commission and the Inter-American Commission on Human Rights of the Organization of American States confirm that torture, prolonged detainment without charge, and summary arrest and execution have become common fare in several Latin American nations.[3] In particular, the governments of Chile, Uruguay, and Argentina have unleashed a war of terror on their populations which can only find comparison in the practices of the European Fascist dictatorships of the 1930s.

It is not really necessary to describe the various modes of torture to which the average political prisoner in Latin America is subjected. Beatings, electric shock administered to all parts of the body, gang rape of female prisoners, confinement in cells whose size permits the prisoner neither to stand nor completely lie down, and enforced isolation during which time a prisoner is permitted no human contact are just part of the practices which have been documented. People are taken from their homes at any hour of the day or night, never to be seen again. In many cases whole families have been taken while their unoccupied apartment or house is sacked by their abductors.

The physical defilement of human beings is but the most overt manifestation of the destruction of law and decency in these societies. The general picture is one of the systemic destruction of constitutional life. As I indicated in congressional testimony:

> Let us be very clear about the current state of human rights and civil liberties in Uruguay. The constitution has been cast aside. Parliament is closed. Newspapers and the electronic media are under complete censorship. The once powerful trade union movement has been destroyed with most of its leaders under arrest, in exile, or dead. Many political parties and newspapers have been declared illegal and all political activity is banned. The university and primary and secondary school system have been intervened by the military with the dismissal of faculty and teachers based on their ideas and beliefs. Literally tons of books, newspapers and periodicals have been destroyed, and the works of many artists and writers prohibited. Anyone can be arrested at any time for any reason and held incommunicado indefinitely. This has created a situation in which Uruguay finds itself ranked number one in the world in terms of the per capita proportion of prisoners charged with political offenses. Hundreds of prisoners have been subjected to psychological and physical torture which in many cases has resulted in death or permanent injury. All this in a nation that until recent years was one of the most open, liberal democratic societies in the world....[4]

Some argue that even if these conditions are true, the U.S. cannot impose its standards on other societies. They take the position that the nations of Latin America do not share our cultural heritage and values and therefore do not have our standards of political and civil rights; that we cannot expect them to, and to impose our standards on them would be a form of cultural imperialism. This argument has merit to the extent that Latin America does not partake of our Anglo-Saxon heritage. But it does share, unlike much of the Third World, a Western and Christian heritage and a long and sometimes forced acquaintanceship with American political and constitutional theory and practice. The fact is that among the worst human rights violators in Latin America in recent years—Chile, Argentina, and Uruguay—are three of the most developed and European in outlook. Two of these countries, Chile and Uruguay, have a contemporary history of stable, civil, and constitutional party politics within the context of scrupulously protected personal and civil liberties. To excuse the practices of the current regimes in these countries by arguing that "what can you expect, they are not like us," is to deny their histories and engage in a thinly disguised racism.

The argument that torture is not new to Latin America also misses the point. While the use of torture per se is not new, what is new is the systematic use of torture as an *instrument of rule*, and the use of it by states now equipped with twentieth century technology that easily turns old-fashioned authoritarianism into barbaric totalitarianism. It is not accidental that those nations which have long been considered among the most developed in Latin American and all of the Third World—Chile, Uruguay, and Argentina—have emerged as the most brutal and repressive as they fell into the hands of a right-wing military. These societies have long enjoyed a reputation for their relatively developed infrastructure and literate and participant populations. To stop the social processes that were at work in these nations required massive and sophisticated repression. The skills and instruments necessary for that repression were available and attainable, frequently with the blessing and cooperation of the United States.

United States Foreign Policy and Human Rights Violations in Latin America

In retrospect, it is now clear that such programs as the Alliance for Progress were only one side of our policy toward Latin America during the 1960s and early 1970s. Another aspect, implemented principally through the Agency for International Development (AID), involved the training and equipping of police and military forces in Latin America against *internal* and not external threats. This counterinsurgency and "antisubversion" programming involved the training of thousands of military and police personnel at such institutions as the School of the Americas in the Canal Zone and the International Police Academy in Washington. Active liaison between security forces in a given nation and U.S. advisors was handled through AID's Public Safety Program or through the Military Advisory and Assistance Group attached to our embassy. As documented by congressional hearings and such exposes as Philip Agee's *Inside the Company: CIA Diary*, these programs involved tens of millions of dollars and the covert intervention in the internal affairs of most of our South American neighbors. The legacy of this policy was not merely the destruction of guerrilla movements in Latin America but resulted in the creation and maintenance of police states throughout the continent.

Perhaps the most ominous trend in human rights violations in Latin America is that the violator nations have often coordinated their activities, thereby transnationalizing their kidnapping, terror, and assassination. Chileans have been killed in Argentina as well as in Washington. Uruguayans were murdered in Buenos Aires and over two dozen others were kidnapped there by Uruguayan and Argentinian military and civilian agents. They were tortured and then illegally transported to Montevideo where the Uruguayan government explained their presence with a cover story announcing that they were captured in Uruguay after secretly returning there to commence guerrilla operations. One of the victims of this bizarre incident, Daniel Rodriguez Larreta, a highly respected, conservative journalist, was released and has borne witness to the details of this story in testimony and press conferences throughout Europe and the United States. He decided to talk in spite of the fact that his son and daughter-in-law were among those kidnapped and were still being held.

In the face of the deterioration in the human rights situation in Latin America and the increased international exposure of this situation, Congress had begun to question our aid programs and most specifically the relationship between such aid and regimes which were rapidly becoming international pariahs. Senators Kennedy and Abourezk and Congressmen Koch, Harkin, and Fraser, to name but a few, began to challenge U.S. policy and to doubt the Kissinger State Department commitment to human rights. The capstone of this struggle between an evasive, if not obstructionist, administration and an increasingly concerned Congress, was the passage of the Harkin Amendment in 1975. In essence, this amendment, Section 116 of the Economic Assistance Act, the primary food and economic aid legislation of the United States, provides that

> no assistance may be provided under this part to the government of any country which engages in a consistent pattern of gross violations of human rights, including torture, or cruel, inhuman or degrading treatment or punishment, prolonged detention without charges, or other flagrant denial of the right to life, liberty and the security of a person, unless such assistance will directly benefit the needy people of such country.

Shortly thereafter, Congressman Donald Fraser of Minnesota was able to get similar legislation incorporated into the Foreign Assistance Act (Section 502B) which governs military assistance to foreign countries.

Kissinger's State Department did all it could to avoid or mitigate the human rights amendments. All forms of aid somehow were justified as "directly benefiting the needy people" of the country in question. When these arguments failed and aid was cut off to Chile, the State Department fell back on the defense that it could not define the concept of "gross violation of human rights" and therefore might not be able to submit the human rights reports required by Section 502B of the Foreign Assistance Act. This stonewalling helped Ed Koch pass an amendment (September

1976) cutting off military aid to Uruguay. Taking a cue from the success of the Koch amendment and increasing Fraser subcommittee interest in Argentina, and wishing to signal its commitment on human rights, the administration announced through Secretary of State Vance that it was reducing its military aid request for Argentina and Ethiopia, and eliminating it entirely for Uruguay, because of the human rights violations of those governments.

The Carter administration accepts the legitimacy of cutting bilateral aid and voting against multilateral aid to regimes that violate the human rights of their citizens, but it does not accept the stringency of "automatic" cutoffs in the style of the Harkin amendment. The administration argues that the threat of a negative vote at, for example, the World Bank or, if necessary, its selective use, gives the United States the flexibility it needs in its conduct with other states. This carrot and stick approach would run the gamut from "quiet diplomacy" to public announcement of aid cuts, thus allowing for a full range of policy options. Unfortunately, this kind of "flexibility" in the past led to a shelving or, potentially even worse, only to a rhetorical commitment to human rights problems, especially in Latin America. Kissinger's vaunted "quiet diplomacy" did little either to improve the human rights situation in the Southern Cone or to elevate the priority of human rights in American policy. In fact, the precarious regimes in Chile and Uruguay were strengthened in their first two to three years in power by the lack of objective statements or comments from the State Department. In the case of Uruguay, our ambassador in Montevideo became a prime apologist for the regime's practices.

It is clear that there could be many reasons why the U.S. government would decide not to vote against aid or loans: security interests, trade concessions, the country's ability to repay its debts and possible weakening of the regime in question might easily lead to the making of exceptions. The flexibility that this administration, like previous ones, has so strenuously fought for, especially in relation to our vote in international lending agencies, will undoubtedly result in watering down the human rights thrust in foreign policy—if for no other reason than that it will leave the formulation of such policy open to the arbitrary interpretation of the executive branch. As long as a regime knows that exceptions will be made and that its World Bank loans will probably be forthcoming, it will not be compelled meaningfully to change its practices. Just as the civil rights struggle in the U.S. really began to make a difference when economic sanctions became operative, so too the conduct of a regime which grossly violates the human rights of its people may be effectively modified as it perceives its economic life-line threatened.

U.S. Human Rights Action Within Regional International Organizations

Recently, those favoring a new approach to U.S. policy toward Latin America and the Third World have been pressing their case. One of the most eloquent statements on human rights in Latin America was put forth by former U.N. Ambassador Andrew Young. Speaking before the U.N.'s Economic Commission on Latin America in Guatemala City on May 3rd, Ambassador Young argued for a broader conception of human rights, one which would tie economic development to social justice. Because it represents a major statement by an important member of the administration's foreign policy team, and because Mr. Young's views are still considered a minority opinion, I have taken the liberty of quoting extensively from his remarks.

> We must unite the concepts of development (which usually means economic growth) with the concept of liberation (which usually means freedom from oppression, poverty, dependence and degradation). This must be done by defining development in terms of the process by which full social justice for all peoples and all persons is realized, rather than just as an economic process.
>
> Separating the economic considerations from the social, political and economic goals is not only an illusion, but ... it produces unintended and harmful effects for both the social and economic process.
>
> Torture and other forms of political repression are not only in violation of our own national commitments to the United Nations, but are also major obstacles to economic and social change ... There can be no real economic development without a free exchange of ideas and a real accountability of the elites who manage society no matter how well-intentioned they may be.[5]

It is unfortunate but not surprising that at this late date, and in the light of the ideas expressed by Ambassador Young, the Latin American dictatorships cling to outmoded justifications and excuses for their terror. In the face of President Carter's statement that we have put the "inordinate fear of communism" behind us in the conduct of our foreign policy, the spokesmen for the Latin American dictatorships still insist on using national security and the "international communist conspiracy" as the rationale for torture and the complete destruction of civil and constitutional liberties. At the 1977 OAS meeting in Grenada, Patricio Carvajal, Chile's foreign minister, argued that "the real cause of supposed repression of human rights is not poverty or economic hardship but subversion and terror sponsored by the Soviet Union." This in the face of a call to decency by Secretary Vance:

> [A] state's efforts to protect itself and secure its society cannot be exercised by denying the dignity of its individual citizens or suppressing political dissent.

The surest way to defeat terrorism is to promote justice in our societies—legal, economic and social justice. Justice that is summary undermines the future it seeks to promote. It produces only more violence, more victims and more terrorism.[6]

The strong stand by the U.S. at Grenada led to the passage of a strongly worded resolution on human rights. Adopted by one vote more than the required 13, despite the opposition of several military regimes, the resolution calls on OAS member states to refrain from "suspending or interfering with the individual's fundamental rights such as security from torture, summary execution, and prolonged detention without the opportunity to test the charges in a fair judicial proceeding." The resolution also moved to improve the effectiveness of the Inter-American Commission on Human Rights by calling for an increase in its resources and on-site visits to all member states. In addition, member states were directed to cooperate with the commission and not retaliate against individuals who testify or submit material to it.

U.S. efforts to strengthen the Inter-American Commission are to be applauded and encouraged. Skeptics will quickly and accurately note that it is difficult to believe that an OAS dominated by military governments will police its own violations in Chile. However, three reports on Chile the Commission has disseminated since the 1973 coup are excellent examples of the objective and professional work that can be done and the kind of public airing which helped reduce human rights violations in that country. The strengthening of the commission indicates U.S. efforts to multilateralize the reporting (and in the future, possibly even the adjudication of human rights violations), thus putting transgressor nations on the defensive, for they can't as easily argue that international investigations of human rights violations represent U.S. interference in their internal affairs.

Another significant step to improve the international legal climate on human rights in the hemisphere, which would also strengthen the OAS and the Inter-American Commission, involves United States ratification of the American Convention on Human Rights. The convention was drafted at the OAS meeting in San Jose, Costa Rica in 1969. At that time 12 states signed, but the U.S. did not. Since then the requisite eleven states have ratified and the convention came into force in July 1978. President Carter has signed the treaty and has sent it to the Senate, with suggested reservations, for ratification.

Human Rights and Private U.S. Investment in the Region

A viable and effective human rights policy must include economic leverage. At a minimum the administration should be able to use its vote in such multilateral lending agencies as the World Bank to oppose loans to those nations which systematically violate the human rights of their citizens. As for the private flow of capital to such nations, the administration should ask for legislation which would prohibit Overseas Private Investment Corporation (OPIC) insurance for private investment abroad in those nations flagrantly transgressing in the area of human rights. Additionally, the administration could support legislation which would reduce or eliminate tax credits for foreign investment in such countries. These measures would put teeth into our human rights policy. Although their passage is far from certain, administration advocacy of such measures would send a clear message to regimes whose intransigence on human rights may lessen as economic sanctions become a real possibility or partial reality.

Conclusions

The United States has yet to establish a consistent human rights policy. If one focuses on the administration's Latin American initiatives, one has grounds for encouragement about such a policy but the picture is still mixed. A loan to Chile is deferred, but military aid to Nicaragua is lobbied through Congress with the aid of a letter in which Terence Todman, assistant secretary of state for inter-American affairs, argued that such aid is necessary for reasons of our national security—a dubious position. In sum, the record remains spotty and unclear. But, unlike the past, human rights is being seriously discussed inside and outside the administration. In itself, this is an encouraging state of affairs. If it results in the kinds of policy changes discussed and advocated in this essay, then U.S. policy will finally achieve a healthy congruence with the ideals and values which have helped democracy here at home and will give impetus to the chance for it to grow abroad.

That North and South America are linked geopolitically is obvious. Less obvious, but of equal importance to the United States are the natural resources that Latin America possesses and the potential and existing markets afforded by this most developed of Third World regions. In this era of rapidly accelerated social and political processes, amidst global demands for equity and social justice, our support of dictatorships which have little or no backing from their populations is a shortsighted policy which cannot serve our national security interests. The past decades have shown that no matter how much repression it engages in, a dictatorship that does not enjoy popular support will fall. Indeed, should such dictatorships fall, a new generation of leaders will perforce not count as allies those forces or nations that supported their predecessors, thereby weakening the position of a United States which has engaged in such policies.

In sum, geopolitics, levels of development, and a shared Western heritage including a meaningful experience with representative institutions and civil liberties, all point toward a continuing close, if not special, relationship between the United States and Latin America. The question thus posed is whether that relationship will include a relevant and meaningful human rights component. I have argued in this essay that if it does not, the long-range security interests and the more broadly defined "national interest" of the United States (contrary to the conventional wisdom) will be jeopardized, if not irreparably damaged.

NOTES

1. Richard J. Barnet, "U.S. Needs Modest, Uniform Standard on Human Rights," *Los Angeles Times*, 13 March 1977.
2. Morris Blachman and Martin Weinstein, "Democratic Theory and Hemispheric Politics: The Case of the Missing Victim," paper presented at the Seminar on Problems of Democracy, Authoritarianism, and Development in Hemispheric Affairs, Spring 1976, at Center for Inter-American Relations, mimeographed.
3. Among the many such reports are the following:

    U.S., Congress, House, *Human Rights in Uruguay and Paraguay*. Hearings before the Subcommittee on International Organizations. Committee on International Relations, 95th Congress, 1977.

    U.S., Congress, House, *Chile: The Situation of Human Rights and Its Relationship to United States Government Assistance Programs*, hearings before the Subcommittee on International Organization, Committee on International Relations, 94th Congress, 1976.

    U.S., Congress, House, *Human Rights in Nicaragua, Guatemala and El Salvador: Implications for United States Policy*, hearings before the Subcommittee on International Organizations, Committee on International Relations, 94th Congress, 1976.

    United Nations. *Protection of Human Rights in Chile*. Report of the Economic and Social Council, 1975 (Document #A-10285); 1976 (#A-31-253); 1977 (#A-32-227).

    Amnesty International. *Amnesty International Briefs: Guatemala*. (London: Russell Press, Ltd., 1976).

    Amnesty International. *Report of Amnesty International: Mission to Argentina*. New York 1976.

    Amnesty International. *Republic of Nicaragua: An Amnesty International Report*. New York 1977.

International Commission of Jurists. *Final Report of Mission to Chile to Study Legal System and the Protection of Human Rights.* Geneva, 1974. Supplements in 1975 and 1976.

International Commission of Jurists. *Report of Mission to Uruguay.* Geneva, 1974. Supplement 1975 and 1977.

International Commission of Jurists. *The Situation of Defense Lawyers in Argentina.* Geneva, 1975.

4. *Human Rights in Uruguay and Paraguay.* Hearings before the Subcommittee on International Organizations and Movements of the House International Relations Committee (Washington: U.S. Government Printing Office, 1976), p. 33.
5. Ambassador Andrew Young, "A New Unity and a New Hope: Economic Growth with Social Justice," United States Mission to the United Nations, press release, 3 May 1977.
6. "Vance Takes Theme of Rights to O.A.S.," *New York Times*, 15 June 1977.

Part IV

Formulation and Implementation of United States Human Rights Policies

Chapter 12

The Influence of Interest Groups on the Development of United States Human Rights Policies

David Weissbrodt

Interest groups afford a potential means for the public to participate in the making of United States foreign policy as to human rights. Since the U.S. government has recently declared that the protection of human rights will be one of its primary international affairs objectives,[1] organizations concerned with human rights may have an important impact on the formulation of U.S. foreign policy.

Even though nongovernmental organizations (NGOs) have probably had very little effect upon fundamental shifts in U.S. foreign affairs during the past 30 years and although foreign policy has not traditionally been a subject for effective public participation,[2] NGOs may be useful in implementing and shaping U.S. human rights policies during the next few years.

Some theorists believe that political decision making can be explained by reference to the competition and cooperation of different groups.[3] In regard to human rights policy for a particular country, one might try to explain and predict U.S. decisions by studying the interplay of such interests as business people who invest in the country, U.S. unions concerned about the loss of jobs through foreign investment, defense industries which may sell arms to the country, companies importing oil from the country, other importers, the U.S. military, the bureaucrats in the State Department, expatriate groups from the country, and other groups which are concerned about human rights issues. Unfortunately, such an analysis is beyond the scope of this chapter and may not, in fact, be possible. There are simply too many such organized and unorganized interest groups, of which only the most obvious on the national level are mentioned above. Also, some of the most powerful groups, for example, the labor unions and business interests, may have no consistent "human rights" policies and their impact may only be felt through processes of influence which are the least accessible to even the best-informed researcher.

Instead, this chapter will only consider the efforts of organized interest groups which attempt to promote the protection of human rights, including international nongovernmental organizations (such as Amnesty International and the International Commission of Jurists); national NGOs concerned with international human rights and centered in Washington, D.C.; and some expatriate or ethnic groups. Such a scope is already quite massive without considering an expansion to include other politically potent factions. This focus on the so-called "human rights lobby" may also be appropriate because most of the academic literature on lobbying has concentrated on major national interest groupings, such as labor, business, farm, and professional organizations. Humanitarian organizations have not generally been the subject of scrutiny.[4]

Also, the theory of competition among interest groups may misconceive at least the self-image, if not the actual role, of some human rights NGOs. Human rights organizations may desire to change the human rights policies of any country, including the United States, which violates human rights. But where U.S. policy in regard to human rights problems abroad is concerned, some international nongovernmental organizations may expressely abstain from attempting to influence U.S. actions. Nevertheless, their information-gathering and publicity about human rights violations may have important impacts on U.S. policy. Accordingly, the competition theory may mistake these international NGOs as just another set of interest groups to balance against the other factions vying for political influence. Instead, international NGOs have the independent capacity to affect human rights problems without invoking U.S. government aid; such organizations deserve consideration separately from other interest groups.

The first section of this chapter sketches the historical background of U.S. human rights policy with some emphasis on the minor role of NGOs. The second section explains some of the reasons for anticipating that interest groups may have a somewhat greater role in shaping U.S. policy during the next few years. The third section discusses the role of international nongovernmental organizations in implementing human rights through independent measures and through U.S. government action. The fourth section analyzes the characteristics, techniques, and effectiveness of national human rights NGOs.

Historical Background of U.S. Policy

During the immediate post-World War II period, the United States and several nongovernmental organizations, centered in this country, were principal participants in framing language for the United Nations Charter,[5] which obligated all member states to take joint and separate action[6] for the achievement of "universal respect for, and observance of, human rights and fundamental freedoms for all without distinction as to race, sex, language or religion."[7] Similarly, the United States and NGOs in this country were among the most influential drafters of the Universal Declaration of Human Rights, which further delineated the human rights obligations of UN members.[8]

Under the impetus of the Bricker Amendment and the cold war, however, U.S. policy underwent a profound shift in the early 1950s: Senator Bricker and his congressional colleagues began to fear that U.N. human rights instruments might be used to criticize the racial policies of the United States.[9] In order to defeat the Bricker Amendment, which would have limited the treaty-making power of the administration,[10] Secretary of State Dulles promised that the United States would not ratify the multilateral human rights treaties,[11] which were then being drafted in the United Nations to further elaborate upon the human rights obligations of governments.[12] The cold war also redirected U.S. government attention to human rights violations in Eastern Europe and other countries where Communists came into power.[13] Of course, interest groups representing emigres from these countries encouraged this cold war concern for human rights.[14]

As detente developed between the United States and the Soviet Union, the U.S. government became more reluctant to talk about human rights even in Communist countries.[15] In addition, the Vietnam conflict made the U.S. government itself directly responsible for serious human rights violations abroad[16] and even less willing to discuss the subject.

During the same period Congress grew increasingly dissatisfied with its secondary role in national leadership and with the Vietnam War. The growing popular disatisfaction with U.S. policy toward Vietnam was expressed by a number of nongovernmental organizations[17] and these interest groups worked with and through Congress to end the war in Indo-China.[18] As congressional pressure was to some extent responsible for ending the Vietnam War[19] and Congress was beginning to insist on a greater role in directing U.S. foreign policy, several members of Congress criticized the U.S. government for not making human rights a greater part of its foreign policy. These congressional critics were joined by a number of international nongovernmental organizations in encouraging greater U.S. concern for human rights.

While campaigning for office, President Carter adopted this human rights theme as a way of criticizing the previous administration and as an example of his commitment to greater public participation in foreign policy. The U.S. government has announced its commitment to the cause of human rights and is developing a strategy for achieving that objective.

It appears from this brief historical sketch that identifiable nongovernmental organizations concerned with human rights have had very little influence on the significant movements in U.S. foreign affairs during the post-World War II era. Nevertheless, nongovernmental organizations may have at the same time provided some assistance in shaping and implementing human rights policies.

A Mandate for Greater NGO Influence in U.S. Human Rights Policies

There are several reasons for anticipating that nongovernmental organizations may in the coming years play a somewhat more important role in U.S. foreign policy on human rights.

First, Secretary of State Vance has stressed the work of nongovernmental organizations in the promotion of human rights:

> This administration's human rights policy has been framed in collaboration and consultation with Congress and private organizations.... Outside the government, there is much that can be done. We welcome the efforts of individual American citizens and private organizations—such as religious, humanitarian, and professional groups—to work for human rights with commitments of time, money and compassion.[20]

Second, Congress has mandated that the administration give consideration to the human rights findings of *international* nongovernmental organizations, in making bilateral, foreign economic, and military aid decisions.[21] Furthermore, Congress has attempted to encourage all aid-recipient governments to cooperate with international NGOs by requiring that such cooperation be considered in aid determinations. For example, as to aid through international financial institutions, Congress has required:

> In determining whether a country is in gross violation of internationally recognized human rights standards ..., the United States government shall give consideration to the extent of cooperation of such country in permitting an unimpeded investigation of alleged violations of internationally recognized human rights by appropriate international organizations in-

cluding, but not limited to, the International Committee of the Red Cross, Amnesty International, the International Commission of Jurists, and groups or persons acting under the authority of the United Nations or the Organization of American States.[22]

These statutes recognize that international nongovernmental organizations are not merely another type of interest group vying for U.S. political influence, but possess independent fact-finding and implementing capabilities. By using this international NGO information in its published human rights reports, the State Department has implicitly indicated that it finds the information to be reliable.[23] The NGO information may force the State Department to consider whether reported human rights violations might suggest some U.S. measures to promote human rights in a particular country. The acts of the State Department may thus reinforce the NGO concern about a particular country[24] and help, in at least some cases, to alleviate the human rights problems.

A third rationale for actual and potential cooperation between the U.S. government and nongovernmental organizations involves economic assistance by the U.S. government. The Agency for International Development has long used NGOs and relief organizations to assist in the distribution and management of economic assistance.[25] Many of these programs have not in the past been conducted in such a way as to promote human rights, but there is some hope that such programs will be redesigned to take account of their human rights impact. For example, the nongovernmental organizations have been and might continue to be useful in aiding the resettlement of former human rights victims as refugees in the United States.[26] Also, nongovernmental organizations might be used by the State Department in assisting the families and attorneys of political prisoners.[27] Some nongovernmental organizations, including the International Commission of Jurists and the International Committee of the Red Cross, have received direct assistance from the U.S. government to support their human rights activities.[28] Furthermore, Congress has considered the establishment of a Human Rights Institute, which would provide substantial funding to nongovernmental organizations that promote international human rights.[29]

The U.S. government might also seek relations with national human rights organizations in other countries. Until recently the U.S. government has largely maintained contacts with other governments and some business interests elsewhere. Perhaps, the U.S. government should try to establish better relations with a broader spectrum of society, including nongovernmental organizations concerned with human rights. These national organizations may be the most effective in fostering human rights on a day-to-day basis.[30]

Yet a fourth reason for expecting nongovernmental organizations to have a larger role in the formulation of basic U.S. human rights policies is that Congress has become an important participant in U.S. foreign policymaking. And Congress is a far more accessible forum for nongovernmental organizations than the State Department or other U.S. agencies with an interest in foreign affairs. The State Department and other federal departments continue to maintain the day-to-day conduct of U.S. foreign relations. But Congress has been demanding and gradually achieving an increasing impact on overall human rights policies.

Nongovernmental organizations have experienced difficulty in piercing the instinctive secrecy and timidity of State Department policymaking processes. Similarly, the State Department has found it hard to respond adequately to public participation. The State Department has largely disregarded nongovernmental advice because "outside" groups were thought generally to lack the expertise necessary for understanding the complexities of foreign affairs.[31]

While these State Department attitudes may be slowly changing[32] and at least some nongovernmental organizations may possess the requisite expertise on human rights issues, Congress remains the traditional focus of nongovernmental organizations activity. Accordingly, with the rise of congressional influence must come a related increase in NGO participation in the making of human rights policies.

A fifth reason for expecting increased NGO influence over U.S. foreign policy in regard to human rights might be found in the characteristics and work of nongovernmental organizations themselves. The past contribution of nongovernmental organizations to U.S. human rights policies and the potential role of such groups vary considerably with the nature of the organizations. There appear to be at least two relevant categories of NGOs concerned with human rights: international nongovernmental organizations and national nongovernmental organizations.

International NGOs

What They Are and What They Do

The major international nongovernmental organizations have central offices and/or at least some membership outside the United States.[33] For example, the International Commission of Jurists has its secretariat in Geneva with a U.N. representative in New York.[34] Members of the commission itself are distinguished lawyers and judges from noncommunist countries; the Commission has national sections in about 50 countries, but most of its operations are conducted by a small staff in Geneva. The International League for Human Rights has a very small staff in New York City and an office with volunteers in Washington, D.C., and is loosely affiliated with national civil liberties organizations in about 25 countries.[35] Amnesty International is one of the largest of these NGOs, with about 100 researchers and administrators in its London secretariat, 35 national sections, and 2,000 prisoner adoption groups, largely in Europe, North America, and Japan.[36] The U.S. national section of Amnesty International also has a small office in Washington, D.C., and larger staffs in New York and San Francisco. While the International Commission of Jurists and the International League for Human Rights deal with a wide variety of human rights issues, Amnesty International concentrates on the release of prisoners of conscience, the prevention of torture, and the abolition of capital punishment.

The International Committee of the Red Cross is centered in Geneva, staffed exclusively by Swiss nationals, and is principally concerned with the conditions of confinement for war prisoners and political prisoners around the world.[37] Other international nongovernmental organizations concerned with human rights include the World Council of Churches,[38] the Minority Rights Group,[39] and the World Conference for Religion and Peace.[40] Many international NGOs have consultative status with the U.N. Economic and Social Council, which relationship permits them to contribute directly to U.N. human rights deliberations.[41] Many of these organizations have an international, rather than a national, focus and attempt to stop human rights violations in more or less the same fashion: by collecting information, using diplomatic means to urge compliance with international minimum standards, directing publicity at violations if diplomacy fails, sending observers to prisons or trials, and using intergovernmental fact-finding procedures.[42]

While most of these measures are directed at the government immediately responsible for the violations, NGOs may urge another government, for example the United States, to use its influence in convincing the target government to cease particular violations. There is no doubt that governments, like the United States, may exert great pressure on nations.[43] Accordingly, there is considerable incentive for NGOs to seek the assistance of "sympathetic" governments. But there are also serious risks in asking the U.S. government, for example, to intervene.

In regard to some human rights violators, the U.S. government may not be the most effective advocate. U.S. relations with Albania, Angola, Cambodia, and Syria, for example, are such that U.S. human rights activity as to these countries may be poorly received and probably would not be particularly effective. Also, the U.S. government is very difficult to motivate into action; the scarce resources of these NGOs might be better spent in more direct approaches. In regard to some countries, U.S. government assistance may also serve to identify the NGO with U.S. policies.[44] The effectiveness of an international NGO's human rights work may depend upon its reputation for impartiality and such a close relationship between the NGO and a particular government may undermine that appearance of impartiality. Finally, international nongovernmental organizations may not want to be identified with some of the measures, such as aid limitations, available to the U.S. government in connection with its attempts to place pressure on governments which violate human rights. Such coercion simultaneously involves great potential for exerting leverage and a serious risk of negative reactions.[45]

Impact of Human Rights Legislation

Even if the international NGOs attempt to keep a certain distance from U.S. human rights activity, it is inevitable that interaction will occur. As the organizations generate information and sometimes publicity about certain prisoners or about human rights violations in particular countries, legislation now requires that the U.S. government consider that information in deciding its own policies.[46]

Indeed, State Department human rights reports indicate that materials from several international nongovernmental organizations—principally Amnesty International, the International Commission of Jurists, and Freedom House—have been consulted.[47] The State Department, however, has begun to implement its legislative mandate by gathering only the most easily accessible of NGO publications.[48] The State Department apparently has not gathered NGO materials on human rights issues systematically and definitely has not used these materials systematically in reporting to Congress.[49]

The legislation certainly gives international nongovernmental organizations—and particularly Amnesty International, the International Commission of Jurists, and the International Committee of the Red Cross—an apparent interest in State Department consideration of human rights issues. To the extent that some of the international nongovernmental organizations may be less concerned than others about overt identification with the U.S. government's (or any government's) policies, the legislation might be read to give nongovernmental organizations a right to demand to be heard in the State Department on particular cases or country situations.

International nongovernmental organizations, however, have thus far taken very little interest in how the State Department is pursuing its mandate to consider human rights information in making foreign policy decisions.[50] The State Department has functioned largely without public scrutiny and under a cloak of secrecy.[51] The State Department has not explicated the procedures which it follows in considering human rights information.[52] Some international nongovernmental organizations might want to demand that the procedures be explained, for example, in regard to when and by whom aid decisions are made, how human rights information is considered, and how international nongovernmental organizations could inject human rights information at the appropriate times and places so as to have an impact on U.S. policy.

If the State Department fails to fulfill its obligations under this legislation, international nongovernmental organizations would have a claim of particular competence to challenge the State Department in congressional oversight hearings. Because they are specifically identified in the human rights legislation, international NGOs may also possess an arguable claim of standing to challenge the State Department in the courts.[53] For example, nongovernmental organizations might argue that the State Department failed to fulfill its statutory obligations to consider human rights in making bilateral and multilateral aid determinations. In such a case NGOs might argue that they represent the human rights victims who have suffered injury in fact from the U.S. government's continued support for repressive regimes.

Areas of Cooperation: Information Gathering and Specific Appeals

For international nongovernmental organizations which are not particularly concerned about identification with the U.S. government's policies, there are several other areas of potential and actual cooperation with the U.S. government. For example, in order to act effectively on human rights problems, both NGOs and the U.S. government must collect accurate information about the situation in many countries and as to what sort of response might be most helpful.[54] Information gathering is, of course, not entirely neutral in effect. The act of gathering information may make the human rights violator far more circumspect or may even cause a cessation of the violations.

In some countries, for example Burma and Afghanistan, the U.S. embassies had better access to information sources and could collect more accurate human rights material than any NGO.[55] In some emergency situations where there is an imminent risk of torture or execution, the contacts of the U.S. government and its international communications system may be far more effective in obtaining information, for example in some Latin American countries, than any NGO.

Accordingly, NGOs have a strong incentive for seeking the assistance of the U.S. government in urgent cases or where the U.S. government may have better sources of information. Several NGOs have sought U.S. government assistance on particular cases with only mixed results.[56] Some requests have been pursued with the urgency they deserve; information has been obtained or, at least, confirmed. In at least a handful of cases prisoners have been released or other human rights violations have been abated. On other occasions, the urgent appeals have been ignored or lost in the endless clearances necessary before the State Department can act. The difference in the handling of these urgent requests may depend less upon U.S. policy than upon the sympathy of the officials contacted and their positions in the State Department hierarchy.[57] Hence, some international nongovernmental organizations have been somewhat reluctant to seek U.S. assistance in such cases, not only because they fear overt identification with the U.S. government, but also because they worry that the information might be leaked or otherwise misused by officers of the U.S. government more sympathetic to the accused government than to human rights.

In some circumstances, the U.S. government may seek the assistance of NGOs to confirm information obtained from other sources or to intervene in situations where the NGOs are better placed for action. For example, the U.S. government may have sought the assistance of certain NGOs in regard to recent threats to U.S. citizens by the government of Uganda.[58] Furthermore, NGO contacts with human rights victims and their families may provide sources of information unavailable to the U.S. government.[59] Accordingly, there is a considerable potential for fruitful exchange of human rights information between international nongovernmental organizations and the State Department. These channels of communication, however, are not as well used as they might be if there were greater trust and fewer risks on both sides.

A related, albeit somewhat distinguishable, area of potential cooperation has arisen in regard to citizen letters written to Congress and the State Department about the status of individual prisoners or other human rights victims abroad.[60] Members of Amnesty International adoption groups, for example, have for several years written to the State Department and to Congress seeking the assistance of the U.S. government in obtaining information about or obtaining the release of their designated prisoners of conscience. The groups found that direct contact with the State Department rarely motivated the State Department to mount an inquiry with the U.S. embassy in the imprisoning country or with the imprisoning government itself. Until recently, most letters to the State Department went unanswered.

Amnesty International local groups found, however, that letters to members of Congress, which were then transmitted to the State Department, achieved greater results. At minimum, the groups received an acknowledgement of their letter from the member of Congress, usually a response from the State Department, and occasionally information from the U.S. embassy abroad or the government concerned. Sometimes such letters of inquiry achieved the release of the adopted prisoners.[61] These letters may have contributed to the human rights consciousness of Congress, the State Department, and the imprisoning government. It is not at all clear whether these low visibility appeals have engendered any substantial risks that Amnesty International will be identified with the actions of the U.S. government.[62]

Such letter writing by U.S. citizen members of international nongovernmental organizations partakes of both international activity and peculiarly national NGO human rights work. When the U.S. government responds to these individual appeals, the individual is at least implicity invoking the considerable power of the U.S. government. Accordingly, these appeals demand careful planning to allow often effective individual humanitarian initiatives, while limiting the substantial risks involved. Perhaps, Amnesty International and other nongovernmental organizations using similar tactics ought to undertake a more careful approach to such requests for U.S. government assistance.

The handling of these individual appeals, however, also demonstrates the general receptiveness of the Congress to such public participation in foreign affairs, the State Department's lower degree of responsiveness to the public, and also the use of Congress to channel public pressure toward the State Department. If the administration really wished to assume leadership in the human rights area, it would be appropriate for the administration to begin responding directly to such public appeals rather than awaiting congressional letters and pressure.

International Procedures

Another area of potential cooperation for international NGOs and the U.S. government may be found in their use of international procedures for human rights implementation.[63] Many international NGOs and the U.S. government have the right to participate in developing human rights standards and implementing human rights through the organs of such intergovernmental organizations as the United Nations,[64] the Organization of American States,[65] the International Labor Organization,[66] and UNESCO.[67] The State Department has occasionally consulted with NGOs on an informal basis as to the position U.S. government representatives might take in such international bodies.[68]

The U.S. government, however, has not generally devoted significant resources to developing the requisite expertise in the procedures of these organizations and has frequently changed representatives for domestic political reasons, thus preventing individuals from acquiring adequate experience. The U.S. government representatives have, of course, great potential influence in such international bodies, if they master the processess well enough to make their positions understood.

The representatives of some nongovernmental organizations have considerable experience and expertise in the procedures of some intergovernmental organizations. Accordingly, there is considerable room for fruitful cooperation between the U.S. government representatives and NGOs in pursuing common human rights objectives through international organizations. NGOs and their lawyers may help delegates of the United States and other nations in preparing for meetings of international bodies.[69] Also, international NGOs may assist in achieving coordination among the representatives of the various governments, including the United States.

From this brief and incomplete catalog one can see that there are many possible areas of human rights cooperation for the U.S. government and international NGOs. Such cooperation has considerable potential for the improvement of human rights practices around the world, but also involves the risk of cooption for NGOs and thus ultimately involves a danger of harm to the entire human rights cause.

National NGOs Concerned With International Human Rights

While the primary question for international nongovernmental organizations may be the extent to which they wish to influence U.S. government policy and also to become identified with those policies, nongovernmental organizations centered in the United States have not been as sensitive to such issues. Such a myopic view of human rights is generated by the nature of such national NGOs and by the fewer options for action apparently available to such organizations.

When a national NGO attempts to influence U.S. foreign policy, its success or failure may depend on a number of factors: the characteristics of the NGO, the techniques employed by the NGO, the nature of the issue pressed by the NGO, the characteristics of the target for NGO activity, and the objectives of the NGO. These broad categories are not discrete; there is much overlap and interaction between them. For example, the characteristics of the NGO can limit the number and efficacy of techniques available to it, and a technique employed may be intimately related to the characteristics of the target or the objective sought by the NGO.

Characteristics of the NGO

The most important organizational characteristics bearing upon an

NGO's influence on U.S. human rights policies include the organization's visibility, constituency, and reputation for accuracy; the legitimacy of its interest in human rights; and its access to decision makers.[70] Decision makers are more likely to view an NGO as reliable if the NGO is nationally prominent and often in the public eye. And, unless the area of organizational activity is within the target official's specialized interest, the target's awareness of the activity will depend on the NGO's general reputation and prominence in the public sphere.[71] Such visibility will benefit an NGO little, however, in the absence of high *credibility*, a major component of which is the significance of its constituency in terms of size and representativeness. Although a very large constituency can be important by way of sheer voting power,[72] target officials may be skeptical as to representativeness when an NGO—for example, a church organization—claims to present the views of millions of members.[73]

Both legislative and administrative targets see the supplying of information by an NGO as one of its most important and helpful functions.[74] Trust by the target of the NGO is essential to effectiveness: targets must perceive NGO representatives and communications as honest, sincere, and dependable.[75] As a corollary to this, the expertise of the NGO in its area of interest is important and may aid in clarifying policy alternatives for both the NGO and its target.[76] It is thus advantageous for an NGO to be in close proximity to developments, so that it may provide original, rather than derivative, information.[77] Also, the influence of an organization generally is limited to those areas in which it has a real interest, even though it may take a stance on issues in other areas.[78] Unfortunately for human rights NGOs, economic interests in foreign policy are more often seen as legitimate than other interests.[79]

For example, the Center for International Policy of the Fund for Peace has recently been one of the most energetic nongovernmental organizations in Washington, D.C. concerned with human rights. The center's director is a former State Department country officer for South Korea,[80] who became dissatisfied with the Kissinger department's inattention to human rights. The center maintains a small office on Capitol Hill with a handful of researchers, who are paid at slightly above subsistence wages, and is largely supported by contributions from charitable organizations.[81] Since the center has not developed a membership constituency, it must rely on the accuracy of its research for its impact on U.S. policy. The center has addressed almost all its efforts at Congress and the congressional control of the foreign aid process as a means of influencing human rights. It has produced a series of well-documented reports on bilateral foreign aid and aid through international financial institutions.[82] Its report on international financial institutions formed the most influential basis for recent legislation requiring U.S. representatives to these international banks to consider human rights in extending loans.[83] The center sought, in testimony before a congressional committee,[84] stringent human rights provisions. The center had little influence on the legislative language, but the information contained in published reports and articles written by the center's staff were frequently cited during congressional debate on the 1977 human rights legislation.[85] The center has been a leader in Washington, D.C. human rights work because of its willingness to generate high quality information not otherwise available on matters of human rights interest.

The Friends Committee on National Legislation is a Washington, D.C. based Quaker organization which lobbies for humanitarian social, economic, and political legislation, and which has taken human rights as a priority issue of concern.[86] The Friends Committee derives its support and staff from the U.S. Quaker community and was one of the first national organizations to devote one of its staff to pressing for general human rights legislation by direct contacts with members of Congress[87] and by testimony before congressional committees.[88]

The Washington office on Latin America is largely sponsored by a coalition of religious organizations, including the National Council of Churches, the United Methodist Church, the Jesuit Conference of the United States, and the Anti-Defamation League.[89] The Washington office was established in 1974 to monitor U.S. government policy concerning economic, social, political, and human rights conditions in Latin America.[90] Its staff of about six[91] have been active in working with members of Congress to prepare and testify at hearings on human rights issues,[92] writing reports on human rights problems in Latin America,[93] and monitoring legislative actions on aid to Latin America.[94]

The Human Rights Working Group has brought together representatives or observers from most of the 20 or 30 organizations in Washington, D.C. concerned about international human rights affairs.[95] The Working Group meets under the auspices of an informal legislative subcommittee of the Coalition for a New Foreign and Military Policy, which is itself a group of 33 national church, labor, professional, and humanitarian NGOs which had coalesced to lobby in Congress against the Vietnam War. After the war the organizations decided to continue their efforts on related issues; since early 1976 the coalition has actively pursued human rights issues on Capitol Hill and in public education projects.

Among the organizations which attend the coalition's Human Rights Working Group as members or observers are the Center for International Policy,[96] the Washington Office on Latin America,[97] and the

Friends Committee on National Legislation.[98] In addition, at least three international nongovernmental organizations have sent observers or representatives to Working Group meetings: the International League for Human Rights,[99] the Washington office of Amnesty International (USA),[100] and the Women's International League for Peace and Freedom.[101] A number of other national organizations send representatives to Working Group meetings and have at least one employee, if not several staff members, engaged in human rights activities in Washington, D.C.; for example, Americans for Democratic Action,[102] Clergy and Laity Concerned,[103] the Council on Hemispheric Affairs,[104] the National Council of Churches,[105] the Transnational Institute,[106] and the United States Catholic Conference.[107]

In addition, the Working Group includes a number of expatriate or specific country groups: the Argentine Commission for Human Rights,[108] the Chile Committee for Human Rights,[109] the Chile Legislative Center,[110] the Friends of the Filippino People,[111] the Movement for a Free Philippines,[112] Nonintervention in Chile,[113] the North American Coalition for Human Rights in Korea,[114] the Panama Committee for Human Rights,[115] Taiwanese Rights and Culture Association,[116] TAPOL,[117] the Urguayan Information Project,[118] and the Washington Office on Africa.[119] Some of these national-oriented organizations are directed by expatriates from particular countries and/or have partisan political positions, which might affect the apparent impartiality of Human Rights Working Group discussions and decisions. Although the leadership of the Working Groups generally derives from somewhat more independent organizations, the political spectrum represented in the Working Group may give the informal coalition a less impartial image for joint human rights efforts than might be desirable.[120] But the Working Group usually serves more as a forum for different groups to exchange information about their individual activities than as a center for systematic coordination.

Techniques

The prinicipal techniques employed by human rights NGOs include the stimulation of letters from organization members, personal contacts with decision makers or staff, testimony before congressional committee hearings, contacts at meetings, the stimulation of letters by a few members of Congress to others (Dear Colleague letters), dissemination of information through the media, educational programs, litigation, and coordination with other NGOs.

Although most studies have indicated that fostering letters from organization members is one of the least effective techniques for influencing U.S. policy,[121] it appears that human rights organizations frequently rely on such efforts.[122] The Americans for Democratic Action, however, has been one of the most active lobbyists on human rights issues and has apparently used more direct contacts with representatives on Capitol Hill.[123] While NGO representatives generally consider the personal presentation of facts and argument to be the most effective technique, some scholars have found that representatives of church, humanitarian, and citizens' NGOs did not consider the technique to be as effective as testimony at committee hearings.[124]

Many of the national human rights NGOs have also appeared at, or submitted material for, congressional committee hearings, including, for example, the American Committee on Africa,[125] the American Jewish Committee,[126] the Armenian Rights Movement,[127] Committee of Concerned Scientists,[128] Episcopal Churchmen for South Africa,[129] the Indochina Resource Center,[130] National Conference on Soviet Jewry,[131] the National Council of Churches,[132] the United Church of Christ,[133] and the U.S. Catholic Conference.[134] An investigative hearing can sometimes be stimulated by an NGO, especially if a close relationship exists between the NGO and a key committee member or principal staff.[135] A trustworthy NGO, if willing to view the issue from the committee's perspective, "may be able to influence who is called, what is said, and perhaps the nuances of what is reported in a relevant investigation."[136]

Some NGOs have convinced members of Congress to write letters to their colleagues on human rights issues.[137] These letters help to raise congressional and public awareness about problems in particular countries,[138] help create a consensus on legislative issues before a formal vote is taken,[139] and may be used to press human rights positions on the State Department.[140] Human rights NGOs have also sought congressional resolutions as another method of influencing U.S. foreign policy.[141] Other NGOs have sought publicity for human rights issues through letters to the editor, press releases, and articles for journals.[142] The human rights organizations also issue their own reports for which they attempt to obtain broad distribution[143] and for which they may seek reprinting in the Congressional Record[144] or in the records of congressional hearings.[145] Some of the NGOs have mounted public education projects, including speakers, films, pamphlets, etc., on human rights issues, often of legislative concern.[146]

In addition, a few nongovernmental organizations have used administrative and judicial processes for raising human rights issues and exerting pressure on U.S. government policymaking.[147] Although litigation activities have just begun to enter within the purview of the Human Rights Working Group, many of these other human rights techniques have been coordinated to some extent through the Human Rights Working Group.[148]

Nature of the Issues Raised, Characteristics of the Target, and Objectives of the NGO

Other factors relevant to the effectiveness of a human rights NGO include the nature of the issues raised by the organization and the relation of the NGO's characteristics to the position espoused,[149] and the choice of the target official. The target might be selected by such considerations as the extent of agreement between the NGO and the possible target official,[150] the NGO's access to the decision maker,[151] the position of the decision maker,[152] and the target's expectation that the public will participate in the decision-making process.[153] And finally, the effectiveness of the NGO may be affected by the goals pursued by the organization.

Some of the national organizations newly concerned with human rights are staffed by veterans of efforts to end the Vietnam War.[154] Much of that campaign was fought through efforts to obtain congressional leverage upon the administration to end the war. The Vietnam conflict was such a large and clear target that it drew the organizations together in common purpose.

Human rights, however, is a much more difficult subject matter. Instead of one clear goal there are as many possible objectives as there are human rights set forth in the International Bill of Human Rights and as there are countries in the world. Instead of seeing this complexity and devising a careful strategy, most of the nongovernmental organizations newly concerned with human rights have directed their energies at one familiar target—Congress—in order to obtain one relatively heavy-handed human rights measure—aid cutoffs.[155] Even if the national NGOs were correct in usually relying on the efficacy of the U.S. government's action to press international human rights issues and careful in selecting which human rights problems to address, such organizations should face another important issue: In order to influence U.S. human rights policy the organizations must determine which parts of the government decide U.S. policy. The nongovernmental organizations, however, do not appear to recognize that Congress is not in charge of the day-to-day conduct of the U.S. human rights policies and most basic policy formulation.[156] Congressional action cannot be honed to take account of the unique and changing relations of the U.S. with each country of the world. While Congress is a more accessible and more familiar sphere of NGO activity, the State Department has available far more effective and delicate tools for achieving human rights objectives, including, for example, diplomacy, publicity, aid, trade, etc. It appears relatively clear that the administration now has the will to use some of these more sensitive tools for achieving human rights improvement.[157] Indeed, the national human rights NGOs have not only ignored the State Department too often, but also have not directed their attention toward the many other agencies of the U.S. government which have the capacity to take measures for human rights objectives, including the Departments of Treasury,[158] Commerce,[159] Defense,[160] and Labor.[161]

In addition, the human rights lobby has had very little to offer administration or congressional decision makers as to concrete, first-hand, reliable information on human rights problems around the world. Instead, these human rights organizations have generally been able to provide only information derived from international nongovernmental organizations, such as the International League for Human Rights, Amnesty International, and the International Commission of Jurists.

Because of the reluctance of some international nongovernmental organizations to become involved directly in U.S. policy formulation, however, national NGOs may have a role in transmitting information generated by the international organizations in a form relevant to U.S. policy makers. As intermediaries, some of the national nongovernmental organizations have been modestly effective in shaping congressional human rights initiatives.

Conclusion

International nongovernmental organizations have an important role in the protection of human rights, quite apart from the efforts of governments to implement human rights principles. There exists considerable basis for cooperation between governments and international NGOs, but such cooperation involves serious risks that the NGOs will be coopted or lose their reputation for impartiality. Both NGOs and governments should be aware of these potential risks and benefits of cooperation to achieve human rights objectives.

National NGOs in the U.S. must similarly be aware of the limits to the efficacy of U.S. human rights policies. Human rights interest groups lack a sufficient constituency to force the administration and Congress to listen. Except for a few organizations, these nongovernmental organizations lack specialized knowledge which they can make available to the legislature or the executive. Lacking a constituency with clout and lacking expertise, these organizations have very little to offer in determining U.S. policy. Such national NGOs might be more effective by having contacts with policymakers and by keeping abreast of affairs.

These human rights organizations should begin to develop a broader and more sophisticated strategy for influencing U.S. policy—not only in Congress, but as to the diverse departments of the executive and as to multinational corporations based in the U.S. which may be responsible for human rights problems. The administration, and particularly the State Department, should develop mechanisms for encouraging public participation in the making of U.S. human rights policies and for obtaining the assistance of those national NGOs which have developed the necessary expertise.[162]

Since one major contribution of human rights has been to establish the individual—not just governments—as a subject of transnational law and policy,[163] it is entirely appropriate that individuals can work through nongovernmental organizations to implement and protect human rights.

NOTES

*The author wishes to thank Elliott Goldsmith, Lynn Roberson, and Michele Timmons for their invaluable assistance in preparing this chapter. This chapter was largely prepared during the summer of 1977 and does not systematically cover events and materials issued since that time.
1. See Oscar Schachter, "International Law Implications of U.S. Human Rights Policies," *New York Law School Law Review* 24 (1978): 63, 63-66; David Weissbrodt, "Human Rights Legislation and U.S. Foreign Policy," *Georgia Journal of International and Comparative Law* 7 (Summer 1977): 231-32, 278-79.
2. See Richard A. Frank, "Public Participation in the Foreign Policy Process," in *The Constitution and the Conduct of Foreign Policy,* eds. Francis O. Wilcox and Richard A. Frank (New York: Praeger, 1976), p. 71.
3. See David B. Truman, *The Governmental Process,* 2d ed. (New York: Knopf, 1971), pp. 10-13; Luther H. Zeigler, *Interest Groups in American Society* (Englewood Cliffs, N.J.: Prentice-Hall, 1964), pp. 6-11; Andrew M. Scott and Margaret A. Hunt, *Congress and Lobbies* (Chapel Hill: University of North Carolina Press, 1965), pp. 9-10; compare Arthur F. Bentley, *The Process of Government* (Cambridge: Belknap Press of Harvard University Press, 1967), pp. 204, 210-12; Gabriel A. Almond and G. Bingham Powell, Jr., *Comparative Politics—A Developmental Approach* (Boston: Little, Brown, 1966), pp. 73-79; David Easton, *A System Analysis of Political Life* (New York: Wiley, 1965), pp. 17-33.
4. For example, compare H.R. Mahood, *Pressure Groups in American Politics* (New York: Scribner, 1967), pp. 77-93, with ibid., pp. 195-224; and compare James Deakin, *The Lobbyists* (Washington, D.C.: Public Affairs Press, 1966), pp. 103-52, with ibid., p. 152. Cf. Harry M. Scoble and Laurie S. Wiseberg, "Human Rights NGOs: Notes Towards Comparative Analysis," *Human Rights Journal* 9 (1976) (concentrating on international NGOs); "The Growing Lobby for Human Rights," *Washington Post,* 12 December 1976, sec. B, p. 1. See also Zygmunt Nagorski, "A Member of the CFR Talks Back," *National Review* 9 December 1977, p. 1416; "The Council on Foreign Relations—Is it a Club? Seminar? Presidium? 'Invisible Government?'" *New York Times,* 21 November 1971.

5. See Louis Henkin, "The United States and the Crisis in Human Rights," *Virginia Journal of International Law* 14 (Summer 1974): 654. See also David Weissbrodt, "The Role of International Nongovernmental Organizations in the Implementation of Human Rights," *Texas International Law Journal* 12 (Spring/Summer 1977): 307, n. 71.
6. See United Nations, *Charter*, art. 55.
7. United Nations, *Charter*, art 56; ibid., art. 1, sec. c. See Louis B. Sohn, "The Human Rights Law of the Charter," *Texas International Law Journal* 12 (Spring/Summer 1977): pp. 129-32.
8. See United Nations, General Assembly, 3rd Session, *Universal Declaration of Human Rights* (G. A. Res. 217A, Doc. A/810), 10 December 1948, p. 56; Weissbrodt, "Human Rights Legislation," p. 234, n. 15.
9. See, for example, Jerome J. Shestack and Roberta Cohen, "International Human Rights: A Role for the United States," *Virginia Journal of International Law* 14 (Summer 1974), p. 688; Weissbrodt, "Human Rights Legislation," pp. 235-36, n. 26.
10. The various versions of the Bricker Amendment are reproduced in "Report on the 1957 Bricker Amendment," *Records of the New York City Bar Association* 12 (June 1957): 343-46. See William W. Bishop, Jr., *International Law,* 3rd ed. (Boston: Little, Brown, 1971), pp. 110-12; Thomas Buergenthal, "International Human Rights: U.S. Policy and Priorities," *Virginia Journal of International Law* 14 (Summer 1974): p. 612.
11. See Buergenthal, "International Human Rights," p. 613; Weissbrodt, "Human Rights Legislation," p. 236, n. 26. Cf. Eleanor C. McDowell, *Digest of United States Practice in International Law, 1975* (Washington, D.C.: Department of State Publication, 1976), p. 180.
12. See Weissbrodt, "Human Rights Legislation," p. 235, n. 26.
13. See ibid., p. 234, nn. 17-20.
14. See U.S. Congress, *Captive Nations Week,* Proclamation 3303, 86th Cong., 1st sess., 17 July 1959; idem, Letter from the League for the Liberation of the Peoples of the U.S.S.R. (Paris bloc), 1 September 1959, *Congressional Record* 105 A7575; idem, Resolution issued by the American Friends of Captive Nations, the Conference of Americans of Central European Descent, and the Assembly of Captive European Nations, on the occasion of the opening of Captive Nations Week, 19 July 1959, *Congressional Record* 105: 14106.

For more recent examples of this phenomenon, see idem, Human Rights in Cuba, 20 July 1977, *Congressional Record* 123:E4656-57 (statement of Cuban Committee Pro Human Rights); idem, Rumania Charged with Discrimination Against Hungarian Minority, 18 July 1977, *Congressional Record* 123 H7318-19 (statement of Committee for Human Rights in Rumania); idem, Remarks of Representative Annunzio discussing Czechoslovak National Council of America, 1 August 1977, *Congressional Record* 123 H8227-28; idem, Commission on Security and Cooperation in Europe, *Basket III: Implementation of the Helsinki Accords, Hearings before the Commission on Security and Cooperation in Europe, Volume II,*

95th Cong., 1st sess., 1977, pp. 42-67 (testimony of Dr. Kazys Bobelis, chairman, Joint Baltic Committee, president, Lithuanian American Council, Inc.); ibid., p. 356 (statement submitted by the American Hungarian Federation).
15. See Weissbrodt, "Human Rights Legislation," pp. 235, 237, n. 27.
16. See Joseph Goldstein et al., *The My Lai Massacre and Its Coverup: Beyond the Reach of Law?* (New York: Free Press, 1976). See, for example, U.S., 92nd Cong., 2d sess., statements regarding American war atrocities, 26 April 1972, *Congressional Record* 118:14379; idem, Declaration of Scholars and Professionals Concerned About U.S. War Crimes in Indochina, 26 April 1972, *Congressional Record* 118:14382; idem, Article concerning torture of political prisoners in Saigon, 16 August 1972, *Congressional Record* 118:28512; idem, Is the War in Vietnam a Racist War?, 18 August 1972, *Congressional Record* 118:29289 (remarks of Congressman Matsunaga); U.S., 93rd Cong., Political Prisoners in South Vietnam, 28 November 1973, *Congressional Record* 119:521250-53 (remarks of Senator Abourezk); idem, Assistance to Police and Prisons in South Vietnam, 17 December 1973, *Congressional Record* 119:523160-61.

When the United States was threatened with an investigation into U.S. racial discrimination and human rights violations in Vietnam, it withdrew its resolution for an investigation of Greece and Haiti by the U.N. Commission on Human Rights. Cf. United Nations, Economic and Social Council, *Official Records* (E14475), supplement 4, 27 February 1968, pp. 68, 76.

17. See, for example, discussion of demonstrations by groups sponsored by the National Peace Action Coalition and supported by the People's Coalition for Peace and Justice, in *Congressional Record*, 118 (26 April 1972): 14492; idem, resolution to end the war by the United Church of Christ in Western Pennsylvania, 19 July 1972, *Congressional Record* 118:24518. See also note 20 below.
18. See, for example, the support of Common Cause for ending the war, in *Congressional Record* 118 (3 May 1972): 15652; polls by Peace Alert U.S.A., acting with the support of 72 members of Congress, ibid., p. 29274; resolution by Norfolk, Connecticut, Stop The War Committee, ibid., p. 37381; International Committee of Conscience on Vietnam, ibid., p. 2672; National Student Lobby, ibid., p. 13975.
19. See W. Taylor Reveley III, "The Power to Make War," in Wilcox and Frank, *The Constitution and the Conduct of Foreign Policy*, p. 110; *War Powers Resolution*, U.S. Code, vol. 50, secs. 1541-48 (1977).
20. Cyrus Vance, secretary of state, address at the University of Georgia Law School, April 1977, reprinted in *Congressional Record* 123 (3 May 1977): H3915-16. See Warren Christopher, deputy secretary of state, address to the American Bar Association, February 1978: "Our human rights initiative has given recognition and a new stimulus to the long-standing efforts of private nongovernmental organizations in this field. We applaud these endeavors and recognize that over time they may well out-distance any governmental ef-

fort." U.S. Department of State, *Human Rights and U.S. Foreign Policy* (Washington, D.C.: Department of State Publication, 1978), p. 13:

> The U.S. human rights initiative has given a boost to the longstanding efforts of private organizations such as the Red Cross, Amnesty International, and the International League for Human Rights. The U.S. government works closely with these organizations and recognizes that over time, their efforts may well outdistance those of any government.

21. U.S. Code, vol. 22, sec. 2151n(c) (1977), amended, Statutes at Large 91:533, 537 (bilateral economic aid; known as section 116 of the Foreign Assistance Act, or the Harkin Amendment); U.S. Code, vol. 22, sec. 2304(b)(1) (1977) (bilateral security assistance; known as section 502B of the Foreign Assistance Act). See U.S., Congress, House, *Providing Increased Participation by the United States in International Financial Institutions*, 28 July 1977, H.R. 5262, *Congressional Record* 123:H8100-01.

    Some commentators have begun to credit nongovernmental lobbyists with the passage of this human rights legislation. See, for example, "The Growing Lobby for Human Rights," *Washington Post*, 12 December 1976, sec. B, p. 5. Cf. U.S., Congress, *Human Rights—Rhetoric and Policy*, 22 July 1977, *Congressional Record* 123:E4742 (remarks of Representative Bonker). In fact, nongovernmental organizations generally concerned with human rights devoted no significant attention to Congress during the critical formative period of 1973 through 1975. Indeed, it was individual members of Congress, including most prominently Senators Abourezk, Cranston, and Humphrey, and Representatives Fraser, Harkin, and Solarz with their staffs, who drafted and generated the political will necessary to achieve passage of Section 502B of the Foreign Assistance Act. Although Representative Harkin may have received assistance from NGOs in drafting section 116 of the Foreign Assistance Act, NGOs had little part in the enactment of the Harkin Amendment. Cf. Edward F. Snyder, "Background Paper on U.S. Human Rights Legislation" (unpublished memorandum, 22 October 1976). A few scholars and international nongovernmental organizations were asked by Congress to provide factual information about human rights violations around the world and about international procedures for human rights implementation. See U.S., Congress, Senate, Committee on Foreign Relations, *Human Rights, Hearings before the Subcommittee on Foreign Assistance of the Senate Committee on Foreign Relations*, 95th Cong., 1st sess., 1977, pp. 10, 53. The impulse for legislative action, however, came almost entirely from Congress—not from the NGOs.

    By January 1976, a group of organizations became attracted to the already-existing human rights activity on Capitol Hill. It took these organizations several months to learn about and to establish themselves in the human rights field. The present version of Section 502B had already been drafted in December 1975 and none of the newly interested organizations had any significant hand in either its drafting or its eventual enactment in June 1976. See Weissbrodt, "Human Rights Legislation," p. 244, n. 48.

    The Center for International Policy had a substantial influence in regards

to the 1977 human rights legislation on the International Financial Institutions. See notes 80-81 below and accompanying text.
22. U.S. Code, vol. 22, sec. 262d(e) (1978). See also idem, vol. 7, sec. 1712(c) (1978); idem, vol. 22, secs. 2151n(c), 2304(b) (1977).
23. See U.S., Congress, House, Committee on International Relations, *Human Rights and U.S. Policy, Argentina, Haiti, Indonesia, Iran, Peru, and the Philippines, Reports submitted to the House Committee on International Relations, by the Department of State*, 94th Cong., 2d sess., 1976 (hereafter cited as U.S. Congress, House, *1976 Human Rights Reports)*; U.S. Congress, Senate, Committee on Foreign Relations, *Human Rights Reports, prepared by the Department of State, submitted to the Subcommittee on Foreign Assistance of the Senate Committee on Foreign Relations*, 95th Cong., 1st sess., 1977 (hereafter cited as U.S., Congress, Senate, Committee on Foreign Relations, *1977 Human Rights Reports*); U.S., Congress, *Country Reports on Human Rights Practices, Report submitted to the House Committee on International Relations and the Senate Committee on Foreign Relations, by the Department of State*, 95th Cong., 2d sess., 1978 (hereafter cited as U.S., Congress, *1978 Country Reports*).
24. See notes 48-50 below and accompanying text.
25. See U.S. Congress, House, Committee on International Relations, *Chile, The Status of Human Rights and its Relationship to U.S. Economic Assistance Programs, Hearings before the Subcommittee on International Organizations of the House Committee on International Relations*, 94th Cong., 2d sess., 1976, pp. 134-93 (hereafter cited as U.S. Congress, House, Committee on International Relations, *1976 Chile Hearings*); U.S. Congress, House Committee on Foreign Affairs, *International Protection of Human Rights, The Work of International Organizations and the Role of U.S. Foreign Policy, Hearings before the Subcommittee on International Organizations and Movements of the House Committee on Foreign Affairs*, 93rd Cong., 1st sess., 1973, p. 453 (hereafter cited as U.S. Congress, House, Committee on Foreign Affairs, *International Human Rights Hearings*) (testimony of Harriet Crowley, deputy assistant administrator, Bureau for Population and Humanitarian Assistance, AID).
26. See U.S. Congress, Senate, Committee on Foreign Relations, *Human Rights, Hearings before the Subcommittee on Foreign Assistance of the Senate Committee on Foreign Relations*, 95th Cong., 1st sess., 1977, p. 10 (hereafter cited as U.S. Congress, Senate, Committee on Foreign Relations, *1977 Human Rights Hearings*).
27. See U.S. Congress, House, Committee on International Relations, *1976 Chile Hearings*, pp. 168-93; U.S., Congress, Senate, Committee on Foreign Relations, *1977 Human Rights Hearings*, p. 52.
28. See U.S., Congress, House, Committee on Foreign Affairs, *International Human Rights Hearings*, p. 814; U.S., Congress, 95th Cong., 1st sess., 1977, H.R. 6689, sec. 105(b), p. 814.

The World Peace Through Law Center has also received U.S. government funds in the hope that the organization would undertake human rights efforts. See U.S., Congress, House, Committee on International Relations, *1976 Chile Hearings*, p. 173; U.S., Congress, House, Committee on Foreign Affairs, *International Human Rights Hearings*, p. 814.

29. On March 7, 1978, Representatives Dante Fascell and Donald Fraser proposed an Institute for Human Rights, which would receive five million dollars in initial funding and would have a primary function of supporting human rights nongovernmental organizations. U.S., Congress, 95th Cong., 2d sess., 1978, H.R. 11326.

Pursuant to Section 116(e) of the Foreign Assistance Act, the Agency for International Development has allocated $675,026 for nongovernmental organizations during fiscal year 1978: American Academy of Arts and Sciences ($48,987), American Society of International Law ($152,414 with total funding $380,580), Asia Society ($20,000), Center for Law and Social Policy ($87,000), Associación Colombiana Por Derechos Humanos ($6,000), Consortium for Peace, Education, and Development ($19,500), Creative Associates ($66,000), Cultural Survival, Inc. ($49,800), University of Wisconsin ($20,000), and Woodstock Theological Center ($196,142). Jonathan Silverstone, "Section 116(e)—Human Rights Initiative" (unpublished memorandum, January 4, 1978).

30. See U.S., Congress, Senate, Committee on Foreign Relations, *1977 Human Rights Hearings*, p. 7. For example, see "Paraguay is Freeing Political Prisoners," *New York Times*, 24 February 1977, p. 6.

31. See Donald C. Blaisdell, "Pressure Groups, Foreign Policies and International Politics," *Annals* 319 (September 1958): 152.

32. See Anita Stockman, State Department Program Officer, letter to David Weissbrodt, 12 August 1977; Charles Runyon, address at Notre Dame, 28 April 1977; Cyrus Vance, address at University of Georgia Law School; U.S., Congress, House, 95th Cong., 1st sess., 1977, H.R. 6689, sec. 113 (authorizing funds to facilitate public participation in State Department proceedings). The State Department has been making greater efforts at least to inform the public of department policies, if not to accept public participation in decision making. See, e.g., National Foreign Policy Conference for leaders of Nongovernmental Organizations, 17-18 May 1977.

33. See Weissbrodt, "Role of International Nongovernmental Organizations," p. 297; Jerome J. Shestack, "Sisyphus Endures: The International Human Rights NGO," *New York Law School Law Review* 24 (1978): 89, 90-95; Kjell Skjelshaek, "The Growth of International Nongovernmental Organizations in the Twentieth Century," in Robert O. Keohane and Joseph S. Nye, Jr., *Transnational Relations and World Politics* (Cambridge, Mass.: Harvard University Press, 1972).

34. See International Commission of Jurists, *Objectives, Organization, Activities* (International Commission of Jurists, 1972); *Yearbook of International Organizations* (Brussels: Union of International Associations, 1974): 15:284-85; Niall MacDermot, *Annual Report on the Activities of the International Commission of Jurists* (International Commission of Jurists, at 1 July 1975, June 1976).

The International Commission of Jurists has submitted statements to congressional hearings. For example, see International Commission of Jurists, "Gross Violations of Human Rights: A Practical Guide for Nongovernmental Organizations Wishing to File Communications with the United Nations," in U.S., Congress, House, Committee on Foreign Affairs, *International Human Rights Hearings,* p. 598; U.S., Congress, House, Committee on International Relations, *Human Rights in Uruguay and Paraguay, Hearings before the Subcommittee on International Organizations of the House Committee on International Relations*, 94th Cong., 2d sess., 1976, pp. 154-55 (hereafter cited as U.S., Congress, House, Committee on International Relations, *Human Rights Hearings on Uruguay and Paraguay*).
35. See Weissbrodt, "Role of International Nongovernmental Organizations," p. 297; Harry M. Scoble and Laurie S. Wiseberg, "The International League for Human Rights: The Strategy of a Human Rights NGO," *Georgia Journal of International and Comparative Law* 7 (Summer 1977): 295-97, 310-11; *Yearbook of International Organizations* (Brussels: Union of International Associations, 1974), 15:399; International League for the Rights of Man, *Annual Review 1974-1975* (International League for the Rights of Man, 1975); "Spotlight on NGOs: The International League for Human Rights," *Human Rights Internet,* January 1977, pp. 7-8.
36. See *Yearbook of International Organizations* (Brussels: Union of International Associations, 1974), 15:29; Amnesty International, *Amnesty International Handbook* (Amnesty International, 1977), pp. 7-8.
    Amnesty International has submitted data regarding certain human rights violators to congressional hearings. See, for example, U.S., Congress, House, Committee on Foreign Affairs, *International Human Rights Hearings*, pp. 782-95 (regarding Chile).
37. See Michel Veuthy, *Guerilla et droit humanitaire* (Geneva: Institut Henry-Dunant, 1976), pp. 51-61, 292-318; International Committee of the Red Cross, *Annual Report 1976* (International Committee of the Red Cross, 1976), pp. 6-28; idem, *Activities, Principles, Organization* (International Committee of the Red Cross, 1971), p. 1; James A. Joyce, *Red Cross International and the Strategy of Peace* (New York: Oceana Publications, 1959), pp. 112-15; Donald D. Tansley, *Final Report: An Agenda for the Red Cross.*
38. See *Yearbook of International Organizations* (Brussels: Union of International Associations, 1974), 15:634. See, for example, Commission of the Churches on International Affairs, "Report on Human Rights" (unpublished memorandum for World Council of Churches Executive Committee, 1977).
39. See Minority Rights Group, *Aims, Work, Reports* (Minority Rights Group, 1976). See also "Spotlighting NGOs: The Minority Rights Group, *Human Rights Internet,* December 1976, pp. 17-18; Minority Rights Group, *Nomads of the Sahel* (Minority Rights Group, 1977).
40. See *Yearbook of International Organizations* (Brussels: Union of International Associations, 1974), 15:701; for example, Homer A. Jack, *Religion and Peace* (Indianapolis: Bobbs-Merrill, 1966).

41. See Weissbrodt, "Role of International Nongovernmental Organizations," p. 296.
42. See ibid., pp. 300, 302-15.
43. See Henkin, "The United States and the Crisis in Human Rights," pp. 666-71; Shestack and Cohen, "International Human Rights," pp. 680-701.
44. See Weissbrodt, "Role of International Nongovernmental Organizations," p. 301. But see "Conference on Implementing a Human Rights Commitment in U.S. Foreign Policy," sponsored by International League for Human Rights and Carnegie Endowment for International Peace, 4 February 1977.
45. See, for example, "El Salvador Rejects U.S. Arms Aid," *Washington Post*, 18 March 1977, sec. A. p. 12; "Guatemala Rejects Aid, Cites Rights Criticism," *Washington Post*, 17 March 1977, sec. A, p. 14.
46. See note 21 above. See also U.S., Congress, Senate, Citation of A.I. report on Argentina in connection with Congress' decision to stop aid on human rights grounds, 15 June 1977, *Congressional Record* 123:S9888-90; idem, China and the United States Today, 29 June 1977, *Congressional Record* 123:S11132 (remarks of Senator Dole); "Hill Panels Cut Foreign Aid and Defense Budget," *Washington Post*, 28 May 1977, sec. A, p. 1.

Several of the international NGOs have testified before congressional committees and thus sought the visibility and impact that such hearings might bring to their views. See, for example, Testimony of Roberta Cohen, Executive Director, International League for Human Rights, in U.S., Congress, House, Committee on International Relations, *Human Rights Hearings on Uruguay and Paraguay*, pp. 105-09; Testimony of Niall MacDermot, Secretary General, International Commission of Jurists, in U.S., Congress, House, Committee on Foreign Affairs, *Human Rights in Chile, Hearing before the Subcommittees on International Organizations and Movements and on Inter-American Affairs of the House Committee on Foreign Affairs*, 93d Cong., 2d sess., 1974, pp. 3-16; Testimony of Martin Ennals, Secretary General, Amnesty International, in U.S., Congress, House, Committee on Foreign Affairs, *International Human Rights Hearings*, p. 252; Testimony of Homer A. Jack, Secretary General, World Conference of Religion for Peace, ibid., pp. 412-21.
47. U.S., Congress, House, *1976 Human Rights Reports*, pp. 2-3, 8, 14, 19-21, 29-30. See generally U.S., Congress, Senate, Committee on Foreign Relations, *1977 Human Rights Reports*; U.S., Congress, *1978 Country Reports*.
48. See Weissbrodt, "Human Rights Legislation," pp. 264, 267-74. See also sources cited in note 47 above.
49. See sources cited in note 23 above; Weissbrodt, "Human Rights Legislation," p. 264, n. 111.
50. On at least one occasion, however, Amnesty International has submitted factual material to a congressional committee, which concluded that a country, Ethiopia, was responsible for "a consistent pattern of gross violations of human rights." The A.I. report was expressly submitted in the context of Section 502B of the Foreign Assistance Act, which provides for the termination of aid to such countries. U.S., Congress, House, Committee on Interna-

tional Relations, *Prepared Statement by Amnesty International Concerning Human Rights in Ethiopia, submitted to the Subcommittee on African Affairs of the House Committee on International Relations,* 95th Cong., 1st sess., 1977. Following that report and a substantial deterioration of U.S. relations with the socialist regime in Ethiopia, military aid was restricted by the administration. "In Rights Push, Vance Asks Cuts to Three Countries," *Washington Post,* 25 February 1977, sec. A, p. 1. Finally, aid was cut off by Congress with the acquiescence of the administration. *Statutes at Large* 90:614, 619-20 (1977). Cf. Coalition for a New Foreign and Military Policy, "Minutes of Human Rights Working Group," 7 June 1977, p. 1 (presentation by Mark Schneider, Deputy Coordinator for Human Rights, Department of State, on the subject of the Carter administration's evolving human rights policies).

51. See generally David Weissbrodt, "Domestic Legal Activity in Futherance of International Human Rights Goals," in William D. Raymond, *Implementing International Human Rights Through the Domestic Legal Process* (Charlottesville, Virginia: John Bassett Moore Society of International Law, 1975); Wilcox and Frank, *The Constitution and the Conduct of Foreign Policy.*

52. See sources cited in note 51 above.

53. See Ted Stein, "Public Interest Litigation and United States Foreign Policy," *Harvard International Law Journal* 18 (Spring 1977): 403-10. There remains, however, the question of whether the human rights legislation (see note 21 above) affords a rule of law which is capable of judicial enforcement. Cf. Simon v. Eastern Kentucky Welfare Rights Organization, 426, U.S. 26, 37-40 (1976); Warth v. Seldin, 422 U.S. 490, 499-502 (1975).

54. See Weissbrodt, "Role of International Nongovernmental Organizations," pp. 300-01; idem, "Human Rights Legislation," pp. 281-83.

For example, in response to enactment of the 1974 Foreign Assistance Act, the State Department cabled instructions to all diplomatic posts, in January and February of 1975, requesting updated reporting on significant human rights developments. U.S., Department of State, *Report to Congress on the Human Rights Situation in Countries Receiving Security Assistance,* March 1975 (hereafter cited as U.S., Department of State, *1975 Report*), appendix, p. 2 (cable of 17 January 1975 to all diplomatic posts). See ibid., appendix, pp. 5-6 (airgram of 14 February 1975). The cable specified that "facts obtained from this reporting would be used in formulating U.S. policy in considering country by country" what the United States should do "to promote respect for an observance of human rights both for their own sake and in response to increasing congressional interest." Ibid., appendix, p. 2. In response to these instructions, each post submitted to the State Department a classified analysis of the human rights situation in the country in which it was located.

55. See U.S., Congress, Senate, Committee on Foreign Relations, *1977 Human Rights Reports,* pp. 3-4, 24.

56. See, for example, American Bar Association, Section of International Law,

Committee on International Human Rights, minutes of 8 August 1977 meeting, pp. 6-10.
57. See note 70 below.
58. See U.S., Congress, Senate, Committee on Foreign Relations, *1977 Human Rights Hearings*, p. 44.
59. See Niall MacDermot, "Human Rights and the Churches" (unpublished memorandum, 15 June 1976), pp. 2-4.
60. This human rights correspondence is a logical extension of the more familiar ombudsman function of Members of Congress who deal with grievances of constituents, particularly vis-à-vis the federal bureaucracy. See generally Donald G. Tacheron and Morris K. Udall, *The Job of the Congressman* (Indianapolis: Bobbs-Merrill, 1966), p. 63; John C. Wahlke et al., *The Legislative System: Explorations in Legislative Behavior* (New York: Wiley, 1962), p. 306. Certainly some representatives have developed an interest in international human rights as a result of a humane concern for the victims of atrocities. In addition, these letters and some congressional human rights activity are outgrowths of the cold war preoccupations with "captive nations" and the resulting need to placate Eastern Europe emigré constituents. A continuing concern on the part of some members of Congress with the special human rights problems of the "captive nations" is reflected in congressional remarks commemorating the 59th anniversary of the Ukraine's independence. *Congressional Record* 123 (26 January 1977): H516. Much of the more recent human rights focus in Congress, however, has a broader and more even-handed character. For example, see U.S., Congress, House, Committee on International Relations, *Human Rights in Indonesia and the Philippines, Hearings before the Subcommittee on International Organizations of the House Committee on International Relations*, 94th Cong., 2d sess., 1976 (hereafter cited as U.S., Congress, House, Committee on International Relations, *Human Rights Hearing on Indonesia and the Philippines*); idem, *Religious Persecution in the Soviet Union, Hearings before the Subcommittes on International Political and Military Affairs and on International Organizations of the House Committee on International Relations*, 94th Cong., 2d sess., 1976.
61. See, for example, Hubert H. Humphrey, letter to Gary King of Amnesty International (U.S.A.) Group 37 regarding the release of a Philippine prisoner, 6 January 1977.
62. Amnesty International members have just recently been instructed to consider carefully whether motivating U.S. government inquiries would be damaging to the organization's independence. Amnesty International, Washington (D.C.) Office, memorandum to local prisoner adoption groups, 15 March 1978, pp. 1-3.
63. See Egon Schwelb, "The International Measures of Implementation of the International Covenant on Civil and Political Rights and the Optional Protocol," *Texas International Law Journal* 12 (Spring/Summer 1977): 149-51, note 40.

The Influence of Interest Groups 257

64. See Weissbrodt, "Role of International Nongovernmental Organizations," p. 296-313.
65. See ibid., pp. 314-15.
66. See ibid., p. 313.
67. See also United Nations, Economic, and Social Council, Session, *Study of the Procedures Which Should be Followed in the Examination of Cases and Questions Which Might be Submitted to UNESCO Concerning the Exercise of Human Rights in the Spheres of its Competence* (UNESCO 102 Ex/19), 7 April 1977, pp. 47-68.
68. For example, on July 29, 1976, Representative Donald Fraser, chairman of the House Subcommittee on International Organizations, held an informal meeting to discuss human rights issues to be considered by the U. N. General Assembly. Participants in the meeting included subcommittee and State Department representatives, academicians, and representatives of concerned NGOs, such as the International League for Human Rights, American Association for the International Commission of Jurists, B'nai B'rith, and others. See also Donald Young, Minutes of Meeting Concerning U.S. Ratification of the U.N. Human Rights Covenants, ad hoc meeting with Congressman Donald Fraser, 13 January 1977.
69. See note 68 above.
70. Clearly, an NGO would benefit by having contacts at all levels in each branch of government, but this is usually impossible due to the cost in time and money. Lester W. Milbrath, *The Washington Lobbyists* (Chicago: Rand McNally, 1963), p. 267. To be effective, therefore, an NGO must choose its contacts carefully. When pursuing a legislative goal, preferred contacts are legislators occupying key positions and their staffs, particularly those on legislative committees which are crucial to passage. See ibid., Abraham Holtzman, *Interest Groups and Lobbying* (New York: Macmillan, 1966), p. 99. Staff assistants may be chosen over legislators as contacts because they often have more time and expertise than their employers. Milbrath, *The Washington Lobbyists,* p. 209.

When an NGO goal involves the State Department, an NGO can maintain contacts with policy and information officials within the appropriate offices of the department.

Pressure groups may have a number of advantages over the State Department in their efforts to obtain their objectives. In the first place, some of these groups can undercut American foreign policy by taking independent actions at home or abroad. In the second place, nongovernmental organizations may be more creditable because the public wants to believe what the group is saying.

William O. Chittick, *State Department, Press, and Pressure Groups* (New York: Wiley-Interscience, 1970), pp. 240-41.
71. Scott and Hunt, *Congress and Lobbies*, pp. 34-35. If the NGO is viewed as prestigious by a member of Congress' constitutents, s/he may infer an influence on voting behavior and listen more carefully. Zeigler, *Interest Groups*, p. 245. Another important determinant of visibility for an NGO is

the media attention given to activity outside the governmental sphere. Vladimer O. Key, Jr., *Politics, Parties, and Pressure Groups* (New York: Crowell, 1956), p. 160. An NGO may attempt to elevate its public status by press releases, advertising, educational aids, and organizational publications. Henry A. Turner, "How Pressure Groups Operate," *Annals* 319 (September 1958): 69, 70-71.
72. Milbrath, *The Washington Lobbyists*, p. 348. But see Zeigler, *Interest Groups*, pp. 240-47, suggesting that even the power of large organizations to guarantee and deliver votes has been exaggerated.
73. Francis O. Wilcox, *Congress, the Executive, and Foreign Policy* (New York: Published for the Council on Foreign Relations by Harper & Row, 1971), p. 117; Chittick, *State Department*, p. 241: "One [State] Department official, for example, objected to the fact that leaders of the National Council of Churches exploit their positions by suggesting that they represent the people in the pews."
An NGO which is based too narrowly, however, may be viewed as insignificant, Scott and Hunt, *Congress and Lobbies*, p. 54.
74. Scott and Hunt, *Congress and Lobbies*, pp. 48-49 (information function vis-à-vis Congress); Chittick, *State Department*, p. 231 (same vis-à-vis State Department). See Emanuel Celler, "Pressure Groups in Congress," *Annals* 319 (September 1958): 3.
75. Holtzman, *Interest Groups*, p. 77; Milbrath, *The Washington Lobbyists*, p. 289.
Although the purpose of a communication may be persuasion, any attempt to convince by providing inaccurate information can destroy whatever cooperation exists between the target and the NGO. Deakin, *The Lobbyists*, p. 194; Milbrath, *The Washington Lobbyists*, p. 211. Since information presented by an interest group may be viewed as slanted, a reputation for impartiality can facilitate the perceived reliability of an NGO's communicated information.
76. See Gabriel A. Almond, *The American People and Foreign Policy*, 2d ed. (New York: Praeger, 1960), p. 236.
77. See Milbrath, *The Washington Lobbyists*, p. 308. International NGOs may be closer than the State Department to developments in a specific country and more able to conduct programs abroad. Chittick, *State Department*, pp. 231-32.
78. B.C. Cohen, "The Influence of Non-Governmental Groups in Foreign Policy-making," in *Studies in Citizen Participation in International Relations*, 2 vols. (Boston: World Peace Foundation, 1959), vol. 2, p. 12.
79. Zeigler, *Interest Groups*, p. 17. "[S]ome groups lack [direct] influence on foreign policy most of the time. This seems to be especially true of the large national organizations commonly placed in the categories of civic, professional, fraternal, women's, ideological, and even religious groups." Ibid., p. 16.
80. See "U.S. Aid Restrictions Called Incomplete," *New York Times*, 17 July 1977, p. 7.
81. See, for example, Center for International Policy, *Human Rights and the U.S. Foreign Assistance Program, Fiscal Year 1978*, 2 pts. (Center for International Policy, 1977), pt. 1: *Latin America*; pp. ii, 63.
82. Ibid.; idem, pt. 2 *East Asia*. See also "U.S. Aid Restrictions Called Incomplete," *New York Times*, 17 July 1977, p. 7.

The Influence of Interest Groups 259

83. See, for example, U.S., Congress, House, *Congressional Record*, 95th Cong., 1st sess., 15 July 1977, 123:E4527 (article by Center for International Policy); idem, World Bank Intends to Loan $2.9 Billion to Human Rights Violators, 18 July 1977, *Congressional Record* 123:S12193 (Center for International Policy data quoted in debate).
84. See U.S., Congress, House, Committee on Appropriations, *Hearings Before a Subcommittee of the House Committee on Appropriations, Foreign Assistance and Related Agencies Appropriations For 1978*, 95th Cong., 1st sess., 1977, pp. 121-126 (testimony of James Morrell); idem, *Hearings Before the Subcommittee on International Development Institutions and Finance of the House Committee on Banking, Finance and Urban Affairs, International Development Institutions Authorizations—1977*, 95th Cong., 1st sess., 1977, pp. 196-218 (testimony of William Goodfellow and James Morrell).
85. See, for example, U.S., Congress, House, *Congressional Record*, World Bank Intends to Loan $2.9 Billion to Human Rights Violators, 95th Cong., 1st sess., 18 July 1977, 123:S12193 (Center for International Policy data quoted in debate).
86. See Friends Committee on National Legislation, "Introduction to the Committee and the Annual Meeting," (Washington, D.C.: 29 March 1972); Friends Committee on National Legislation, "Friends Committee on National Legislation Washington Newsletter," (Washington, D.C.: April 1977), No. 391, p. 3.
87. See note 123, *infra*.
88. See, for example, U.S., Congress, Senate, Committee on Foreign Relations, *1977 Human Rights Hearings*, pp. 33-41 (testimony of Edward F. Snyder).
89. See Washington Office on Latin American, "Update: Latin America," (Washington, D.C., May-June 1977), p. 1; Joseph T. Eldridge, codirector of the Washington Office on Latin America, letter to David Weissbrodt, 15 December 1976, Human Rights Library, University of Minnesota Law School, Minneapolis, MN; Washington Office on Latin America, "Official List of Members of the Latin American Strategy Committee (LASC)," (Washington, D.C.: 3 December 1976); See also, Note, "The Role of Nongovernmental Organizations in Implementing Human Rights in Latin America," *Georgia Journal of International and Comparative Law* 7 (Summer 1977): 477, 487.
90. See Joseph T. Eldridge, codirector of the Washington Office on Latin America, letter to David Weissbrodt, 15 December 1976, Human Rights Library, University of Minnesota Law School, Minneapolis, MN.
91. Ibid., p. 1.
92. See U.S., Congress, House, Committee on International Relations, *Human Rights in Nicaragua, Guatemala, and El Salvador: Implications for U.S. Policy: Hearings Before the Subcommittee on International Organizations of the House Committee on International Relations*, 94th Cong., 2d sess., 8-9 June 1976, pp. 155-57 (memo from the Washington Office on Latin America to participants in the hearings regarding preparation of testimony), (hereafter cited as U.S., Congress, House, Committee on International Relations, *Human Rights in Nicaragua, Guatemala, and El Salvador*); Joseph T. Eldridge, codirector of the Washington Office on Latin America, letters to David Weissbrodt, 15 December 1977 and 12 May 1977, Human Rights

Library, University of Minnesota Law School, Minneapolis, MN; Cressida S. McKean, Washington Office on Latin America, letter to David Weissbrodt, 17 July 1977, Human Rights Library, University of Minnesota Law School, Minneapolis, MN. The Washington Office on Latin America has also been instrumental in arranging for meetings between prominent Latin American political figures and administration officials.

93. See, for example, Washington Office on Latin America, "Update: Latin America," (Washington, D.C., May-June 1977), pp. 5-8.
94. See, for example, Washington Office on Latin America, "Legislative Update: Latin America," (Washington, D.C., January-February 1977); idem, "Update: Latin America," (May-June 1977), pp. 1-3.
95. See Coalition for a New Foreign and Military Policy, "What is the Human Rights Working Group?" (Washington, D.C.: undated 1977).
96. Coalition for a New Foreign and Military Policy, "Human Rights Working Group Minutes," (Washington, D.C.: 12 July 1977), p. 1 (hereafter cited as Coalition, "Minutes").
97. Coalition, "Minutes," (7 April 1977), p. 1.
98. Coalition, "Minutes," (12 July 1977), p. 1.
99. See, for example, ibid., p. 1.
100. Ibid.
101. Ibid., see Brooks and Ramsey, "What Does the Legislative Office Do?," *Peace and Freedom* 37 (January 1977): 10-11; Austin, "Carter Hypocritical on Human Rights?" *Peace and Freedom* 37 (April-May 1977): 3; Women's International League for Peace and Freedom, "Legislative Alert," (Washington, D.C.: 18 August 1977), p. 2; Women's International League for Peace and Freedom, "Chile—The Hard Facts," (Washington, D.C.: 1976).
102. Coalition, "Minutes," (12 July 1977), p. 1.

Americans for Democratic Action is a liberal NGO primarily concerned with legislative and political reform and maintains a national office in Washington, D.C., and autonomous state, regional, city, and college chapters. The Washington office maintains a legislative lobbying department. Americans for Democratic Action publishes periodicals and an annual *Voting Record* which records key votes and rates legislators according to ADA standards.

See V. Aregay, Americans for Democratic Action, introductory leaflet (Washington, D.C.: 1975); See also U.S., Congress, Senate, Committee on Foreign Relations, *1977 Human Rights Hearings*, pp. 18-33 (testimony of Bruce Cameron, Legislative Representative for Americans for Democratic Action on the subject of human rights and security assistance).

103. See Coalition, "Minutes," (12 July 1977), p. 1.

Clergy and Laity Concerned is a religious-based organization concerned with societal and humanitarian issues. It has 38 chapters and affiliates throughout the United States. See Clergy and Laity Concerned, "Our Allies' Secret Agents Have Come to the United States...," (Washington, D.C., 1977), p. 6. Clergy and Laity Concerned maintains a Human Rights Coordinating Center in Washington, D.C., in addition to its regular offices there. See Clergy and Laity Concerned, "Proposal for CALC's Program on Human Rights and U.S. International Relations," (Washington, D.C., 1976). CALC has about 20,000 contributors and one-third of its approximately 50 employees is now devoted to human rights matters. Interview with

C. Nelson, Minnesota Chapter of Clergy and Laity Concerned, 30 August 1977.
104. See Coalition, "Minutes," (12 July 1977), p. 1.
Both Senator James Abourezk and Representative Donald Fraser are members of the Board of Trustees of the Council on Hemispheric Relations, an NGO concerned with U.S.-Latin American relations. Shortly after the formation of the Council, Senator Abourezk announced its founding to the Senate and entered statements by members of the Council's Board of Trustees into the Congressional Record. U.S., Congress, Senate, *Congressional Record*, 94th Cong., 2d sess., 4 August 1976, 122:S13444.
105. Coalition, "Minutes," (7 June 1977), p.1.
The National Council of Churches is an interdenominational organization comprised of Christian churches which has established an office of human rights in New York. The National Council's Division of Church and Society also maintains an office of Haitian Refugee Affairs in Washington, D.C., which coordinates activities on behalf of Haitian refugees and prisoners. See, for example, Office of Haitian Refugee Concerns, National Council of Churches, Washington, D.C., 15 March 1977. The National Council is also active in trying to stop U.S. aid for repressive regimes. See Note, "The Role of Nongovernmental Organizations in Implementing Human Rights in Latin America," *Georgia Journal of International and Comparative Law* 7 (Summer 1977), pp. 486-87.

See, for example, an open letter to presidential candidates Ford and Carter from the National Council of Churches noting, *inter alia*, the organization's "sense of shame [regarding] the degree to which the United States government has provided economic, military, and political support to some of the most flagrant [human rights] violators." "Open Letter Sent to Candidates," *Christian Science Monitor*, 12 October 1976, p. 27; campaign of the Office of Haitian Refugees, National Council of Churches, to send letters to Attorney General Bell, Secretary of State Vance, and Assistant Secretary of State Todman (with copies to legislators) on behalf of Haitian refugees and political prisoners in Office of Haitian Refugee Concerns, Division of Church and Society, National Council of Churches, "Refugee Legislation V/V Human Rights," (Washington, D.C., 22 March 1977); Testimony of Dr. Claire Randall, General Secretary, National Council of Churches, in U.S., Congress, Senate, Committee on Foreign Relations, *Foreign Policy Choices for the Seventies and Eighties: Hearing Before the Senate Committee on Foreign Relations*, 94th Cong., 1st and 2d sess., 1975 and 1976, p. 238; Testimony of Leonard C. Meeker on behalf of the Committee on the Caribbean and Latin America, National Council of Churches, U.S., Congress, House, Committee on International Relations, *1976 Chile Hearings*, pp. 3-13.
106. See Coalition, "Minutes," (7 February 1977), p. 1.
The Transnational Institute publishes pamphlets, reprints, and special reports on economic and political developments abroad, including the role of the United States, multinational banks, and multinational corporations. See, "TNI Publications 1977," Transnational Institute, Washington, D.C., 1977. See, for example, Richard J. Barnet, *The Crisis of the Corporation* (Washington, D.C.: Transnational Institute, 1975); Howard M. Wachtel, *The New Gnomes: Multinational Banks in the Third World* (Washington, D.C.: Transnational Institute, 1977).

107. See Coalition, "Minutes," (7 June 1977), p. 1.

The United States Catholic Conference is the social action secretariat of the National Conference of Catholic Bishops. See *Encyclopedia Americana*, 1974, "National Conference of Catholic Bishops." The U.S. Catholic Conference maintains an office of International Justice and Peace at its headquarters in Washington, D.C., which has been active in promoting human rights in Latin America and elsewhere. See U.S. Catholic Conference, *Justice and Peace* 1 (February/March 1977); Note, "The Role of Nongovernmental Organizations in Implementing Human Rights in Latin America," *Georgia Journal of International and Comparative Law* 7 (Summer 1977), pp. 484-86; Rev. James S. Rausch, general secretary, U.S. Catholic Conference, open letter to Secretary of State Henry Kissinger, Washington, D.C., 7 April 1976 (supporting black majority participation in the government of South Africa); Testimony of Rev. J. Bryan Hehir, associate secretary, Office of International Justice and Peace, U.S. Catholic Conference, in U.S., Congress, House, Committee on Foreign Affairs, *Torture and Oppression in Brazil; Hearing Before the Subcommittee on International Organizations and Movements of the House Committee on Foreign Affairs*, 93d Cong., 2d sess., 11 December 1974, pp. 15-32; Testimony of Thomas Quigley, Latin American Bureau, U.S. Catholic Conference, in U.S., Congress, House, Committee on Foreign Affairs, *International Human Rights Hearings*, pp. 195-99; Testimony of James Jennings, associate director, division of Justice and Peace, U.S. Catholic Conference, ibid., p. 64.

The Office of International Justice and Peace, U.S. Catholic Conference, publishes essays, educational materials, reprints of organization testimony before Congress, and statements, which include human rights materials. See Office of International Justice and Peace, U.S. Catholic Conference, "Publications List," (Washington, D.C., Winter 1976-77). See, for example, idem, "Human Rights/Human Needs: An Unfinished Agenda," (Washington, D.C., January 1978); idem, "A Primer for Teachers," (educational packet, 1972); idem, "Human Rights: A Question of Conscience," (Washington, D.C., 1974).

108. See Coalition, "Minutes," (12 July 1977), p. 1.

Representatives from the Argentine Commission for Human Rights testified at the hearings on Argentina held by Representative Donald Fraser. See Argentine Commission for Human Rights Washington Information Bureau, Argentine Commission for Human Rights (Washington, D.C., undated 1977). Representatives from the Argentine Commission also testified before the Senate Subcommittee on Foreign Assistance on April 25, 1977. See Argentine Commission for Human Rights, "Update on Legislation Regarding Military Aid to Argentina," (Washington, D.C., 6 May 1977), p. 1. The Argentine Commission was a principal lobbyist for congressional action cutting off aid to that country on human rights grounds. See U.S., 91 Stat. 614, 619-20 (1977); U.S., Congress, Senate, *Congressional Record*, 95th Cong., 1st sess., 15 June 1977, 123:S9888-94 (discussion of Amnesty International and Argentine Commission reports in connection with Senate adoption of Foreign Assistance Act Section 620B).

109. See Coalition, "Minutes," (7 April 1977), p. 1.

The Chile Committee for Human Rights is a Washington, D.C., based NGO headed by Isabel Letelier. Its sponsors include seven members of Congress and a number of prominent national figures from many fields. See

Chile Committee for Human Rights, "Newsletter," (Washington, D.C., May 1977), p. 5. (Reprinting Amnesty International materials for campaign for Chile's disappeared; Chile Committee for Human Rights, "Newsletter," (Washington, D.C., March 1977) (containing information concerning human rights violations in, and U.S. foreign policy toward, Chile).

110. See Coalition, "Minutes," (12 July 1977), p. 1.

The Chile Legislative Center, an office of the National Coordinating Center in Solidarity with Chile, publishes a newsletter on Chilean human rights developments. See, for example, Chile Legislative Center, "Chile Legislative Center Bulletin," (Washington, D.C., November 1976).

111. See Coalition, "Minutes," (12 July 1977), p.1.

Friends of the Filipino People operates a Congress Education Project for the purpose of supplying information to Congress on U.S.-Philippine relations. Friends of the Filipino People, "An Organizational Description," (Washington, D.C., and New York, 28 July 1977). Techniques employed by the organization include letter-writing campaigns, distribution of literature, contacts with legislators or other governmental officials, and coalition work with other NGOs. See, for example, Friends of the Filipino People, "Stop U.S. Aid to the Philippine Dictatorship!" (New York, 1977); Friends of the Filipino People, "U.S. Bases in the Philippines: A Position Paper by the Friends of the Filipino People," (New York, 1977); Friends of the Filipino People, Anti-Martial Law Coalition (Philippines), "A Reply to the State Department," (Washington, D.C., 11 January 1977).

112. See Coalition, "Minutes," (7 February 1977), p. 1.

The goal of the Movement for a Free Philippines is to promote a more democratic government in the Philippines, e.g., representative elected leadership and a return to 1935 constitutional provisions. The organization is headed by Raul Monglapus, an expatriate Philippines Senator and diplomat who has been living in the United States since the imposition of martial law by President Marcos in 1972. Gary King, Twin Cities Chapter, Movement for a Free Philippines, (telephone interview, 1 September 1977).

113. See Coalition, "Minutes," (12 July 1977), p. 1.

See, for example, campaign for the "disappeared" in Chile, in coordination with Amnesty International, Chile Committee for Human Rights, and other groups in Non-Intervention in Chile, "Chile Newsletter," (Berkeley, Cal., June/July 1977), p. 1; campaign to persuade the U.S. government to withhold all forms of aid so long as gross human rights violations continue in Chile, ibid., p. 6; participation in coalition campaign urging senators to vote yes on Abourezk-Hatfield amendment to H.R. 5262, ibid., p. 11.

114. See Coalition, "Minutes," (12 July 1977), p. 1.

See, for example, testimony of James P. Sinnott, later of the North American Coalition for Human Rights in South Korea, former vicar general of the Roman Catholic Diocese of Inchon, Korea, in U.S., Congress, Senate, Foreign Relations Committee, *Foreign Assistance Authorization: Hearings Before the Subcommittee on Foreign Assistance of the Committee on Foreign Relations*, 94th Cong., 1st sess. (3 and 13 June, 17, 21, 23 and 29 July, 17 and 23 September 1975), pp. 462-70.

115. See Coalition, "Minutes," (12 July 1977), p. 1.

116. See Coalition, "Minutes," (7 February 1977), p. 1.

The Taiwanese Rights and Culture Association has utilized press releases on the subject of human rights in Taiwan. See, for example, Taiwanese

Rights and Culture Association, "Political Condition and Human Rights in Taiwan," (press release, 28 February 1977). The wife of a prisoner in Taiwan announced a press conference regarding her husband's situation on the letterhead of the organization. Taiwanese Rights and Culture Association, "Urgent Press Conference Invitation," (January 1977).

117. See Coalition, "Minutes," (3 March 1977), p. 1.

See, for example, testimony of Carmel Budiardjo, a member of TAPOL (Campaign for the Release of Indonesian Political Prisoners), in U.S., Congress, House, Committee on International Relations, *Human Rights Hearings on Indonesia and the Philippines*, p. 2.

118. See Coalition for the New Foreign and Military Policy, "What is the Human Rights Working Group?" (Washington, D.C., undated 1977).

In January 1977, the Uruguay Information Project submitted to Representative Donald Fraser an analysis and response to a State Department document on human rights in Uruguay. Louise Popkin and Juan R. Ferreira, letter to Representative Donald Fraser, Uruguay Information Project, Washington, D. C., January 1977.

119. See Coalition, "Minutes," (12 July 1977), p. 1. The Washington Office on Africa has a small staff on Capitol Hill and concentrates its efforts almost entirely on issues relating to southern Africa. See, for example, Washington Office on Africa, "Washington Notes on Africa," (Washington, D.C., Summer 1977).

120. See note 141, below. For an extreme example, Representative McDonald attacked the Coalition for a New Foreign and Military Policy for urging aid to so-called "new communist terrorist regimes." The American Committee on Africa, American Friends Service Committee, Americans for Democratic Action, Clergy and Laity Concerned, and other NGOs were mentioned in Representative McDonald's accusations. U.S., Congress, House, *Congressional Record*, 95th Cong., 1st sess. (28 July 1977):123:E4912.

121. "Considered singly, the letter-writing campaign is probably the least effective and most relied upon lobbying technique." Zeigler, *Interest Groups*, p. 272. Wilcox, *Congress, the Executive, and Foreign Policy*, p. 115; Scott and Hunt, *Congress and Lobbies*, pp. 72-74; Milbrath, *The Washington Lobbyists*, p. 247. Targets may find form letters offensive, irritating, uninformed, and unrepresentative, because such form letters require so little thought and effort from the sender. Holtzman, *Interest Groups*, p. 102; Bertram M. Gross, *The Legislative Struggle* (New York: McGraw-Hill, 1953), p. 162. In sufficient volume, however, such grass roots communication may represent considerable political weight to the target or demonstrate that people are aware of the issue. Scott and Hunt, *Congress and Lobbies*, pp. 74, 76; Milbrath, *The Washington Lobbyists*, p. 245.

To be effective, letters to legislators must be personal, thoughtful, and informed expressions of individual views. Wilcox, *Congress, the Executive, and Foreign Policy*, p. 115; Scott and Hunt, *Congress and Lobbies*, p. 72; Milbrath, *The Washington Lobbyists*, p. 249. Effectiveness is further facilitated by the prominence of the sender, especially in the target's constitutency. Holtzman, *Interest Groups*, p. 103.

Letter-writing can be effective vis-à-vis the State Department and other administrative agencies:

As a rule of thumb, information officers attempt to determine the source of opposition whenever they receive ten letters expressing the same view on the same issue in one week. Public correspondence is particularly useful in anticipating organized campaigns against various features of American policy abroad.

Chittick, *State Department*, p. 164.
122. For example, the American Committee on Africa urged letters to Senators, especially Senator Inouye as chairman of the Foreign Operations Subcommittee of the Senate Appropriations Committee, asking inclusion of Mozambique and Angola in the foreign aid appropriations bill. American Committee on Africa, "ACOA Action News," (New York, July-August 1977), p. 2. See also, for example, Friends of the Filipino People, "Stop U.S. Aid to the Philippines Dictatorship!" (New York, 1977); Friends of the Filipino People, "To Another Year for the Marcos Dictatorship," (Cambridge, Mass., 1976); Human Rights Coordinating Center, Clergy and Laity Concerned, "Action Alert," (Washington, D.C., 27 June 1977); Coalition, "Minutes," (12 January 1977), p. 2.

The Citizen's Action Guide to Human Rights distributed by the Human Rights Working Group, provides instructions which enhance the effectiveness of letter-writing, such as citing documented facts and asking a question which cannot be answered with a form letter. Coalition for a New Foreign and Military Policy, "Citizen's Action Guide to Human Rights," (Washington, D.C., 1977), p. 7. The guide also discusses how to arrange and utilize personal visits with legislators, and the use of phone calls and telegrams to legislators. Ibid. The Guide notes that "[p]etitions count for very little in Washington, and post cards and form letters are *much* less effective than personal letters." Ibid.

A few of the U.S. human rights organizations have begun to communicate directly with embassies and governments responsible for human rights violations, rather than consistently seeking U.S. government leverage. See, for example, United States Committee for Justice to Latin American Prisoners, "USLA Reports," (New York, Winter 1977), p. 15; Chinese Human Rights Society, introductory letter (New York, 29 December 1976).

Some U.S. professional organizations have begun to make appeals to the U.S. government and to other countries on behalf of the human rights of their fellow professionals imprisoned in other countries. See, for example, American Bar Association, "Minutes of Meeting of the Committee on International Human Rights," section on International Law (Chicago, 8 August 1977); American Bar Association, "Resolution of the American Bar Association Home of Delegates," (24-25 February 1975); American Academy of Arts and Sciences, "Scientific Freedom and Responsibility Committee Appointed." *Science* 193 (1976): 877; "Scientists Tortured in South America," *Christian Science Monitor*, 6 July 1977, pp. 1-3 (discussing efforts of American Physical Society and American Academy for the Advancement of Science).

International NGOs possess far greater flexibility in this sort of activity, because they can ask citizens of different countries to express their concern over human rights problems. U.S. organizations can only rely on U.S. citizens and the human rights concerns of U.S. citizens may be less credible in regard to some countries than as to others. Nevertheless, U.S. NGOs might make greater use of these direct approaches. While studies have indicated that stimulated letter-writing campaigns are not particularly effective in influencing U.S. policy, (see note 121 above), there is some evidence that foreign government officials are so unaccustomed to such grass-roots campaigns that stimulated letters are quite effective on specific human rights problems.

For example, if there is concern that a prisoner might be tortured or killed, Amnesty International uses its Urgent Action Network. Thousands of notices are sent to individual AI members all over the world, who in turn send telegrams and letters to specific government officials who may have influence over the fate of the prisoner.

The results are quite impressive. For example, in 25% of the cases where the grass-roots technique was used, the situation improved. Amnesty International, "How Effective are Urgent Actions?" mimeographed (1977), p. 2. That is, torture stopped, the arrest was acknowledged by the authorities, or the disappeared person located. In another 22% of the cases, the prisoners were released. It should be noted that the Urgent Action notices, in general, are not aimed at the release of prisoners, but to protect their fundamental rights to life and the integrity of the person. Nevertheless, the pressure resulted in their being released. In 28% of the cases, there was additional information as a result of all those Urgent Action letters, but there was no indication of an improvement of the situation. In 20% of the cases no new information was received. And finally, in 5% of the cases, the situation worsened, despite the appeals. That is, in 47% of the cases, the situation definitely improved, and although it is difficult to establish a direct correlation between the Urgent Actions and the subsequent improvements, there is some evidence of the relative value of this technique.

123. See, for example, Bruce P. Cameron, legislative representative, Americans for Democratic Action, letter to Senator Hubert H. Humphrey (Washington, D.C.: Americans for Democratic Action, 30 August 1976) (urging Senator Humphrey to request State Department reports on human rights in eight countries pursuant to Section 502B of the International Security Assistance and Arms Export Control Act of 1976, 22 U.S.C.A. § 2304(c). (Supp. 1977)). Representatives of Americans for Democratic Action visited four House committee members on the issue of aid to the Philippines, on May 4, 1976. Americans for Democratic Action, "Action for Human Rights," (Washington, D.C., 1977).

Similarly, Roger Rumpf, of the Human Rights Coordinating Center, Clergy and Laity Concerned, met with Representative Fraser about U.S. policy toward South Korea. Coalition, "Minutes," (12 January 1977), p. 2.

The Friends Committee on National Legislation helped organize a delegation of religious representatives to discuss human rights with then President-elect Carter's deputy director of issues on October 2, 1976, and with State Department representatives on October 19, 1976. Friends Committee on National Legislation, "Annual Report & Legislative Summary 1976," (Washington, D.C., 1976), p. 4. The Friends Committee also participated in a delegation to the State Department urging a visa for Carmel Budiardjo of TAPOL to speak on political prisoners in Indonesia. (Ibid.) Representatives of the Human Rights Working Group met with State Department staff, including Patt Derian, Coordinator for Human Rights and Humanitarian Affairs. Coalition, "Minutes," (3 March 1977), p. 2.

124. It should be noted, however, that this finding was based on the responses a decade ago of only, seven church, humanitarian, and citizens' NGO

representatives. Lester W. Milbrath, "Lobbying as a Communications Process," in Samuel C. Patterson, *American Legislative Behavior* (Princeton, N.J.: Van Nostrand, 1968), pp. 307-8.
125. Michael Davis, of the American Committee on Africa, testified before the House Subcommittee on International Organizations on the subject of racism and repression in Namibia, in U.S., Congress, House, Committee on International Relations, *Namibia: The United Nations and U.S. Policy: Hearings Before the Subcommittee on International Organizations of the House Committee on International Relations*, 94th Cong., 2d sess. (24 and 27 August 1976), pp. 21-37.
126. U.S., Congress, House, Committee on Foreign Affairs, *International Human Rights Hearings*, pp. 359-66 (testimony of Sidney Liskofsky, American Jewish Committee); U.S., Congress, Commission on Security and Cooperation in Europe, *Basket Three: Implementation of the Helsinki Accords: Hearings Before the Commission on Security and Cooperation in Europe, Volume II*, 95th Cong., 1st sess. (15 and 17 March 1977), pp. 72-74 (testimony of Rabbi Marc Tanenbaum, member of the American Jewish Committee, coleader of the National Interreligious Task Force on Soviet Jewry).
127. Dicran Simsarian, chairman of the Armenian Rights Movement, testified on the subject of Turkish oppression of its Armenian population. U.S., Congress, House, Committee on International Relations, *Investigation into Certain Past Instances of Genocide and Exploration of Policy Options for the Future: Hearings Before the Subcommittee on Future Foreign Policy Research and Development of the House Committee on International Relations*, 94th Cong., 2d sess. (11 May and 30 August 1976), pp. 41-45.
128. U.S., Congress, Commission on Security and Cooperation in Europe, *Basket Three Hearings, Volume III* (testimony by Robert Adelstein, cochairman of the Committee of Concerned Scientists and head of the Molecular Cardiology Section of the NIH).
129. U.S., Congress, House, Committee on International Relations, *Resources in Namibia: Implications for U.S. Policy: Hearings Before the Subcommittee on International Resources, Food, and Energy of the House Committee on International Relations*, 94th Cong., 1st sess. (10 June 1975 and 13 May 1976), p. 44 (testimony of William O. Johnston, president of Episcopal Churchmen for South Africa).
130. Fred Branfman and D. Gareth Porter, codirectors of the Indochina Resource Center, testified before the House Subcommittee on Asian and Pacific Affairs on the subject of aid to Indochina. U.S., Congress, House, Committee on Foreign Affairs, *Political Prisoners in South Vietnam and the Philippines: Hearings Before the Subcommittee on Asian and Pacific Affairs of the House Committee on Foreign Affairs*, 93rd Cong., 2d sess. (1 May and 5 June 1974), pp. 18-49 (testimony of Mr. Branfman, pp. 18-38; testimony of Mr. Porter, pp. 38-46).
131. A written statement detailing the case of an individual Soviet prisoner was submitted to the House Subcommittee on International Organizations by Alan G. Howard of the National Conference of Soviet Jewry. U.S., Congress, House, Committee on International Relations, *Anti-Semitism and Reprisals Against Jewish Emigration in the Soviet Union: Hearings Before the Subcommittee on International Organizations of the House Committee on International Relations*, 94th Cong., 2d sess. (27 May 1976), pp. 20-26.

132. U.S., Congress, House, Committee on International Relations, *Human Rights in Nicaragua, Guatemala, and El Salvador*, pp. 78-88 (testimony of Rev. William L. Wipfler, director, Caribbean and Latin America Department, National Council of Churches).
133. U.S., Congress, House, Committee on International Relations, *Human Rights Hearings on Indonesia and the Philippines*, pp. 60-68, 81-98 (testimony of Rev. Harold K. Schulz, executive director of the United Church of Christ Center for Social Action and Dr. George Otto, conference minister, Rocky Mountain Conference of the United Church of Christ).
134. Thomas Quigley, of the Office of International Justice and Peace, United States Catholic Conference, testified before the House Subcommittee on International Organizations on the subject of religious persecution in El Salvador. U.S., Congress, House, Committee on International Relations, "Report of July 21, 1977, Hearing before the Subcommittee on International Organizations of the House Committee on International Relations," memorandum, 22 July 1977.
135. Milbrath, *The Washington Lobbyists*, p. 233. See Lewis A. Dexter, *How Organizations Are Represented in Washington* (Indianapolis, Bobbs-Merrill, 1969), p. 74; Gross, *The Legislative Struggle*, pp. 285-86. From a long-range perspective, NGOs may also attempt to influence the composition of committees by pressing for the assignment of their congressional supporters. Donald C. Blaisdell, *American Democracy Under Pressure* (New York: Ronald Press Co., 1957), p. 111; Gross, *The Legislative Struggle*, pp. 275-76.
136. Dexter, *How Organizations Are Represented*, pp. 75-76. See note 92 above. There is no guarantee that committee members are really listening and lending weight to testimony, however, nor that they and their nonmember colleagues will read the printed records; in fact, many committee members may already have made up their minds on the issue. Milbrath, *The Washington Lobbyists*, p. 310; Zeigler, *Interest Groups*, p. 254. Effectiveness may ultimately depend on how well-prepared and confidence-inspiring the particular witness is. Scott and Hunt, *Congress and Lobbies*, p. 79. In this regard, NGOs which are primarily involved in expanding their membership and collecting dues will be minimally effective:

> Many of these groups have no contact with the legislative process except at formal hearings at committees, and they are treated with patient tolerance by veteran legislators who have developed a good knowledge of the relative merits of interest groups (Zeigler, *Interest Groups*, p. 267).

Also, if the relevant committee has a convenor or outspoken member who is hostile to the interests of the NGO, the effectiveness of any attempt to utilize hearings will be minimal. Ibid., p. 225.

An NGO can get publicity for its stand on an issue through media coverage of committee hearings, and this exposure may actually reach more legislators than the testimony itself or the printed committee reports. Milbrath, *The Washington Lobbyists*, p. 231; Dexter, *How Organizations Are Represented*, p. 76. Another advantage of testifying at hearings is the opportunity to gain the trust of members and initiate contacts with them for future activities. Zeigler, *Interest Groups*, p. 256.

137. See Blaisdell, *American Democracy,* pp. 105-07, 111. Legislators who are willing to be "inside lobbyists" by writing Dear Colleague letters help legitimize and publicize the NGO's position. Sympathetic legislators can also help by inserting speeches, statements, and letters of NGO representatives into the Congressional Record. Turner, "How Pressure Groups Operate," p. 66; Milbrath, *The Washington Lobbyists,* p. 234. But see Milbrath, p. 172:

> In this writer's opinion, people in Washington overplay the importance and value of appearing on the record. Washington folklore insists that there is something sacred about getting on the record and that great benefits will follow. Those who believe this seem to assume that masses of people (as well as congressmen) read the record or that they listen to persons who do read the record; neither assumption is justified by the evidence available.

Sympathetic legislators also may influence their colleagues in an informal fashion which is perceived as a mutual exchange of views, rather than as a source of influence. Lewis A. Dexter, "What Do Congressmen Hear?" in Nelson W. Polsby, ed., *Congressional Behavior* (New York: Random House, 1971), p. 37.

138. Ten House members utilized information from Amnesty International on "disappeared persons" in Chile, in a Dear Colleague letter sent to other House members on June 24, 1977. See Amnesty International U.S.A., Chile Coordination Group, Campaign for Disappeared Prisoners in Chile, 7 July 1977. Representative Ketchum inserted in the Congressional Record a Dear Colleague letter he had received, which solicited cosponsors for a resolution. The resolution, H. R. Con. Res. 137, 95th Cong., 1st sess., 1977, expressed support for the Carter administration's stance on human rights, reaffirmed the commitment to obtaining compliance with the Helsinki Accords, and urged the president to support human rights in non-Eastern European countries as well. The letter was signed by Representative Pease, and listed 34 cosponsors of the resolution. *Congressional Record* 123 (21 March 1977): H2344.

139. Senator Hatfield inserted in the Congressional Record a Dear Colleague letter sent to members of the Senate by Representative Badillo. The letter discussed the potential effectiveness of the Abourezk-Hatfield amendment to a bill authorizing increased United States participation in international lending institutions. U.S., Congress, House, *An Act to Provide For Increased Participation by the United States in the International Bank for Reconstruction and Development, the International Development Association, etc.,* Pub. L. 95-118, 95th Cong., 1st sess., 1977, H.R. 5262. See *Bretton Woods Agreement Act, U.S. Code Annotated,* vol. 22, sec. 262(d) (supp. no. 4, 1978). The amendment mandated a "no" vote by U.S. representatives to such institutions on loans to countries that consistently violate human rights, unless the loan directly benefits the needy. The letter urged Senate support for the amendment. *Congressional Record* 123 (14 June 1977): S9710.

140. For example, Senator Proxmire inserted in the Congressional Record a letter sent by 15 senators to Secretary of State Vance; the letter urged United States diplomatic action on behalf of Kurdish refugees in Iran and Iraq, through direct and third-party approaches. *Congressional Record* 123 (26 July 1977):

S12833. See also a letter of April 2, 1976, from 119 members of Congress to President Ford, regarding oppression in South Korea, in U.S., Congress, Senate, Committee on Foreign Relations, *International Security Assistance, Hearings before the Subcommittee on Foreign Assistance of the Senate Committee on Foreign Relations*, 94th Cong., 2d sess., 1976, pp. 88-89; a letter of April 19,1976, from Senator Kennedy to Secretary of State Kissinger, requesting communications of U.S. concern to Brazilian authorities regarding the removal of political rights from two members of the Brazilian Congress; and letters of March 15, 1976, from senators Humphrey and McGee, and 30 other congressional representatives, to Secretary of State Kissinger, requesting immediate action by the State Department to obtain the release of Olga Talamante, an American citizen jailed and tortured in Argentina.

Members of Congress have in recent years also effectively utilized correspondence in the form of questions as one means of forcing the State Department to formulate and articulate its position on matters affecting human rights. See, for example, the State Department's responses to questions submitted by Representative Fraser, in U.S., Congress, House, Committee on International Relations, *Human Rights Hearings on Uruguay and Paraguay*, app. 4, p. 145; an exchange of correspondence between Representative Fraser and Deputy Secretary Kempton B. Jenkins, regarding the position of the United States on Chile, in U.S., Congress, House, Committee on Foreign Affairs, *Review of the U.N. Commission on Human Rights, Hearings before the Subcommittee on International Organizations and Movements of the House Committee on Foreign Affairs*, 93rd Cong., 2d sess., 1974, app. 3, p. 68; and a letter of December 22, 1976 from Kempton B. Jenkins, acting assistant secretary for congressional relations, to Representative Fraser. Such congressional correspondence may be drafted or generated by NGOs.

141. For example, see the introduction of a resolution, H.R. Con. Res. 224, 95th Cong., 1st sess., 1977, that supported Soviet prisoners of conscience Rudenko, Tykhy, Moroz, and Shukhevych, in *Congressional Record* 123 (5 August 1977): H8831; Representative Koch's remarks about meeting with a delegation from the United Ukranian American Organizations and receiving two petitions, in ibid., pp. H8830-31; the debate on S. Con. Res. 7, 95th Cong., 1st sess., 1977, wherein data from the National Conference on Soviet Jewry is cited by Representative Fascell, in ibid., p. H2364; support for S. Con. Res. 7 by the Committee for the Defense of Valentyn Moroz, cited by Representative LeFante in ibid., p. H2372; and the work of the Greater New York Council on Soviet Jewry, cited by Representative Badillo in ibid., p. H2373.

142. See American Association for the Advancement of Science, *A.A.A.S. News*, 1 July 1977, pp. 40-41. See also a letter to the editor of the *New York Times* from Paul Irish, executive associate of the American Committee on Africa, on the subject of barring aid to Mozambique. *New York Times*, 14 July 1977, p. 38. This letter prompted an editorial in the *Times* that mentioned the letter and urged the removal of Mozambique from the foreign aid "blacklist," "Aiding Mozambique," *New York Times*, 17 July 1977, p. 20.

The Council on Hemispheric Affairs issues numerous press releases on human rights developments in Latin America. For example, see Council on Hemispheric Affairs, "Charge Made that Full-Blown Anti-Semitism Exists in Argentina," press release, 20 May 1977; idem, "On Vance's O.A.S.

Human Rights Speech," press release, 15 June 1977. Charges made by the Council were reported in an article in the *Washington Post*. "Chilean Protest Seeks Missing-Person Probe," *Washington Post*, 16 June 1977, sec. A, p. 34.

143. See, for example, Richard Barnet, *The Crisis of the Corporation* (Washington, D.C.: Transnational Institute, 1975); Howard M. Wachtel, *The New Gnomes: Multinational Banks in the Third World* (Washington, D.C.: Transnational Institute, 1977); World Council of Churches, Commission of the Churches on International Affairs, newsletter, no. 3 (1976), p. 1; Lutheran Council in the U.S.A., Office for Governmental Affairs, "Focus on Governmental Affairs" (newsletter, April 1977); North American Congress on Latin America "NACLA Publications" (brochure); Washington Office on Latin America, "Update: Latin America" (newsletter, May-June 1977; and idem, "Legislative Update: Latin America" (newsletter, January-February 1977).

In the process of determining their position, formalizing their views, or seeking publicity, NGOs sometimes pass resolutions on human rights issues. See, for example, "Statement on Ratification of the Genocide Convention," Lutheran Council U.S.A. Annual Meeting Minutes, 1973 Meeting, pp. 18-19. American Association for the Advancement of Science, *A.A.A.S. News*, 1 July 1977, p. 40.

The Human Rights Working Group's *Citizen's Action Guide to Human Rights* (Washington, D.C.: Coalition for a New Foreign and Military Policy, 1977), p. 15, contains a form resolution urging elected officials to implement and extend existing human rights legislation; the *Guide* urges organizations to sign the resolution and send copies to legislators.

144. See, for example, the insertion by Representative Fraser of a "balanced and useful analysis of the issue of the United States and the ILO," prepared by the Overseas Development Council, in *Congressional Record* 123 (5 August 1977): E5176-77; and "Uncivil Strife in El Salvador," *Sojourners*, July 1977, an article by two associates of the Washington Office on Latin America, which was inserted by Senator Kennedy into *Congressional Record* 123 (4 August 1977): S13801-04.

The National Captive Nations Committee has generated a number of insertions in the Congressional Record and discussion on the effort of Congress to commemorate Captive Nations Week and to raise public consciousness about human rights problems in Eastern Europe. For example, see "Captive Nations Week, 1977," *Congressional Record* 123 (21 July 1977): E4689; and "Captive Nations Week, 1977," *Congressional Record* 123 (20 July 1977): H7476-97.

145. See, for example, "Southern Africa: The U.S. Record at the U.N., 1972," prepared by the Africa Fund of the American Committee on Africa, in U.S., Congress, House, Committee on Foreign Affairs, *International Human Rights Hearings*, p. 638; and "Statement on Political Repression and Terror in Brazil," prepared by the Latin America Department of the National Council of Churches, in ibid., p. 672.

146. At a meeting of the Human Rights Working Group in January 1977, representatives of the Human Rights Education Project discussed plans for a mobile educational unit to be used around the country for education on human rights violations in Chile, Argentina, and Uruguay, and the role of the United States vis-à-vis these countries. Coalition for a New Foreign and

Military Policy, Human Rights Working Group Minutes, meeting of 12 January 1977, p. 1. Human Rights Working Group members collaborated on a human rights guide for distribution to the public; the publication discusses violating countries, human rights legislation, and suggestions for organizing community campaigns for human rights. Coalition for a New Foreign and Military Policy, *Citizen's Action Guide*.

Nonintervention in Chile provides films and speakers for educational presentations on Chile and the "disappeared." "Non-Intervention in Chile," *Chile Newsletter* (June-July 1977).

Most of the nongovernmental organizations concerned with human rights are nonprofit organizations which cannot regularly engage in a substantial amount of legislative activity without losing their tax-exempt status. Internal Revenue Service, *Internal Revenue Code*, secs. 501(c)(3), 501(h)(3)-(5) (1978). There are thus just a few NGOs, such as Americans for Democratic Action, which actively engage in lobbying work and have registered as lobbyists under the *Federal Regulation of Lobbying Act, U.S. Code*, vol. 2, secs. 261-270 (1977). All of the Washington, D.C. human rights NGOs, whether nonprofit or not, engage in some lobbying activities, but must also devote substantial efforts in education and other activities not directly related to the legislative process. See generally Boris L. Bittker and George K. Rahdert, "The Exemption of Nonprofit Organizations from Federal Income Taxation," *Yale Law Journal* 85 (January 1976): 299; and E. Sachs, "Lobby Act Reform" (memorandum, Congressional Research Service, 29 June 1977).

147. Clement E. Vose, "Litigation as a Form of Pressure Group Activity," *Annals* 319 (September 1958): 20.

The Center for Law and Social Policy, the International Human Rights Law Group, the Lawyers' Committee for Civil Rights Under Law (Africa Assistance Project), the Lawyers' Committee for International Human Rights, the Center for Constitutional Rights, and the Interfaith Center on Corporate Responsibility have been the organizations most engaged in these litigation activities. David Weissbrodt, "Domestic Legal Activity in Furtherance of International Human Rights Goals," in *Implementing International Human Rights Through the Domestic Legal Process*, ed., William D. Raymond (Charlottesville: Moore Society, 1975), pp. 10-12; Lawyers' Committee for Civil Rights Under Law, Africa Legal Assistance Project, "Interim Report," mimeographed (Washington, D.C., 1974); Center for Constitutional Rights, "Docket Report," mimeographed (New York, 1974), p. 18; Richard B. Lillich, "The Enforcement of International Human Rights Norms in Domestic Courts," in *International Human Rights Law and Practice*, ed., James C. Tuttle (Philadelphia: American Bar Association, 1978); Richard B. Lillich, "The Role of Domestic Courts in Promoting International Human Rights Norms," *New York Law School Law Review* 24 (1978): 153; Stein, "Public Interest Litigation," pp. 375-401.

See, for example, Diggs v. Richardson, 555 F.2d 848 (D.C. Cir. 1976) and associated administrative proceedings, 40 Fed. Reg. 28, 469 (1975); 41 Fed. Reg. 7510 (1976) (granting waiver for seal skins from South Africa); 41 fed. Reg. 7537 (1976) (decision of director of National Marine Fisheries Service); 41 Fed. Reg. 10, 940 (1976) (supplemental decision declining to amend waiver and regulations to permit import of seal skins from Namibia) (suit by individuals and the South West Africa Peoples Organization challenging the legality of Commerce Department action in regard to a proposed waiver of the import prohibition of the Marine Mammals Protection Act, 16 U.S.C.A. § 1361 et seq. (Supp. 1977), by allowing importation of seal skins from Namibia. Plaintiffs asserted that the proposed waiver would breach U.S. international obligations under U.N. Security Council Resolutions 276 and 301); Edlow International Co., 3 N.R.C. 563 (1976) (suit by Sierra Club, the Union of Concerned Scientists, and the Natural Resources Defense Council attempting to prevent the issuance of licenses to allow the export of enriched uranium to be used for fuel at the Tarapur Atomic Power Station in India or to condition the issuance of the licenses on India's acceptance of restrictions on its nuclear program); Diggs v. Civil Aeronautics Board (CAB), CAB South African Airways—Docket No. 24944 (OSN 73-10-2) (Sept. 5, 1973), aff'd 516 F.2d 1248 (1975), cert. denied 425 U.S. 910 (1976) (suit by Members of the House of Representatives, the American Committee on Africa, Black United Front of Washington, African Heritage Studies Association, and IFCO-Action appealing from an order of CAB, approved by the president, authorizing South African Airways to service a new route between South Africa and New York. Petitioners asserted that the CAB's order violated §§ 402(b) and 404(b) of the Federal Aviation Act, 49 U.S.C. §§ 1372(b) and 1374(b), contending that these sections prohibit the CAB from issuing a permit to a foreign carrier which discriminates among its passengers on a racial basis.); Sisters of the Precious Blood, Inc. v. Bristol-Myers Co., 431 F. Supp. 385 (S.D.N.Y. 1977) (challenge to corporate failure to inform shareholders as to the nature of the company's infant formula business in Third World countries.)

These cases are by no means regularly successful. Diggs v. Richardson was dismissed in the Court of Appeals because certain parts of Security Council Resolution 301 were held to be non-self-executing. The District Court held that even if they were self-executing, the suit must be dismissed for nonjusticiability. Diggs v. CAB was dismissed for lack of jurisdiction, and Edlow was dismissed for extraterritorial application of NEPA. Participation by NGOs in public interest litigation has been severely curtailed by standing requirements, political question problems, requirements for a causal nexus, nonjusticiability, extraterritorial application of federal law, political questions, and non-self-executing treaty problems. See Stein, "Public Interest Litigation," pp. 401-426.

148. The Human Rights Working Group has considered requests under the Freedom of Information Act, *U.S. Code*, vol. 5, sec. 552 (1977), for human rights documents generated by the State Department. See, for example, Coalition for a New Foreign and Military Policy, "Human Rights Working Group Minutes," mimeographed (Washington, D.C., 12 July 1977), p. 2.

More typical examples of Working Group coordination include: Seven NGOs collaborated on a paper responding to State Department reports on human rights in five foreign countries. "Human Rights and U.S. Foreign Policy: A Response by Non-Governmental Organizations to the State Department Reports on Argentina, Haiti, Indonesia, Iran and the Philippines," (Paper prepared by Americans for Democratic Action, Anti-Martial Law Coalition, Argentine Commission on Human Rights, Clergy and Laity Concerned, Friends of the Filipino People, National Council of Churches, and Washington Office on Latin America), 14 January 1977. See also Memorandum to House and Senate Conferees on the Appropriations Bill for

Foreign Assistance and Related Programs, Fiscal Year 1977, from representatives of 14 NGOs, Sept. 14, 1976 (memorandum urging prohibition of all military assistance to Uruguay, signed by representatives of religious, labor, political, and humanitarian NGOs, including the National Council of Churches, Mennonite Central Committee, Network, Friends Committee on National Legislation, Americans for Democratic Action, Coalition for a New Foreign and Military Policy, United Auto Workers, Washington Office on Latin America, and others); see sources cited in notes 95-120 above.

Coalitions are useful to NGOs with limited financial, political, and administrative resources; they serve to widen the range of contacts, techniques, and information available to its members; and coordination allows for efficient division of labor. Holtzman, *Interest Groups*, p. 86; Milbrath, *The Washington Lobbyists*, pp. 170-71. Also, sympathetic governmental contacts may actively participate in the formulation and activities of such coalitions. Ibid., p. 173.

Coalitions of NGOs may be formed in a number of ways. One NGO may operate as a catalyst for other NGOs; several NGOs may establish a coordinating center or committee; or informal contacts between NGOs may be formalized. Blaisdell, *American Democracy*, pp. 112-13. Coalitions may exist only as long as the unifying issue exists, or may be more permanent, depending on the nature of their common interest. Holtzman, *Interest Groups*, p. 87; Milbrath, *The Washington Lobbyists*, p. 170; Blaisdell, *American Democracy*, p. 113.

Coalitions may not be effective in all situations. The sincerity of coalitions whose common interest is tangential to their individual major interests may be doubted. Milbrath, *The Washington Lobbyists*, p. 170. The inclusion in a coalition of an NGO which certain decision makers find offensive will prove an obstacle to its effectiveness. Ibid., p. 171; see sources cited in notes 108-120 above. Finally, the coordination and management of coalitions and their activities may be difficult, because organizations will usually possess different priorities. Ibid.

149. When the issue is a controversial one, legislators are more likely to see the NGO as important to relevant legislation, perhaps as a result of the greater visibility of NGOs involved in such issues. See Scott & M. Hunt, *Congress and Lobbies*, p. 34. Since controversial issues by their very nature provoke opposition, however, competing pressures may cancel each other's influence:

> [T]he [State] Department is subject to such a wide range of group pressures on any given issue that these pressures offset each other, leaving the State Department free to determine its own policy. As one Department official stated, "We always welcome opposite views because that enables us to make a decision quite apart from these pressures."

Chittick, *State Department*, pp. 237-38 (footnote omitted); Cohen, "The Influence of Non-Governmental Groups," p. 19. If the issue is perceived by the target to be one in which the NGO has merely a tangential interest or one in which the target has little interest, influence on that issue will be lessened. Ibid.; Scott & Hunt, *Congress and Lobbies*, p. 54. Also, NGOs are less effective when the issue is one of broad policy; their greatest impact is apparently on details and specific language. Milbrath, *The Washington Lobbyists,* pp. 343-44.

Governmental shapers of foreign policy may be skeptical that an NGO has the expertise necessary to deal with foreign policy issues; as a result, information and advice offered by the NGO may be discounted. Donald C. Blaisdell, "Pressure Groups, Foreign Policies and International Politics," *Annals* 319 (September 1958): 149, 152. An NGO needs to "prove itself" by supplying consistently accurate information, being in close proximity to developments, and having foreign policy specialists on its staff. Also, officials may believe that NGOs lose sight of the broad perspective and ramifications of foreign policy and "resent efforts by such groups to impose their narrowly conceived views on the Department and the government." Chittick, *State Department,* p. 240; Blaisdell, "Pressure Groups," p. 152. Finally, the policy advocated by the NGO must be in "consonance ... with the prevailing political temper of the times." Cohen, "The Influence of Non-Governmental Groups," p. 19.

150. A supportive target may decide to become actively involved in furthering the NGO's interests. See sources cited in note 137 above. It has been suggested that "legislators who are not personally involved in the attainment of interest group goals are most likely to be open to the representations of any group which they believe to have a legitimate claim." Wahlke, Eulau, Buchanan, Ferguson, *The Legislative System,* p. 341. Attempts to influence known opponents of the advocated policy can arouse hostility on the part of the target and adversely affect any existing NGO-target relationship; the target may then take action *against* the NGO. Dexter, *Organizations in Washington,* pp. 68-69. Holtzman, *Interest Groups,* p. 81; see, for example, note 117 above. One observer notes that influence is inversely related both to the target's perception that pressure is being applied and to hostility toward the NGO's goals. See Chittick, *State Department,* p. 242. Contact with a known opponent of the NGO's position can be made through others whose efforts will be perceived as more legitimate by the hostile target. See Holtzman, *Interest Groups,* p. 82.

151. NGOs usually have access to targets who are receptive to their policy proposals dues to a similarity of background, occupational affiliation, or policy objectives. Richard W. Gable, "Political Interest Groups as Policy Shapers," *Annals* 319 (September 1958), 84, 91; Zeigler, *Interest Groups,* pp. 268-69; Chittick, *State Department,* p. 242. The ease of approaching targets known to be receptive, however, may cause NGOs to overlook points of access more promising in terms of fulfilling their objectives. For example, habitual legislative approaches through congressional contacts may be overemphasized to the exclusion of more useful approaches through the State Department and other administrative agencies. See Dexter, *How Organizations Are Represented,* p. 42.

Access to decision makers may be had through their staff assistants. Since staff assistants process information for their superiors, they have a degree of influence on what their superiors will see and hear; they may, in fact, allow their own policies to affect their processing of information:

> Staff persons are appointed by their superiors and are supposed to be alter egos for them, but since staff members are individuals, they may

have some political convictions which intrude into the performance of their tasks.

Milbrath, *The Washington Lobbyists*, pp. 239-40.
152. The position of the target may also affect how NGOs are perceived. Factors to be considered include congressional seniority, administrative level, and official duties. For legislative targets, those with lower seniority may see NGOs as more important than do those with a higher seniority; members of Congress with low seniority and with smaller staffs are more reliant on NGOs for information and aid specific issues. Scott & Hunt, *Congress and Lobbies*, p. 65. In administrative agencies, officials of different levels have different degrees of policymaking authority; officials with greater authority may see their relationships with NGOs as more antagonistic than do those with less authority. See Chittick, *State Department*, pp. 248-49. In general, NGOs are less effective with State Department targets since the State Department is less reliant on NGOs for information. Ibid., p. 238.
153. The expectations of the target that the public will participate in a certain area may affect the amount of NGO influence which can be exerted. Grassroots NGO efforts may be more effective on issues whose targets do not expect to generate much public activity. Also, such public participation may have more effect on targets in branches of the government which ordinarily are not subject to much public contact and expression of opinion.

In the past, the American public has been relatively indifferent to foreign policy issues which do not adversely affect the United States. Cf. George E. Reedy, "Secrecy Versus National Unity," in Francis O. Wilcox & Richard A. Frank, *The Constitution and the Conduct of Foreign Policy* (New York: Praeger, 1976) pp. 58, 60-61. Also, public involvement in foreign policymaking has been discouraged:

> The failure to permit or invite public involvement is usually justified on the grounds that participation is inconsistent with the requirements of secrecy, speed, and unity and is ill-advised because the public is not equipped to deal with the complexities of foreign affairs problems.

Richard A. Frank, "Public Participation in the Foreign Policy Process," in Francis O. Wilcox & Richard A. Frank, *The Constitution and the Conduct of Foreign Policy* (New York: Praeger, 1976), pp. 66, 71.
154. See Note, "Role of Nongovernmental Organizations," pp. 505-06, n. 218.
155. Weissbrodt, "Human Rights Legislation," pp. 256-62; see e.g., "Twelve Groups Draw Carter on Human Rights Overseas," *Washington Post*, 17 January 1977, sec. A, p. 2.
156. Weissbrodt, "Human Rights Legislation," pp. 278-87.
157. See Warren Christopher, deputy secretary of state, address to American Bar Association, August 1977; Cyrus Vance, secretary of state, address at the University of Georgia Law School, April 1977.
158. See Gene E. Godley, assistant secretary for legislative affairs, Department of the Treasury, letter to Representative Donald Fraser, 10 June 1977, Human Rights Library, University of Minnesota.

In coordinating the U.S. position on human rights issues, the Treasury works with other U.S. agencies through the InterAgency Group on Human

Rights and Foreign Assistance. The Treasury oversees U.S. participation in the international development banks: the World Bank, the Inter-American Development Bank, the Asian Development Bank, and the African Development Fund. The secretary instructs the U.S. representatives in these institutions on the positions they are to take on issues.

Under present legislation the U.S. representatives to these banks are directed to consider which countries may be engaged in gross violations of internationally recognized human rights when voting on loans.

Actions which may be taken include a U.S. statement at the banks' board of directors or a consultation with the management of the institutions and executive directors from other countries with a view to advancing the cause of human rights.

The Treasury has assured Representative Fraser that it will encourage the channeling of resources from the development banks to countries which do not consistently violate human rights and to encourage assistance to the needy people in developing countries.

159. See Juanita M. Kreps, secretary of commerce, letter to Representative Donald Fraser, 21 June 1977, Human Rights Library, University of Minnesota.

The Commerce Department participates in the Commission on Security and Cooperation in Europe which monitors compliance with the Helsinki Final Act. Commerce also administers the antiboycott policy of the Export Administration Act in regard to discrimination against U.S. citizens or firms on the basis of race, color, religion, national origin, or sex. In addition, Commerce has license control over equipment exports to foreign police, in consultation with the State Department. For example, Commerce has recently refused licenses for the export to Chilean and South African police of computerized fingerprint processing systems. Commerce also manages the embargo on exports to Rhodesia of U.S. origin commodities or technical data, the embargo of arms, munitions, military equipment for South Africa.

160. See David E. McGiffert, assistant secretary of defense, letter to Representative Donald Fraser, June 1977, Human Rights Library, University of Minnesota.

The Department of Defense has assured Representative Fraser that no U.S. security assistance will be used for civilian police or law enforcement purposes. Foreign students attending U.S. military training should receive instruction embracing the Geneva conventions and other principles of moral military conduct. Defense is examining these curricula to see if more should be done to broaden the focus to include instruction in internationally recognized human rights principles such as those embodied in the Universal Declaration of Human Rights.

Military attaches and security assistance personnel abroad are subject to the control and supervision of the Chiefs of the Diplomatic Missions, thereby assuring to some extent consistency in interchanges with host country officers.

Defense Department regulations require security assistance organizations abroad to monitor the use of equipment provided under the security assistance programs to assure that the items are used for the purposes for which they were provided and are not put to other uses.

The human rights record of a government is one of the factors considered in symbolic and ceremonial matters such as high-level military personnel visits, port calls, and exchanges of awards.

Defense is currently working with the State Department's coordinator for human rights and humanitarian affairs to see what additional steps Defense might take to further the cause of human rights.

161. See Ray Marshall, secretary of labor, letter to Representative Donald Fraser, 24 May 1977, Human Rights Library, University of Minnesota.

The principal activity of Labor relating to human rights has been its participation in the work of the International Labor Organization.

Most of Labor's international assistance activities involve technical cooperation agreements in such fields as vocational training, statistics, and manpower planning, most of which are sponsored and financed by the State Department or the Agency for International Development.

162. See "The Growing Lobby For Human Rights," *Washington Post*, 12 December 1976, sec. B, p. 1. A few of the national NGOs develop their own original information and thus have a claim to expertise, which might make them influential, including the Center for International Policy, the Washington Office on Latin America, the National Council of Churches, the U.S. Catholic Conference, and the Transnational Institute. The State Department has recently appointed Roberta Cohen, a former executive director of the International League for Human Rights, to be a State Department liason with human rights organizations.

163. Hersch Lauterpacht, ed., *International Law; A Treatise* (London, New York: Longmars, Green, 1955), pp. 117-18, 736-53; Rosalyn Higgins, "Conceptual Thinking About the Individual in International Law," *New York Law School Law Review* 24 (1978): 11, 16-19.

Chapter 13

The Role of Congress in Deciding United States Human Rights Policies

Robert B. Boettcher

President Jimmy Carter came into office with a professed commitment to human rights in foreign policy. It was a major theme of his election campaign and was to become a major feature of the foreign policy of his administration. The emphasis he placed on human rights from the outset represented perhaps the most notable shift from the foreign policy of the previous administration and gave rise to public discussion over how this new element could become a workable part of American diplomacy.

Early Congressional Initiatives

It was known that human rights had become an increasingly popular issue in Congress and that it had been the subject of disputes between Secretary of State Henry Kissinger and congressional human rights advocates over the amount of aid for countries where serious violations of human rights had been reported. What is perhaps less well known is the extent to which one subcommittee of Congress and its chairman had been addressing their work systematically to the very questions faced by the new Carter administration—how to make human rights a major factor in U.S. foreign policy and integrate it into the regular process of diplomacy. Since 1973, the Subcommittee on International Organizations of the House International Relations Committee, chaired by Representative Donald M. Fraser of Minnesota, has held more than 100 hearings on human rights in foreign policy, studying the implications to the United States of human rights issues in international organizations and human rights violations in 28 different countries. The subcommittee has issued numerous publications, including a 1974 report with 29 recommendations for United States policy.

President Carter inherited a State Department which had already undergone important administrative changes and some degree of policy reevaluation in favor of human rights as a result of Fraser's persistent efforts. A review of the work of the Fraser subcommittee can serve as a case study of how a congressional subcommittee can have a long-range impact on foreign policy as well as shed light on the question of what, respectively, are the most desirable roles of the executive and legislative branches in the conduct of foreign policy in this particular field.

Prior to Fraser's opening round of hearings in 1973, Congress already evinced a growing interest in international protection of human rights. Reports of South Vietnam's treatment of political prisoners led to increased congressional criticism of the U.S. policy in support of that country. Concern in Congress over the repressive acts of the military junta in Greece brought serious—although ultimately unsuccessful—attempts to halt military aid and to prevent homeporting in Greece by the U.S. Navy's Sixth Fleet. The public safety assistance program of the Agency for International Development was terminated because Congress perceived it as contributing to repression in aid-receiving countries. And in 1973, an amendment by Senator James Abourezk to the Foreign Assistance Act expressed the sense of Congress that the president should deny military and economic assistance to governments which hold political prisoners.

Fraser was an active supporter of these early expressions of congressional interest in human rights in foreign policy. A quiet, conscientious, and hard-working Minnesota Democrat, Fraser had been a liberal activist on the House Foreign Affairs Committee since he first came to Congress in 1963. Having acquired enough seniority to become a subcommittee chairman in 1971, he chose the Subcommittee on International Organizations, which has jurisdiction over United Nations affairs, because of the importance he attached to the development of effective international systems of law and accepted procedure for maintaining world order. As subcommittee chairman he held hearings on various aspects of U.S. participation in the United Nations system and decided to devote some special attention to human rights, initially because he felt the United States should place more stress on making the United Nations and related organizations more effective in promoting worldwide observance of internationaliy guaranteed human rights. His concern emanated from a conviction that the way a government treats its own people is a legitimate concern of the international community. Such concern, he believed, was both justified and made imperative by the fact that many nations, including the United States, are either signatories to international covenants on human rights or have voiced support for them. Through the years he had heard American leaders reiterate support for human rights principles in international relations but saw the subject relegated to a low priority in the actual conduct of foreign relations.

Returning from a visit to the Soviet Union toward the end of 1972, where he saw evidence of flagrant human rights violations, he directed that a major series of hearings be organized around the subject of international protection of human rights. His long-term objectives were: (1) to raise the priority of the human rights factor in U.S. foreign policy decision making; and (2) to strengthen the capacity of international organizations to ensure protection of human rights.

The goals were ambitious, so Fraser embarked upon the original project with modest expectations. He hoped that the planned hearings would be educational for the public and members of Congress, that some increase of executive branch interest might be achieved, and that the subcommittee might be able to produce a few constructive recommendations. For the purpose of assisting in organizing the hearings, he hired an experienced human rights specialist, John Salzberg, to work with the subcommittee staff for a period expected to be not more than about six months. The fact that four years and 100 hearings later, John Salzberg is still working full-time on human rights for the Fraser subcommittee is one indication that the project far exceeded original expectations. Indeed, John Salzberg's thorough, methodical, and expert performance through the years stands as a model of effective congressional staff work and he deserves a large measure of credit for the success of the Fraser subcommittee's human rights endeavors.

The subcommittee's claim of jurisdiction in the human rights field rested on several points. The rules of the Committee on International Relations state that the Subcommittee on International Organizations will "deal with oversight of, and legislation pertaining to, the United Nations, its related agencies, and other international organizations...."
The preamble to the Charter of the United Nations expresses the determination of the peoples of the United Nations "to reaffirm faith in fundamental human rights," and goes on to list as one of the four principal purposes of the United Nations, "promoting and encouraging respect for human rights and fundamental freedoms for all without distinction as to race, sex, language, or religion." The Universal Declaration of Human Rights, adopted by the U.N. General Assembly in 1948, has become a major instrument for promoting human rights observance and is widely regarded as customary international law. Viewed from the perspective of United Nations interest in human rights, the subcom-

mittee's jurisdiction was not challenged. After the initial series of broad-based hearings, subsequent hearings concentrated on the bilateral implications of human rights violations in particular countries, since United States action in those cases seemed more likely to have a decisive effect than would the United States position on resolutions and procedures in the United Nations, especially in view of the large amount of military and economic assistance the United States gave those countries. In the course of these hearings the Fraser subcommittee consulted with appropriate regional subcommittees and sometimes held joint hearings. Jurisdictional problems within the International Relations Committee have been minimal due to an attitude of mutual accommodation among subcommittee chairmen and their general acknowledgement of the special role assumed by the Subcommittee on International Organizations with respect to human rights.

The subcommittee held its original series of 15 hearings in the fall of 1973. Witnesses included current and former U.S. government officials, representatives of nongovernmental organizations, representatives of U.N. agencies, scholars, and members of Congress. Topics ranged from the general to the specific—including racial discrimination, torture of political prisoners, human rights in armed conflicts, the status of women, U.S. procedures for dealing with human rights problems, the relationship between foreign aid and human rights, U.N. human rights covenants, the organization of the State Department, and a few case studies of selected countries where serious violations had been reported.

The Subcommittee Report and Obstacles to Its Implementation

Two published documents resulted from these hearings: the published record of the hearings entitled "International Protection of Human Rights" and a special report, "Human Rights in the World Community: A Call for U.S. Leadership." The latter was a summary of the major findings of the hearings and contained 29 recommendations for U.S. policy, most of them addressed to the State Department. The experience with these hearings was educational—perhaps as much for Congressman Fraser, the subcommittee members and staff as for anyone—not only in that the hearings constituted lessons about the status of human rights observance and protection, but also because the subcommittee came to realize the magnitude of the challenge of grappling with human rights as a factor in international relations. Fraser chose to accept the challenge, and so indicated in his preface to the published hearings:

> The subcommittee's concern for international protection of human rights does not end with the publication of its report. The report, in fact, con-

stitutes an agenda for work in the human rights field, upon which efforts can be made toward forthright action by the United States government consistent with the recommendations.

Pressing for action by the executive branch and Congress, Fraser and fellow human rights advocates succeeded in having a number of the recommendations implemented, in whole or in part, during the Nixon and Ford administrations:

1. State Department reports on human rights conditions in aid-receiving countries;
2. Withdrawal or reduction of military assistance to violator nations through legislation initiated by Congress;
3. Legislation restricting economic assistance to violator nations;
4. Appointment of an assistant legal adviser for human rights in the State Department;
5. Assignment of human rights officers for each of the regional bureaus in the State Department;
6. Creation of a coordinator for human rights and humanitarian affairs in the State Department;
7. Increased U.S. support for the efforts of black majorities in southern Africa to achieve self-determination;
8. Active U.S. support for United Nations efforts to combat the practice of torture; and
9. Stronger expressions of U.S. support for human rights within the Organization of American States.

While Henry Kissinger was Secretary of State, a climate of confrontation prevailed between the State Department and human rights activists in Congress. Kissinger's concept of world order through balance among the most powerful nations allowed little room for active concern over human rights. He mounted stiff resistance to congressional pressure for a firm stance by the United States toward governments who were gross violators of human rights. Human rights advocates in Congress reacted with alarm over Kissinger's embrace of the military junta in Chile, his lack of interest in the problems of white-minority rule in southern Africa before the Portuguese colonies became independent, his intense pursuit of detente with the Soviet Union while largely overlooking the plight of Soviet dissidents and of Jews who wished to emigrate, and his determination to maximize the special U.S. supportive relationships with increasingly repressive governments in the Philippines and South Korea. His negative attitude toward human rights was demonstrated in an incident involving the American ambassador to Chile, David Popper. The *New York Times* reported that after Kissinger read a telegram from the embassy in Santiago describing a conversation in which the Ambassador expressed concern about human rights practices to Chilean leaders, Kissinger wrote in the margin of the telegram: "Tell Popper to cut out the political science lectures." The State Department did not deny the accuracy of the newspaper story. With regard to South Korea the following year, at the very time the American ambassador was making representations to the Seoul government about its human rights record, in Washington the State Department was engaged in an all-out effort to defeat a congressional amendment which would have reduced military aid to South Korea because of human rights violations.

Congressional Human Rights Standards for Security and Development Assistance

The Kissinger State Department responded more positively, however, to congressional recommendations for organizational changes, such as the establishment of new offices and positions related to human rights. Still, Kissinger's basic disagreement with the notion that human rights should be a major factor in foreign policy collided with the growing support on Capitol Hill for emphasizing human rights, with the result that Congress enacted tough legislation over objections of the executive branch. The most significant legislative measures are in the foreign assistance acts: Section 502B on human rights and security assistance; and Section 116 on human rights and development assistance (see Appendix). Also important are human rights amendments aimed at the international financial institutions such as the World Bank and the regional development banks. These measures provide a general framework within which the executive branch is expected to shape security and development assistance programs with appropriate attention to the human rights performance of recipient governments. Neither law dictates decisions with respect to specific countries; rather, the executive branch is given the flexibility to shape policies to particular circumstances.

Section 502B, introduced by Congressman Fraser, prohibits military aid and sales to governments engaged in a consistent pattern of gross violations of internationally recognized human rights except under extraordinary national security circumstances. Congress placed importance on restricting military assistance because military equipment and power often are used by governments to oppress their own people. The relationship between human rights and development assistance raises questions which are more difficult to answer than is the case with regard to military assistance. Too stringent implementation of Section 116 runs the risk of penalizing the poor because the government is repressive. The prevailing attitude in Congress when this measure was adopted appeared to be that in certain serious cases, such as Chile, the U.S. government was using economic aid to prolong the staying power of dictatorships rather than to help needy people. Similar in concept to Section 116, the legislation on human rights and the multilateral banks requires that U.S. delegates vote against loans to repressive governments unless the loan directly benefits needy people. In 1977, Congress rejected an alternative approach sponsored by House Banking and currency Committee Chairman Henry Reuss of Wisconsin. The Reuss amendment recommended that the administration encourage the multilateral banks to give priority to loans to countries with good human rights records, conversely giving lower priority to repressive governments.

Congressional Investigation of Contrary Records on Human Rights

The record of the Subcommittee on International Organizations reflects attention to human rights violations in countries of all political coloration. Apparently ideology is not a dependable indicator of the extent to which a government allows its citizens to enjoy fundamental freedoms. Even among communist states there are significant differences. Governments from extreme left to extreme right, and many in between, are guilty of flagrant abuses of human rights. The activities of the Fraser subcommittee have responded to reliable reports of violations without regard to the ideology of the state or its political attitude toward the United States. If human rights are indeed universal and the United States has a legally valid commitment to work to uphold human rights, then systematic gross violations regardless of who commits them, should be given serious attention along with other important factors in formulating U.S. policies toward violator governments. The subcommittee has taken that position, both in its hearings and in frequent recommendations to the State Department by Chairman Fraser. Among the governments whose human rights records have been considered at hearings by the subcommittee: (1) five are communist—the Soviet Union, Cuba, Cambodia, North Korea, and Vietnam; (2) two are neutral—India and Indonesia; (3) two are controlled by white-minority governments—South Africa and Rhodesia; (4) 13 are members of some form of alliance with the United States—Chile, the Philippines, South Korea, Argentina, Uruguay, Paraguay, El Salvador, Guatemala, Nicaragua, Iran, Haiti, Taiwan, and Thailand; (5) 15 were recipients of U.S. military assistance or sales at some time since 1974—Argentina, Iran, Chile, the Philippines, South Korea, Uruguay, Paraguay, El Salvador, Guatemala, Nicaragua, Haiti, Israel, Taiwan, Indonesia, and Thailand; (6) 14 were recipients of U.S. bilateral economics assistance at some time since 1974—Argentina, the Philippines, Indonesia, India, Uruguay, Paraguay, Chile, South Korea, El Salvador, Guatemala, Nicaragua, Iran, Haiti, and Thailand.

It is obvious that the policies of the United States may have greater potential for limiting or contributing to repression in countries with whom the United States has a supportive relationship than in other countries. In countries such as Cambodia and North Korea, with whom the United States does not even have diplomatic relations, there can be little if any expectation that effective influence can be brought to bear on human rights practices. In countries with closer relations with the United States, such as Argentina or the Philippines, the potential for leverage is greater. But even governments receiving substantial American political, economic, or military support may not respond positively to pressure. Dictators who resort to repression are not likely to change their ways readily. Repression may in fact be necessary for them to remain in power. However, it is still important for the United States to disassociate itself from such regimes by limiting or refraining from special supportive relationships in the absence of compelling or overriding reasons of U.S. national security. The Fraser subcommittee has found that to do otherwise can have the effect of actually contributing to repression. The way repressive governments cleverly take advantage of the support implied by visits of high American officials, and the specter of American tanks surrounding demonstrators testify to this unpleasant fact.

Advent of Carter Human Rights Concern and Congressional Response

After the election of Jimmy Carter there was wide speculation as to how and whether Carter would put into practice the statements about human rights in foreign policy made during his campaign for the presidency. More to the point with regard to Congress, human rights advocates on Capitol Hill were asked what stance they would take toward a president who placed strong emphasis on human rights. Would they be less aggressive dealing with a Democratic president since most of them are Democrats? Had their clamor about human rights been merely a useful political weapon to do battle with a Republican administration? During the early months of the Carter administration, it became clear that they were taking an attitude of "wait and see," at least insofar as proposing additional tough legislation was concerned. Congressman Fraser, for example, decided against offering another amendment to cut military aid to South Korea in 1977. He and like-minded colleagues were willing to give the new administration some time to try new initiatives in human rights diplomacy before making judgments. However, one important congressional vote did go against the Carter administration early in 1977. The administration had supported the unsuccessful Reuss Amendment which would have instructed U.S. representatives to the international financial institutions to encourage loans to countries with good human rights records rather than to vote against loans to gross violator governments. The opposition to the Reuss Amendment was led by two Democrats, Representative Tom Harkin of Iowa and Representative Herman Badillo of New York.

Members of Congress in the "wait and see" camp, while refraining from bold public pronouncements, were quietly urging the new administration to implement the spirit as well as the letter of the human rights legislation enacted over the objections of the previous administration. They were also holding meetings among themselves and with executive branch officials with the objective of accomplishing Senate ratification of the three United Nations covenants on human rights which had just entered into force without U.S. ratification although they had been adopted by the U.N. General Assembly some 10 years earlier: The international Convention on the Elimination of All Forms of Racial Discrimination, the International Covenant on Economic, Social, and Cultural Rights, and the International Covenant on Civil and Political Rights. It had been clear since adoption of the treaties by the UN General Assembly that Senate ratification could not be achieved without the solid support of the president of the United States. During 1977, President Carter signed all three conventions, as well as the Inter-American Convention on Human Rights. In February 1978, the president sent all four treaties to the Senate with a strong appeal that the Senate advise and consent to their ratification, with appropriate reservations regarding treaty provisions inconsistent with U.S. law.

Congressional human rights advocates seemed encouraged, if not completely satisfied, with the Carter record. They agree generally that the administration had been working conscientiously to make human rights a significant factor in foreign policy. Executive branch efforts included: (1) quiet diplomatic talks with representatives of foreign governments, at the most senior levels of government; (2) more frequent acts or declarations by the U.S. government with respect to human rights problems in a particular country; (3) reductions or terminations of military assistance or military sales to some of the most repressive governments, as intended by congressionally initiated legislation; (4) reductions or terminations of bilateral development assistance, as intended by congressionally initiated legislation; (5) at the international financial institutions, use of American influence to persuade governments with serious human rights problems to withdraw loan applications for projects appearing not to be directly beneficial to needy people until the human rights situation has improved, or when they were not withdrawn, the United States has voted "no" or abstained; (6) urging the United

Nations and the Organization of American States to act with respect to egregious situations in particular countries.

The Carter human rights record has also drawn criticism on Capitol Hill. Some legislators say it is too zealous; others say it is too timid. At a hearing of the Fraser subcommittee to review the administration's human rights performance, Representative Edward Derwinski, an Illinois conservative Republican, charged that Carter's foreign policy has ignored rights violations by leftist governments and taken a tough stance only toward anticommunist countries. He asked, "Why is anticommunism no longer a part of our policy? Why are we embracing Cuba and rejecting a long-time ally like Argentina?" Another member of the subcommittee, Representative Leo Ryan, a liberal Democrat from California, complained that the administration is "being bold where it's safe and good politics—like criticizing the treatment of Soviet Jews—while expressing only mild disapproval" when dealing with allies such as South Korea and the Philippines. Testifying for the administration, Deputy Assistant Secretary of State Mark Schneider replied that the administration's concern over human rights applies to every country, whether friend or foe. However, he acknowledged a problem by saying:

> The major difficulty is that human rights is a new policy. It's hard to define, and it cuts across the entire range of interests that the United States has with other governments. Therefore, these interests have to be integrated with human rights and taken into consideration.

Recently, a new and slightly different human rights proposal was made on Capitol Hill. Congressman Fraser and Congressman Dante Fascell (D-Fla.) introduced a bill to create an Institute for Human Rights and Freedom. The board members of the institute, although appointed by the president, would work independently of the State Department. Charged with responsibility to promote the observance of international human rights and fundamental freedoms, the institute would provide assistance, financial and otherwise, for: (1) private individuals and nongovernmental organizations that are promoting human rights; (2) conferences and seminars for the promotion of human rights; (3) the publication and display of books and artistic works which have been supressed for political reasons; (4) fellowships and research activities in the field; (5) nongovernmental organizations which are helping victims of repression and their families; and (6) private legal groups within the United States which extend legal assistance to persons and groups overseas whose rights are being violated.

Conclusions

As of early 1978, the climate of confrontation over human rights between Capitol Hill and the State Department had been replaced by a climate of cooperation. This new situation is regarded by congressional human rights advocates as a definite improvement. They recognize that while Congress has major responsibilities in foreign relations, it cannot actually implement foreign policy. Only the executive branch has the resources to do that. They recognize also that diplomacy is conducted between the executive branch and representatives of foreign governments. If Congress and the executive branch are at loggerheads over a particular policy, the result in the conduct of diplomacy is either confusion or the foreign government taking advantage of the more favorable position, whether that of Congress or the executive branch. Congress has the prerogative to enact legislation over the objections of a reluctant executive branch, but the executive branch can implement legislation with varying degrees of forthrightness. The human rights legislation of recent years was enacted as a last resort by Congress after human rights advocates had tried unsuccessfully to persuade the executive branch to accord human rights a high priority in foreign policy. But even now that human rights has become a significant element in the president's foreign policy, Congress has by no means abdicated. The international organization subcommittee continues to hold hearings, and concerned members of Congress continue to press the administration for more attention to particular problems.

However, the new spirit of cooperation should auger well for the chances of conducting U.S. foreign relations with a coherent, significant, and hopefully effective human rights component.

Chapter 14

The Contribution of the United States to the Promotion and Protection of International Human Rights

Richard B. Lillich

Six years ago the Subcommittee on International Organizations of the House Committee on Foreign Affairs began a series of seminal hearings on the international protection of human rights.[1] These hearings, plus the subcommittee's follow-up report in 1974, entitled "Human Rights in the World Community: A Call for U.S. Leadership,"[2] contained a multitude of innovative recommendations not only for strengthening the United Nations capability in this field, but even more importantly for increasing the priority given to human rights concerns in the United States foreign policy process.

Many of the latter subsequently were adopted administratively or enacted into law, and therefore were in place for President Carter's use when he assumed office and began his remarkable "consciousness-raising" effort to make international human rights law a matter of international as well as national concern. This effort cannot be praised too much. Indeed, in view of the critical tone of many of the remarks that follow, I wish to underscore that I fully recognize that I am indulging today in the luxury of criticizing a basically sound policy. This luxury was in short supply before January 20, 1977, when the president reactivated the human rights concerns that, at their best, have guided U.S. foreign policy.

Thus, it seems self-evident that there could be no better time than the present for an assessment of where the United States stands and where it should go regarding the implementation of international human rights norms.³ In addition to the criticism from its usual detractors, the Carter administration's record on human rights has come under increasing scrutiny and even occasional attack recently from some of its former friends. The train may be on the right track, they say, but it seems to have lost some steam. Thus Congressman Bonker, current chairman of the Subcommittee on International Organizations, in the context of hearings held in 1978 on U.S. private investment in South Africa, remarked that "[i]t seems we have reached an impasse between our policies and rhetoric on one hand, and our ineffectiveness to do anything on the other."⁴ The former chairman of the subcommittee, Congressman Fraser, in the recent inaugural issue of the journal *Universal Human Rights*, also has affirmed that "within the Congress and the Administration a crossroads has been reached on the promotion of human rights."⁵

Looking down the track, one can discern a cluster of signals pointing towards various areas where changes or improvements in our approach to implementing international human rights norms are most urgent. I would like to concentrate upon five of these areas, interspersing my descriptive remarks with occasional suggestions of steps that the executive branch or Congress should take to effectuate the proclaimed human rights policies of the U.S. more fully. The areas are:

1. The ratification by the United States of pending international human rights agreements;
2. The making and clarification of United States domestic law to implement the commitments and to achieve our goals in the human rights area;
3. The need to coordinate and support the emerging international human rights bureaucracy in the executive branch to enable it to initiate and carry out an effective human rights policy;
4. The importance of an expanded and permanent congressional oversight role to guarantee that its legislative mandate is being followed by the executive branch in the human rights area; and
5. The domestic implementation of and compliance with international human rights norms.

I. U.S. Ratification of Pending International Human Rights Agreements

Contrary to popular assumptions, there is plenty of international human rights law on the books. A report submitted by the Department of State to the Senate Committee on Foreign Relations in early 1979 lists 35 principal treaties and agreements concluded under the auspices of the UN, the OAS, the ILO, and other international bodies and conferences.⁶ In addition, it mentions seven other nontreaty and agreement international human rights instruments—such as the Universal Declaration of Human Rights, the Standard Minimum Rules for the Treatment of Prisoners, and the Helsinki Final Act—which, while not creating formal legal obligations, arguably reflect norms of customary international law or, at the very least, standards of behavior by which states may be judged.[7] Thus, while the implementation of this considerable body of substantive law leaves much to be desired, at least it already exists. Several additional human rights treaties—on the taking of hostages,[8] the elimination of torture,[9] and the rights of the child[10]—are also in various stages of the drafting process.

A major problem from our foreign policy perspective lies in the fact that the United States is a party to only 11 of the 35 treaties and agreements.[11] While it has signed another nine (only six of which have been submitted to the Senate), in 15 instances the United States has not even signed the international instrument in question.[12] The most charitable reason for this sad ratification record, as Professor Louis Henkin noted some five years ago, is that

> [t]he United States has seen international human rights law as designed for others only. Our respect for human rights, we believe, already surpasses any foreseeable, acceptable, international standard; the need is to bring the blessings of liberties to others.[13]

This self-satisfied, parochial attitude is increasingly costly: the U.S. suffers charges of hypocrisy; it cannot participate in or take advantage of the enforcement mechanism these instruments establish; and, last but not least, its citizens cannot invoke these treaties internationally or domestically.

This situation seemed to improve when President Carter assumed office. In 1977 he committed his administration to seek Senate approval of the Genocide Convention[14]—which has been pending before the Senate for 30 years—and, on February 23, 1978, he sent to the Senate four major treaties (three of which he had signed): the Covenant on Civil and Political Rights, the Covenant on Economic, Social and Cultural Rights, the Convention on the Elimination of All Forms of Racial Discrimination, and the American Convention on Human Rights.[15]

The four treaties were encumbered with over two dozen proposed reservations, understandings, declarations and statements which, in the words of Professor David Weissbrodt, "appear either trivial, unnecesssary, violative of international law, or a combination of the above."[16] They thus substantially undermine the lofty expectations created by the president's pledge to work for their prompt ratification. Moreover, subsequent developments, or more accurately the lack thereof, bring even this pledge into doubt. For despite considerable rhetorical support for their ratification by the president and members of the executive branch, the willingness to expend even a small portion of political capital to achieve the Senate's advice and consent appears lacking.

The situation with the Genocide Convention, in particular, is what would have been labeled "a national disgrace" during the 1976 presidential campaign. Here is the first and foremost international human rights treaty that has been adopted by 84 countries, that has been pending before the Senate for three decades, and that has been reported out favorably several times in the past decade.[17] Yet, during this session of Congress there has been little enthusiasm shown by the Senate leadership, much less by the chairman of the Foreign Relations Committee for acting on it.[18] Moreover, despite all the president's occasional rhetorical exhortations, there has been no concerted effort by the White House to nudge the Senate along in the ratification process. Given these facts, it is up to nongovernmental organizations and interested citizens to lobby the Senate for its prompt advice and consent to the convention's ratification.

Additionally, such organizations and citizens should bring pressure upon the Senate to give its advice and consent to the other human rights conventions pending before it, including the four treaties which the president sent up in early 1978. As in the case of the Genocide Convention, the Senate may wish to attach several reservations and understandings to each of these treaties.[19] However, petty or unnecessary reservations, like most of those suggested by the president in his message of transmittal, should not be added. By ratifying these treaties, the United States will obtain the tools and the credibility that it badly needs if it is to pursue successfully its proclaimed human rights policy abroad and at home.

II. Making and Clarifying U.S. Domestic Law

Congress has played an important role in promoting and institutionalizing U.S. concern for human rights since 1973 by enacting a series of statutes linking economic and military assistance with the human rights record of recipient countries. Sections 116[20] and 502B[21] of the Foreign Assistance Act, both in place by the end of 1976 and therefore ready for the Carter administration's use, have been clarified and supplemented since then by additional statutes that either have strengthened the statutory language on the books or extended it to such other areas as agricultural commodity sales,[22] OPIC insurance[23] or—in the case of exports to South Africa—Eximbank facilities.[24]

Somewhat surprisingly, from its earliest days in office, the Carter Administration demonstrated little enthusiasm for such legislative initiatives. It raised the standard objections of the executive branch that statutory directives would "tie its hands" and deny it the "flexibility" needed to achieve its human rights objectives.[25] Moreover, during the past year, whatever tepid enthusiasm it occasionally had mustered for such initiatives has turned into outright opposition to any additional human rights legislation.[26] In the case of Uganda, this opposition culminated in what Congressman Solarz characterized as a "morally and politically untenable"[27] position, namely, the administration's opposing a proposed trade embargo—which, fortunately, was enacted anyway—against the former regime of Idi Amin on the almost laughable ground that it would violate "the principles of free trade" to which the United States is committed.[28] That the administration still opposes any new human rights legislation was made clear in April by Deputy Assistant Secretary for Human Rights Mark L. Schneider who, in responding to a question following a speech to the International Human Rights Law Group in Washington, stated flatly that "we have enough law to do what we want to do."[29]

This statement may well be correct—but only if one assumes, as its critics do, that the administration's human rights policy is primarily an effort in rhetoric. If one accepts the good faith of the administration's human rights commitment, then surely Mr. Schneider's response must strike one as naive. The present hodgepodge of patchwork prohibitions is so laced through with exceptions and limited in scope that any serious attempt by the U.S. to bring economic pressures to bear upon a gross human rights violator is doomed to ultimate failure from the start. If the administration does not perceive this fact, then the Congress should proceed to enact legislation mandating those policies that are likely to achieve the administration's self-proclaimed objectives. I will summarize briefly under the headings of "plugging loopholes" and "extending coverage" those areas that I believe warrant serious attention and possibly legislative initiatives by Congress.

Plugging Loopholes

"Needy People" Exceptions. Section 116(a) of the Foreign Assistance Act provides that no economic assistance may be given to a gross human rights violator "unless such assistance will directly benefit the needy people in such country."[30] Similar exceptions are found in Section 112 of the Agricultural Trade Development and Assistance Act[31] that governs agricultural commodity sales and Section 239(1) of the Foreign Assistance Act [32] that covers OPIC insurance. Unfortunately, no criteria are set out in the legislation to guide the executive branch[33] in its determination of whether "needy people" actually are involved and, if so, whether the assistance will "directly benefit" them. Deputy Secretary of State Christopher's testimony before the Subcommittee on International Organizations in May that "economic assistance that directly benefits the needy is rarely disapproved, even to governments with poor human rights records"[34] indicates that the exception is invoked regularly and in-

terpreted broadly by the administration. Because "needy people," like the poor, will be with us for some time, Congress should consider defining the term and the criteria for determining when assistance "directly benefits" such a class. While the definitional difficulties are obvious, failure to grapple with them could lead to the vitiation of Section 116.

"National Security" Exceptions. Section 502B of the Foreign Assistance Act states that no military assistance may be given to a gross human rights violator unless there exist "extraordinary circumstances" that make it in the "national interest" to provide such assistance.[35] Similarly, Section 239(1), covering OPIC insurance, also contains a "national security interest" exception.[36] As is the case with the "needy people" exception, no criteria are provided in the above statutes to guide the executive branch[37] in determining whether national security interests truly are involved. At present, the exception, in the words of Congressman Harkin,[38] is being "exploited" to permit large-scale military assistance to several repressive regimes, including Indonesia, the Philippines, and South Korea. In a working paper published in 1978, he caustically remarked that "Congress did not intend to provide the Pentagon with a loophole large enough to drive a tank through."[39] Harkin noted that the reasons for invoking the exception are, to say the least, "not always clear," adding that "I simply fail to see how stopping or reducing our military aid to the Philippines would jeopardize our national interests. In fact, the opposite may be true."[40] Whether national security interests actually are involved, of course, is a "judgment call," but if this exception continues to be exploited excessively, Congress should consider amending Section 502B to circumscribe the administration's gloss on the section. Otherwise, its purpose, like that of Section 116, will be undercut.

Extending Coverage

Although Congress has linked direct United States economic and military aid to the human rights record of recipient countries in the statutes discussed above, indirect aid through multilateral economic assistance programs has gone largely unregulated. Since "[e]conomic aid increasingly flows through multi-lateral institutions," as Congressman Harkin reminds us, "any successful attempt to pursue our human rights goals must extend to include these important channels for U.S. foreign aid."[41] Additionally, serious consideration must be given to extending human rights criteria to the private sector—including banking, trade, and investment. As Sandra Vogelgesang notes in a recent article in *Foreign Affairs,* "[m]ore and more members of Congress see trade and aid as part of a continuum of tools to affect performance on human rights."[42] Let us examine five areas in which, in my opinion, human

rights concerns should be taken into account by executive branch policymakers, if not voluntarily, then pursuant to Congress's mandate.
International Monetary Fund (IMF). International financial institutions (IFIs), the foremost of which is the World Bank, have been remarkably reluctant to consider human rights factors in loan decisions or the human rights implications of their financial operations. Thus, some of the world's most repressive regimes—Brazil, Indonesia, and the Philippines—have been among the most active borrowers from the IFI. This result, which undercuts the U.S. policy of denying economic and military assistance to gross human rights violators, is especially ironic when one considers that we now channel 40 percent of our foreign aid appropriations through IFIs.[43]

Accordingly, Congress in 1977 enacted the Harkin Amendment that instructed U.S. executive directors on the World Bank and five other IFIs "to oppose any loan, any extension of financial assistance, or any technical assistance to [a gross human rights violator], unless such assistance is directed specifically to programs which serve the basic human needs of the citizens of such country."[44] The United States has opposed approximately two dozen loans on human rights grounds over the past one and one-half years, and while all were approved—since the U.S. does not have a veto power in these institutions—the policy has caused other loans to be deferred or withdrawn.[45] Moreover, if the administration is successful in carrying out Congress' mandate to enlist the support of bank members in this human rights effort,[46] either by their adopting a policy similar to that of the United States or by amending the charters of their respective institutions to incorporate human rights criteria, a powerful economic lever will have been fashioned to encourage compliance with basic international human rights norms.

During the last Congress, the House by a voice vote attached a human rights amendment to pending legislation authorizing U.S. financial participation in the IMF Supplementary Financing [Witteveen] Facility.[47] This amendment required the U.S. executive director on the IMF not only to use his best efforts to see that IMF transactions contribute to meeting basic human needs, but also to oppose any such transactions that would contribute to the violation of basic human rights. Unfortunately, the Senate refused to approve a similar amendment.[48] The argument that was raised was that to do so would politicize an international lending institution.[49] Writing in human rights conditions to bilateral aid programs was acceptable to most senators, but it was regarded as "mischief," to quote Senator Church, insofar as the IMF was concerned.[50] The United States, he declared, should not "lay down conditions on . . . the International Monetary Fund that have to do with certain political objectives of the United States. . . ."[51]

This attitude reveals a complete misperception of what "basic human rights"—the phrase used in the amendment and defined therein in some detail—is all about. Certainly, human rights concerns have become and hopefully will long remain a key factor in U.S. foreign-policy decision making, but to characterize such internationally recognized human rights as mere "political objectives" of the U.S. is to ignore their universality and undercut their importance. Moreover, as Congressman Harkin has noted, "[i]t is naive to suppose that the IMF operates in a political and moral vacuum."[52] The conditions attached to its loans, as he demonstrates, often lead borrowing countries to adopt repressive measures in order to carry out austerity programs. Furthermore, its loans frequently bail out or prop up the most repressive governments. A 1976-1977 IMF aid package to South Africa of $464 million (of which we provided $107 million through our IMF contribution) allowed that country to increase its military budget by exactly the same amount.[53] Since South Africa hardly can be said to face hostile neighbors, the increased military expenditures obviously were intended to strengthen its capability to deal with internal disorders resulting from its apartheid policy. Recent accounts that the IMF was considering a large loan to Nicaragua, at the very time that the corrupt Somoza regime was on its last legs, support the thesis that the IMF all too often comes to the aid of authoritarian regimes in their hour of need.[54] Surely the Senate should reconsider its decision of last year and, acting in conjunction with the House, extend the Harkin Amendment to the IMF as well as to the IFIs.

Export-Import Bank (Eximbank). The Eximbank loans money to foreign countries at low interest rates, thus enabling them to buy products made in the United States. Since the bank is funded exclusively by government money, there is even less reason to exempt it from human rights concerns than in the case of the IMF. Yet in past years, Congress has refused to extend the Harkin Amendment to the bank on the ground that, in the words of Senator Javits, it was "inappropriate to mix up [human rights concerns] with these banking efforts. . . ."[55] (Congress in 1978 did pass the compromise Evans Amendment,[56] which effectively prohibits Eximbank financing of exports to the South African government or its agencies; it also bars the financing of exports to other purchasers in South Africa, unless the purchaser has endorsed and is implementing the fair employment principles of the Sullivan Code).

With all due respect, this argument is the reddest of herrings. Since public funds are being used to stimulate United States exports, "there is no reason to make this branch of foreign policy exempt from human rights considerations."[57] Two years ago, when an unsuccessful attempt was made in the House to extend the Harkin Amendment from IFI to

Eximbank decisions, Congressman Hyde made this point in eloquent fashion:

> I am a little confused as to why there is such a difference between trade and aid. I know the superficial differences, but it seems to me where there is a profit to be made, our commitment to a strong, Puritan ethic is watered down considerably.
> Where it is a matter of multilateral aid, we are mandating a no vote, but here when there are a few bucks to be made, then we suddenly say, well, you know, take a sidelong glance at the human rights situation, but for God's sake, don't kill the deal.[58]

Obviously, requiring the Eximbank to take human rights concerns into account occasionally will impact negatively upon exports, but it is a price that must be paid if the principle behind our human rights policy is to be maintained. Thus, Congress should enact legislation extending the Harkin Amendment to Eximbank decisions.

Private Commercial Banks. Cutting off U.S. military or economic aid to a country that grossly violates the human rights of its citizens will have little impact if that country is able to obtain funds from private sources. To be truly effective, a human rights policy designed to bring economic pressure to bear upon a human rights violator must extend to the private as well as the public sector. Yet several of the worst violators have been able to thumb their noses at the U.S. government because private commercial banks, including several of the largest in this country, have rushed to extend them credit. By so doing, these banks undercut the proclaimed foreign policy goals of the Carter administration in the most serious fashion.

Chile is an excellent case in point. When the United States withheld $27.5 million in economic assistance in 1977,[59] this action had about as much effect on the Pinochet regime as an attack upon a rogue elephant with a pea shooter. Why? According to a report issued by the Institute for Policy Studies, while bilateral assistance to Chile dried up during 1975-1976, commercial bank loans increased 500 percent.[60] In 1977 alone, U.S. banks provided $514 million in loans and credits.[61] Given this access to private funds, Chile had little to fear when the United States government tightened the economic screws that year. Indeed, Chile has continued to borrow heavily from U.S. banks. In January and April 1978, despite near-universal condemnation of the junta's abysmal human rights record, the Wells Fargo Bank and Morgan Guaranty Trust headed consortia loans to Chile of $125 and $210 million, respectively.[62] More recently, despite Congressman Reuss's appeal to Secretary of State Vance that U.S. banks should be requested to discontinue making such loans, the banks actually appear to have stepped up their lending activities.[63]

Thus we have here the classic example of slapping the wrist while greasing the palm. What is particularly unsettling is the fact that administration officials—Mr. Schneider, mentioned above, is a good example—either do not perceive that private commercial bank lending buttresses and maintains many repressive regimes such as Chile's, or, if they do, they are unwilling or unable to do anything about it—even when its continuation makes a mockery of the administration's human rights policy. Indeed, the principal actor in this exercise of naiveté or worse is the president himself. When asked during his Brazilian new conference in 1978 whether Congress should condition United States commercial bank loans upon human rights considerations, he prefaced his answer with a typical banker's response, stressing the soundness of loans to Brazil. He then concluded as follows:

> It would be inconceivable to me that Congress would try to restrict the lending of money by American private banks to Brazil under any circumstances. This would violate the principles of our own free enterprise system. And if such an act was passed by Congress, I would not approve it.[64]

What can be said about this attitude except that it is truly sad to see it held by a president who has made human rights the centerpiece of U.S. foreign policy? Professor Richard Fagen—in a recent article in *Foreign Affairs* aptly entitled "The Carter Administration and Latin America: Business as Usual?"—cogently remarks that "[o]ne cannot continue to subscribe to and even celebrate banker's rules in public and private international capital markets that operate to deepen indebtedness, repression and inequality while at the same time claiming that one has policies designed to address basic human needs and encourage democracy."[65] The Carter administration, he adds, "apparently refuses to face up to the fact that what is good for U.S. business . . . interests, as conventionally conceived, may in fact be quite disastrous for human rights."[66]

Given this attitude by the executive branch, it clearly becomes Congress' responsibility to address the issue. I am not as yet prepared to say what legislation should ultimately be enacted. My intention has been to identify, not resolve, what I perceive to be one of the major weaknesses of United States human rights policy. Last year Congressman Harkin introduced a bill that would have required U.S. commercial banks to inform the Departments of State and Treasury when they intended to make loans to countries determined to be gross human rights violators.[67] This mild reporting bill, which would not have precluded banks from proceeding to lend, was not enacted, but it would have been an important first step in formulating a comprehensive human rights policy to cover the private as well as the public sector. The Subcommittee on International Organizations and the appropriate Senate subcommittees should schedule hearings on the lending policies of private commercial banks vis-á-vis such contries as Brazil, Chile, Indonesia, South Africa, and South Korea, out of which hopefully legislation might come that would be designed to make these policies compatible with the proclaimed human rights objectives of the Carter administration.

Trade Restrictions (Embargoes and Controls). A trade embargo ranks among the severest forms of economic pressure. The U.S. unilaterally maintains such embargoes against Cambodia, Cuba, North Korea, and Vietnam.[68] As mentioned above,[69] Congress enacted legislation establishing an embargo against Uganda in 1978 over executive branch objections that, with the ouster of General Amin, is in the process of being repealed.[70] Moreover, pursuant to several UN Security Council resolutions,[71] implemented by executive orders issued pursuant to the UN Participation Act, [72] the United States participates in multilateral economic sanctions against Rhodesia and in a multilateral arms embargo against South Africa. Trade embargoes for human rights purposes, however, undoubtedly will continue to be rare exceptions to the traditional "free trade" policy of the United States.

What are more likely to be used are selective export controls. Under Section 3(2) of the Export Administration Act of 1969, the president is authorized to use export controls "to the extent necessary to further significantly the foreign policy of the United States and to fulfill its international responsibilities . . . ."[73] Under this act, the Department of Commerce, which with input from the Departments of State and Treasury administers export control policies, has refused to license the sale of various items—say, a Sperry Univac computer to the Soviet Union or Allis-Chalmers turbine generators to Argentina—for human rights purposes. The reaction to these license denials by the business community, especially during the past year, has been outspoken.[74] Congressman Bingham, writing in *Foreign Affairs,* rightly notes that "there is probably no type of foreign policy that sends businessmen up the wall faster. Besides the unpredictability of the controls (why are they applied to some human rights violators more than others?), businessmen argue that their unilateral nature merely guarantees that the business will go to other countries and the target country will still get the trade."[75]

With the large trade deficit being run by the U.S, the encouragement of exports certainly must be a major policy objective. Amendments to the Export Administration Act considered by Congress underscore this objective by placing the burden of proof upon proponents of export controls for foreign policy—including human rights—purposes.[76] Although the amendments apparently still permit the president to deny export licenses for human rights reasons, the criteria set out and the procedural requirements involved probably will have a "chilling effect" upon the use of export controls for such purposes.[77] While the United States obviously cannot cut off all trade with every country governed by a repressive regime, neither should it utilize the much-abused policy of "free trade" in order to justify the indiscriminate sale of goods to any country, no matter how dismal its human rights record. The shocking revelation by the Russian dissident Vladimir Bukovsky—"I was taken out of the Soviet Union in handcuffs on which it was labelled, 'Made in U.S.A.' "[78]—should serve as a warning in this regard.

Foreign Investment. The longstanding policy of the U.S., reaffirmed by the Carter administration in 1977, is neither to promote nor discourage private foreign investment.[79] This policy has resulted in a "hands-off" attitude toward the investment decisions of corporations owned by the United States. Thus, last year the executive branch opposed bills introduced by Congressmen Bingham, Diggs, and Solarz that would have prohibited all new U.S. investments in South Africa.[80] Yet our investments, like loans from our private commercial banks, merely strengthen an economy resting upon the apartheid system. Indeed, U.S. money and skills are building a series of giant coal-conversion plants that will help South Africa withstand the effects of a U.N. oil embargo, should one be imposed in the future.[81]

Because U.S. investment, like trade and loans, can help keep a gross human rights violator afloat long after the termination of economic and military assistance, Congress should enact legislation that at least prescribes conditions under which new investment to such countries might be cut off. The five Nordic countries already have banned new investments in South Africa,[82] and at least one ot them—Sweden—has adopted a Code of Conduct for its corporations doing business there.[83] The EEC approved a similar code for its corporations operating in South Africa in 1977,[84] as did Canada in 1978.[85] Therefore, even if there is insufficient support in Congress for an investment ban, several excellent models exist that could be used to adopt a fair employment code to which United States corporations with investments in South Africa would have to comply.[86] In short, as an absolute minimum, Congress should mandate that U.S. corporations doing business in South Africa adhere to the principles of the Sullivan Code,[87] as certain South African corporations now are required to do so under the Evans Amendment.[88]

III. Coordination and Support of Executive Branch Human Rights Bureaucracy

The legislation enacted by Congress since 1973, in addition to the Carter administration's human rights initiatives, have generated an awesome task for the Department of State's Bureau of Human Rights and Humanitarian Affairs—that part of the executive branch primarily entrusted with shaping and implementing our human rights policy. While its staff has increased substantially over the past two years, it still needs additional personnel to perform its mandated functions and to coordinate the department's policies with the positions of other departments and agencies. Moreover, the latter, which often pay little attention to human rights matters, each needs additional staff to focus exclusively on human rights matters. As Roberta Cohen, now with the Human Rights Office, has suggested, "consideration should be given to the appointment of senior-level human rights advisors in these departments to integrate human rights concerns in their programs."[89]

The foregoing general comments can be transformed into specific operational recommendations only after a thorough review of the responsibilities that the Congress has assigned to the executive branch and the duties the latter has assumed in order to implement President Carter's proclaimed human rights policy. Accordingly, Congress should hold hearings to review these matters, concentrating upon what additional personnel and research support is required to facilitate the development and carrying out of a coordinated policy in this area. Among the many suggestions that could be made, the following three items may be mentioned.

First, a new, high-level Inter-Agency Human Rights Committee is needed to integrate human rights concerns into all aspects of U.S. foreign policy. At present, there exists an Inter-Agency Committee on Human Rights and Foreign Assistance, chaired by Deputy Secretary of State Christopher, but its competence is limited to examining bilateral and multilateral economic assistance decisions for their human rights import. Military assistance decisions are reviewed by the Arms Export Control Board, into which the Human Rights Office has an input, albeit at a lower level. Over a year ago, in response to Congressman Fraser's question about the need for an overarching committee to embrace both economic and military assistance, Mr. Schneider replied that a military assistance committee to parallel the Christopher Committee was "under review," and that the review was "nearing completion."[90] He also asserted that the establishment of such a committee was "a live possibility...."[91] At the very least, Congress should inquire about what happened to this idea.

Secondly, not only does the Human Rights Office need additional staff, but many other bureaus and offices in the Department of State either are woefully understaffed or have no human rights personnel at all. In the Office of the Legal Adviser, for instance, one assistant legal adviser is responsible for all international human rights law matters. As Ms. Cohen states, surely "[a]dditional human rights staff should be appointed, thus enabling the office to keep pace with the myriad of legal issues arising in response to the new policy."[92] Other offices undoubtedly need similar help. Who within the department has the responsibility for and actually has prepared the series of much-needed position papers on human rights issues—on geographical areas, particular countries, specific rights, questions of linkage, coordination with allies, and so on? Who has the responsibility for anticipating and perhaps "gaming" human rights crises, such as the one that occurred in Nicaragua over the past two years? Are the necessary funds available to have such work done within the department, or by outside consultants through the Office of External Research? These and other questions must be asked and answered if an effective follow-up by the executive branch in human rights matters is to be expected.

Thirdly, any effective human rights policy must extend beyond the Department of State to cover other departments and agencies as well. Too often the policies and actions of the latter—such as the Department of Commerce's licensing of "gray area" sales to South Africa, or the Department of the Treasury's instructions to U.S. representatives on the IFIs or the IMF—conflict with or actually undercut our human rights policies. Such policies, being one factor in the foreign policy process, upon occasion must give way to other considerations, but only after a careful and coordinated evaluation of just what is in the best long- as well as short-range interests of the United States. In addition to the departments mentioned, the Departments of Defense and Justice also need to be brought into the human rights picture to a much greater extent. Increased reachout by Department of State personnel may be helpful in achieving coordinated positions, but ultimately what is needed is building a human rights component into the internal decision-making processes of such departments. A useful first step would be the appointment of senior-level human rights officers in each department, as suggested by Ms. Cohen, so that in approaching a particular decision—say, the attitude toward Haitian refugees to be taken by the Department of Justice[93]—persons within and without the department would know who in it was to speak out for human rights.

IV. Congressional Oversight Role

In order to guarantee that its mandate is being followed, Congress must review and oversee various reports and actions of the executive branch in a far more serious and sustained fashion than it has done in the past. To date, congressional scrutiny has focused primarily upon the president's exercise of his waiver authority under the Jackson-Vanik Amendment[94] and the annual reports on economic and military assistance prepared by the Department of State pursuant to Sections 116(d) and 502B(b) of the Foreign Assistance Act.[95] These reports, while still leaving something to be desired, have improved greatly in the last two years.[96] Moreover, they probably would improve even more in the future if they received more than a desultory review from the Subcommittee on International Organizations and its Senate counterpart. A systematic assessment of the reports, under which certain countries or areas or rights or other categories would be examined each year on a rotating basis, is one approach worth considering. Additionally, the reporting requirement should be expanded to cover all countries, not just recipients of U.S. assistance, so that the reports will reflect a better view of the worldwide human rights picture.

In addition to examining the annual reports on human rights, Congress has numerous other review and oversight responsibilities, many of which apparently it has neglected to fulfill. The following statutory provisions provide a useful checklist to determine just how effective Congress has been in monitoring executive branch compliance with the spirit as well as the letter of existing law.

Section 116 of the Foreign Assistance Act. Gross human rights violators are denied economic assistance by Section 116(a), unless it will directly benefit the needy people in the country.[97] To determine whether this exception has been invoked properly, Section 116(b) provides that the Senate Committee on Foreign Relations or the House Committee on Foreign Affairs may require the executive branch "to submit in writing information demonstrating that such assistance will directly benefit the needy people in such country, together with a detailed explanation of how such assistance will directly benefit the needy people in such country."[98] If either committee disagrees with this justification, it may initiate action to terminate such assistance by a concurrent resolution. No such termination has taken place to date, but in view of Deputy Secretary of State Christopher's recent testimony that the Carter administration is interpreting the "needy people" exception liberally, Congress may wish to begin reviewing such economic assistance decisions more carefully.[99]

Section 112 of the Agricultural Trade Development and Assistance Act. Section 112(a) prohibits the sale of agricultural commodities to gross human rights violators unless the sale will benefit the country's needy people.[100] To determine the propriety of this exception's invocation, Section 112(b) provides that the Senate Committee on Agriculture, Nutrition and Forestry or the House Committee on Foreign Affairs may require the president "to submit in writing information demonstrating that an agreement will directly benefit the needy people in a country."[101] Whether either committee ever has made such a request is unknown. If one is made, it is for information purposes only, because the statute does not permit Congress to override the president's decision by concurrent resolution. Nevertheless, for the reasons given above, Congress may wish to initiate requests in the future.

Section 240A of the Foreign Assistance Act. This section states that in its annual report to Congress, OPIC shall describe projects where, despite the fact that the country involved was a gross human rights violator, it provided insurance, reinsurance, guaranty, financing, or financial support on the ground that "the project will directly benefit the needy people in the country in which the project is located...."[102] The appropriate committees reviewing OPIC's annual reports should pay special attention to whether OPIC has invoked this exception and, if so, under what circumstances.

Section 502B(c) of the Foreign Assistance Act. This section parallels Section 116 by denying military assistance to gross human rights violators unless "extraordinary circumstances" exist that make it in the "national interest" to continue such assistance.[103] To determine whether this exception has been invoked properly, the Senate Committee on Foreign Relations or the House Committee on Foreign Affairs may require the secretary of state to submit a statement within 30 days, justifying the continuation of assistance. Upon the transmittal of a statement, "the Congress may at any time thereafter adopt a joint resolution terminating, restricting, or continuing security assistance for such country."[104] No such joint resolution has yet been adopted. Indeed, apparently only once, in 1976, has the Committee on Foreign Affairs actually requested such statements.[105] Recalling Congressman Harkin's comment on the executive branch's abuse of this exception,[106] and noting his observation that last year's Congressional Presentation Document on military assistance justified such aid to countries like Indonesia and Nicaragua "on the most flimsy and tenuous grounds,"[107] Congress should take advantage of this section and initiate a thorough and critical evaluation of military assistance to all gross human rights violators.

Section 502B(2) of the Foreign Assistance Act. This section as amended in 1978 provides, inter alia, that:

> [s]ecurity assistance may not be provided to the public, domestic intelligence, or similar law enforcement forces of a country, and licenses may not be issued under the Export Administration Act of 1969 for the export

of crime control and detection instruments and equipment to a country [which is a gross human rights violator] unless the President certifies in writing to the [House and the Senate] that extraordinary circumstances exist warranting provision of such assistance and issuance of such licenses.[108]

Contingency assistance to such countries may be provided also only upon a similar written certification by the president. Congress should ascertain whether certifications have been issued in either instance and, if so, whether "extraordinary circumstances" actually existed.

Section 31 of the Bretton Woods Agreement Act. This section, also added in 1978, requires the secretary of the treasury to submit an annual report to Congress on the human rights situation in countries drawing on funds made available under the IMF Supplementary Financing [Witteveen] Facility.[109] In view of the concern of many members of Congress with the IMF's apparent failure to take human rights factors into account when attaching conditions to its loans, these reports should be reviewed carefully to determine whether additional legislation may not be needed.[110]

Section 701 of the International Financial Institutions Act. This section, which requires the U.S. executive directors of the six IFIs to oppose loans or assistance to gross human rights violators unless directed specifically to programs serving the basic human needs of the citizens of such countries, also requires the secretaries of state and treasury to report annually to the House and the Senate on the progress toward achieving the statute's goals.[111] As in the case of the IMF above, Congress' concern with the IFIs warrants its careful review of these reports, both to see if its mandate is being carried out and to determine whether additional legislation is needed.

Section 703 of the International Financial Institutions Act. This section enjoins the secretaries of state and treasury to develop a plan for meeting basic human needs and protecting human rights, as well as "a mechanism for acting together to insure that the rewards of international economic cooperation are especially available to those who subscribe to such standards and are seen to be moving toward making them effective in their own systems of governance."[112] Not later than one year after the section's enactment (by October 3, 1978), the secretaries were to have reported to both the Senate and the House on the progress made in carrying out its terms.[113] Congress should learn whether the report has been submitted and, if it has, evaluate its recommendations.

Section 611 of the Foreign Assistance and Related Programs Appropriations Act, 1979. This section, added in 1978, also commands the president to direct the U.S. governor of the six IFIs to propose and seek adoption of provisions requiring their institutions to establish human rights standards to be taken into account when considering applications for assistance.[114] Congress should inquire about the progress that has been made in the case of each institution.

Section 3 of the Export Administration Act. This section authorizes the president to control exports, inter alia, for foreign policy— including human rights—purposes.[115] Unfortunately, Congress has not monitored the export licensing process, administered by the Department of Commerce, and thus does not have an adequate data base to refute recent charges by the business community that license denials do not help human rights abroad and are costly to United States exporters and to the economy in general.[116] Amendments to the Export Administration Act, currently being debated in Congress, may circumscribe somewhat the president's current power to restrict exports for human rights purposes.[117] Whether they do or not, Congress should adopt some method of monitoring the export licensing process in the future to insure that it is supportive of the human rights policy of the United States.

Section 2(b)(1)(B) of the Export-Import Bank Act. This section, added in 1978, in indicative of the current proexport attitude in Congress, in that it instructs the Eximbank to deny applications for credit only in cases where the president determines that such action "would clearly and importantly advance United States policy" in four areas, one of which fortunately is human rights.[118] Congress, as in the case of the export licensing process, should adopt some method of monitoring the Eximbank's decisions authorizing or denying loans or guarantees where human rights factors are involved.

Section 2(b)(8) of the Export-Import Bank Act. This section, the Evans Amendment, also was added in 1978. It prohibits, inter alia, Eximbank guarantees and insurance and extensions of credit to purchasers in South Africa unless the secretary of state certifies that the purchaser has endorsed and is implementing the Sullivan Code.[119] According to the *Financial Mail* of South Africa, in late January 1979 the secretary had not begun the certification process, yet Eximbank facilities were being extended automatically to purchasers who had signed the Sullivan Code.[120] The newsweekly added pointedly that "no inspection is carried out to see whether they are actually adhering to it."[121] If this report is accurate, the executive branch clearly is violating both the letter and the spirit of the Evans Amendment. Congress should look into the matter and regularly review the secretary's certification decisions.

Section 4(m)(1) of the Export Administration Act. This section, added in 1978, provides that "[c]rime control and detection instruments and equipment shall be approved for export by the secretary of commerce only pursuant to a validated export license."[122] Congress should request a list of such licenses annually, both to doublecheck executive branch compliance with Section 502B(a)(2) of the Foreign Assistance Act and to monitor just what crime control equipment is being shipped to countries who are *not* gross human rights violators.[123]

Section 543(3) of the Foreign Assistance Act. This section, also a 1978 addition to the statute books, provides that the curricula of international military education and training courses should be revamped "to increase the awareness of nationals of foreign countries participating in such activities of basic issues involving internationally recognized human rights."[124] Since the future leaders of many countries participate in such programs, Congress should review their content from a human rights perspective.

Section 610(b) of the Foreign Relations Authorization Act, Fiscal Year 1979. By this 1978 statute, Congress urged the president to move aggressively to support multilateral action by the UN or other international organizations, and to encourage bilateral actions by countries having more extensive relations with Cambodia, to bring an end to the gross human rights violations in that country.[125] Under Section 610(c), the secretary of state was requested to transmit not later than January 20, 1979, a report to the House and Senate "describing fully and completely actions taken pursuant to [Section 610(b)]."[126] Congress should determine whether the report has been made and, if so, review its conclusions.

* * *

The above survey of the human rights laws that Congress has enacted in recent years reveals review and oversight responsibilities that, with all due respect, it has not yet fully appreciated, much less fulfilled. If the Congress is to continue to play a significant role in the formulation of U.S. human rights policy, at the very least it must monitor executive branch compliance with the laws that it has passed to help shape that policy. These oversight activities, in my opinion, are important and time-consuming enough to warrant the division of the Subcommittee on International Organizations of the House Committee on Foreign Affairs into two subcommittees—one on International Organizations and the other on International Human Rights (with a full-time staff for the latter as well). Additionally, the Senate Committee on Foreign Relations should establish a permanent Subcommittee on International Human Rights. The two new subcommittees then could perform, perhaps jointly, these important and so far neglected review and oversight functions.

V. Domestic Implementation of and Compliance with International Human Rights Law

In the area of international human rights, as in all areas of law generally, the "mirror image" principle must be kept in mind: namely, that the claims one projects against others inevitably will result in similar claims against oneself. Given the obviousness of this principle, it is no surprise that the Soviet Union responded to President Carter's expressions of concern over its treatment of human rights activist Anatoly Scharansky by singling out North Carolina's treatment of the Wilmington 10. What does cause wonderment is the fact that this response came as a surprise to the president. Clearly, the Carter Administration, at least in its early days, did not expect the actions of the United States to be measured against international human rights law. Nor did it contemplate using this law as a lever to upgrade or buttress domestic constitutional or statutory law. In short, to paraphrase an earlier quote from Professor Henkin, the Carter administration faithfully followed the traditional U.S. view that regarded international human rights law as designed for others only.

There were some notable exceptions. Early on, the president backed the repeal of the Byrd Amendment, thereby allowing the United States to resume compliance with the UN's sanctions program against Rhodesia.[127] The president also signed the McGovern Amendment, which liberalized U.S. visa policies to conform them with the Helsinki Final Act.[128] INS procedures governing the treatment of refugees, tested repeatedly by Haitian "boat people," have been modified in the direction of the standards set out in the Refugees Protocol, one of the few UN human rights treaties to which the United States is a party.[129] What changes have been made, however, have occurred on an ad hoc basis. No systematic effort has been undertaken to review U.S. legal standards and, where necessary, to attempt to bring them into line with international human rights law. That is doubly regrettable: first, because an opportunity to upgrade U.S. law is being passed up; and, secondly, because a foreign policy based upon human rights concerns can retain credibility overseas only if such concerns are seen to be effectively at work in the U.S. This corollary to the "mirrow image" principle warrants much greater attention by the executive branch as well as by Congress.

First, all departments and agencies should review the statutes and regulations they administer to insure their conformity with international human rights law. Such a study is already underway in the Department of Justice, initiated by the Civil Rights Division, but similar surveys should be undertaken across-the-board.[130]

Secondly, Congress should assess all proposed legislation against the standards of international human rights law. If a bill violates that body of law—as do current bills seeking to terminate U.S. participation in the UN's sanctions program against Rhodesia—it should not be enacted into law.[131] Conversely, Congress should seek out areas where legislation is needed to bring United States law up to the level of its international counterpart. Legislation prohibiting the use of dum-dum bullets by law enforcement officers in the U.S. would be a good example. The United States already is committed under the Geneva Convention to forego their use in international conflicts: why should a policeman in the U.S. be allowed to use this weapon against a civilian when a GI may not use it against an enemy soldier?[132]

Third, both the executive branch and the Congress should commence serious efforts to monitor our compliance with the Helsinki Final Act.[133] The president took the first step in this direction on December 6, 1978, when, in a brief memorandum to various departments and agencies, he instructed them to cooperate with the Department of State and the Commission on Security and Cooperation in Europe (the Fascell Commission) "to assess implementation and identify areas where American performance can be improved."[134] The Fascell Commission held a one-day hearing in April 1979 on possible U.S. violations of Helsinki's human rights standards, during the course of which the chairman took pains to point out that the commission as presently constituted lacked the resources to carry out a general oversight function within the federal government.[135] Clearly, some follow-up to the president's memorandum and Congressman Fascell's lament is required.

VI. Conclusion

In brief conclusion, I wish to reiterate what I stated at the outset of this chapter: the United States has reached a cross-roads with respect to the implementation of its human rights policy. Over the past three years, President Carter's initiatives, often built upon the legislative foundation previously laid down by the Congress, have helped shape a new U.S. foreign policy that has as its centerpiece the president's oft-proclaimed concern for human rights. Experience has revealed, however, that concern is not enough, that further steps need to be taken if our human rights policy is to be made genuinely effective. This chapter suggests a few such remedial steps, many of which Congress and the executive branch will regard as too controversial or too costly to implement. Until most of them are acted upon, however, it is difficult to see how the United States can achieve a more than marginally relevant human rights policy.

NOTES

* © The Procedural Aspects of International Law Institute, Inc., 1979. The writer wishes to thank Amy Young-Anawaty, Esq., executive director, International Human Rights Law Group, Washington, D.C., for her research assistance in connection with Part II of this chapter. This chapter was completed in the summer of 1979.

1. *International Protection of Human Rights: Hearings Before the Subcomm. on International Organizations and Movements of the House Comm. on Foreign Relations,* 93rd Cong., 1st Sess. (1973).
2. *Subcomm. on International Organizations and Movements of the House Comm. on Foreign Affairs, 93rd, Cong., 2d. Sess., Human Rights in The World Community: A Call for U.S. Leadership,* (Comm. Print 1974).
3. For a preliminary assessment made in mid-1977, see Lillich, "A United States Policy of Humanitarian Intervention and Intercession," in *Human Rights and American Foreign Policy,* edited by D. Kommers and G. Loescher, 1979.
4. *United States Private Investment in South Africa: Hearings Before the Subcomms. on Africa and on International Economic Policy and Trade of the House Comm. on International Relations,* 95th Cong., 2d Sess. 179 (1978).
5. Fraser and Salzberg, "Foreign Policy and Effective Strategies for Human Rights," *Universal Human Rights* 1 (1979):11.
6. See *International Human Rights Treaties and Agreements,* (Jan. 1979). (Report from the Dept. of State to the Senate Comm. on Foreign Relations).
7. *Id.* at 131-48. Many scholars, for instance, now regard the Universal Declaration as being part of customary international law. See, e.g., Humphrey, "The International Bill of Rights: Scope and Implementation," *William and Mary Law Review* (1976): 527.
8. 34 UN GAOR, Supp. (No. 39) 23, UN Doc. A/34/39 (1979).
9. 35 UN ESCOR, Supp. (No. 6) 1, UN Doc. E/CN.4/1347 (1979).
10. 35 UN ESCOR, Supp. (No. 6) 60, UN Doc. E/CN.4/1347 (1979).
11. *International Human Rights Treaties and Agreements, supra,* note 6, at 2-88. The 11 treaties and agreements to which the U.S. is a party are the United Nations Charter, *id.* at 2; the Slavery Convention, *id.* at 4; the Protocol Amending the Slavery Convention, *id.* at 7; the Supplementary Convention on the Abolition of Slavery and Institutions and Practices Similar to Slavery, *id.* at 9; the Inter-American Convention on the Granting of Political Rights to Women, *id.* at 12; the Convention on the Political Rights of Women, *id.* at 13; the Geneva Convention Relative to the Treatment of Prisoners of War, *id.* at 17; the Geneva Convention for the Amelioration of the Conditions of the Wounded and Sick in Armed Forces in the Field, *id.* at 26; the Geneva Convention Relative to the Protection of Civilian Persons in Time of War, *id.* at 31; and the Protocol Relating to the Status of Refugees, *id.* at 38.
12. *Id.* at 91-131. The treaties and agreements that the United States has signed but not ratified are the Convention on the Prevention and Punishment of the Crime of Genocide, *id.* at 46; the Convention Concerning the Abolition of Forced Labor, *id.* at 51; the Convention on the Consent to Marriage; Minimum Age for Marriage and Registration of Marriage, *id.* at 54; the Inter-

national Convention on the Elimination of All Forms of Racial Discrimination, *id.* at 57; the International Covenant on Civil and Political Rights, *id.* at 63; the International Covenant on Economic, Social and Cultural Rights, *id.* at 71; the American Convention on Human Rights, *id.* at 78; the Protocol I Additional to the Geneva Conventions of Aug. 12, 1949, and Relating to the Protection of Victims of International and Armed Conflicts, *id.* at 86; and the Protocol II Additional to the Geneva Conventions of Aug. 12, 1949, and Relating to the Protection of Victims of Non-International Armed Conflicts, *id.* at 88.

Those treaties and agreements which the U.S. has not signed are the Convention Concerning Freedom of Association and Protection of the Right to Organize, *id.* at 91; the Convention Concerning the Application of the Principles of the Right to Organize and to Bargain Collectively, *id.* at 93; the Convention for the Suppression of the Traffic in Persons and of the Exploitation of the Prostitution of Others, *id.* at 96; the Convention Concerning Equal Remuneration for Men and Women Workers for Work of Equal Value, *id.* at 98; the Convention on the International Right of Correction, *id.* at 100; the Convention Relating to the Status of Stateless Persons, *id.* at 102; the Convention of the Nationality of Married Women, *id.* at 106; the Convention Concerning Discrimination in Respect to Employment and Occupation, *id.* at 108; the Convention Against Discrimination in Education and Its Protocol, *id.* at 111; the Convention on the Reduction of Statelessness, *id.* at 117; the Convention Concerning Employment Policy, *id.* at 119; the Optional Protocol to the International Covenant on Civil and Political Rights, *id.* at 121; the Convention on the Non-Applicability of Statutory Limitations to War Crimes Against Humanity, *id.* at 124; the Convention Concerning Protection and Facilities to be Afforded Workers' Representatives in the Undertaking, *id.* at 126; and the International Convention on the Suppression and Punishment of the Crime of Apartheid, *id.* at 128.

13. Henkin, "The United States and the Crisis in Human Rights," *Virginia Journal of International Law* (1974):653.
14. 1 Pub. Papers 449, 450 (1977).
15. S. Exec. Doc. Nos. C, D, E & F, 95th Cong., 2d Sess. (1978).
16. Weissbrodt, "United States Ratification of the Human Right Covenants," Minnesota Law Review 63 (1978):35.
17. S. Exec. Doc. no. 25, 91st Cong., 1st Sess. (1970); S. Exec. Doc. no. 6, 92d Cong., 1st Sess. (1971); S. Exec. Doc. no. 5, 93rd Cong., 1st Sess. (1973); S. Exec. Doc. no. 23, 94th Cong., 2d Sess. (1976).
18. Senator Church, who faces a 1980 challenge from a right-wing Republican candidate who opposes U.S. ratification of the Genocide Convention, reportedly wants to postpone a Senate vote on the Convention until the next session of Congress.
19. For instance, it is universally agreed that a reservation to Article 20 of the UN Covenant on Civil and Political Rights will be required in order to preserve first amendment free speech rights. See, e.g., "Report of the Committee on Human Rights," *1977-1978 American Branch International Law Association Proceedings* (1978): 53.

20. Foreign Assistance Act of 1961, § 116, 22 U.S.C. § 2151 (1976).
21. Foreign Assistance Act of 1961, § 502B, 22 U.S.C.A. § 2304 (1979).
22. Agricultural Trade Development And Assistance Act of 1954, § 112, 7 U.S.C. § 1712 (Supp. I 1977).
23. Foreign Assistance Act of 1961, § 239(1), 22 U.S.C.A. § 2199 (1979).
24. Export-Import Bank Act of 1945, § 2 (b)(8), 12 U.S.C.A. § (1979).
25. *To Extend and Amend the Export-Import Bank Act of 1945; Hearings on H.R. 5501 Before the Subcomm. on International Trade, Investment and Monetary Policy of the House Comm. on Banking, Finance and Urban Affairs,* 95th Cong., 1st Sess. 69 (1977). (Statement of Hon. Patricia Derian.)
26. During 1978, for instance, the Department of State, Treasury, and Commerce opposed any additional human rights legislation with respect to South Africa. See *United States Private Investment in South Africa: Hearings Before the Subcomms. on Africa and on International Economic Policy and Trade of the House Comm. on International Relations,* 95th Cong., 2d Sess. 166-78 (1978). (Testimony of Hon. Richard Moose, Hon. Stanley J. Marcuss, and Hon. C. Fred Bergsten.)
27. *United States-Uganda Relations: Hearings Before the Subcomms. on Africa, International Organization, and International Economic Policy and Trade of the House Comm. on International Relations,* 95th Cong., 2d Sess. 111 (1978).
28. *Id.* at 98-102 (statement of Hon. Julius L. Katz).
29. Statement of Hon. Mark L. Schneider, Deputy Assistant Secretary for Human Rights, in Washington, D.C. (Apr. 10, 1979).
30. Foreign Assistance Act of 1961, § 116(a), 22 U.S.C. § 2151 (1976).
31. Note 22 *supra.*
32. Note 23 *supra.*
33. Or, for that matter, Congress in its oversight role to be discussed at notes 97-102 *infra.*
34. New York *Times,* May 3, 1979, at A2, Col. 3.
35. Note 21 *supra.*
36. Note 23 *supra..*
37. Or, once again, Congress in its oversight role to be discussed at notes 103-107 *infra.*
38. T. Harkin, "Human Rights and Foreign Aid: Forging an Unbreakable Link 14" (Oct. 6, 1978), (Working paper published by the Center for Philosophy and Public Policy of the University of Maryland).
39. *Id.*
40. *Id.*
41. *Id.* at 7.
42. Vogelgesang, "What Price Principle? U.S. Policy on Human Rights," *Foreign Affairs* 16 (1978):819.
43. Hovey, "White House is Fighting to Prevent Congress' Crippling of World Bank," *New York Times,* March 28, 1978, at C53, Col. 4. *Cf.* Marmorstein, "World Bank Power to Consider Human Rights Factors in Loan Decisions," 13 *Journal of Economic Law and Economics* (1978): 113, in which the author

concludes that the World Bank's Articles already allow it to take human rights concerns into account in making loan decisions.
44. International Financial Institutions Act of 1977, 701, 22 U.S.C. § 262d (Supp. I 1977).
45. Harkin, *supra* note 38, at 9.
46. Foreign Assistance and Related Programs Appropriations Act, 1979, § 611, 22 U.S.C.A. § 262d note (1979).
47. 124 Cong. Rec. S12,145 (daily ed. July 31, 1978).
48. *Id.* at S12,148. For text of the amendment, see *id.* at S12,086.
49. *Id.* at S12,144 (remarks of Sen. Javits).
50. *Id.* at S12,145 (remarks of Sen. Church).
51. *Id.*
52. Harkin, *supra,* note 38, at 12.
53. *Id.* at 3.
54. *Washington Post,* July 7, 1979, at A1, col. 5.
55. Note 47 *supra,* at S12,097 (remarks of Sen. Javits).
56. Note 24 *supra.*
57. Harkin, *supra,* note 38, at 12. Indeed, it is already subject to human rights considerations. Section 2(b)(1)(B) of the Export-Import Bank Act of 1945, as amended last year, provides that human rights factors are one of only four nonfinancial or noneconomic reasons that the president can rely upon when ordering the Eximbank to deny applications for credit. 12 U.S.C.A. § 635 (1979).
58. *To Extend and Amend the Export-Import Bank Act of 1945; Hearings on H.R. 5501 Before the Subcomm. on International Trade, Investment and Monetary Policy of The House Comm. on Banking, Finance and Urban Affairs,* 95th Cong., 1st Sess. 255 (1977).
59. Under the International Security Assistance and Arms Export Control Act of 1976, § 406, 22 U.S.C. 2370 note (1976), military assistance to Chile was terminated, and a $27.5 million ceiling was put on economic assistance. Chile responded by formally notifying the U.S. that it no longer wished to receive economic assistance. *New York Times,* October 21, 1976, at A8, col. 1.
60. I. Littelier and M. Moffit, Transnational Institute, *Human Rights, Economic Aid and Private Banks: The Case of Chile,* in Report to the Subcomm. on Prevention of Discrimination and Protection of Minorities, UN Comm. on Human Rights, at 19 (1978).
61. Country Exposure Lending Survey, Red. Res. Bd. Press Release, January 16, 1978.
62. I. Lettelier and M. Moffit, *supra* note 60, at 20, Table II.
63. *Financial Times* (London), May 22, 1979, at 22, col. 5.
64. *New York Times,* March 31, 1978, at A12, col. 1.
65. Fagen, The Carter Administration and Latin America: Business as Usual? *Foreign Affairs* 57 (1979): 652, 669.
66. *Id.*
67. H.R. 12,568, 95th Cong., 2d Sess. (1978). Senator Kennedy also has made a similar proposal. *New York Times,* May 5, 1978, at A7, col. 1.

68. *United States-Uganda Relations, supra* note 27, at 98-99.
69. See text at note 28 *supra*.
70. Export Administration Act of 1969, § 4(m), 50 U.S.C.A. app. § 2403 (1979).
71. See, e.g., S.C. Res. 232, 21 U.N. SCOR, Res. and Dec., at 7 (1966); S.C. Res. 253, 23 U.N. SCOR, Res. and Dec., at 5 (1968); S.C. Res. 418, 32 U.N. SCOR, Res. and Dec. at 5-6 (1977).
72. See, e.g., Exec. Order No. 11,419, 3 C.F.R. § 731 (1966-1970 compilation), reprinted in 22 U.S.C. § 287c app. at 324 (1976).
73. Export Administration Act of 1969, § 3(2), 50 U.S.C. ap. § 2402 (1976).
74. For evidence of business community opposition to export controls for human rights purposes, see generally R. Lillich and F. Newman, *International Human Rights: Problems of Law and Policy* 842-63 (1979).
75. Bingham and Johnson, "A Rational Approach to Export Controls," Foreign Affairs 57 (1979): 894, 911.
76. The House and the Senate have pending before them similar versions of a proposed new Export Administration Act of 1979 that emphasize the priority of exports and the importance of limiting export controls. H.R. 4034, 96th Cong., 1st Sess. (1979); S. 737, 96th Cong., 1st Sess. (1979).
77. The reports accompanying H.R. 4034 and S. 737 bear out the statement in the text. H.R. Rep. No. 96-200, 96th Cong., 1st Sess. (1979), S. Rep. No. 96-109, 96th Cong., 1st Sess. (1979). The latter notes that "[n]o aspect of U.S. export control policy received sharper criticism during committee and subcommittee hearings than controls maintained for foreign policy purposes." *Id.* at 6.
78. *Basket Three: Implementation of the Helsinki Awards, Vol. I: Hearings Before the Commission on Security and Cooperation in Europe,* 95th Cong., 1st Sess. 33 (1977).
79. *United States Private Investment in South Africa, supra* note 4, at 172 (statement of Hon. C. Fred Bergsten).
80. *Id.* at 166-78 (testimony of Hon. Richard H. Moose, Hon. Stanley J. Marcuss and Hon. C. Fred. Bergsten).
81. *Washington Post,* April 27, 1979, at A25, col. 1.
82. *United States Private Investment in South Africa, supra* note 4, at 28.
83. Sweden enacted this law June 1, 1979. Interview with Martin Grundity, First Secretary, Swedish Embassy, in Washington, D.C., August 7, 1979.
84. R. Lillich and F. Newman, *supra* note 74, at 465-68.
85. *United States Private Investment in South Africa, supra* note 4 at 86-88.
86. For instance, Congressman Solarz's bill, in addition to prohibiting new U.S. investments in South Africa, also established "a fair employment code of conduct to which American citizens and corporations with existing investments in South Africa would have to comply..." *Id.* at 2.
87. *United States Private Investment in South Africa, supra* note 4, at 90-94. Reverend Sullivan last year expanded the principles to include, among other things, a provision that black workers be free to provide their own unions. *Washington Post,* July 6, 1978, at D5, col. 6.
88. Note 24 *supra*.
89. Cohen, "Human Rights Decision-Making in the Executive Branch: Some

Proposals for a Coordinated Strategy, in *Human Rights and American Foreign Policy,* edited by D. Kommers and G. Loescher, pp. 216, 236 (1979).
90. *Foreign Assistance Legislation for Fiscal Year 1979 (Part 4): Hearings Before the Subcomm. on International Organizations of the House Comm. on International Relations,* 95th Cong., 2d Sess. 7 (1979).
91. *Id.*
92. Cohen, *supra* note 89, at 235.
93. During the appeal of a case alleging that the Immigration and Naturalization Service did not afford an adequate hearing on their claim for asylum, as required by the UN Protocol Relating to the Status of Refugees, signed January 31, 1967, entered into force October 4, 1967, 19 U.S.T. 6223, T.I.A.S. No. 6577, 606 U.N.T.S. 267, the Department of Justice intervened to state that the INS had changed its procedures and hence the case was moot. Department of Justice Memorandum Suggesting Mootness at 1, 2, *Pierre v. United States,* 434 U.S. 962 (1977). Having a permanent human rights officer in the department certainly would sensitize it to international human rights law factors in other such cases.
94. Trade Act of 1974, § 402, 19 U.S.C. § 2432 (1976).
95. Foreign Assistance Act of 1961, § 116(d), 22 U.S.C. § 2151 (1976); Foreign Assistance Act of 1961, § 502B(b), 22 U.S.C.A. § 2304 (1979).
96. Falk, The Human Rights County Reports, *World Issues* (Oct./Nov. 1978): 19.
97. Note 30 *supra.*
98. Foreign Assistance Act of 1961, § 116(b), 22 U.S.C. § 2151 (1976).
99. *Id.*
100. *Agricultural Trade Development and Assistance Act of 1954,* § 112(a), 7 U.S.C. § 1712 (Supp. I 1977).
101. Agricultural Trade Development and Assistance Act of 1954, § 112(b), 7 U.S.C. § 1712 (Supp. I 1977).
102. Foreign Assistance Act of 1961, § 240A, 22 U.S.C.A. § 2200a (1979). This section also contains a "national security interest" exception.
103. Foreign Assistance Act of 1961, § 502B(c), 22 U.S.C.A. § 2304 (1979).
104. *Id.*
105. Department of State, 94th Cong., 2d Sess., *Human Rights and U.S. Policy: Argentina, Haiti, Indonesia, Iran, Peru, and The Philippines,* Reports submitted to the House Comm. on International Relations 36 (Comm. Print 1976).
106. *See* text at notes 38-40 *supra.*
107. Note 47 *supra* at H2458. (Remarks of Congressman Harkin.)
108. Foreign Assistance Act of 1961, § 502B(a) (2), 22 U.S.C.A. § 2304 (1979).
109. Bretton Woods Agreement Act, § 31, 22 U.S.C.A. § 286-10 (1979). Also relevant in this regard is Section 30(b), which requires the U.S. Governor of the IMF to submit an annual report to Congress evaluating the effect of IMF-induced policies on the basic human needs of the poor majority within those countries. Bretton Woods Agreement Act, § 30, 22 U.S.C.A. § 286e-9 (1979). Congress in its oversight function should examine these reports carefully.

110. In its oversight function, Congress also should ascertain the extent to which its injunction in Section 30(a)—to the effect that the U.S. executive director on the IMF initiate a "wide consultation" with other directors to encourage the formulation of stabilizing programs designed to meet basic human needs—actually has been carried out. Bretton Woods Agreement Act, § 30(a), 22 U.S.C.A. § 286e-a (1979).
111. Note 44 *supra*.
112. International Financial Institutions Act of 1977, § 703, 22 U.S.C. § 262c note (Supp. I 1977).
113. *Id.*
114. Note 46 *supra*.
115. Export Administrative Act of 1969, § 3, 50 U.S.C. app. § 2402 (1976).
116. Such charges are reported in Bingham and Johnson, "A Rational Approach to Export Controls, *Foreign Affairs* 57 (1979): 894.
117. *See* text at note 77 *supra*. While legislative history shows that the president's power has not been restricted by Congress in a literal sense, as a practical matter the president is likely to be discouraged from using export controls as frequently as in the past.
118. Export-Import Bank Act of 1945, § 2(b)(1)(B), 12 U.S.C.A. § 635 (1979).
119. Note 24 *supra*.
120. *Financial Mail*, January 26, 1979, at 214.
121. *Id.*
122. Export Administration Act of 1969, § 1969, § 4(m)(1), 50 U.S.C.A. app. § 2403 (1979).
123. Note 108 *supra*. Section 502B(a)(2) refers only to "gross human rights violations," but many countries may still violate human rights without having crossed the threshold that qualifies them as "gross violators."
124. Foreign Assistance Act of 1961, § 543(3), 22 U.S.C.A. § 2347b (1979).
125. Foreign Relations Authorization Act, Fiscal Year 1979, § 610(b), 22 U.S.C.A. § 2151 note (1979).
126. Foreign Relations Authorization Act, Fiscal Year 1979, § 610(c), 22 U.S.C.A. § 2151 note (1979).
127. See R. Lillich and F. Newman, *supra* note 74, at 433-35.
128. Act to Provide Certain Basic Authority for the Department of State, § 21, 22 U.S.C. § 2691 (Supp. I 1977).
129. Protocol Relating to the Status of Refugees, signed January 31, 1967, entered into force October 4, 1967, 19 U.S.T. 6223, T.I.A.S. No. 6577, 606 U.N.T.S. 267.
130. The study is being conducted by the author as legal consultant to the Civil Rights Division of the Department of Justice.
131. See, e.g., S. 996, 96th Cong., 1st Sess. (1979). Since UN sanctions laid down in 1966 and 1968 (see note 71 *supra*) remain legally binding upon the United States under Article 25 of the UN Charter, all current bills permitting the resumption of economic relations with Rhodesia necessarily violate international law.

132. See Paust, *Does Your Police Force Use Illegal Weapons? A Configurative Approach to Decision Integrating International and Domestic Law*, 18 *HARV. INT'L L. J.* 19 (1977).
133. Final Act — Conference on Security and Cooperation in Europe (Helsinki Accord), signed Aug. 1, 1975, 73 *Department of State Bulletin* 323 (1975).
134. Memorandum from President Carter to various departments, December 6, 1978, Sixth Annual Report by the President to the Commission on Security and Coordination in Europe on the Implementation of the Helsinki Final Act, Dec. 1, 1978 - May 31, 1979, at 52 app.
135. *3 Basket Three: Implementation of the Helsinki Accords: Hearings Before the Commission on Security and Cooperation in Europe*, 96th Cong., 1st Sess. 383-84 (1979). (Remarks of Hon. Dante B. Fascell.) The most recent report devotes only 10 of 52 pages to U.S. compliance with the Helsinki standards. Sixth Annual Report by the President to the Commission on Security and Coordination in Europe on the Implementation of the Helsinki Final Act, December 1, 1978 - May 31, 1979.

Appendices

A. A UNIVERSAL DECLARATION OF HUMAN RIGHTS

Preamble

Whereas recognition of the inherent dignity and of the equal and inalienable rights of all members of the human family is the foundation of freedom, justice and peace in the world,

Whereas disregard and contempt for human rights have resulted in barbarous acts which have outraged the conscience of mankind, and the advent of a world in which human beings shall enjoy freedom of speech and belief and freedom from fear and want has been proclaimed as the highest aspiration of the common people,

Whereas it is essential, if man is not to be compelled to have recourse, as a last resort, to rebellion against tyranny and oppression, that human rights should be protected by the rule of law,

Whereas it is essential to promote the development of friendly relations between nations,

Whereas the peoples of the United Nations have in the Charter reaffirmed their faith in fundamental human rights, in the dignity and worth of the human person and in the equal rights of men and women and have determined to promote social progress and better standards of life in larger freedom,

Whereas Member States have pledged themselves to achieve, in cooperation with the United Nations, the promotion of universal respect for and observance of human rights and fundamental freedoms,

Whereas a common understanding of these rights and freedoms is of the greatest importance for the full realization of this pledge,

Now, therefore,
The General Assembly
Proclaims this Universal Declaration of Human Rights as a common standard of achievement for all peoples and all nations, to the end that every individual and every organ of society, keeping this Declaration

constantly in mind, shall strive by teaching and education to promote respect for these rights and freedoms and by progressive measures, national and international, to secure their universal and effective recognition and observance, both among the peoples of Member States themselves and among the peoples of territories under their jurisdiction.

Article 1

All human beings are born free and equal in dignity and rights. They are endowed with reason and conscience and should act towards one another in a spirit of brotherhood.

Article 2

Everyone is entitled to all the rights and freedoms set forth in this Declaration, without distinction of any kind, such as race, colour, sex, language, religion, political or other opinion, national or social origin, property, birth or other status.

Furthermore, no distinction shall be made on the basis of the political, jurisdictional or international status of the country or territory to which a person belongs, whether it be independent, trust, non-self-governing, or under any other limitation of sovereignty.

Article 3

Everyone has the right to life, liberty and the security of person.

Article 4

No one shall be held in slavery or servitude; slavery and the slave trade shall be prohibited in all their forms.

Article 5

No one shall be subjected to torture or to cruel, inhuman or degrading treatment or punishment.

Article 6

Everyone has the right to recognition everywhere as a person before the law.

Article 7

All are equal before the Law and are entitled without any discrimination to equal protection of the law. All are entitled to equal protection against any discrimination in violation of this Declaration and against any incitement to such discrimination.

Article 8

Everyone has the right to an effective remedy by the competent national tribunals for acts violating the fundamental rights granted to him by the constitution or by law.

Article 9

No one shall be subjected to arbitrary arrests, detention or exile.

Article 10

Everyone is entitled in full equality to a fair, and public hearing by an independent and impartial tribunal, in the determination of his rights and obligations and of any criminal charge against him.

Article 11

1. Everyone charged with a penal offence has the right to be presumed innocent until proved guilty according to law in a public trial at which he has had all the guarantees necessary for his defence.
2. No one shall be held guilty of any penal offence on account of any act or omission which did not constitute a penal offence, under national or international law, at the time when it was committed. Nor shall a heavier penalty be imposed than the one that was applicable at the time the penal offence was committed.

Article 12

No one shall be subjected to arbitrary interference with his privacy, family, home or correspondence, nor to attacks upon his honour and reputation. Everyone has the right to the protection of the law against such interference or attacks.

Article 13

1. Everyone has the right to freedom of movement and residence within the borders of each State.

2. Everyone has the right to leave any country, including his own, and to return to his country.

Article 14

1. Everyone has the right to seek and to enjoy in other countries asylum from persecution.
2. This right may not be invoked in the case of prosecutions genuinely arising from non-political crimes or from acts contrary to the purposes and principles of the United Nations.

Article 15

1. Everyone has the right to a nationality.
2. No one shall be arbitrarily deprived of his nationality nor denied the right to change his nationality.

Article 16

1. Men and women of full age, without any limitation due to race, nationality or religion, have the right to marry and to found a family. They are entitled to equal rights as to marriage, during marriage and at its dissolution.
2. Marriage shall be entered into only with the free and full consent of the intending spouses.
3. The family is the natural and fundamental group unit of society and is entitled to protection by society and the State.

Article 17

1. Everyone has the right to own property alone as well as in association with others.
2. No one shall be arbitrarily deprived of his property.

Article 18

Everyone has the right to freedom of thought, conscience and religion; this right includes freedom to change his religion or belief, and freedom, either alone or in community with others and in public or private, to manifest his religion or belief in teaching, practice, worship and observance.

Article 19

Everyone has the right to freedom of opinion and expression; this right includes freedom to hold opinions without interference and to seek, receive and impart information and ideas through any media and regardless of frontiers.

Article 20

1. Everyone has the right to freedom of peaceful assembly and association.
2. No one may be compelled to belong to an association.

Article 21

1. Everyone has the right to take part in the government of his country, directly or through freely chosen representatives.
2. Everyone has the right of equal access to public service in his country.
3. The will of the people shall be the basis of the authority of government; this will shall be expressed in periodic and genuine elections which shall be by universal and equal suffrage and shall be held by secret vote or by equivalent free voting procedures.

Article 22

Everyone, as a member of society, has the right to social security and is entitled to realization, through national effort and international cooperation and in accordance with the organization and resources of each State, of the economic, social and cultural rights indispensable for his dignity and the free development of his personality.

Article 23

1. Everyone has the right to work, to free choice of employment, to just and favourable conditions of work and to protection against unemployment.
2. Everyone, without any discrimination, has the right to equal pay for equal work.
3. Everyone who works has the right to just and favourable remuneration ensuring for himself and his family an existence worthy of human dignity, and supplemented, if necessary, by other means of social protection.
4. Everyone has the right to form and to join trade unions for the protection of his interests.

Article 24

Everyone has the right to rest and leisure, including reasonable limitation of working hours and periodic holidays with pay.

Article 25

1. Everyone has the right to a standard of living adequate for the health and well-being of himself and of his family, including food,

clothing, housing and medical care and necessary social services, and the right to security in the event of unemployment, sickness, disability, widowhood, old age or other lack of livelihood in circumstances beyond his control.

2. Motherhood and childhood are entitled to special care and assistance. All children, whether born in or out of wedlock, shall enjoy the same social protection.

Article 26

1. Everyone has the right to education. Education shall be free, at least in the elementary and fundamental stages. Elementary education shall be compulsory. Technical and professional education shall be made generally available and higher education shall be equally accessible to all on the basis of merit.

2. Education shall be directed to the full development of the human personality and to the strengthening of respect for human rights and fundamental freedoms. It shall promote understanding, tolerance and friendship among all nations, racial or religious groups, and shall further the activities of the United Nations for the maintenance of peace.

3. Parents have a prior right to choose the kind of education that shall be given to their children.

Article 27

1. Everyone has the right freely to participate in the cultural life of the community, to enjoy the arts and to share in scientific advancement and its benefits.

2. Everyone has the right to the protection of the moral and material interests resulting from any scientific, literary or artistic production of which he is the author.

Article 28

1. Everyone is entitled to a social and international order in which the rights and freedoms set forth in this Declaration can be fully realized.

Article 29

1. Everyone has duties to the community in which alone the free and full development of his personality is possible.

2. In the exercise of his rights and freedoms, everyone shall be subject only to such limitations as are determined by law solely for the purpose of securing due recognition and respect for the rights and freedoms of others and of meeting the just requirements of morality, public order and the general welfare in a democratic society.

3. These rights and freedom may in no case be exercised contrary to the purposes and principles of the United Nations.

Article 30

Nothing in this Declaration may be interpreted as implying for any State, group or person any right to engage in any activity or to perform any act aimed at the destruction of any of the rights and freedoms set forth herein.

B. INTERNATIONAL COVENANT OF CIVIL AND POLITICAL RIGHTS, 1966

The States Parties to the present Covenant,

Considering that, in accordance with the principles proclaimed in the Charter of the United Nations, recognition of the inherent dignity and of the equal and inalienable rights of all members of the human family is the foundation of freedom, justice and peace in the world,

Recognizing that these rights derive from the inherent dignity of the human person,

Recognizing that, in accordance with the Universal Declaration of Human Rights, the ideal of free human beings enjoying civil and political freedom and freedom from fear and want can only be achieved if conditions are created whereby everyone may enjoy his civil and political rights, as well as his economic, social and cultural rights,

Considering the obligations of States under the Charter of the United Nations to promote universal respect for, and observance of, human rights and freedoms,

Realizing that the individual, having duties to other individuals and to the community to which he belongs, is under a responsibility to strive for the promotion and observance of the rights recognized in the present Covenant,

Agree upon the following articles:

PART I

Article 1

1. All peoples have the right of self-determination. By virtue of that right they freely determine their political status and freely pursue their economic, social and cultural development.

2. All peoples may, for their own ends, freely dispose of their natural wealth and resources without prejudice to any obligations arising out of international economic co-operation, based upon the principle of mutual benefit, and international law. In no case may a people be deprived of its own means of subsistence.

3. The States Parties to the present Covenant, including those having responsibility for the administration of Non-Self-Governing and Trust Territories, shall promote the realization of the right of self-determination, and shall respect that right, in conformity with the provisions of the Charter of the United Nations.

PART II

Article 2

1. Each State Party to the present Covenant undertakes to respect and to ensure all individuals within its territory and subject to its jurisdiction the rights recognized in the present Covenant, without distinction of any kind, such as race, colour, sex, language, religion, political or other opinion, national or social origin, property, birth or other status.

2. Where not already provided for by existing legislative or other measures, each State Party to the present Covenant undertakes to take the necessary steps, in accordance with its constitutional processes and with the provisions of the present Covenant, to adopt such legislative or other measures as may be necessary to give effect to the rights recognized in the present Covenant.

3. Each State Party to the present Covenant undertakes:

(*a*) To ensure that any person whose rights or freedoms as herein recognized are violated shall have an effective remedy, notwithstanding that the violation has been committed by persons acting in an official capacity:

(*b*) To ensure that any person claiming such a remedy shall have his right thereto determined by competent judicial, administrative or legislative authorities, or by any other competent authority provided for by the legal system of the State, and to develop the possibilities of judicial remedy;

(*c*) To ensure that the competent authorities shall enforce such remedies when granted.

Article 3

The States Parties to the present Covenant undertake to ensure the equal right of men and women to the enjoyment of all civil and political rights set forth in the present Covenant.

Article 4

1. In time of public emergency which threatens the life of the nation and the existence of which is officially proclaimed, the States Parties to the present Covenant may take measures derogating from their obligations under the present Covenant to the extent strictly required by the exigencies of the situation, provided that such measures are not inconsistent with their other obligations under international law and do not involve discrimination solely on the ground of race, colour, sex, language, religion or social origin.
2. No derogation from articles 6, 7, 8 (paragraphs 1 and 2), 11, 15, 16 and 18 may be made under this provision.
3. Any State Party to the present Covenant availing itself of the right of derogation shall immediately inform the other States Parties to the present Covenant, through the intermediary of the Secretary-General of the United Nations, of the provisions from which it has derogated and of the reasons by which it was actuated. A further communication shall be made, through the same intermediary, on the date on which it terminates such derogation.

Article 5

1. Nothing in the present Covenant may be interpreted as implying for any State, group or person any right to engage in any activity or perform any act aimed at the destruction of any of the rights and freedoms recognized herein or at their limitation to a greater extent than is provided for in the present Covenant.
2. There shall be no restriction upon or derogation from any of the fundamental human rights recognized or existing in any State Party to the present Covenant pursuant to law, conventions, regulations or custom on the pretext that the present Covenant does not recognize such rights or that it recognizes them to a lesser extent.

PART III

Article 6

1. Every human being has the inherent right to life. This right shall be protected by law. No one shall be arbitrarily deprived of his life.
2. In countries which have not abolished the death penalty, sentence of death may be imposed only for the most serious crimes in accordance with the law in force at the time of the commission of the crime and not contrary to the provisions of the present Covenant and to the Convention on the Prevention and Punishment of the Crime of Genocide. This

penalty can only be carried out pursuant to a final judgement rendered by a competent court.

3. When deprivation of life constitutes the crime of genocide, it is understood that nothing in this article shall authorize any State Party to the present Covenant to derogate in any way from any obligation assumed under the provisions of the Convention on the Prevention and Punishment of the Crime of Genocide.

4. Anyone sentenced to death shall have the right to seek pardon or commutation of the sentence. Amnesty, pardon or commutation of the sentence of death may be granted in all cases.

5. Sentence of death shall not be imposed for crimes committed by persons below eighteen years of age and shall not be carried out on pregnant women.

6. Nothing in this article shall be invoked to delay or to prevent the abolition of captial punishment by any State Party to the present Covenant.

Article 7

No one shall be subjected to torture or to cruel, inhuman or degrading treatment or punishment. In particular, no one shall be subjected without his free consent to medical or scientific experimentation.

Article 8

1. No one shall be held in slavery; slavery and the slave-trade in all their forms shall be prohibited.

2. No one shall be held in servitude.

3. (a) No one shall be required to perform forced or compulsory labour;

(b) Paragraph 3 (a) shall not be held to preclude, in countries where imprisonment with hard labour may be imposed as a punishment for a crime, the performance of hard labour in pursuance of a sentence to such punishment by a competent court;

(c) For the purpose of this paragraph the term "force or compulsory labour" shall not include:

(i) Any work or service, not referred to in sub-paragraph (b), normally required of a person who is under detention in consequence of a lawful order of a court, or of a person during conditional release from such detention;

(ii) Any service of a military character and, in countries where conscientious objection is recognized, any national service required by law of conscientious objectors;

(iii) Any service exacted in cases of emergency or calamity threatening the life or well-being of the community;

(iv) Any work or service which forms part of normal civil obligations.

Article 9

1. Everyone has the right to liberty and security of person. No one shall be subjected to arbitrary arrest or detention. No one shall be deprived of his liberty except on such grounds and in accordance with such procedure as are established by law.
2. Anyone who is arrested shall be informed, at the time of arrest, of the reasons for his arrest and shall be promptly informed of any charges against him.
3. Anyone arrested or detained on a criminal charge shall be brought promptly before a judge or other officer authorized by law to exercise judicial power and shall be entitled to trial within a reasonable time or to release. It shall not be the general rule that persons awaiting trial shall be detained in custody, but release may be subject to guarantees to appear for trial, at any other stage of the judicial proceedings, and, should occasion arise, for execution of the judgement.
4. Anyone who is deprived of his liberty by arrest or detention shall be entitled to take proceedings before a court, in order that that court may decide without delay on the lawfulness of his detention and order his release if the detention is not lawful.
5. Anyone who has been the victim of unlawful arrest or detention shall have an enforceable right to compensation.

Article 10

1. All persons deprived of their liberty shall be treated with humanity and with respect for the inherent dignity of the human person.
2. (*a*) Accused persons shall, save in exceptional circumstances, be segregated from convicted persons and shall be subject to separate treatment appropriate to their status as unconvicted persons;
  (*b*) Accused juvenile persons shall be separated from adults and brought as speedily as possible for adjudication.
3. The penitentiary system shall comprise treatment of prisoners the essential aim of which shall be their reformation and social rehabilitation. Juvenile offenders shall be segregated from adults and be accorded treatment appropriate to their age and legal status.

Article 11

No one shall be imprisoned merely on the ground of inability to fulfil a contractual obligation.

Article 12

1. Everyone lawfully within the territory of a State shall, within that territory, have the right to liberty of movement and freedom to choose his residence.
2. Everyone shall be free to leave any country, including his own.
3. The above-mentioned rights shall not be subject to any restrictions except those which are provided by law, are necessary to protect national security, public order *(ordre public),* public health or morals or the rights and freedoms of others, and are consistent with the other rights recognized in the present Covenant.
4. No one shall be arbitrarily deprived of the right to enter his own country.

Article 13

An alien lawfully in the territory of a State Party to the present Covenant may be expelled therefrom only in pursuance of a decision reached in accordance with law and shall, except where compelling reasons of national security otherwise require, be allowed to submit the reasons against his expulsion and to have his case reviewed by, and be represented for the purpose before, the competent authority or a person or persons especially designated by the competent authority.

Article 14

1. All persons shall be equal before the courts and tribunals. In the determination of any criminal charge against him, or of his rights and obligations in a suit at law, everyone shall be entitled to a fair and public hearing by a competent, independent and impartial tribunal established by law. The Press and the public may be excluded from all or part of a trial for reasons of morals, public order *(ordre public)* or national security in a democratic society, or when the interest of the private lives of the parties so requires, or to the extent strictly necessary in the opinion of the court in special circumstances where publicity would prejudice the interests of justice; but any judgement rendered in a criminal case or in a suit at law shall be made public except where the interest of juvenile persons otherwise requires or the proceedings concern matrimonial disputes or the guardianship of children.
2. Everyone charged with a criminal offence shall have the right to be presumed innocent until proved guilty according to law.
3. In the determination of any criminal charge against him, everyone shall be entitled to the following minimum guarantees, in full equality:

   (*a*) To be informed promptly and in detail in a language which he understands of the nature and cause of the charge against him;

(*b*) To have adequate time and facilities for the preparation of his defence and to communicate with counsel of his own choosing;

(*c*) To be tried without undue delay;

(*d*) To be tried in his presence, and to defend himself in person or through legal assistance of his own choosing; to be informed, if he does not have legal assistance, of this right; and to have legal assistance assigned to him, in any case where the interests of justice so require, and without payment by him in any such case if he does not have sufficient means to pay for it;

(*e*) To examine, or have examined, the witnesses against him and to obtain the attendance and examination of witnesses on his behalf under the same conditions as witnesses against him;

(*f*) To have the free assistance of an interpreter if he cannot understand or speak the language used in court;

(*g*) Not to be compelled to testify against himself or to confess guilt.

4. In the case of juvenile persons, the procedure shall be such as will take account of their age and the desirability of promoting their rehabilitation.

5. Everyone convicted of a crime shall have the right to his conviction and sentence being reviewed by a higher tribunal according to law.

6. When a person has by a final decision been convicted of a criminal offence and when subsequently his conviction has been reversed or he has been pardoned on the ground that a new or newly discovered fact shows conclusively that there has been a miscarriage of justice, the person who has suffered punishment as a result of such conviction shall be compensated according to law, unless it is proved that the non-disclosure of the unknown fact in time is wholly or partly attributable to him.

7. No one shall be liable to be tried or punished again for an offence for which he has already been finally convicted or acquitted in accordance with the law and penal procedure of each country.

Article 15

1. No one shall be held guilty of any criminal offence on account of any act or omission which did not constitute a criminal offence, under national or international law, at the time when it was committed. Nor shall a heavier penalty be imposed than the one that was applicable at the time when the criminal offence was committed. If, subsequent to the commission of the offence, provision is made by law for the imposition of a lighter penalty, the offender shall benefit thereby.

2. Nothing in this article shall prejudice the trial and punishment of any person for any act or omission which, at the time when it was committed, was criminal according to the general principles of law recognized by the community of nations.

Article 16

Everyone shall have the right to recognition everywhere as a person before the law.

Article 17

1. No one shall be subjected to arbitrary or unlawful interference with his privacy, family, home or correspondence, nor to unlawful attacks on his honour and reputation.
2. Everyone has the right to the protection of the law against such interference or attacks.

Article 18

1. Everyone shall have the right to freedom of thought, conscience and religion. This right shall include freedom to have or to adopt a religion or belief of his choice, and freedom, either individually or in community with others and in public or private, to manifest his religion or belief in worship, observance, practice and teaching.
2. No one shall be subject to coercion which would impair his freedom to have or to adopt a religion or belief of his choice.
3. Freedom to manifest one's religion or beliefs may be subject only to such limitations as are prescribed by law and are necessary to protect public safety, order, health, or morals or the fundamental rights and freedoms of others.
4. The States Parties to the present Covenant undertake to have respect for the liberty of parents and, when applicable, legal guardians to ensure the religious and moral education of their children in conformity with their own convictions.

Article 19

1. Everyone shall have the right to hold opinions without interference.
2. Everyone shall have the right to freedom of expression; this right shall include freedom to seek, receive and impart information and ideas of all kinds, regardless of frontiers, either orally, in writing or in print, in the form of art, or through any other media of his choice.
3. The exercise of the rights provided for in paragraph 2 of this article carries with it special duties and responsibilities. It may therefore be subject to certain restrictions, but these shall only be such as are provided by law and are necessary:
    (a) For respect of the rights or reputations of others;
    (b) For the protection of national security or of public order *(ordre public)*, or of public health or morals.

Article 20

1. Any propaganda for war shall be prohibited by law.
2. Any advocacy of national, racial or religious hatred that constitutes incitement to discrimination, hostility or violence shall be prohibited by law.

Article 21

The right of peaceful assembly shall be recognized. No restrictions may be placed on the exercise of this right other than those imposed in conformity with the law and which are necessary in a democratic society in the interests of national security or public safety, public order *(ordre public),* the protection of public health or morals or the protection of the rights and freedoms of others.

Article 22

1. Everyone shall have the right to freedom of association with others, including the right to form and join trade unions for the protection of his interests.
2. No restrictions may be placed on the exercise of this right other than those which are prescribed by law and which are necessary in a democratic society in the interests of national security or public safety, public order *(ordre public),* the protection of public health or morals or the protection of the rights and freedoms of others. This article shall not prevent the imposition of lawful restrictions on members of the armed forces and of the police in their exercise of this right.
3. Nothing in this article shall authorize States Parties to the International Labour Organisation Convention of 1948 concerning Freedom of Association and Protection of the Right to Organize to take legislative measures which would prejudice, or to apply the law in such a manner as to prejudice, the guarantees provided for in that Convention.

Article 23

1. The family is the natural and fundamental group unit of society and is entitled to protection by society and the State.
2. The right of men and women of marriageable age to marry and to found a family shall be recognized.
3. No marriage shall be entered into without the free and full consent of the intending spouses.
4. States Parties to the present Convenant shall take appropriate steps to ensure equality of rights and responsibilities of spouses as to marriage, during marriage and at its dissolution. In the case of dissolution, provision shall be made for the necessary protection of any children.

Article 24

1. Every child shall have, without any discrimination as to race, colour, sex, language, religion, national or social origin, property or birth, the right to such measures of protection as are required by his status as a minor, on the part of his family, society and the State.
2. Every child shall be registered immediately after birth and shall have a name.
3. Every child has the right to acquire a nationality.

Article 25

Every citizen shall have the right and the opportunity, without any of the distinctions mentioned in article 2 and without unreasonable restrictions:

(*a*) To take part in the conduct of public affairs, directly or through freely chosen representatives;

(*b*) To vote and to be elected at genuine periodic elections which shall be by universal and equal suffrage and shall be held by secret ballot, guaranteeing the free expression of the will of the electors;

(*c*) To have access, on general terms of equality, to public service in his county.

Article 26

All persons are equal before the law and are entitled without any discrimination to the equal protection of the law. In this respect, the law shall prohibit any discrimination and guarantee to all persons equal and effective protection against discrimination on any ground such as race, colour, sex, language, religion, political or other opinion, national or social origin, property, birth or other status.

Article 27

In those States in which ethnic, religious or linguistic minorities exist, persons belonging to such minorities shall not be denied the right, in community with the other members of their group, to enjoy their own culture, to profess and practise their own religion, or to use their own language.

PART IV

Article 28

1. There shall be established a Human Rights Committee (hereinafter referred to in the present Covenant as the Committee). It shall consist of eighteen members and shall carry out the functions hereinafter provided.
2. The Committee shall be composed of nationals of the States Parties to

the present Covenant who shall be persons of high moral character and recognized competence in the field of human rights, consideration being given to the usefulness of the participation of some persons having legal experience.
3. The members of the Committee shall be elected and shall serve in their personal capacity.

Article 29

1. The members of the Committee shall be elected by secret ballot from a list of persons possessing the qualifications prescribed in article 28 and nominated for the purpose by the States Parties to the present Covenant.
2. Each State Party to the present Covenant may nominate not more than two persons. These persons shall be nationals of the nominating State.
3. A person shall be eligible for renomination.

Article 30

1. The initial election shall be held no later than six months after the date of the entry into force of the present Covenant.
2. At least four months before the date of each election to the Committee, other than an election to fill a vacancy declared in accordance with article 34, the Secretary-General of the United Nations shall address a written invitation to the States Parties to the present Covenant to submit their nominations for membership of the Committee within three months.
3. The Secretary-General of the United Nations shall prepare a list in alphabetical order of all the persons thus nominated, with an indication of the States Parties which have nominated them, and shall submit it to the States Parties to the present Covenant no later than one month before the date of each election.
4. Elections of the members of the Committee shall be held at a meeting of the States Parties to the present Covenant convened by the Secretary-General of the United Nations at the Headquarters of the United Nations. At that meeting, for which two thirds of the States Parties to the present Covenant shall constitute a quorum, the persons elected to the Committee shall be those nominees who obtain the largest number of votes and an absolute majority of the votes of the representatives of States Parties present and voting.

Article 31

1. The Committee may not include more than one national of the same State.

2. In the election of the Committee, consideration shall be given to equitable geographical distribution of membership and to the representation of the different forms of civilization and of the principal legal systems.

Article 32

1. The members of the Committee shall be elected for a term of four years. They shall be eligible for re-election if renominated. However, the terms of nine of the members elected at the first election shall expire at the end of two years; immediately after the first election, the names of these nine members shall be chosen by lot by the Chairman of the meeting referred to in article 30, paragraph 4.
2. Elections at the expiry of office shall be held in accordance with the preceding articles of this part of the present Covenant.

Article 33

1. If, in the unanimous opinion of the other members, a member of the Committee has ceased to carry out his functions for any cause other than absence of a temporary character, the Chairman of the Committee shall notify the Secretary-General of the United Nations who shall then declare the seat of that member to be vacant.
2. In the event of the death or the resignation of a member of the Committee, the Chairman shall immediately notify the Secretary-General of the United Nations, who shall declare the seat vacant from the date of death or the date on which the resignation takes effect.

Article 34

1. When a vacancy is declared in accordance with article 33 and if the term of office of the member to be replaced does not expire within six months of the declaration of the vacancy, the Secretary-General of the United Nations shall notify each of the States Parties to the present Covenant, which may within two months submit nominations in accordance with article 29 for the purpose of filling the vacancy.
2. The Secretary-General of the United Nations shall prepare a list in alphabetical order of the persons thus nominated and shall submit it to the States Parties to the present Covenant. The election to fill the vacancy shall then take place in accordance with the relevant provisions of this part of the present Covenant.
3. A member of the Committee elected to fill a vacancy declared in accordance with article 33 shall hold office for the remainder of the term of the member who vacated the seat on the Committee under the provisions of that article.

Article 35

The members of the Committee shall, with the approval of the General Assembly of the United Nations, receive emoluments from United Nations resources on such terms and conditions as the General Assembly may decide, having regard to the importance of the Committee's responsibilities.

Article 36

The Secretary-General of the United Nations shall provide the necessary staff and facilities for the effective performance of the functions of the Committee under the present Covenant.

Article 37

1. The Secretary-General of the United Nations shall convene the initial meeting of the Committee at the Headquarters of the United Nations.
2. After its initial meeting, the Committee shall meet at such times as shall be provided in its rules of procedure.
3. The Committee shall normally meet at the Headquarters of the United Nations or at the United Nations Office at Geneva.

Article 38

Every member of the Committee shall, before taking up his duties, make a solemn declaration in open committee that he will perform his functions impartially and conscientiously.

Article 39

1. The Committee shall elect its officers for a term of two years. They may be re-elected.
2. The Committee shall establish its own rules of procedure, but these rules shall provide, *inter alia*, that:
    (*a*) Twelve members shall constitute a quorum;
    (*b*) Decisions of the Committee shall be made by a majority vote of the members present.

Article 40

1. The States Parties to the present Covenant undertake to submit reports on the measures they have adopted which give effect to the rights recognized herein and on the progress made in the enjoyment of those rights:
    (*a*) Within one year of the entry into force of the present Covenant for the State Parties concerned;
    (*b*) Thereafter whenever the Committee so requests.

2. All reports shall be submitted to the Secretary-General of the United Nations, who shall transmit them to the Committee for consideration. Reports shall indicate the factors and difficulties, if any, affecting the implementation of the present Covenant.
3. The Secretary-General of the United Nations may, after consultation with the Committee, transmit to the specialized agencies concerned copies of such parts of the reports as may fall within their field of competence.
4. The Committee shall study the reports submitted by the States Parties to the present Covenant. It shall transmit its reports, and such general comments as it may consider appropriate, to the States Parties. The Committee may also transmit to the Economic and Social Council these comments along with the copies of the reports it has received from States Parties to the present Covenant.
5. The States Parties to the present Covenant may submit to the Committee observations on any comments that may be made in accordance with paragraph 4 of this article.

Article 41

1. A State Party to the present Covenant may at any time declare under this article that it recognizes the competence of the Committee to receive and consider communications to the effect that a State Party claims that another State Party is not fulfilling its obligations under the present Covenant. Communications under this article may be received and considered only if submitted by a State Party which has made a declaration recognizing in regard to itself the competence of the Committee. No communication shall be received by the Committee if it concerns a State Party which has not made such a declaration. Communications received under this article shall be dealt with in accordance with the following procedure:

(*a*) If a State Party to the present Covenant considers that another State Party is not giving effect to the provisions of the present Covenant, it may, by written communication, bring the matter to the attention of that State Party. Within three months after the receipt of the communication, the receiving State shall afford the State which sent the communication an explanation or any other statement in writing clarifying the matter, which should include, to the extent possible and pertinent, reference to domestic procedures and remedies taken, pending, or available in the matter.

(*b*) If the matter is not adjusted to the satisfaction of both States Parties concerned within six months after the receipt by the receiving State of the initial communication, either State shall have the right to refer the matter to the Committee, by notice given to the Committee and to the other State.

(*c*) The Committee shall deal with a matter referred to it only after it has ascertained that all available domestic remedies have been invoked and exhausted in the matter, in conformity with the generally recognized principles of international law. This shall not be the rule where the application of the remedies is unreasonably prolonged.

(*d*) The Committee shall hold closed meetings when examining communications under this article.

(*e*) Subject to the provisions of sub-paragraph (*c*), the Committee shall make available its good offices to the States Parties concerned with a view to a friendly solution of the matter on the basis of respect for human rights and fundamental freedoms as recognized in the present Covenant.

(*f*) In any matter referred to it, the Committee may call upon the States Parties concerned, referred to in sub-paragraph (*b*), to supply any relevant information.

(*g*) The States Parties concerned, referred to in sub-paragraph (*b*), shall have the right to be represented when the matter is being considered in the Committee and to make submissions orally and/or in writing.

(*h*) The Committee shall, within twelve months after the date of the receipt of notice under sub-paragraph (*b*), submit a report:
  (i) If a solution within the terms of sub-paragraph (*e*) is reached, the Committee shall confine its report to a brief statement to the facts and of the solution reached:
  (ii) If a solution within the terms of sub-paragraph (*e*) is not reached, the Committee shall confine its report to a brief statement of the facts; the written submissions and record of the oral submissions made by the States Parties concerned shall be attached to the report.
In every matter, the report shall be communicated to the States Parties concerned.

2. The provisions of this article shall come into force when ten States Parties to the present Covenant have made declarations under paragraph 1 of this article. Such declarations shall be deposited by the States Parties with the Secretary-General of the United Nations, who shall transmit copies thereof to the other States Parties. A declaration may be withdrawn at any time by notification to the Secretary-General. Such a withdrawal shall not prejudice the consideration of any matter which is the subject of a communication already transmitted under this article; no further communication by any State Party shall be received after the notification of withdrawal of the declaration has been received by the

Secretary-General, unless the State Party concerned had made a new declaration.

Article 42

1. (*a*) If a matter referred to the Committee in accordance with article 41 is not resolved to the satisfaction of the States Parties concerned, the Committee may, with the prior consent of the States Parties concerned, appoint an *ad hoc* Conciliation Commission (hereinafter referred to as the Commission). The good offices of the Commission shall be made available to the States Parties concerned with a view to an amicable solution of the matter on the basis of respect for the present Covenant;

(*b*) The Commission shall consist of five persons acceptable to the States Parties concerned. If the States Parties concerned fail to reach agreement within three months on all or part of the composition of the Commission, the members of the Commission concerning whom no agreement has been reached shall be elected by secret ballot by a two-thirds majority vote of the Committee from among its members.

2. The members of the Commission shall serve in their personal capacity. They shall not be nationals of the States Parties concerned, or of a State not party to the present Covenant, or of a State Party which has not made a declaration under article 41.

3. The Commission shall elect its own Chairman and adopt its own rules of procedure.

4. The meetings of the Commission shall normally be held at the Headquarters of the United Nations or at the United Nations Office at Geneva. However, they may be held at such other convenient places as the Commission may determine in consultation with the Secretary-General of the United Nations and the States Parties concerned.

5. The secretariat provided in accordance with article 36 shall also service the commissions appointed under this article.

6. The information received and collated by the Committee shall be made available to the Commission and the Commission may call upon the States Parties concerned to supply any other relevant information.

7. When the Commission has fully considered the matter, but in any event not later than twelve months after having been seized of the matter, it shall submit to the Chairman of the Committee a report for communication to the States Parties concerned:

(*a*) If the Commission is unable to complete its consideration of the matter within twelve months, it shall confine its report to a brief statement of the status of its consideration of the matter;

(*b*) If an amicable solution to the matter on the basis of respect for human rights as recognized in the present Covenant is reached, the Commission shall confine its report to a brief statement of the facts and of the solution reached;

(c) If a solution within the terms of sub-paragraph *(b)* is not reached, the Commission's report shall embody its findings on all questions of fact relevant to the issues between the States Parties concerned, and its views on the possibilities of an amicable solution of the matter. This report shall also contain the written submissions and a record of the oral submissions made by the States Parties concerned;

(d) If the Commission's report is submitted under sub-paragraph (c), the States Parties concened shall, within three months of the receipt of the report, notify the Chairman of the Committee whether or not they accept the contents of the report of the Commission.

8. The provisions of this article are without prejudice to the responsibilities of the Committee under article 41.

9. The States Parties concerned shall share equally all the expenses of the members of the Commission in accordance with estimates to be provided by the Secretary-General of the United Nations.

10. The Secretary-General of the United Nations shall be empowered to pay the expenses of the members of the Commission, if necessary, before reimbursement by the States Parties concerned, in accordance with paragraph 9 of this article.

Article 43

The members of the Committee, and of the *ad hoc* conciliation commissions which may be appointed under article 42, shall be entitled to the facilities, privileges and immunities of experts on mission for the United Nations as laid down in the relevant sections of the Convention on the Privileges and Immunities of the United Nations.

Article 44

The provisions for the implementation of the present Covenant shall apply without prejudice to the procedures prescribed in the field of human rights by or under the constituent instruments and the conventions of the United Nations and of the specialized agencies and shall not prevent the States Parties to the present Covenant from having recourse to other procedures for settling a dispute in accordance with general or special international agreements in force between them.

Article 45

The Committee shall submit to the General Assembly of the United Nations, through the Economic and Social Council, an annual report on its activities.

PART V

Article 46

Nothing in the present Covenant shall be interpreted as impairing the provisions of the Charter of the United Nations and of the constitutions of the specialized agencies which define the respective responsibilities of the various organs of the United Nations and of the specialized agencies in regard to the matters dealt with in the present Covenant.

Article 47

Nothing in the present Covenant shall be interpreted as impairing the inherent right of all peoples to enjoy and utilize fully and freely their natural wealth and resources.

PART VI

Article 48

1. The present Covenant is open for signature by any State Member of the United Nations or member of any of its specialized agencies, by any State Party to the Statute of the International Court of Justice, and by any other State which has been invited by the General Assembly of the United Nations to become a party to the present Covenant.
2. The present Covenant is subject to ratification. Instruments of ratification shall be deposited with the Secretary-General of the United Nations.
3. The present Covenant shall be open to accession by any State referred to in paragraph 1 of this article.
4. Accession shall be effected by the deposit of an instrument of accession with the Secretary-General of the United Nations.
5. The Secretary-General of the United Nations shall inform all States which have signed this Covenant or acceded to it of the deposit of each instrument of ratification or accession.

Article 49

1. The present Covenant shall enter into force three months after the date of the deposit with the Secretary-General of the United Nations of the thirty-fifth instrument of ratification or instrument of accession.
2. For each State ratifying the present Covenant or acceding to it after the deposit of the thirty-fifth instrument of ratification or instrument of accession, the present Covenant shall enter into force three months after the date of the deposit of its own instrument of ratification or instrument of accession.

Article 50

The provisions of the present Covenant shall extend to all parts of federal States without any limitations or exception.

Article 51

1. Any State Party to the present Covenant may propose an amendment and file it with the Secretary-General of the United Nations. The Secretary-General of the United Nations shall thereupon communicate any proposed amendments to the States Parties to the present Covenant of States Parties for the purpose of considering and voting upon the proposals. In the event that at least one third of the States Parties favours such a conference, the Secretary-General shall convene the conference under the auspices of the United Nations. Any amendment adopted by a majority of the States Parties present and voting at the conference shall be submitted to the General Assembly of the United Nations for approval.
2. Amendments shall come into force when they have been approved by the General Assembly of the United Nations and accepted by a two-thirds majority of the States Parties to the present Covenant in accordance with their respective constitutional processes.
3. When amendments come into force, they shall be binding on those States Parties which have accepted them, other States Parties still being bound by the provisions of the present Covenant and any earlier amendment which they have accepted.

Article 52

Irrespective of the notifications made under article 48, paragraph 5, the Secretary-General of the United Nations shall inform all States referred to in paragraph 1 of the same article of the following particulars:

 (*a*) Signatures, ratifications and accessions under article 48;

 (*b*) The date of the entry into force of the present Covenant under article 49 and the date of the entry into force of any amendments under article 51.

Article 53

1. The present Covenant, of which the Chinese, English, French, Russian and Spanish texts are equally authentic, shall be deposited in the archives of the United Nations.
2. The Secretary-General of the United Nations shall transmit certified copies of the present Covenant to all States referred to in article 48.

C. INTERNATIONAL COVENANT ON ECONOMIC, SOCIAL AND CULTURAL RIGHTS, 1966

THE STATES PARTIES TO THE PRESENT COVENANT

Considering that, in accordance with the principles proclaimed in the Charter of the United Nations, recognition of the inherent dignity and of the equal and inalienable rights of all members of the human family is the foundation of freedom, justice and peace in the world,

Recognizing that these rights derive from the inherent dignity of the human person,

Recognizing that, in accordance with the Universal Declaration of Human Rights, the ideal of free human beings enjoying freedom from fear and want can only be achieved if conditions are created whereby everyone may enjoy his economic, social and cultural rights, as well as his civil and political rights,

Considering the obligation of States under the Charter of the United Nations to promote universal respect for, and observance of, human rights and freedoms,

Realizing that the individual, having duties to other individuals and to the community to which he belongs, is under a responsibility to strive for the promotion and observance of the rights recognized in the present Covenant,

Agree upon the following articles:

PART 1

Article 1

1. All peoples have the right of self-determination. By virtue of that right they freely determine their political status and freely pursue their economic, social and cultural development.
2. All peoples may, for their own ends, freely dispose of their natural wealth and resources without prejudice to any obligations arising out of international economic co-operation, based upon the principle of mutual benefit, and international law. In no case may a people be deprived of its own means of subsistence.
3. The States Parties to the present Covenant, including those having responsibility for the administration of Non-Self-Governing and Trust Territories, shall promote the realization of the right of self-determination, and shall respect that right, in conformity with the provisions of the Charter of the United Nations.

PART II

1. Each State Party to the present Covenant undertakes to take steps, individually and through international assistance and co-operation, especially economic and technical, to the maximum of its available resources, with a view to achieving progressively the full realization of the rights recognized in the present Covenant by all appropriate means, including particularly the adoption of legislative measures.
2. The States Parties to the present Covenant undertake to guarantee that the rights enunciated in the present Covenant will be exercised without discrimination of any kind as to race, colour, sex, language, religion, political or other opinion, national or social origin, property, birth or other status.
3. Developing countries, with due regard to human rights and their national economy, may determine to what extent they would guarantee the economic rights recognized in the present Covenant to non-nationals.

Article 3

The States Parties to the present Covenant undertake to ensure the equal right of men and women to the enjoyment of all economic, social and cultural rights set forth in the present Covenant.

Article 4

The States Parties to the present Covenant recognize that, in the enjoyment of those rights provided by the State in conformity with the present Covenant, the State may subject such rights only to such limitations as are determined by law only in so far as this may be compatible with the nature of these rights and solely for the purpose of promoting the general welfare in a democratic society.

Article 5

1. Nothing in the present Covenant may be interpreted as implying for any State, group or person any right to engage in any activity or to perform any act aimed at the destruction of any of the rights or freedoms recognized herein, or at their limitation to a greater extent than is provided for in the present Covenant.
2. No restriction upon or derogation from any of the fundamental human rights recognized or existing in any country in virtue of law, conventions, regulations or custom shall be admitted on the pretext that the present Covenant does not recognize such rights or that it recognizes them to a lesser extent.

PART III

Article 6

1. The States Parties to the present Covenant recognize the right to work, which includes the right of everyone to the opportunity to gain his living by work which he freely chooses or accepts, and will take appropriate steps to safeguard this right.
2. The steps to be taken by a State Party to the present Covenant to achieve the full realization of this right shall include technical and vocational guidance and training programmes, policies and techniques to achieve steady economic, social and cultural development and full and productive employment under conditions safeguarding fundamental political and economic freedoms to the individual.

Article 7

The States Parties to the present Covenant recognize the right of everyone to the enjoyment of just and favourable conditions of work which ensure, in particular:

(*a*) Remuneration which provides all workers, as a minimum, with:

(i) Fair wages and equal remuneration for work of equal value without distinction of any kind, in particular women being guaranteed conditions of work not inferior to those enjoyed by men, with equal pay for equal work;

(ii) A decent living for themselves and their families in accordance with the provisions of the present Covenant;

(*b*) Safe and healthy working conditions;

(*c*) Equal opportunity for everyone to be promoted in his employment to an appropriate higher level, subject to no considerations other than those of seniority and competence;

(*d*) Rest, leisure and reasonable limitation of working hours and periodic holidays with pay, as well as remuneration for public holidays.

Article 8

1. The States Parties to the present Covenant undertake to ensure:

(*a*) The right of everyone to form trade unions and join the trade union of his choice, subject only to the rules of the organization concerned, for the promotion and protection of his economic and social interests. No restrictions may be placed on the exercise of this right other than those prescribed by law and which are necessary in a democratic society in the interests of national security or public order or for the protection of the rights and freedoms of others;

(*b*) The right of trade unions to establish national federations or confederations and the right of the latter to form or join international trade-union organizations;

(c) The right of trade unions to function freely subject to no limitations other than those prescribed by law and which are necessary in a democratic society in the interests of national security or public order or for the protection of the rights and freedoms of others;

(d) The right to strike, provided that it is exercised in conformity with the laws of the particular country.

2. This article shall not prevent the imposition of lawful restrictions on the exercise of these rights by members of the armed forces or of the police or of the administration of the State.

3. Nothing in this article shall authorize States Parties to the International Labour Organization Convention of 1948 concerning Freedom of Association and Protection of the Right to Organize to take legislative measures which would prejudice, or apply the law in such a manner as would prejudice, the guarantees provided for in that Convention.

Article 9

The States Parties to the present Covenant recognize the right of everyone to social security, including social insurance.

Article 10

The States Parties to the present Covenant recognize that:

1. The widest possible protection and assistance should be accorded to the family, which is the natural and fundamental group unit of society, particularly for its establishment and while it is responsible for the care and education of dependent children. Marriage must be entered into with the free consent of the intending spouses.

2. Special protection should be accorded to mothers during a reasonable period before and after childbirth. During such period working mothers should be accorded paid leave or leave with adequate social security benefits.

3. Special measures of protection and assistance should be taken on behalf of all children and young persons without any discrimination for reasons of parentage or other conditions. Children and young persons should be protected from economic and social exploitation. Their employment in work harmful to their morals or health or dangerous to life or likely to hamper their normal development should be punishable by law. States should also set age limits below which the paid employment of child labour should be prohibited and punishable by law.

Article 11

1. The States Parties to the present Covenant recognize the right of

everyone to an adequate standard of living for himself and his family, including adequate food, clothing and housing, and to the continuous improvement of living conditions. The States Parties will take appropriate steps to ensure the realization of this right, recognizing to this effect the essential importance of international co-operation based on free consent.

2. The States Parties to the present Covenant, recognizing the fundamental right of everyone to be free from hunger, shall take, individually and through international co-operation, the measures, including specific programmes, which are needed:

(*a*) To improve methods of production, conservation and distribution of food by making full use of technical and scientific knowledge, by disseminating knowledge of the principals of nutrition and by developing or reforming agrarian systems in such a way as to achieve the most efficient development and utilization of natural resources;

(*b*) Taking into account the problems of both food-importing and food-exporting countries, to ensure an equitable distribution of world food supplies in relation to need.

Article 12

1. The States Parties to the present Covenant recognize the right of everyone to the enjoyment of the highest attainable standard of physical and mental health.

2. The steps to be taken by the States Parties to the present Covenant to achieve the full realization of this right shall include those necessary for:

(*a*) The provision for the reduction of the stillbirth-rate and of infant mortality and for the healthy development of the child;

(*b*) The improvement of all aspects of environmental and industrial hygiene;

(*c*) The prevention, treatment and control of epidemic, endemic, occupational and other diseases;

(*d*) The creation of conditions which would assure to all medical service and medical attention in the event of sickness.

Article 13

1. The States Parties to the present Covenant recognize the right of everyone to education. They agree that education shall be directed to the full development of the human personality and the sense of its dignity, and shall strengthen the respect for human rights and fundamental freedoms. They further agree that education shall enable all persons to participate effectively in a free society, promote understanding, tolerance and friendship among all nations and all racial, ethnic or religious groups, and further the activities of the United Nations for the maintenance of peace.

2. The States Parties to the present Covenant recognize that, with a view to achieving the full realization of this right:

   (*a*)   Primary education shall be compulsory and available free to all;

   (*b*)   Secondary education in its different forms, including technical and vocational secondary education, shall be made generally available and accessible to all by every appropriate means, and in particular by the progressive introduction of free education;

   (*c*)   Higher education shall be made equally accessible to all, on the basis of capacity, by every appropriate means, and in particular by the progressive introduction of free education;

   (*d*)   Fundamental education shall be encouraged or intensified as far as possible for those persons who have not received or completed the whole period of their primary education;

   (*e*)   The development of a system of schools at all levels shall be actively pursued, an adequate fellowship system shall be established, and the material conditions of teaching staff shall be continuously improved.

3. The States Parties to the present Covenant undertake to have respect for the liberty of parents and, when applicable, legal guardians to choose for their children schools, other than those established by the public authorities, which conform to such minimum educational standards as may be laid down or approved by the State and to ensure the religious and moral education of their children in conformity with their own convictions.

4. No part of this article shall be construed so as to interfere with the liberty of individuals and bodies to establish and direct educational institutions, subject always to the observance of the principles set forth in paragraph 1 of this article and to the requirement that the education given in such institutions shall conform to such minimum standards as may be laid down by the State.

Article 14

Each State Party to the present Covenant which, at the time of becoming a Party, has not been able to secure in its metropolitan territory or other territories under its jurisdiction compulsory primary education, free of charge, undertakes, within two years, to work out and adopt a detailed plan of action for the progressive implementation, within a reasonable number of years, to be fixed in the plan, of the principle of compulsory education free of charge for all.

Article 15

1. The States Parties to the present Covenant recognize the right of everyone:

   (*a*)   To take part in cultural life;

(b) To enjoy the benefits of scientific progress and its applications;

(c) To benefit from the protection of the moral and material interests resulting from any scientific, literary or artistic production of which he is the author.

2. The steps to be taken by the States Parties to the present Covenant to achieve the full realization of this right shall include those necessary for the conservation, the development and the diffusion of science and culture.

3. The States Parties to the present Covenant undertake to respect the freedom indispensable for scientific research and creative activity.

4. The States Parties to the present Covenant recognize the benefits to be derived from the encouragement and development of international contacts and co-operation in the scientific and cultural fields.

PART IV

Article 16

1. The States Parties to the present Covenant undertake to submit in conformity with this part of the Covenant reports on the measures which they have adopted and the progress made in achieving the observance of the rights recognized herein.

2. (a) All reports shall be submitted to the Secretary-General of the United Nations, who shall transmit copies to the Economic and Social Council for consideration in accordance with the provision of the present Covenant.

(b) The Secretary-General of the United Nations shall also transmit to the specialized agencies copies of the reports, or any relevant parts therefrom, from States Parties to the present Covenant which are also members of these specialized agencies in so far as these reports, or parts therefrom, relate to any matters which fall within the responsibilities of the said agencies in accordance with their constitutional instruments.

Article 17

1. The States Parties to the present Covenant shall furnish their reports in stages, in accordance with a programme to be established by the Economic and Social Council within one year of the entry into force of the present Covenant after consultation with the States Parties and the specialized agencies concerned.

2. Reports may indicate factors and difficulties affecting the degree of fulfillment of obligations under the present Covenant.

3. Where relevant information has previously been furnished to the United Nations or to any specialized agency by any State Party to the present Covenant, it will not be necessary to reproduce that information, but a precise reference to the information so furnished will suffice.

Article 18

Pursuant to its responsibilities under the Charter of the United Nations in the field of human rights and fundamental freedoms, the Economic and Social Council may make arrangements with the specialized agencies in respect of their reporting to it on the progress made in achieving the observance of the provisions of the present Covenant falling within the scope of their activities. These reports may include particulars of decisions and recommendations on such implementation adopted by their competent organs.

Article 19

The Economic and Social Council may transmit to the Commission on Human Rights for study and general recommendations or, as appropriate, for information the reports concerning human rights submitted by States in accordance with articles 16 and 17, and those concerning human rights submitted by the specialized agencies in accordance with article 18.

Article 20

The States Parties to the present Covenant and the specialized agencies concerned may submit comments to the Economic and Social Council on any general recommendation under article 19 or reference to such general recommendation in any report of the Commission on Human Rights or any documentation referred to therein.

Article 21

The Economic and Social Council may submit from time to time to the General Assembly reports with recommendations of a general nature and a summary of the information received from the States Parties to the present Covenant and the specialized agencies on the measures taken and the progress made in achieving general observance of the rights recognized in the present Covenant.

Article 22

The Economic and Social Council may bring to the attention of other organs of the United Nations, their subsidiary organs and specialized agencies concerned with furnishing technical assistance any matters arising out of the reports referred to in this part of the present Covenant which may assist such bodies in deciding, each within its field of competence, on the advisability of international measures likely to contribute to the effective progressive implementation of the present Covenant.

Article 23

The States Parties to the present Covenant agree that international action for the achievement of the rights recognized in the present Covenant includes such methods as the conclusion of conventions, the adoption of recommendations, the furnishing of technical assistance and the holding of regional meetings and technical meetings for the purpose of consultation and study organized in conjunction with the Governments concerned.

Article 24

Nothing in the present Covenant shall be interpreted as impairing the provisions of the Charter of the United Nations and of the constitutions of the specialized agencies which define the respective responsibilities of the various organs of the United Nations and of the specialized agencies in regard to the matters dealt with in the present Covenant.

Article 25

Nothing in the present Covenant shall be interpreted as impairing the inherent right of all peoples to enjoy and utilize fully and freely their natural wealth and resources.

PART V

Article 26

1. The present Covenant is open for signature by any State Member of the United Nations or member of any of its specialized agencies, by any State Party to the Statute of the International Court of Justice, and by any other State which has been invited by the General Assembly of the United Nations to become a party to the present Covenant.
2. The present Covenant is subject to ratification. Instruments of ratification shall be deposited with the Secretary-General of the United Nations.
3. The present Covenant shall be open to accession by any State referred to in paragraph 1 of this article.
4. Accession shall be effected by the deposit of an instrument of accession with the Secretary-General of the United Nations.
5. The Secretary-General of the United Nations shall inform all States which have signed the present Covenant or acceded to it of the deposit of each instrument of ratification or accession.

Article 27

1. The present Covenant shall enter into force three months after the date of the deposit with the Secretary-General of the United Nations of

the thirty-fifth instrument of ratification or instrument of accession.

2. For each State ratifying the present Covenant or acceding to it after the deposit of the thirty-fifth instrument of ratification or instrument of accession, the present Covenant shall enter into force three months after the date of the deposit of its own instrument of ratification or instrument of accession.

Article 28

The provisions of the present Covenant shall extend to all parts of federal States without any limitations or exceptions.

Article 29

1. Any State Party to the present Covenant may propose an amendment and file it with the Secretary-General of the United Nations. The Secretary-General shall thereupon communicate any proposed amendments to the States Parties to the present Covenant with a request that they notify him whether they favour a conference of States Parties for the purpose of considering and voting upon the proposals. In the event that at least one third of the States Parties favours such a conference, the Secretary-General shall convene the conference under the auspices of the United Nations. Any amendment adopted by a majority of the States Parties present and voting at the conference shall be submitted to the General Assembly of the United Nations for approval.

2. Amendments shall come into force when they have been approved by the General Assembly of the United Nations and accepted by a two-thirds majority of the States Parties to the present Covenant in accordance with their respective processes.

3. When amendments come into force they shall be binding on those States Parties which have accepted them, other States Parties still being bound by the provisions of the present Covenant and any earlier amendment which they have accepted.

Article 30

Irrespective of the notifications made under article 26, paragraph 5, the Secretary-General of the United Nations shall inform all States referred to in paragraph 1 of the same article of the following particulars:

(*a*) Signatures, ratifications and accessions under article 26;

(*b*) The date of the entry into force of the present Covenant under article 27 and the date of the entry into force of any amendments under article 29.

Article 31

1. The present Covenant, of which the Chinese, English, French, Rus-

sian and Spanish texts are equally authentic, shall be depositied in the archives of the United Nations.
2. The Secretary-General of the United Nations shall transmit certified copies of the present Covenant to all States referred to in article 26.

D. TABLE OF SIGNATURES AND RATIFICATIONS

As of December 1979

S - Signature
R - Ratification or Accession

State	Covenant on Civil & Political Rights	Covenant on Economic, Social & Cultural Rights
Algeria	S	S
Argentina	S	S
Australia	S	R
Austria	S	S
Barbados	R	R
Belgium	S	S
Bulgaria	R	R
Byelorussian SSR	R	R
Canada	R	R
Chile	R	R
Colombia	R	R
Costa Rica	R	R
Cyprus	R	R
Czechoslovakia	R	R
Denmark	R	R
Dominican Republic	R	R
Ecuador	R	R
Egypt	S	S
El Salvador	S	R
Finland	R	R
German Democratic Republic	R	R
Germany, Federal Republic of	R	R
Guinea	R	R
Guyana	R	R

Appendix 357

State	Covenant on Civil & Political Rights	Covenant on Economic, Social & Cultural Rights
Honduras	S	S
Hungary	R	R
Iceland	S	S
Iran	R	R
Iraq	R	R
Ireland	S	S
Israel	S	S
Italy	S	S
Jamaica	R	R
Japan	R	R
Jordan	R	R
Kenya	R	R
Lebanon	R	R
Liberia	S	S
Libyan Arab Republic	R	R
Luxembourg	S	S
Madagascar	R	R
Mali	R	R
Malta	R	S
Mauritius	R	R
Mongolia	R	R
Morocco	R	R
Netherlands	R	R
New Zealand	R	R
Norway	R	R
Panama	R	R
Peru	R	R
Philippines	S	R
Poland	R	R
Portugal	R	R
Romania	R	R
Rwanda	R	R
Senegal	R	R
Spain	R	R
Surinam	R	R
Sweden	R	R
Syrian Arab Republic	R	R
Tunisia	R	R
Ukrainian SSR	R	R
U.S.S.R.	R	R

State	Covenant on Civil & Political Rights	Covenant on Economic, Social & Cultural Rights
United Kingdom	R	R
U. Rep. of Tanzania	R	R
U. States of America	S	S
Uruguay	R	R
Venezuela	R	R
Yugoslavia	R	R
Zaire	R	R

* Gambia, India, Trinidad, and Tobago have also ratified both treaties.

E. SECTIONS 502B AND 116 OF THE FOREIGN ASSISTANCE ACT

Section 502 B

(a) (1) It is the policy of the United States, in accordance with its international obligations as set forth in the Charter of the United Nations and in keeping with the constitutional heritage and traditions of the United States, to promote and encourage increased respect for human rights and fundamental freedoms for all without distinction as to race, sex, language, or religion. To this end, a principal goal of the foreign policy of the United States is to promote the increased observance of internationally recognized human rights by all countries.

(2) It is further the policy of the United States that, except under circumstances specified in this section, no security assistance may be provided to any country the government of which engages in a consistent pattern of gross violations of internationally recognized human rights.

(3) In furtherance of the foregoing policy the President is directed to formulate and conduct international security assistance programs of the United States in a manner which will promote and advance human rights and avoid identification of the United States, through such programs, with governments which deny to their people internationally recognized human rights and fundamental freedoms, in violation of international law or in contravention of the policy of the United States as expressed in this section or otherwise.

(b) The Secretary of State shall transmit to the Congress, as part of the presentation materials for security assistance programs proposed for each fiscal year, a full and complete report, prepared with the assistance of the Coordinator for Human Rights and Humanitarian Affairs, with respect to practices regarding the observance of and respect for internationally recognized human rights in each country proposed as a recipient of security assistance. In determining whether a government falls within the provisions of subsection (a) (3) and in the preparation to any report or statement required under this section, consideration shall be given to—

> (1) the relevant findings of appropriate international organizations, including nongovernmental organizations, such as the International Committee of the Red Cross; and

> (2) the extent of cooperation by such government in permitting an unimpeded investigation by any such organization of alleged violations of internationally recognized human rights.

(c) (1) Upon the request of the Senate or the House of Representatives by resolution of either such House, or upon the request of the Committee on Foreign Relations of the Senate or the Committee on International Relations of the House of Representatives, the Secretary of State shall, within thirty days after receipt of such request, transmit to both such Committees a statement, prepared with the assistance of the Coordinator for Human Rights and Humanitarian Affairs, with respect to the country designated in such request, setting forth—

> (A) all the available information about observance of and respect for human rights and fundamental freedom in that country, and a detailed description of practices by the recipient government with respect thereto:

> (B) the steps the United States has taken to—

>> (i) promote respect for and observance of human rights in that country and discourage any practices which are inimical to internationally recognized human rights, and

>> (ii) publicly or privately call attention to, and disassociate the United States and any security assistance provided for such country from, such practices;

(C) whether, in the opinion of the Secretary of State, notwithstanding any such practices—

(i) extraordinary circumstances exist which necessitate a continuation of security assistance for such country, and, if so, a description of such circumstances and the extent to which such assistance should be continued (subject to such conditions as Congress may impose under this section), and

(ii) on all the facts it is in the national interest of the United States to provide such assistance; and

(D) such other information as such committee or such House may request.

(2) (A) A resolution of request under paragraph (1) of this subsection shall be considered in the Senate in accordance with the provisions of section 601 (b) of the International Security Assistance and Arms Export Control Act of 1976.

(B) The term "certification," as used in section 601 of such Act, means for the purposes of this subsection, a resolution of request of the Senate under paragraph (1) of this subsection.

(3) In the event a statement with respect to a country is requested pursuant to paragraph (1) of this subsection but is not transmitted in accordance therewith within thirty days after receipt of such request, no security assistance shall be delivered to such country except as may thereafter be specifically authorized by law from such country unless and until such statement is transmitted.

(4) (A) In the event a statement with respect to a country is transmitted under paragraph (1) of this subsection, the Congress may at any time thereafter adopt a joint resolution terminating, restricting, or continuing security assistance for such country. In the event such a joint resolution is adopted, such assistance shall be so terminated, so restricted, or so continue, as the case may be.

(B) The term "certification," as used in section 601 of such Act, means for the purposes of this subsection, a resolution of request of the Senate under paragraph (1) of this subsection.

(C) The term "certification," as used in section 601

of such Act, means, for the purposes of this paragraph, a statement transmitted under paragraph (1) of this subsection.

(d) For the purposes of this section—

(1) the term "gross violations of internationally recognized human rights" includes torture or cruel, inhuman, or degrading treatment or punishment, prolonged detention without charges and trial, and other flagrant denial of the right to life, liberty, or the security of person; and

(2) the term "security assistance" means—

(A) assistance under chapter 2 (military assistance) or chapter 4 (security supporting assistance) or chapter 5 (military education and training) of this part or part VI (assistance to the Middle East) of this Act;

(B) sales of defense articles or services, extensions of credits (including participations in credits, and guarantees of loans under the Arms Export Control Act); or

(C) any license in effect with respect to the export of defense articles or defense serviced to or for the armed forces, police, intelligence, or other internal security forces of a foreign country under section 38 of the Arms Export Control Act.

Section 116

(a) No assistance may be provided under this part to the government of any country which engages in a consistent pattern of gross violations of internationally recognized human rights, including torture or cruel, inhuman, or degrading treatment or punishment, prolonged detention without charges, or other flagrant denial of the right to life, liberty, and the security of person, unless such assistance will directly benefit the needy people in such country.

(b) In determining whether this standard is being met with regard to funds allocated under this part, the Committee on International Relations of the House of Representatives may require the Administrator primarily responsible for administering part I of this Act to submit in writing information demonstrating that such assistance will directly benefit the needy people in such country, together with a detailed explanation of the assistance to be provided (including the dollar amounts of such assistance) and an explanation of how such assistance will directly benefit the needy people in such country. If either committee or either House of Congress disagrees with the Administrator's justification it may initiate action to terminate assistance to any country by a concurrent resolution under section 617 of this Act.

(c) In determining whether or not a goverment falls within the provisions of subsection (a), consideration shall be given to the extent of cooperation of such government in permitting an unimpeded investigation of alleged violations of internationally recognized human rights by appropriate international organizations, including the International Committee of the Red Cross, or groups or persons acting under the authority of the United Nations or of the Organization of American States.

(d) The President shall transmit to the Speaker of the House of Representatives and the Committee on Foreign Relations of the Senate, in the annual presentation, materials on proposed economic development assistance programs, a full and complete report regarding the steps he has taken to carry out the provisions of this section.

CONTRIBUTORS

BRUNO V. BITKER (LL.B., Cornell University, 1921). Bruno V. Bitker currently is a practicing attorney in Milwaukee. He has held many positions in and out of goverment: U.S. delegate in Teheran, Iran, 1968; consultant with the Department of State, 1968-73; and delegate to the Human Rights Conference at Uppsala, University of Sweden, 1972. Cochairman of the American Bar Association's National Institute of the Law of Human Rights, 1978. He is the author of "The Constitutionality of International Agreements on Human Rights" (*Santa Clara Lawyer*, Vol. 12, 1972) and other articles.

ROBERT B. BOETTCHER (B.A., Auburn University, 1964; M.S. in Foreign Services, Georgetown University, 1965). Robert B. Boettcher is now staff director of the Korean Investigation for the Subcommittee on International Organizations, of the House Committee on International

Relations. He had the principal staff responsibility in the House for the repeal of the Byrd Amendment. He has organized 76 subcommittee hearings on human rights in foreign policy during the past three years. He has also taken part in drafting of legislation concerning U.S. policy on Namibia, restrictions on military assistance to repressive governments, and other international human rights issues.

ROBERT L. BOROSAGE (B.A., Michigan State University, 1966; M.A., George Washington University, 1968; J.D., Yale Law School, 1971). Robert L. Borosage presently serves as the director of the Institute for Policy Studies, Washington, D.C. He is the former director of the Center for National Security Studies, and has coauthored several books, including *Exploring Contradictions* with Brenner and Weidner (McKay, 1974), *The CIA File* with Marks (Grossman, 1975), and *The Lawless State: Crimes of the U.S. Intelligence Agencies* with Berman, Halperin, and Marwick (Penguin, 1976). He has also written several newspaper and journal articles on the activities of U.S. intelligence agencies.

WALKER CONNOR (B.A., University of Massachusetts, 1951; M.A., Georgetown University, 1958; Ph.D., Georgetown University, 1962). Walker Connor is currently a professor of political science at the State University of New York at Brockport. During the academic year 1977-1978 he was at St. Antony's College, Oxford University, England as a Rhodes Fellow and Visiting Fellow of Race Relations. He is the author of *The National Question in Marxist Theory and Strategy*, *The Ethnic Strain in World Politics,* and *Ethnic Nationalism and Political Disintegration.*

RICHARD A. FALK (B.S. in economics from Wharton School, University of Pennsylvania, 1952; LL.B., Yale Law School, 1955; J.S.D., Harvard University, 1962). Richard A. Falk is Albert G. Milbank professor of international law and practice and director of the American Participation in the World Order Models Project (WOMP). He has written numerous articles and is currently on the editorial boards of *Foreign Policy Magazine, American Journal of International Law*, and *Alternatives*. He is the author of *Law, War and Morality in the Contemporary World* (Praeger, 1963), *The Status of Law in International Society* (Princeton University Press, 1970), *A Global Approach to National Policy* (Harvard University Press, 1975), and *A Study of Future Worlds* (Free Press, 1975). He is also coeditor of *The Future of the International Legal Order* with Cyril E. Black (Princeton University Press, 1969, 1970, 1971, 1972). He is currently working on a series of related essays dealing with human rights.

C. CLYDE FERGUSON, JR. (A.B., Ohio State University, 1948; LL.B., Howard University, 1951; LL.D., Rutgers University, 1966). C. Clyde Ferugson is a professor of law at Harvard University. He has been the United States ambassador to Uganda (1970-1972) and a United States representative on the United Nations Commission on Racial Discrimination. From 1962 to the present he has been on the board of directors of the legal defense and education fund of the NAACP. He is the author of "The United Nations Human Rights Covenants: Problems of Ratification and Implementation" (American Society of International Law Proceedings, 1968).

PAUL KATTENBURG (B.A., University of North Carolina, 1943; M.A., George Washington University, 1946; Ph.D., Yale University, 1949). Dr. Kattenburg is a professor in the Department of Goverment and International Studies at the University of South Carolina. He is a retired Foreign Service officer, a specialist in U.S. foreign policy and Southeast Asian affairs, and author of numerous studies in the field. He is author of *The Vietnam Trauma in American Foreign Policy, 1945-75* (Transaction Books, 1980).

RICHARD B. LILLICH (A.B., Oberlin College, 1954; LL.B., Cornell University, 1957; LL.M., New York University, 1959; J.S.D., New York University, 1960). Richard B. Lillich is Howard W. Smith professor of law at the University of Virginia School of Law. He is the president of the Procedural Aspects of the International Law Institute and is a former member of the Executive Council of the American Society of International Law, the Rapporteur of its Panel on State Responsibility, and an editor of its *Journal*. Included among his most recent publications are: *Humanitarian Intervention and the United Nations* (University Press of Virginia, 1973); *International Claims: Their Settlement by Lump Sum Agreements*, with Burns H. Weston (University Press of Virginia, 1975); and *International Human Rights: Problems of Law and Policy*.

MARCUS G. RASKIN (B.A., University of Chicago; LL.D., University of Chicago). In 1963 Marcus G. Raskin cofounded the Institute for Policy Studies, an independent center devoted to research on public policy questions and is currently a Fellow there. Between 1965 and 1972 he was a member of the board of trustees of Antioch College. He has written and coauthored *The Limits of Defense* (Doubleday, 1962), *After Twenty Years* (Random House, 1965), *The Vietnam Reader* (Random House, 1971), and most recently, *Notes on the Old System: To Transform American Politics* (David McKay, 1974). He is currently the editor of the *Journal of Social Reconstruction* and the author of the forthcoming book, *The Common Good* (Simon and Schuster).

LOUIS BRUNO SOHN (Dipl. Sc. M. and L.L.M. in 1935 from John Casimir University of Lwow, Poland; LL.M., Harvard Law School, 1940; S.J.D., Harvard Law School, 1958). Louis B. Sohn is Bemis professor of international law and John Harvey Gregory lecturer on world organization at the Harvard Law School. Professor Sohn serves as a member of the United States delegation to the United Nations Law of the Sea Conference. He is the chairman of the Commission to Study the Organization of Peace, a member of the American Society of International Law, a vice president of the American branch of the International Law Association, and a member of the editorial board of the American Journal of International Law. His publications include *World Peace Through World Law* (3rd. ed.) written with Grenville Clark (Harvard University Press, 1966), *Cases on United Nations Law* (2d ed., Foundation Press, 1967), *Basic Documents of African Regional Organizations* (4 vols, Oceana, 1971-72), *International Protection of Human Rights*, with Thomas Buergenthal (Bobbs-Merrill, 1973).

MARTIN WEINSTEIN (B.A., Columbia University; M.A., Ph.D., New York University). Martin Weinstein is associate professor of political science at William Patterson College in New Jersey and serves as a special consultant to the Council on Hemispheric Affairs. He is the author of *Uruguay: The Politics of Failure* (Greenwood Press, 1975) and the editor of *Revolutionary Cuba in the World Arena* (Institute for the Study of Human Issues, 1979). Other writings and research center on U.S.-Latin American relations and problems of ideology and development in Latin America. Professor Weinstein has also testified before the House International Relations Committee on Human Rights in Uruguay (1976).

PETER WEISS (B.A., St. John's, Annapolis, Md.; LL.B., Yale). Peter Weiss is the chairman of the board of the Institute for Policy Studies. He is the vice president of the Center for Constitutional Rights in New York. An international lawyer, he has served on many human rights missions and litigations.

DAVID WEISSBRODT (B.A., Columbia College, Columbia University, 1966; J.D., University of California Law School, 1969). David Weissbrodt is presently an associate professor at the University of Minnesota Law School. His publications include "Exhaustion of Remedies in the Context of the Racial Discrimination Convention," with Schaffer (*Human Rights Journal*, 1969), "Conscientious Objection to Military Service as a Human Right," with Schaffer (*Review of the International Commission of Jurists*, 1972), "The Role of Non-governmental Organizations in the Implementation of Human Rights" (*Texas International Law Journal*, 1977), and "U.S. Foreign Policy and Human Rights" (*Georgia Journal of International & Comparative Law*, 1977). He serves on the Advisory Board of the U.S. Institute of Human Rights, as well as being a member of the American Association for the International Commission of Jurists and the International League for Human Rights.

ANN C. WILCOX (B.A., Wittenberg University, 1977). Ann C. Wilcox has been associated with the Institute for Policy Studies in Washington since 1976, holding a variety of research and administrative positions. She majored in history at Wittenberg University in 1977 and has studied the Russian language in Leningrad, USSR. She is currently administrative assistant to the director of the Institute for Policy Studies and is a member of the editorial working group of the *Journal of Social Reconstruction*.

ROBERT G. WIRSING (B.A., Colorado State College, 1958; M.A., University of Denver, 1970; Ph.D., University of Denver, 1971). Robert G. Wirsing is an associate professor in the Department of Government and International Studies at the University of South Carolina. He is the editor of *International Relations & the Future of Ocean Space* (University of South Carolina Press, 1973); and author of *Socialist Society and Free Enterprise Politics* (Carolina Academic Press, 1977).

University of South Carolina Project Working Group

M. GLENN ABERNATHY (B.S., Birmingham Southern University, 1942; M.A., University of Alabama, 1947; Ph.D., University of Wisconsin, 1953). Dr. Abernathy is Olin D. Johnston professor of political science. He is a specialist in constitutional law and is the author of *Civil Liberties Under the Constitution*, 3rd edition (Harper and Row, 1977).

MORRIS J. BLACHMAN (B.A., Brandeis University, 1961; M.A., University of South Carolina, 1968; Ph.D., New York University, 1976). Dr. Blachman is an associate professor in international studies. He is a specialist in Latin American affairs, a coeditor of *Terms of Conflict: Ideology in Latin American Politics*, with Hellman (ISHI Press, 1977) and is the author of *Eve in Adamocracy: The Politics of Women in Brazil* (ISHI Publications, 1978).

NATALIE KAUFMAN HEVENER (B.A., University of Pennsylvania, 1963; Ph.D., University of Virginia, 1966). Dr. Hevener is an associate professor of international studies. She is a specialist in international law whose articles have appeared in the *International and Comparative Law Quarterly*, *Middle East Journal*, the *International Journal of Women's Studies*, and the *Harvard Women's Law Journal*.

PAUL M. KATTENBURG (see contributors list).

WILLIAM P. KREML (B.A., Northwestern University, 1962; J.D., Northwestern University, 1965; M.A., University of Tennessee, 1968; Ph.D., Indiana University, 1972). Dr. Kreml is an associate professor of government. He is a specialist in law and political economy and is the author of *The Anti-Authoritarian Personality* (Pergamon Press, 1977) and *The Middle Class Burden* (Carolina Academic Press, 1979).

MICHAEL R. WEISSER (B.A., The City College of New York, 1967; Ph.D., Northwestern University, 1972). Dr. Weisser is an associate professor of history. He is a specialist in European affairs and is the author of *Crime and Punishment in Early Modern Europe, 1350-1850* (Harvester Press, 1978).

ROBERT G. WIRSING (see contributors list).

Additional Faculty Participants

Dr. Shahrough Akhavi
Dr. Paul W. Blackstock
Dr. Mark W. DeLancey
Dr. Charles W. Kegley, Jr.
Dr. D. Bruce Marshall
Dr. Harvey B. Silverstein

Graduate Student Participants

Catherine C. Farrow
Steven A. Mosher (assistant to editor)
Amy Pitts (assistant to editor)
Carl Young (assistant to editor)

Index

Abourezk, James, 220, 280
Adams, John Quincy, 111
Agee, Philip, 219
Agency for International Development (AID), 219, 233
Agricultural Trade Development and Assistance Act, 295, 305-06
Allende, Salvador, 12, 14
American Bar Association (ABA), 66, 89, 90, 130
American Convention on Human Rights of 1968, 91, 223, 293
American Declaration of the Rights and Duties of Man, 139
Americans for Democratic Action (ADA), 244, 260n
Amin, Idi, 13, 24, 295
Amnesty International, 23, 125, 183 184, 217, 230, 233, 236, 238-39, 246, 266n
apartheid, 7, 19, 46, 203-13
Argentina, 218-20, 286, 288
arms control, 6, 146-48
Arms Export Control Board, 303
authoritarianism, 219

Badillo, Herman, 287
balance of power, 21, 39, 102
Barr, Stringfellow, 129
Bingham, John, 301, 302
Blanco, Carrero, 185
Bonker, Don, 292
Bretton-Woods Agreement, 307
Brezhnev, Leonid, 15
Bricker Amendment, 45, 65, 90, 231
brinkmanship, 142, 216
Brzezinski, Zbigniew, 42, 49, 54
Buckley, William F., 38
Buergenthal, Thomas, 84
Bukovsky, Vladimir, 302

Buñuel, Luis, 216
Byrd Amendment, 310

Capotorti, Francesco, 190, 199n
Carter, James, administration, 11, 13, 17, 34, 38, 40-42, 45, 68, 72, 96, 114-15, 123-24, 129, 189, 212, 294-95, 310; and human rights, 2, 30, 34, 49, 53-62, 224, 232, 279, 286-88, 291, 303; and foreign policy, 1, 49-50, 215, 221, 299, 331; speech to the Organization of American States (1977), 125; speech to the United Nations (1977), 124
Castro, Fidel, 12, 14, 33
Center for International Policy of the Fund for Peace, 241, 242
Central Intelligence Agency (CIA), 11, 12, 14, 29, 47, 48, 49, 58, 217, 219
Chamberlain, Neville, 21
Chen, Lung-Chu, 191
Chile, 123, 127, 216, 217, 218, 220 223, 283, 299-302
Chomsky, Noam, 39-40
Christopher, Warren, 50n, 125, 130 249n, 295, 303, 305
Church, Frank, 297
Clark, Ramsey, 38
Claude, Inis, 12, 22, 163, 181
Cleaver, Eldridge, 18
Clemenceau, Georges, 15
Clergy and Laity Concerned, 260n
Cohen, Roberta, 303-04
cold war, 30, 33, 60, 62, 70, 216, 231
Committee on the Present Danger, 55
Communist Manifesto, 118n
Conference on Security and Cooperation in Europe (Helsinki Conference), 85, 108, 140

Congress, United States, 53, 59, 66, 126; House International Relations Committee, Subcommittee on International Organizations, 279-84, 291, 295-96, 301, 309
Connor, Walker, 174
Constitution, United States, 65, 87, 94; Bill of Rights, 1, 59, 83
Convention on the Freedom of Association, 66
Convention on the Political Rights of Women, 88, 90
counterforce strategy, 21
Cranston, Maurice, 12
customary international law, 29

Dean, Vera Micheles, 81
Declaration of Independence, United States, 1, 6, 77, 79, 80, 110
Declaration of the Rights of Man and Citizen, France, 78, 103
DeGaulle, Charles, 13, 15, 101
Democratic Republic of Vietnam (DRV), 15, 21, 280, 301
Derwinski, Edward, 288
detachment, "bureaucratic," 13; games theory, 13
détente, 140, 167, 231
Diggs, Charles, 302
Dulles, John Foster, 33, 90, 139-40, 206, 231
Dumbarton Oaks, 81-82
Dworkin, Ronald, 129

Eisenhower, Dwight, 33, 90, 96, 139
Emancipation Proclamation, 79, 80
Employment Act of 1947, United States, 61
Equal Rights Amendment, United States, 60
European Convention on Human Rights, 153n
Export Administration Act of 1969, 301-02, 306; Section 3, 308; Section 4, 308-09
Export-Import Bank, 298-99
Export-Import Bank Act of 1945, 95; Evans Amendment, 298, 302, 308; Section 2, 308

fascism, 136, 166, 217
Fagen, Richard, 300

Falk, Richard, 12
Fascell Commission on Security and Cooperation in Europe, 311
Fascell, Dante, 288, 311
Federal Bureau of Investigation (FBI), 11, 49, 58
Fisher, Roger, 23
Ford, Gerald, 17, 38, 96, 110, 216 283
Foreign Assistance Act of 1961, 94 220, 280; Section 116, 94, 284-85, 294-96, 305, 359; Section 240A, 306; Section 293(1), 295, 296; Section 502B, 94, 95, 220, 284, 294, 296, 305-07, 309, 356-59; Section 543, 309
Foreign Assistance and Related Programs Appropriations Act of 1979, 307-08
Foreign Relations Authorization Act (FY 1979), 309
Frankel, Charles, 12, 13
Fraser, Donald, 40-41, 45, 220-21, 279-83, 284-88, 292, 303
Freedom House, 236
French Revolution, 16
Friends Committee on National Legislation, 242

Gandhi, Mohandas, 101
Geneva Conventions on War of 1949, 146, 150-51
genocide, see International Convention on the Prevention and Punishment of the Crime of Genocide
George, Lloyd, 15
Goldwater, Barry, 38
Greeley, Andrew, 188

Hague Regulations of 1907, 144
Hampton, Fred, 58
Harkin Amendment of 1975, 220 287, 296, 297-99, 306
Helsinki Conference, see Conference on the Security and Cooperation of Europe
Henkin, Louis, 293, 310
Herman, Edward, 39
Hewlett, Sylvia A., 128
Hitler, Adolf, 20, 174, 182
Hobbes, Thomas, 15, 39
Horowitz, Irving L., 13

Housing Act of 1949, United States, 61
Human Rights and Humanitarian Affairs, Bureau of, 303-04
Human Rights Institute, 233
Human Rights Working Group, 242-44, 273n
Hungarian Revolution of 1956, 140
Hyde, Henry, 299

India, 13, 179, 181, 188
Institute for Policy Studies, 299
International Bill of Rights, 81-84 86, 91, 96, 245
International Commission of Jurists, 125, 183, 217, 230, 233, 234, 235, 236, 246, 252n
International Committee of the Red Cross, 70, 233, 235
International Convention on the Elimination of All Forms of Racial Discrimination, 48, 56, 65, 91, 164, 167, 294
International Convention on the Prevention and Punishment of the Crime of Genocide of 1948, 29, 34, 48, 56, 64, 88-89, 90, 142, 164, 167, 173, 187, 293-94, 311
International Court of Justice, 85, 126, 206
International Covenant on Civil and Political Rights, 5, 6, 48, 56, 60, 65, 66, 83, 86, 90, 92-94, 97, 125, 130, 152, 164-65, 171, 190, 293; Optional Protocol, 83; text, 325-43
International Covenant on Economic, Social, and Cultural Rights, 5, 6, 48, 56, 59, 60, 68, 83, 86, 90, 91-92, 97, 124, 129, 152, 171, 293; text, 344-54
International Financial Institutions Act, 95; Section 701, 307; Section 703, 307
International Labor Organization (ILO), 239, 292
International League for Human Rights, 125, 217, 235, 246
International Monetary Fund (IMF), 297-98
International Telephone and Telegraph (ITT), 11, 14

interventionist foreign policy, 1, 8, 38, 62, 70, 72, 148, 177; United States in Guatemala (1954), 217; Bay of Pigs (1961), 217; United States in Dominican Republic (1965), 217
isolationism, 1, 17
Israel, 172, 175, 181, 186

Jackson-Vanick Amendment (1974 Trade Act), 95, 210n, 305
Japan, 23, 26
Javits, Jacob, 298
Jenks, C. Wilfred, 3
Jessup, Phillip, 64, 82
Johnson, Lyndon B., 33, 96
jus cogens, 29

Kastenmeier Bill (H.R. 8688), 144-45
Kellog-Briand Pact of 1928, 144
Kelsen, Hans, 137
Kennedy, Edward M., 220
Kennedy, John F., 14, 15, 33, 49, 66, 96; Alliance for Progress, 33, 219
kin-state, 181-83
King, Martin Luther, Jr., 14, 58
Kissinger, Henry, 1, 11, 13, 14, 33, 38, 54, 117, 124, 146-47, 215, 220, 241, 279, 283-84; Sonnefeldt Doctrine, 121n
Koch Amendment (1976), 220-21
Korean War, 25
Kurds, 176, 182, 187

Lauterpracht, Hersch, 138
League of Arab States, 175
League of Nations, 6, 80, 109, 136-37, 162-64, 165, 166, 178, 180, 193
LeFevre, Ernest, 12
Letelier, Orlando, 127, 130
Levesque, René, 188
Lincoln, Abraham, 78-79
Locke, John, 77
Louis Napoleon, 104

McCarran Act, 56-57
McCarthy, Eugene, 38
McCarthy, Joseph, 70
Machiavelli, Nicolo, 14
McCloy-Zorin Eight Points, 147
McGovern Amendment, 310
McGovern, George, 38

MacNamara, Robert, 128, 133n
Magna Carta, 77
manifest destiny, 111
Mao Tse-Tung, 18
Marcos, Ferdinand, 182
Marx, Karl, 18, 53, 104
Mazzini, Giuseppe, 107
Minority Rights Group, 172, 235
Monroe Doctrine, 111, 112
Monroe, James, 111
Montesquieu, 77
Morgenthau, Hans, 12
Moynihan, Daniel Patrick, 34, 44-46
Murray, Courtney, S.J., 12
Mussolini, Benito, 15
Mutual Assured Destruction (MAD), 21

Namibia, 109-13
National Council of Churches, United States, 242, 261n
national security, 11-14, 54-55, 70-71, 128, 146-49, 189, 216, 224, 296
National Security Agency, 58
Nazism, 160, 166, 172, 181
Nixon, Richard M., 1, 13, 14, 17, 25, 33, 96, 114, 123, 124, 216, 283
Noble, Lela G., 173
North Atlantic Treaty Organization (NATO), 85, 203
Nuremberg, 14, 135, 137-38, 143, 144-45, 152

Official Accountability Act, United States, 152
Organization of African Unity, 108
Organization of American States, 7, 233, 239, 288, 292; Inter-American Commission on Human Rights, 217, 223
Overseas Private Investment Corporation (OPIC), 224, 294-96

Palestine Liberation Organization (PLO), 174-75
Palme, Olav, 24
Panama Canal, 38, 56
Paris Treaty of Peace with Great Britain of 1783, 79
Parti Québécois, Canada, 188
Peace Corps, 33

People's Republic of China (PRC), 17, 26, 101, 178, 182, 188
Philippines, 18, 40, 42, 54, 112, 126, 128, 181, 283, 286, 296
Pinochet, Augusto, 123, 127, 299
Polish Minorities Treaty, 162
Porter, John, 179
Potsdam Conference, 166
Protocol Relating to the Status of Refugees, 310
Proxmire, William, 90
Public Law 95-105, United States, 94; Section 109, 94
Public Law 480, United States, 95; Section 112, 95
Puerto Rican Constitution of 1952, 139

racial discrimination, see International Convention on the Elimination of All Forms of Racial Discrimination
Radio Free Europe, 55
Ramsey, Paul, 12
Reagan, Ronald, 38
realpolitik, 11, 14, 180, 215-16
refugees, see Protocol Relating the Status of Refugees
reification, 13-14
Reuss, Henry, 90, 285, 286, 299
Roosevelt, Eleanor, 84, 138
Roosevelt, Franklin D., 32, 96, 139; and the "four freedoms," 32, 43, 49, 60, 81
Roosevelt, Theodore, 15, 53, 217
Rostow, Eugene, 128
Russell, Bertrand, 24
Russell, Ruth B., 81
Ryan, Leo, 288

Sakharov, Andrei, 55, 123
Salzburg, John, 281
Santayana, George, 26, 27n
Schlesinger, Arthur, 54
Schneider, Mark, 288, 295, 300, 303
Schransky, Anatoly, 310
Select Committee on Nutrition and Human Needs, 61
self-protection of minorities, 185-86
Senate, United States, 5; Committee on the Intelligence Agencies, 57; Foreign Relations committee, 82, 88, 292-94; and treaty ratification, 38, 56, 73-74, 88-89, 189, 223, 287, 293-94

Simon, William, 127
Slavery Convention of 1926, 80
Social Security Act of 1949, United States, 61
Sohn, Louis, 84, 85
Solarz, Stephen, 295, 302
Solzhenitsyn, Alexander, 20, 23
Somoza Debayle, Anastasio, 298
South Africa, Republic of, 7, 46, 109, 113, 126, 173, 184, 203-05, 294, 298, 302; Color Ban Act of 1911, 204; Natives Land Act of 1913, 204; Group Areas Act of 1950, 204; Suppression of Communism Act, 204; Sullivan Code, 302, 308; Terrorism Act, 204
sovereignty, 158, 175
Stalin, Joseph, 101
Stockholm International Peace Research Institute, 154n
Straatsrašon, 16-17, 25, 26
Strategic Arms Limitation Talks, 146-47, 150, 152
Suhrke, Astri, 173
Supreme Court, United States, 110

Taft-Hartley Bill, 129
Taft, Robert, 38
Teheran Proclamation, 85
Terrorism, 23
Thomson, James, 13
Todman, Terence, 224
Transnational Institute, 130, 261n
Truman Doctrine, 33, 73
Truman, Harry S., 33, 96, 166, 187

U Thant, 170
Union of Soviet Socialist Republics (U.S.S.R.), 15, 20, 25, 29-30, 34, 44, 46, 54, 55, 65, 101, 105, 117, 167, 184, 188, 281
United Nations (U.N.), 6, 7, 34, 46, 48, 55, 63-66, 67-68, 73, 109, 164-65, 167, 189, 239, 280, 292; Commission on Human Rights, 55, 66, 83, 93, 165, 217; Commission on the Racial Situation in South Africa, 206; Conference on the Law of the Sea; 190; Economic and Social Council, 81-82, 165, 235; Economic, Social, and Cultural Organization (UNESCO), 206, 239; General Assembly, 5, 22, 44, 46, 56, 73, 82-83, 167; General Assembly Resolution 132-30, 131, 205-07; Participation Act, 301; San Francisco Conference, 81-83, 88; Security Council, 73, 113, 173, 207, 210-11; Subcommittee on the Prevention of Discrimination and the Protection of Minorities, 177, 190 220n
United Nations Charter, 67, 81-82, 84, 97, 107-08, 110, 137-39, 142-43, 144, 231, 281; Article 2 (7), 205, 207-08; Article 6, 209; Article 7, 211; Article 27, 210-11
United States Information Agency (U.S.I.A.), 48
Universal Declaration of Human Rights, 3, 5, 6, 18, 19, 24, 29, 33, 43, 83-84, 85-87, 95, 97, 137, 139, 140, 144, 152, 231, 281, 292; text, 319-25
Universal Human Rights, 292
universal suffrage, 16
Uruguay, 219-21.

Vance, Cyrus, 42, 54, 60, 124, 221, 223, 299; Law Day address at the University of Georgia Law School, 124, 125
Vandenburg, Arthur H., 73, 82
Versailles, Treaty of, 80, 160-61
Vietnam, 1, 4, 11, 12, 13, 24-25, 30, 45, 54, 114, 127, 152, 187, 216, 231, 245
Vogelgesang, Sandra, 296
Voice of America, 48, 55
Voltaire, 77
Vorster, John, 211

Watergate, 1, 11, 24, 30, 54, 152, 216
Webster, Daniel, 110
Weissbrodt, David, 293
Westphalia, 26
Wilmington Ten, 310
Wilson, Woodrow, 15, 49, 101, 104, 111, 112, 161, 166, 173, 191, 197n
Wolfers, Arnold, 12, 19
World Bank, 68, 128, 221, 224, 284, 297
World Conference for Religion and Peace, 235
World Council of Churches, 235

World Health Organization
 (W.H.O.), 206
Wounded Knee, 59
Wright, Quincy, 111

Young, Andrew, 35, 46, 222